MEMOIRS OF A RENAISSANCE POPE

THE COMMENTARIES OF PIUS II

MEMOIRS OF A RENAISSANCE POPE

THE COMMENTARIES OF PIUS II

An Abridgment

TRANSLATED BY *Florence A. Gragg*

EDITED, WITH INTRODUCTION, BY *Leona C. Gabel*

Capricorn Books   NEW YORK

MEMOIRS OF A

RENAISSANCE POPE

THE COMMENTARIES OF PIUS II

Capricorn Books Edition, 1962

Fourth Impression

© 1959

BY FLORENCE A. GRAGG AND LEONA C. GABEL

Library of Congress Catalog

Card Number: 59-5680

FOREWORD

FOREWORD

THE present volume is an abridgment of the *Commentaries of Pius II* published for the first time *in extenso* in English translation by F. A. Gragg and L. C. Gabel in the Smith College Studies in History, volumes XXII, XXV, XXX, XXXV and XLIII, and based on the original Vatican manuscript.

The principle guiding the selection of passages for this abridgment was initially that the content be at first hand, the Pope writing either as observer of or as participant in the events related. This eliminated a substantial body of historical material taken by the author—sometimes word for word—from other sources. A further reduction was effected by cutting or omitting certain blocks of subject matter of interest mainly to the specialist and available to him in the complete edition. The author's fondness for repetition and for lengthy speeches offered still another possibility for abbreviation, though care has been taken to preserve characteristic examples. There remained the task of giving to the material thus selected such coherence and fluency as the original work may be said to have without altering its sequence or phraseology. Transitional words and phrases for this purpose are in every instance drawn from the author's own words; there is no rewording of the text itself. The editor has dispensed with the necessarily cumbersome apparatus showing the location and content of omitted passages. The Topical Guide to the complete edition mentioned above may be consulted for subject matter not here included.

The volume is designed for the general reader—not the specialist—interested in the Renaissance. The aim has been to *abridge,* not to change the original work; to convey the full flavor of this unique Renaissance document. The editor is acutely aware of the arbitrariness of the process involved. Its justification must lie in the wish to make the *Commentaries* accessible to a wider circle of readers than would otherwise be possible. And in the hope, be it added, that some may be led thereby to the august author's great work in its unabridged form.

FOREWORD

Thanks are due to Smith College and to the Smith College Studies in History for permission to use that edition of the *Commentaries* for purposes of the present abridgment. I am also deeply indebted to my colleague, Florence Alden Gragg, for helpful suggestions as well as for her consent to entrust the translation to my reluctant pruning.

Finally, in this 500th anniversary of his elevation to the throne of St. Peter, this volume offers tribute to the memory of Pius II, brilliant, genial and true spokesman of the Italian Renaissance.

LEONA C. GABEL

Smith College
Northampton, Massachusetts
June, 1958

CONTENTS

TOPICAL GUIDE BY BOOKS

In lieu of a Table of Contents which in the nature of the *Commentaries* would assume the proportions of an Index, the following list is appended as a convenient guide to the main subject matter of the individual Books. It is not exhaustive; the sequence of topics merely approximates that of a given Book. Topics in brackets may be found in the unabridged edition in the Smith College Studies in History.

CONTENTS

CONTENTS

The illustrations mentioned *passim* in the text (e.g., "(Fig. 1)") could not be included in this inexpensive edition.

MEMOIRS OF A RENAISSANCE POPE

THE COMMENTARIES OF PIUS II

INTRODUCTION

THE *Commentaries* of Pius II—statesman, poet, humanist, incorrigible traveler and nature lover, who ascended the papal throne in 1458—constitute one of the most revealing documents of the Renaissance, an epoch singularly rich in literary and artistic expression. Like its author, erstwhile Aeneas Sylvius Piccolomini, the work fits into no category, combining the features of autobiography, memoir, diary and history. In its pages is mirrored for us the dynamic, engaging, versatile personality of its genial author; in it is unfolded the drama of that many-faceted era of crisis and tension and glorious creativity—an era no longer medieval and not yet wholly modern. After centuries of obscurity in a Latin edition rigorously expurgated and falsely attributed to another author, the publication for the first time of a complete English edition based on the original manuscript makes available the riches of this unique work. As an abridgment of that edition the present volume aims to preserve unimpaired the qualities which make the *Commentaries* a vital human document setting forth the history of an era and the portrait of one of its most eloquent spokesmen.

THE MAN, THE POPE, AND HIS TIMES

The author of the *Commentaries* chose to write in the third person, a literary device presumably borrowed from Julius Caesar. Whether this choice was dictated by the desire for anonymity or for greater freedom from the normal restraints of modesty, the end result is a remarkable self-portrait of a Renaissance Italian. Without the aid of contemporary biographers we recognize in him a vibrant, genial, self-aware personality, a man of eloquent speech and facile pen. His boundless vitality makes few concessions to the gout and other ills that plagued him. His vanity is breath-taking and disarming. He tells us, for example, that he held an audience so spellbound for two hours that no one even spat. Nor did a stomach attack on another occasion dim the brilliance of a three-hour speech. Equally characteristic is his hearty enjoyment of a joke, of good sport, of people. A boyish zest comes through his vivid descriptions of races which, he insists, he watched from the corner of his eye while engaged in weightier concerns of state. The woes of the puppy Musetta are related with touching pathos; the antics of his niece's baby find a place among the "memorable events" of his times. Flashes of peppery temper liven more than one scene, as when he bade a French cardinal, "Go to the devil, you and your threats! And your money go to hell with you!"

Described as "the man who had a heart for everything," Pius exhibits the many-sided interests of the Renaissance. With startling candor he admits us to the unrehearsed councils of the papal court, gives a back-stage view of his own election, relays the subtle game of European politics. Well-known personalities are captured for all time in unforget-table pen pictures; classical authors inspire his pages, ancient ruins are lovingly depicted. His many writings cover a wide range of subject matter. From the literary "wild oats" of his early career, which he felt called upon as Pope to retract—asking Christendom to "reject Aeneas and accept Pius"—his works include histories, treatises, orations and a voluminous correspondence. It is noteworthy that a copy of his *Historia rerum ubique gestarum,* a work never completed containing much geographical material, was the object of close study and elaborate an-notation by Christopher Columbus.

His was a pontificate of the open road. The Signatura is held in a shaded nook "by the sweet murmur of the stream," Consistory "under the chestnuts" and embassies are heard in the meadow. Drinking freely at the fountain of antiquity and of nature, Pius was at one with his times in sensing no incompatibility between the Christian and classical worlds. He remained Christian—as did the Renaissance—but Heaven receded as earth grew more fair.

Our author's career before becoming Pope took him over the length and breadth of Europe. Born in 1405 of the noble but impoverished Sienese family of the Piccolomini who with others of their class had suffered political ostracism at the hands of Siena's bourgeoisie, the young humanist early sought his fortune elsewhere. The wider arena of European politics beckoned when a papal mission under Bishop Albergati was sent to arrange a peace between France and England. Taking service as the Bishop's secretary, Aeneas traveled as far north as Scotland. The misfortune of freezing his feet in that northern clime resulted in a lifelong affliction. During much of his pontificate he had to be borne about in a sedan chair.

The mission to France ending in failure, Aeneas betook himself to Basle where the Council, now in open breach with the Pope at Rome, offered a field for his talents. Ironically, the future Pope Pius II here became secretary to an antipope Felix V, making his political debut as defender of the conciliar theory which was later to be anathematized in his Bull *Execrabilis*! His indiscretions were thus not solely literary. Of his new master he was later to write:

> For the barber's razor had removed ... a real and becoming ornament, i.e., a long, full beard which covered all the blemishes on his face and ... lent a kind of dignity; and when he appeared without it, with his insignificant face, slanting eyes (for he squinted) and flabby cheeks, he looked like a very ugly monkey.

Nor had Aeneas long to wait before the dubiousness of his position became clear. The course of events soon began to augur badly for the Council at Basle; Aeneas' very successes there might yet prove an embarrassing liability.

A way out of the dilemma presented itself. To the north lay the sprawling, chaotic Holy Roman Empire presided over by Frederick III whose attitude toward the conflict between the rival popes was one of neutrality. From the Emperor came an invitation to Aeneas to enter his service, an offer as timely as it was flattering. If the waters of neutrality did not lead to Rome, neither did they head for the rocks of schism. Aeneas accordingly accepted the post of secretary to the Emperor, a position which in due course brought the poet's crown and the Cardinal's hat in its train. With a sound instinct for realities, he turned to good account his mission from Frederick to Pope Eugenius IV at Rome, effecting both his own and the Emperor's reconciliation with the Roman See. The years in Frederick's service brought to the future Pius II first-hand acquaintance with the anarchy that prevailed in Germany and Austria, the Hussite nationalism of Bohemia and the independent spirit of Hungary. Now master and man, later as joint heads of Christendom, Frederick and his Italian secretary had good reason to appreciate the explosive forces threatening the decadent Empire.

From Aeneas the career diplomat to Pius the Pope the ladder of ascent is clear-cut in its externals. Less clear is the inner transformation from humanist to churchman. The author of the *Commentaries* does not give indication of deep spirituality. Lacking a vocation for the religious life, he had put off the issue of Holy Orders until it became imperative to ecclesiastical advancement. From this frank, transparently revealing document there emerges nothing of the mystic or the zealot or the reformer. Humility is conspicuously absent from his temperament, and a natural skepticism characterizes his intellectual attitude. On the other hand there is every reason to assume that the traditional religious observances were an accepted part of his personal life and that the growing laxity in the Church profoundly disturbed him. Indifference or insincerity in regard to religion formed no part of his character; his natural impulse was to invest religion with grandeur and majesty and to maintain the exalted dignity of the papal office. It is at the close of his career when the impending advance of the Turks, the defaulting of his allies and the approach of death threatened the collapse of all his hopes that the ailing Pontiff gives expression to a vital religious faith—both in word and deed.

Pius' life (1405–1464) spans a tumultuous half century. It saw the second half of the Hundred Years' War immortalized for him as for us in the figure of Joan of Arc. It witnessed the mounting chaos in the Holy Roman Empire. The Pope's own Italy was hardly less turbulent as the *Commentaries* well attest, the city-states in their rivalries paying scant heed to the Turkish threat on the eastern horizon. The efforts of the French to wrest the Kingdom of Naples, a papal fief, from its Aragonese ruler added further complications, posing a threat to the papacy itself.

The Church as spiritual guardian of strife-torn Christendom was in no better way. It still bore the scars of the Great Schism and the papacy's long absence from Rome. Church councils had endeavored to set its house in order, proclaiming for the purpose the doctrine of the supremacy of councils over popes. Incorporated in the Pragmatic Sanction of Bourges, the conciliar doctrine moreover became a political weapon to be brandished by French kings in their dealings with the Holy See. The instrument of reform thus appeared as a sword of Damocles to the restored papacy. Ecclesiastical corruption and exploitation were rife; rumblings of discontent were to be heard on every hand. None of this was lost upon Pius, to whose pen we owe a graphic description of the corrosive forces in the Church in the half century before the Reformation. Yet he let himself be carried along by the currents which were to bring disaster to the Church, of which perhaps the most subtle was the changing outlook upon life summed up in the term Renaissance and nowhere more clearly reflected than in Pius himself.

For it was the period of the early Renaissance, the generation which saw the feverish enthusiasm for classical learning, the collecting of libraries, the revival of Greek studies; which witnessed the flowering of Italian art associated with such names as Masaccio, Leon Battista Alberti, Brunelleschi and Donatello. It was an age of thriving merchants—the far-flung banking empire of the Medici, the still formidable mercantile empire of Venice. With the race of trading folk, however, Pius was thoroughly out of tune. Impecunious himself, of a nobility which had been supplanted by Siena's bourgeoisie, he did not conceal his contempt for this upstart class whose power he could not ignore, whose aid he could not dispense with. By the very scorn he heaps upon the merchant republics Pius pays tribute to their decisive role in Italian politics.

This then was the *quattrocento,* not yet at its peak, which furnished the setting for Pius' career. He ascended the papal throne in 1458, schooled, as he points out, in the service of three popes, an antipope and an emperor, and in that service had traveled extensively. His insatiable curiosity and eager mind had allowed him to miss nothing; he arrived at the highest dignity in Western Christendom one of the best informed men in Europe. The fruits of this wide experience were to be seen not, as the literary world expected, in a pontificate notable for the patronage of letters, but in the political arena both European and Italian. His individualism as a humanist followed him to the papal throne; he remained too much the performer ever to become the patron.

THE *Commentaries* AS A DOCUMENT

The *Commentaries* have a dramatic history of their own. Remaining in manuscript form for more than a century, the work made its debut into print in the later sixteenth century with the double handicap of disguised authorship and an expurgated text. The deception as to authorship had been made possible by Pius himself by writing in the third person; his copyist, Gobellinus, by signing the finished copy as was customary, unwittingly lent his name to the disguise. That is to say, the *Commentaries* saw the light in printed form not as the work of Pius but of one of his secretaries, a German ecclesiastic named John Gobel, who, as it turned out, had merely made a fair copy of the original. It was moreover in the chastened and sober Italy of the Counter Reformation that the *Commentaries* first appeared in print; in the circumstances it was deemed wise by his kinsmen to allow the deception to stand. Nor was this enough. Still better to safeguard the good name of its Renaissance author the work was subjected to a judicious pruning of passages likely to offend. The *Commentaries* thus came down almost to our own century expurgated and as the work of another.

Scholarly detective work was long active in ferreting out the truth. It was the Catholic historian Ludwig Pastor who towards the end of the nineteenth century finally identified the Vatican Codex Reginensis 1995 as the original manuscript of the *Commentaries* written in part in the Pope's own hand, in part dictated to amanuenses. Thus was exposed the double deception as to authorship and content. The evidence is clear. Gobellinus makes it plain at the beginning and end of his manuscript that he has copied this work at the request of the Pope, its author. It is referred to by both contemporary biographers of Pius— Platina and Campano. A letter by Campano reveals that the Pope had asked him to correct the original draft: "He gave them to me to correct. I did not correct them." The most compelling evidence, however, would seem to reside in the work itself which in its freshness, its immediateness to the events recorded, and in the nature of much of its content could only have been written by the chief actor in the story. The discovery of the original draft put the matter beyond doubt.

Taken as a whole, the *Commentaries* lack organization and proportion. The work consists of twelve Books covering the years 1458–1463, to which an uncompleted thirteenth was later added. The "memorable events of his times" are recorded in larger or smaller installments as they came to the knowledge of the author, thus giving the work something of the character of a diary rather than of memoirs. Now and again the Pope reaches into the past to provide the historical background for his theme; sometimes he supplies actual documents. Interspersed at random are speeches, inimitable character sketches, and descriptions of rare beauty—whether of city or countryside, of architecture ancient or new, of the pageantry of the Church or the amusements of humble folk. With his usual candor Pius laments that his work is "rude and unorganized" and hopes that "perhaps someone else will undertake the task of putting each detail in its proper order.... We have not had the time." That task has fortunately never been undertaken.

Instead, it has been the privilege of the present writer, in collaboration with Professor Florence Alden Gragg, to publish an English translation of this original draft of the *Commentaries* as they came from the hand of the Pope without alteration, correction or deletion. The necessary function of historical criticism and amplification has been relegated to accompanying notes. By means of italics (retained in the present volume) the passages deleted or revised in the early editions are readily distinguishable. In them is to be found some of the most important and revealing material in the entire work. The account of his election to the papacy, for example, has an earthy flavor which conveys more of the human than of the divine at work. A scathing indictment of the Curia in explicit terms by the Archbishop of Mainz forms part of the narrative of that unedifying contest. The portrait of the Cardinal of Arras emerges as from an all too candid camera; the wickedness of Sigismondo Malatesta and other unsavory characters is spelled out in lurid detail. Erotic sensuality is portrayed with a realism reminiscent of the author's youthful poetry and his *Euryalus and Lucrezia*. Scattered throughout the work are derogatory allusions to the French and the Venetians which betray a deep-seated and outspoken hostility. That these passages would cause embarrassment or arouse resentment is plain to see. Less understandable the omission of homely anecdote written with irresistible charm, like the tale of the puppy Musetta, the passages vibrant with the warmth of an outgoing, colorful personality. The *Commentaries* and their author have suffered indeed at the hands of their well-wishers.

MAJOR THEMES OF THE *Commentaries*

Four major themes, largely political, wind their way through the *Commentaries*. There is first of all the kaleidoscopic Italian scene dominated by two conflicts which in effect impinge on each other: on the one hand the Pope's protracted struggle with Sigismondo Malatesta of Rimini to recover lands wrested from the Church; on the other the exhausting war waged with the aid of Francesco Sforza in support of Ferrante, King of Naples, against a rival French claimant to the throne. Peninsula-wide in its scope, this theme offers interesting sidelights upon persons and attitudes in fifteenth-century Italy. Out of the turmoil rises the sinister figure of Sigismondo Malatesta, of a wickedness so diabolical as to win for him the unique distinction of being canonized to hell. The Pope's fury against him will tolerate nothing short of complete humiliation. Venice is seen as an arrogant power bent on the subjugation of Italy. A sordid race of traders, the Venetians care nothing for religion. Yet their enemies are, fortunately, numerous. "We shall see many snows," he assures us, "before the Venetians bridle Italy." The Florentines fare no better though Cosimo de' Medici is referred to as "more cultured than merchants usually are." The Pope's own Siena is a thorn in the flesh of its distinguished son, resisting all his efforts to restore his noble class to political power. The mercenary character of Italian warfare is graphically set forth and given a strong note of anti-clericalism. A captain is quoted as saying: "I should be happy if I could see every priest in the world hanged."

Both contests in Italy are brought to a successful conclusion but at tremendous cost to the papal treasury. Ferrante's victory yielded important advantages to the Pope's family in the elevation of his nephew Antonio to princely rank with marriage to Ferrante's illegitimate daughter.

The second major theme moves into the wider European arena. Here the villain of the piece is France. With an eye to Milan and Naples, France has already shown its hand in the Neapolitan wars. On the ecclesiastical front it has reared the standard of Gallican liberties in the so-called Pragmatic Sanction of Bourges, armed, as we have seen, with the threat of a council. Any move of the papacy, whether to assert its suzerainty over Naples or to free itself from the yoke of the conciliar theory thus ran afoul of France. In the diplomatic contest that ensued it early became clear that the stakes were the crown of Naples and the Pragmatic Sanction of Bourges. The contest called for a matching of wits with that wiliest of fifteenth-century monarchs, Louis XI; each contestant held a bait of major attraction for his opponent. From this contest Pius emerged as victor, having gained the revocation of the obnoxious Sanction without yielding on the subject of Naples; he had shown himself a master of a new school of statecraft.

A third theme is occupied with the amorphous Holy Roman Empire whose disintegration poses problems no less serious to Pius than to his former employer, Frederick III. Here the author of the *Commentaries* draws upon knowledge gained at first hand during his years of service there. The bitter conflict between Frederick III and his brother Albert, Archduke of Austria, found Pius solidly on the side of the Emperor. The nationalistic movements in Bohemia and Hungary to free themselves from the Empire on the other hand created for the Pope a diplomatic tightrope; he could not openly support them against the Emperor, neither could he afford to antagonize countries in the vanguard of a crusade against the Turk. In the case of Bohemia the dilemma was finally resolved for him by the resurgence of the Hussite heresy there. With Hungary the case was different. It lay in the immediate path of the Turkish advance; its energetic king and strong nationalist spirit offered vastly greater promise of resistance to the invader than did the dilatory Frederick.

In the war-ridden German realms of the Emperor where political chaos reigned, Pius enters the lists on his own account in a long and violent conflict with Diether von Isenburg, Archbishop of Mainz. The point at issue was Diether's alleged defaulting in the payment of fees due to the papal court, an issue which was permitted to reach the proportions of open war. Between the lines one can see that Diether's quarrel with the Holy See was that of all Germany. His violent denunciation of papal exploitation arouses suspicions not intended by the author of the *Commentaries*. The papal victory achieved at terrific cost to this unhappy land fails somehow to win one's applause. The records of the papal treasury moreover show Diether to have been correct on the central issue.

The fourth theme of the *Commentaries,* finally, is one which Pius regards as pivotal for his whole pontificate—a crusade against the Turk. "Among all the purposes he had at heart," he tells us, "none was dearer than that of rousing Christians against the Turks and declaring war against them." Herein lay not only the defense of Christendom but its moral and spiritual regeneration as well.

The narrative is studded with defeats dramatically told. His pontificate opens with a summons to the princes of Christian Europe to a congress at Mantua to draw up plans for a concerted offensive against the invader at the gates. The feeble response merely underscored European indifference to Pope and Turk alike. Embassies to individual courts encountered evasions or excuses. In 1462 the Pope announced his intention to lead a crusade in person with his one dependable ally, Philip, Duke of Burgundy, and soon thereafter dramatized his appeal to Christendom at large through the spectacular reception of the head of St. Andrew—a sacred relic saved from infidel hands. But even Philip failed at the last, whether willingly or under pressure from the King of France is not clear. Thus at the end of his life only one expedient remained to Pius as the alternative to defeat—to lead a crusade single-handed. The expedition to Ancona, undertaken despite rapidly declining health and disillusionment, climaxes his efforts. His death there sealed the failure of an enterprise already foredoomed.

The question of Pius' motivation and sincerity in regard to the crusade has been under dispute from his own day to ours. Was he the last great Crusader whose campaign ends on a note of martyrdom? Or was he the shrewd politician who saw in a crusade the means of recovering the papacy's lost prestige in Europe? The *Commentaries* provide significant insights which render either of these extreme views unlikely. Composed piecemeal during the years of his pontificate, the *Commentaries* permit one to assess the degree of interest in a crusade at any given time; it is clear that affairs nearer home take first place for some time after the fiasco at Mantua. What is more, Pius admits it. In a remarkable speech to a small group of Cardinals in 1462 he offers an analysis of the mood of Europe as discerning as it is frank. To the modern reader it points to one inescapable conclusion confirmed by subsequent events: fifteenth-century Europe had outgrown the medieval concept of a crusade without having yet awakened to the realities of the Turkish threat to Europe itself. For Pius Western civilization was at stake; only a gigantic defense operation could save it. The language of his appeal was still medieval; nor was he modern enough to consider coming to terms with the infidel. One has only to consult Pius himself to learn that a variety of motives—some practical, some personal, some idealistic—impelled him to this venture. Nor can a final appraisal leave out of account the undeniable heroism of the concluding act of his career. It is at this point that his religious appeal takes on an authentic quality, his final act a note of religious dedication.

To conclude, the *Commentaries of Pius II* depict an epoch of mounting crisis on many fronts as viewed by an informed European from the throne of St. Peter. They mirror too the pulsating cultural forces, the love of life, a this-worldliness of the Renaissance. It was an era in which a new world was being born, an old world struggling to survive. In the author himself these conflicting currents come alive. He gave utterance to them in bidding Christendom to "reject Aeneas and accept Pius." To separate one from the other, however, was no longer possible either for him or his times.

PREFACE

PREFACE

IF the soul dies with the body, as Epicurus wrongly supposed, fame can advantage it nothing. If on the other hand the soul lives on after it is released from this corporeal frame, *as Christians and the noblest philosophers tell us,* it either suffers a wretched lot or joins the company of happy spirits. Now in wretchedness is no pleasure even from renown and the perfect felicity of the blest is neither increased by the praise of mortals nor lessened by their blame. Why then do we so strive for the glory of a fair name? Do souls in Purgatory perhaps taste some sweetness from the reputation they left on earth? But let the argumentative think what they please *about the dead,* provided they do not deny that while men live they take pleasure in the glory of the present, which they hope will continue after death. It is this which sustains the most brilliant intellects and even more than the hope of a celestial life, which once begun shall never end, cheers and refreshes the heart of man. This is especially true of the Pope of Rome, whom almost all men abuse while he lives among them but praise when he is dead. We ourselves have seen Martin V, Eugenius IV, Nicholas V, and Calixtus III condemned by the populace while they lived and extolled to the skies when they were dead. His vicars follow in the footsteps of their Lord. Men said of Christ, our Saviour, while He lived, that He had an evil spirit, but when He hung upon the cross, they acknowledged Him to be the Son of God. The servant is not greater than his master and the treacherous tongue that has not spared so many of Christ's vicars or Christ Himself will not spare Pope Pius II. *He is accused and censured while he lives among us. When he is dead, he will be praised; and men will desire him when they can no longer have him.* After his death Envy will be still and when those passions which warp the judgment are no more, true report will rise again and number Pius among the illustrious popes. (Fig. 1)

Meantime we purpose to write the history of his pontificate and it will not be out of place to set down very briefly by way of introduction a few facts about the origin of his family and his doings before he became pope, that after-generations may understand how he who had before been called Aeneas Sylvius came to sit in St. Peter's chair and to assume the name of Pius II. You who may sometime read these pages, be gracious to them, but show no mercy if they lie.

BOOK I

THE Piccolomini, who came to Siena from Rome [1] and were counted among the oldest and noblest families of the state, were illustrious in arms and letters and possessed many castles and fortresses so long as the aristocrats were in power; but when the government passed from the nobles to the people, the house of Piccolomini was humbled with the rest. Enea Silvio, grandfather of the present writer, retained however a not inconsiderable fortune, which enabled him to live in a dignified fashion. He died while still a young man, leaving his wife, Montanina, with child. She bore a son who was called Silvio. During his minority his property was squandered by his guardians and agents, though he was brought up like a gentleman and sent to school, where he received a thorough training in the liberal arts. When he grew up, he became a soldier, but after divers misfortunes at length came home and having recovered a small part of his patrimony, married a poor but noble girl, Vittoria, of the family of the Forteguerri, who are the patrons of the cathedral of Siena. She was so fruitful that she often gave birth to twins and by her he had eighteen children, though there were never more than ten living at once. He brought up his family in poverty in Corsignano, [2] a town in the valley of the Orcia, but the cruel plague finally carried off all but Enea and his sisters Laodamia and Catherina.

Enea received his father's name, Silvio, and out of reverence for the apostle who was flayed by the barbarous Indians, he was given a third name and was called Enea Silvio Bartolommeo. He was born at dawn on St. Luke's day, October 18, 1405. When he was three years old, while playing with other children, he fell from a high wall onto a rock, receiving a severe wound in the head, which, contrary to the apprehensions and expectations of his parents, was soon healed by his godfather, Niccolò Monticuli, an untrained and so-called empiric physician. In his

[1] This is doubtful. The notion may have originated with the flatterers of Aeneas Sylvius after his accession to the pontificate.
[2] Renamed Pienza by A. S. after he became Pope.

29

eighth year he was tossed by a charging bull and escaped death more
by the help of Heaven than through any human aid.

After remaining for some time in his father's house performing all
sorts of rustic duties, he went, when he was eighteen, to the city, where
he was welcomed by his kinsmen, who thought that so promising a
youth ought to have his chance. He began to study under the gram-
marians, then became an eager follower of poets and orators, and finally
applied himself to civil law. When he had spent some years listening to
the professors of this subject, the outbreak of a serious war between
Siena and Florence forced him to interrupt his literary studies and leave
the beloved soil of his native city.

Now it happened that Domenico Capranica, *a man of noble character
and intellect,* who had been raised to the cardinalate by Martin V and
repudiated by his successor, Eugenius IV, was then at Siena. At that
time a council had been called at Basle,[3] a city of Switzerland on the
Rhine, and was already in session. Domenico, who was in disgrace at
Rome, resolved to defend his claims at Basle. He appointed Aeneas his
secretary and took him with him to Piombino, a town called by some
Populino, which is built on the ruins of the ancient Populonia. There,
when he had decided to go to Genoa by the Ligurian Gulf (because the
way by land was blocked) and when the ship in which he meant to
cross was already in sight, the lord of the place, Jacopo Appiani, though
he pretended to be friendly, forbade any boat to carry him out. But
Domenico, when he realized this treachery, left the town with only one
companion and fled to the coast, where he procured a light skiff and
hastened out to the ship which was sailing to and fro in open sea. When
the tyrant learned of this, he allowed all the rest of Domenico's party
to embark, thinking there was no point in chasing the feathers when
he had lost the meat.

The next day Aeneas and Piero da Noceto, who was also Domenico's
secretary, and all his servants, who had spent a very chilly night in the
open air on the island of Elba, joined Domenico on his ship. But when
they were making for Genoa, they were buffeted by violent gales and
driven off their course to within sight of Africa, so that the sailors were
in terror of being carried into harbors of barbarians. Though it sounds
marvelous and almost incredible, still it is an undoubted fact that in one
day and night after leaving Italy they were driven between Elba and
Corsica to Africa and then, when the wind changed, drifted rather than
sailed back again between Corsica and Sardinia and put in at Porto

[3] 1431–1448.

Venere. Here they procured a galley and had a successful voyage to Genoa, going from there over land to Milan, where they saw the great and illustrious Duke Filippo Maria. After a brief stay they continued their journey and by way of the St. Gotthard Alps, steep mountains towering to the skies and covered deep with snow and ice, they came to Basle.

In Basle Domenico pressed his claim to the cardinalate before the Synod and through the advocacy of Aeneas was restored to his high office. But since Domenico was in financial difficulties because Eugenius forbade his kinsmen to give him any aid, Aeneas transferred his services to Nicodemo della Scala, Bishop of Freising, whose father had been lord of Verona, and then, when Nicodemo left Basle, to Bartolommeo Visconti, Bishop of Novara, serving both as private secretary.

Some time after this Aeneas accompanied Bartolommeo to the court of Eugenius, who was then established at Florence. From there he made a trip on important business to see Niccolò Piccinino, the most celebrated general of the age, who was taking the baths at Siena, and then for the first time he revisited his kinsmen and his old friends, remaining with them five days. When he returned to Florence, he found that Bartolommeo had been accused of grave offenses before Eugenius and was on trial for his life. Therefore Aeneas took refuge with Niccolò, Cardinal of Santa Croce, a most eminent and highly esteemed senator, who appointed him his secretary and rescued Bartolommeo from Eugenius. This he did at the earnest solicitation and recommendation of his major-domo, Tommaso of Sarzana, who afterward ascended the papal throne as Nicholas V, and of Piero da Noceto, who has been mentioned above. The Cardinal of Santa Croce had at that time been appointed ambassador to France to arrange a peace between Charles of France and Henry of England. With him Aeneas saw for the third time Milan and the Duke and from there he visited Monte Giove, which is today better named Mt. St. Bernard, to see Amadeo, Duke of Savoy, who had renounced the world and was living a life of pleasure rather than of penitence in a hermitage at Thonon above Lake Geneva together with six knights, who with him had assumed the hermit's cloak and staff; waiting, I suppose, for an event which happened eight years later, his summons to the papal throne by the cardinals assembled at Basle; for even then the rumor was current that Amadeo was to be pope. *This report was said by some to have originated with women who tell fortunes and have the gift of prophecy, who are very numerous in the mountains of Savoy.*

After paying him his respects the Cardinal went on to Basle and
then sailed down the Rhine to Cologne. Here he again took horse and
proceeded by way of Aix, Liége, Louvain, Douai, and Tournai to Arras,
where a congress of all the French and English cardinals was in session.

Philip, Duke of Burgundy, was at this time siding with the English
against the King of France, who had put his father to death. The Cardinal's first object was to bring about a general truce. When he failed
to accomplish this, he succeeded in reconciling Philip with the King
of France after obtaining his release from the allegiance he had sworn
to the King of England on the ground that that monarch had a claim
to the French throne. At that time too Aeneas sent Philip a letter in
verse on the blessings of peace. But before Philip broke with the English, the Cardinal sent Aeneas to Scotland to restore a certain prelate to
the King's favor.

When Aeneas arrived at Calais, a town on the seacoast opposite
England, he found himself at once an object of suspicion to the English.
Therefore he was put under the charge of his host and permitted to go
neither forward nor back, till the Cardinal of Winchester, who was
returning from Arras, came to his aid and ordered his release. When
however Aeneas went to the King of England and asked for a safe-
conduct to Scotland, he was ordered to go back again, because the
English feared that he would plot some mischief against them with
their enemy, the King of Scotland; for it was well known that he was
secretary to the Cardinal of Santa Croce, who had incurred the bitter
hatred of the English by alienating the Duke of Burgundy. All this was
unknown to Aeneas, who was forced to return much against his will,
having braved the perils of the sea to no purpose. Still he was glad to
have seen the rich and populous city of London, the famous church of
St. Paul, the wonderful tombs of the kings, the Thames which is swifter
at the flow than at the ebb of the tide, the bridge like a city, the village
where men are said to be born with tails,[4] and, more famous than all
the rest, the golden mausoleum of Thomas of Canterbury covered with
diamonds, pearls, and carbuncles, where it is considered sacrilegious to
offer any mineral less precious than silver.

Having therefore crossed the Channel again, he went to the town of
Bruges and then to Sluys, the busiest port in all the West. There he took
ship for Scotland, but was driven to Norway by two violent gales, one
of which kept them in fear of death for fourteen hours. The other

---

[4] Strood, in Kent. The inhabitants of this district were said to have cut off the tail of
St. Thomas à Becket's horse, and were thus fittingly punished by divine justice.

pounded the ship for two nights and a day, so that she sprang a leak
and was carried so far out to sea toward the north that the sailors, who
could no longer recognize the constellations, abandoned all hope. But
the Divine Mercy came to their aid, raising north winds, which drove
the vessel back toward the mainland and finally on the twelfth day
brought them in sight of Scotland.

When they had made harbor, Aeneas in fulfillment of a vow walked
barefoot ten miles to the Blessed Virgin of Whitekirk. After resting
there two hours he found on rising that he could not stir a step, his feet
were so weak and so numb with cold. It was his salvation that there
was nothing there to eat and that he had to go on to another village.
While he was being carried rather than led there by his servants, he got
his feet warm by continually striking them on the ground, so that he
unexpectedly recovered and began to walk.

When he was at last admitted to the King's presence, he obtained all
he had come to ask.[5] He was reimbursed for his traveling expenses and
was given fifty nobles for the return journey and two horses called
trotters.

The following facts about Scotland seem worth recording. It is an
island two hundred miles long and fifty wide, connected with Britain
and extending toward the north. It is a cold country where few things
will grow and for the most part has no trees. Below the ground is found
a sulphurous rock, which they dig for fuel. The cities have no walls.
The houses are usually constructed without mortar; their roofs are
covered with turf; and in the country doorways are closed with oxhides.
The common people, who are poor and rude, stuff themselves with meat
and fish, but eat bread as a luxury. The men are short and brave; the
women fair, charming, and easily won. Women there think less of a
kiss than in Italy of a touch of the hand. They have no wine except
what they import. Their horses are all small and natural trotters. They
keep a few for breeding and castrate the rest. They do not curry them
with iron or comb them with wooden combs or guide them with bridles.
The oysters are larger than those in England *and many pearls are
found in them*. Leather, wool, fish, and pearls are exported from Scotland to Belgium. There is nothing the Scotch like better to hear than
abuse of the English. It is said there are two Scotlands, one cultivated,

[5] Aeneas's unaccustomed brevity here suggests an unwillingness to divulge the nature
of his errand. If the real object was to arouse James of Scotland against England, he was
not successful. James refused to begin war but agreed to send agents to negotiate for
peace, and to refrain from giving aid henceforth to England—so according to Campano.

the other wooded with no open land. The Scots who live in the latter part speak a different language and sometimes use the bark of trees for food. There are no wolves in Scotland. Crows are rare and therefore the trees in which they nest are the property of the royal treasury. *Aeneas also used to say that, before he went to Scotland, he had heard there were trees there growing along a river, the fruit of which rotted, if it fell on the ground, but if it fell into the water, came to life and turned into birds;* [6] *but, when he eagerly investigated this marvel on the spot, he found that it was all a lie or, if true, had been moved on to the Orcades Islands. He did, however, vouch for the truth of the following statement:* at the winter solstice (Aeneas was there then) the day in Scotland is not more than four hours long.

When he had finished his business and was ready to return, the skipper who had brought him over promptly came and offered him his old quarters on his ship. But Aeneas, not so much foreseeing the future peril as remembering the past, said, "If he who has twice been in danger has no right to accuse Neptune, what is to be said to the man who suffers shipwreck a third time? I prefer to trust to the mercy of men rather than of the sea." So he sent the sailor away and chose to travel through England. And very soon after the ship sailed, in the sight of all she ran into a storm, which broke her up and sank her, and the skipper, who was going back to Flanders to marry a young bride, was drowned with everyone else on board except four men who caught hold of some planks and managed to swim to land.

Then Aeneas, realizing that he had been saved by a beneficent God, disguised himself as a merchant and left Scotland for England. A river, [7] which rises in a high mountain, separates the two countries. When he had crossed this in a small boat and had reached a large town about sunset, he knocked at a farmhouse and had dinner there with his host and the parish priest. Many relishes and chickens and geese were served, but there was no bread or wine. All the men and women of the village came running as if to see a strange sight and as our people marvel at Ethiopians or Indians, so they gazed in amazement at Aeneas, asking the priest where he came from, what his business was, and whether he was a Christian. Aeneas, having learned of the scanty entertainment to be found on his journey, had obtained at a certain monastery several

---

[6] Obviously the legend of the Bernacle Geese. *Cf.* Hakluyt, *Voy.* II, 1, 63: "There stand certaine trees upon the shore of the Irish Sea, bearing fruit like unto a gourd, which .... doe fall into the water, and become birds called Bernacles."—1599.

[7] The Tweed.

loaves of bread and a jug of wine and when he brought these out, they excited the liveliest wonder among the barbarians, who had never seen wine or white bread. Pregnant women and their husbands kept coming up to the table, touching the bread and sniffing the wine and asking for some, so that he had to divide it all among them.

When the meal had lasted till the second hour of the night, the priest and the host together with all the men and children took leave of Aeneas and hastened away, saying that they were taking refuge in a tower a long way off for fear of the Scots, who were accustomed, when the river was low at ebb tide, to cross by night and make raids upon them. They could not by any means be induced to take him with them, although he earnestly besought them, nor yet any of the women, although there were a number of beautiful girls and matrons. For they think the enemy will do them no wrong—not counting outrage a wrong. So Aeneas remained behind with two servants and his one guide among a hundred women, who made a circle around the fire and sat up all night cleaning hemp and carrying on a lively conversation with the interpreter.

But after a good part of the night had passed, *two young women showed Aeneas, who was by this time very sleepy, to a chamber strewn with straw, planning to sleep with him, as was the custom of the country, if they were asked. But Aeneas, thinking less about women than about robbers, who he feared might appear any minute, repulsed the protesting girls, afraid that, if he committed a sin, he would have to pay the penalty as soon as the robbers arrived. So he remained alone among the heifers and nanny goats, which prevented him from sleeping a wink by stealthily pulling the straw out of his pallet. Some time after midnight* there was a great noise of dogs barking and geese hissing, at which all the women scattered, the guide took to his heels, and there was the wildest confusion as if the enemy were at hand. Aeneas however was afraid that if he rushed outside, in his ignorance of the road he might fall a prey to the first person he met. Accordingly he thought best to await events in his own room (it was the stable) and very soon the women returned with the interpreter, saying that nothing was wrong and that the newcomers were friends, not enemies. *Aeneas thought this was the reward of his continence.*

At daybreak Aeneas proceeded on his journey and came to Newcastle, which is said to have been built by Caesar. There for the first time he seemed to see again a familiar world and a habitable country; for Scotland and the part of England nearest it are utterly unlike the country we inhabit, being rude, uncultivated, and unvisited by the winter sun. Next he came to Durham, where today men go to see the tomb of the holy abbot, the Venerable Bede, which is piously revered by the inhabitants of the region. He went also to York, a large and populous city, where there is a cathedral notable in the whole world for its size and architecture and for a very brilliant chapel whose glass walls are held together by very slender columns. As he rode along he was joined by an English judge, who was hurrying up to London to court. He told Aeneas what had happened at Arras, supposing him to know nothing about it, and cursed the Cardinal of Santa Croce roundly, calling him a wolf in sheep's clothing. Who would not be amazed at such a coincidence? Aeneas was brought safely to London by a man who, if he had known who he was, would at once have had him put in prison.

In London however, Aeneas found that the King had forbidden any foreigner to leave the island unless he had a royal passport, and he did not think it safe to ask for one. Therefore he bribed the keepers of the port (a thing which is easy enough to do, as this class of men loves nothing more than gold) and so sailed from Dover to Calais, going from there to Basle and straight on to Milan. Having learned there that the Cardinal of Santa Croce had been dispatched from Florence and was on his way to Basle by way of the valley of the Adige and the Arlberg, he set out to join him by crossing the Alps at Brig and proceeding up the valley of the Sion.

When Aeneas had followed the Cardinal so far and had learned that no one was acceptable to Eugenius who had been on the side of the Council of Basle and that any mention of the Bishop of Novara might do him harm, in order not to waste his time at the Roman Curia, he returned, with the Cardinal's approval, to Basle and betook himself to Juan, the influential and holy Cardinal of San Pietro in Vincoli, who was afterward made Bishop of Ostia.

I will now relate briefly what happened at the Council of Basle and Aeneas's distinguished achievements there. At that time they were considering transferring the Council to some other place, to which it was thought the Greeks might come, and the choice lay among four cities which offered to pay the expenses of the Greeks: Florence, Udine, Pavia, and Avignon. Eloquent speeches had been made in the great hall in praise of three of these and only Pavia had no one to plead her cause, because Isidoro Rosati, whom Filippo Maria, Duke of Milan, had sent for that purpose, had spoken so badly and stupidly that he had been bidden to hold his tongue. Aeneas, stirred by the humiliation of a noble city and of that prince, composed a speech that night. The next day he came into the Council and having got permission to speak through the influence of Giuliano, the papal legate, he spoke for two hours to a most attentive and admiring audience, and afterward everyone present had a copy of the speech made for himself.

From that time Aeneas was more popular in the Council and in high favor with the Duke of Milan; for, although his official title was merely psalmist, he acted as secretary and abbreviator and often sat on the Committee of Twelve. This post, though it was held for only three months, carried great weight, since no deputation might engage in the debate unless its subject had been approved by the Twelve nor was anyone admitted to the Council without their permission. In his own deputation (which was called Deputation of the Faith) he often presided. He often kept the keys to the lead which was used to seal the letters of the synod. None of the secretaries was oftener chosen rescribendarius and among the abbreviators he had the rank of the upper bar. When representatives of the various nations were chosen for important matters, he was almost always one. He went on embassies for the Council three times to Strasbourg, twice to Constance, once each to Frankfort, *Trent,* and Savoy, and always with success. When the provost of San Lorenzo at Milan died, Francesco, Bishop of Milan, a man greatly respected for his learning and piety, at once with the approval of the Council appointed Aeneas in his place, though there were not a few scholars and important men among the Milanese themselves who hoped for advancement.

When Aeneas arrived in Milan,[8] he found that by the Duke's orders the chapter had called to the provostship and installed in office a noble of the great house of the Landriani. Aeneas was so high in favor with the prince and the court that he soon obliged his rival to surrender the post to him, but after entering upon it he suddenly came down with a severe fever. Filippo sent to see him every day his own physician, Filippo of Bologna, a learned and delightful man, who afterward entered the service of Pope Nicholas. During this illness, when Aeneas had taken a drug which had no effect and the physician had prepared another draught to be taken the next night, at the very moment when the second drug was to be administered his bowels began to work and caused him such discomfort that he had to get up ninety times. This made him delirious and brought him to the very gates of death (as the

[8] He had come to claim the provostship of San Lorenzo to which he had been appointed.

saying is) and there is no doubt that, if he had drunk the second draught, he would have been so weakened and exhausted that he would have died. Recognizing this as clear evidence of divine mercy, although for seventy-five days he was racked with continuous fever, he could never be induced to listen to magic-workers, though a man was brought to him who was said very recently to have cured of fever two thousand men in the camp of Niccolò Piccinino. But putting his trust in God, by whose aid his life had been spared, he set out while still feverish and returned to Basle, having recovered as he rode along.

At Basle the feast of St. Ambrose of Milan was being celebrated and at the invitation of the Archbishop Aeneas delivered the eulogy of the saint before the synod, though the theologians objected, because they wanted to perform this function themselves. But Aeneas was preferred before them all and was listened to with incredible attention by the entire audience.

In the meantime the Emperor Sigismund had died and Albert [9] had been elected in his place. When Bartolommeo, Bishop of Novara, who had been sent to Albert by Filippo, Duke of Milan, arrived at Basle, he induced Aeneas by his earnest entreaties to accompany him to Austria. Aeneas however, disliking the customs in Austria, with which he had not yet become fully acquainted, parted from Bartolommeo at Vienna and returned to Basle with Lodovico, Patriarch of Aquileia, a noble of the house of the Dukes of Teck, not knowing that a great part of his future life was to be spent in Austria. No man may say, "I will not go to this place," for "God in His wisdom shrouds the future in dark night." [10]

That year [11] was not a good one in Germany for either wine or wheat. In Bavaria boys and girls begged bread from passers-by and fought for the morsels tossed them as dogs fight for bones. And before long there came a frightful plague which spread all over Germany. At Basle it snuffed out the life of the Patriarch Lodovico and of Lodovico, the Roman Protonotary, who was called "the light of the law"; it carried off many prelates and laid low innumerable commoners; and the sickness raged so fiercely that they buried more than three hundred corpses in one day.

But the plague did not spare him either and when he realized that he was infected, he called his attendants and urged them to leave him, that they might not catch the sickness by remaining with a dying man.

[9] Albert of Austria, son-in-law of Sigismund.
[10] Horace, *Carm*. 3. 29. 29.   [11] Probably 1438.

When he found that there were two celebrated doctors in the city, one from Paris, learned but unlucky, the other lucky but ignorant, Aeneas preferred luck to learning—reflecting that no one really knew the proper treatment for the plague. The following was the treatment he was actually given. Since his left thigh was infected, they opened a vein in his left foot. Then, after being kept awake all that day and part of the night, he was made to drink a powder, the nature of which the physician would not tell. Sometimes chopped-up pieces of green, juicy radish and sometimes bits of moist clay were applied to the sore and to the infected place. Under this treatment the fever increased accompanied by a violent headache and his life was despaired of. Therefore he had a priest summoned, made his confession, and received Communion and Extreme Unction. Soon after, he began to wander in his mind and gave meaningless answers to questions. Then the rumor got abroad that he had died, a circumstance which cost him his provostship at Milan, for it was given to another, who, on account of the schism in the Church, could not be ousted. But, after six days, by God's mercy he recovered. When he offered his doctor a fee of six florins (for the man's kindness and faithfulness had been remarkable and perhaps unprecedented in a physician), the latter, thinking he was not worth so much, said, "if you really wish me to take all this money, I will attend six poor men without charge"; and he bound himself by an oath to do so.

When at this time the canonry and the prebend of the cathedral of Trent became vacant by the death of the Pole, Johann Andreas, although the candidates were numerous and not to be disdained, the Council conferred these benefices on Aeneas with its distinguished approval. When he went to take possession of his benefices, he found that a certain German named Vilichinus, a quarrelsome, sly fellow, had pushed himself into them on the authority of the chapter; but Aeneas won the canons over to his side and forced him out.

At this time the Council of Basle had by its decrees deposed Pope Eugenius and, being concerned about a successor, they had chosen eight men from each nation so that there should be thirty-two to whom the power of electing a pope should be delegated. When the Italians were named, Aeneas was one and because the fact that he was not yet in holy orders seemed to make him ineligible for that duty, he was given a document which entitled him to disregard the time fixed by law and assume the ranks of subdeacon and deacon together with the minor orders in one day. He was however unwilling to enter upon an ecclesiastical career for such a reason, but he was present in the conclave as

Clerk of Ceremonies and witnessed all the proceedings by which the
Council of Basle elected Amadeo, Duke of Savoy, Pope Felix V.

Aeneas went at once to the Duke, who was still living in his hermitage, became his secretary and continued in his service at Ripaille,
Thonon, Geneva, Lausanne, and Basle, until Frederick III, King of the
Romans, who had succeeded to the throne on the death of Albert, was
crowned at Aix on his way to Frankfort and Lower Germany. When
Felix sent ambassadors to him, he bade Aeneas accompany them, and
thus Aeneas, who had frequent conversations with Frederick's counsellors, became friendly with a learned and influential man, Sylvester,
Bishop of Chiemsee. He also met and came to know intimately Jacob,
Archbishop of Trier and Imperial Elector, who was as virtuous as he
was noble. After he had been introduced to the Emperor's favor by
these two men and had received the laurel crown with all the privileges
belonging to poets,[12] the Emperor invited him to enter his service and
remain at his court. Aeneas replied that, although there was no one
who had a better right to his services, *seeing that he had been born
under the empire,* yet, as he was still Felix's secretary, he thought it
would not be proper to go over to another master without his permission; he would however return to Basle to ask Felix's consent and if
he could obtain it, he would gladly come to the imperial court. The
Emperor, who was just going to Basle himself, approved this answer.

But Aeneas, when he returned to Felix, was unable by his own efforts
to obtain his release. Finally however through the intervention of
friends he was set free and joining Frederick at Basle on his way back
from Burgundy he was appointed his secretary and protonotary in the
imperial chancery. He took the oath of allegiance to the Emperor at
Brixen, where Caspar Schlick was appointed Chancellor, an office he
had held under Sigismund and Albert. He was a noble knight, a man
of ready wit and an effective speaker, who had the unprecedented or
at least very rare distinction of serving three emperors as chancellor.
While he was acting as the Emperor's legate at Nuremberg, he delegated his authority in the chancery to Wilhelm Tacz, a Bavarian who
hated all Italians. This man insulted Aeneas outrageously, but Aeneas,
having made up his mind to conquer evil with good, laid back his ears
like a stubborn ass when its burden is too heavy for its back, and so,
though he was considered the meanest of all there and did not have a

---

[12] Diploma dated at Frankfort, July 27, 1442. The privileges attached to this honor
included the right to publish and to lecture publicly, to wear a gown embroidered with
gold, etc. This coronation was the first of its kind to occur on German soil.

proper place at table or a suitable room and was despised and laughed at as if he were a hateful heretic or a Jew, he bore everything calmly.

Among his fellow secretaries however was Michael Pfullendorf, who, because he loved the gentler Muses and was engaged in humane studies, bade Aeneas be of good courage, for when the Chancellor returned he would find things better. Nor was he mistaken, for when Caspar returned and tested Aeneas's worth in one way and another, finding him talented, industrious, and able to stand hard work, he began to think highly of him and to show him preference. Furthermore, when Caspar was at Siena at the time when the Emperor Sigismund was there, he had been entertained at the house of the distinguished Niccolò Lolli and his wife, the noble lady, Bartolommea Tolommei, Aeneas's aunt, and had stood godfather to the child of their daughter Margarita, whom he named Gaspare for himself. All this endeared Aeneas the more to him. The next time he went away on an embassy Aeneas was left in charge of the chancery and thereafter he presided over it whenever Caspar was absent. Wilhelm, who had begun by trampling on Aeneas, was now forced to stand in awe of him, so that all might know that meekness is easily exalted and pride still more easily brought low. He was however unable to endure his unpopularity and soon withdrew from the court. All the rest were reconciled with Aeneas, whose influence with the Emperor increased daily so that he was called upon in many important and difficult matters and finally made a member of the Privy Council.

His first mission was to the Trientines, whom he persuaded to swear allegiance to the Emperor, administering the oath himself. Later, when the Emperor and the Electoral Princes were endeavoring at Nuremberg to end the bitter schism between Eugenius IV and Felix V, they decided that the Emperor should choose four men, each Elector two, and the other princes one each, to hear the spokesmen of Eugenius and Felix and see that the Christian state should suffer no harm. The Emperor Frederick named the following: Sylvester, Bishop of Chiemsee, the theologian Thomas Haselbach, the jurisconsult Ulrich Sonnenberg, and Aeneas, *the poet, though the last-named still favored the cause of Basle and Frederick more than he did Eugenius. For the enthusiasm he had felt at Basle had not died down nor had he yet grasped the principles on which Eugenius's case rested, and associating as he did with one side only, he despised the other. (Later however, seeing that the Basle party shrank from a trial, he gradually turned away from them.) Therefore at Nuremberg he stubbornly supported the side of*

*Basle and it was owing to his efforts that the terms of peace offered to
the opposing factions were less favorable to Eugenius than to Basle;
for when they decided to try to restore peace to the Church by calling
another council to which both Eugenius and the delegates at Basle
should come, the place named was the city of Constance in the province
of Mainz, very far from Eugenius and near Basle.*

Meantime Aeneas had received from the Emperor the parish church
of the Valle Sarantana, which brought him a yearly income of sixty
florins. This valley, lying among the Alps which separate Germany
from Italy, has only one entrance and that one very high and difficult,
and for three quarters of the year it is buried under snow and thick ice.
The inhabitants remain in their houses all winter making boxes and
other pieces of carpentry, at which they are very skillful, which they
sell in the summer in Bolzano and Trent. They while away a good deal
of time playing chess and dicing, games at which they are extraordinarily clever. They have no fear of war nor are they tormented by any
ambition nor consumed by greed for gold. Their wealth is in their
flocks, which they feed on hay in the winter, and they also live on them.
There are men among them who have never drunk anything, with
whom milky food takes the place of drink. Those who live far from the
church place the bodies of those who die during the winter out of doors
and keep them frozen till summer; then the priest, as he goes the rounds
of the parish, heads a long funeral train and pronouncing the last words,
receives into the cemetery many bodies at one time, while the people
follow the procession dry-eyed. They might be the happiest of mortals,
if they realized their blessings and bridled their lust; but they spend
day and night in revelry indulging in promiscuous intercourse and no
girl is ever a virgin when she marries.

After this, when the Council of Basle had rejected the proposed terms
of peace, Aeneas was sent to confer with Eugenius. But when he reached
Siena, his kinsmen were unanimous in trying to deter him from going
to Rome, because he had been against Eugenius at Basle. *For Eugenius,
they declared, remembered nothing so long as an injury and was both
vindictive and cruel.* Aeneas on the contrary said that he could not think
Rome was unsafe for the Emperor's ambassador and that he must either
perform the duty he had undertaken or die in the attempt. Therefore
in spite of the entreaties of his weeping family he continued on his way.

An old intimate of his, Gerardo Landriano, Cardinal of Como, like
the good senator and faithful friend he was, introduced him to the
presence of Eugenius. I should like to quote here the words of Aeneas

to the Pope, for they are few and worth recording. By the Pope's side stood two cardinals, those of Como and Amiens, who first by apostolic authority absolved Aeneas of all blame which he had incurred by taking the side of the Council of Basle. When therefore he came before Eugenius and had been permitted to kiss his foot, hand, and cheek, having presented his credentials and been bidden to speak, he said, "Your Holiness, before I deliver the Emperor's message, I will say a few words about myself. I know that many tales about me that are neither creditable nor fit to be repeated have been poured into your ears. Nor have those who have given you these reports of me lied. At Basle I said, wrote, and did many things *against you*. I deny none of them. But my purpose was not so much to hurt you as to help the Church of God. *For in attacking you I thought I was showing obedience to God*. I was wrong (who can deny it?) but wrong in the company of men neither few nor mean. I followed the lead of Giuliano, Cardinal of Sant' Angelo, Niccolò, Archbishop of Palermo, and Lodovico Pontano, notary of Your Holiness's see, who were thought to be the very eyes of the law and the teachers of truth. I will say nothing of the University *of Paris* and other schools all over the world, of which so many were opposed to you. Who might not have erred in company with such great names? But I confess that when I realized the error of the Council, I did not make all haste to go to you, as many did, but fearing to fall from one error into another, as those who try to avoid Charybdis often fall into Scylla, I betook myself to those who were considered neutral, that I might not pass from one extreme to the other without time for reflection. Therefore I stayed three years with the Emperor, where I heard more and more of the dispute between the Council and your legates, till finally I came to have no shadow of doubt that the truth was on your side. Thus it happened that when the Emperor desired to send me to Your Clemency, I gladly obeyed, thinking that it would afford me an opportunity of regaining your favor. Now I stand before you and because I sinned in ignorance, I beg you to forgive me. After that I will set forth the Emperor's cause."

Eugenius replied, "We know that you have sinned grievously against us, but since you confess your error, we must pardon you. For the Church is a loving mother, who never remits the due penalty when a son denies his sin nor insists upon it when he confesses. You now know the truth. See that you do not let it go and that you seek by good works to regain the Divine Grace *which you lost by wicked acts*. You are now in a position where you can defend the truth and be of service to the

Church. Hereafter we shall forget past wrongs and so long as you do well, we shall love you well." After this they proceeded to speak of ecclesiastical matters, about which Eugenius wished time to meditate.

Meanwhile, when Aeneas was looking for the Cardinal of Aquileia, he chanced to meet Tommaso of Sarzana, then Bishop of Bologna.[13] When he was on the point of greeting him in accordance with their old friendship, he found that he drew back and tried to avoid him with every sign of loathing; for he supposed that Aeneas was still on the side of the Council of Basle, which he himself hated above all things. Aeneas, surprised at this and somewhat indignant, stopped short and made no further effort to speak to him; but some days later, when Aeneas lay ill with a painful attack of colic at the house of Giuliano Baratto, an old friend of his from Basle, Tommaso was sorry for him and sent his faithful and tried friend, the Spaniard Martino, to comfort the sick man and offer him money to pay his physicians. Cardinals sent to inquire for him and the Pope himself sent the distinguished Giovanni of Padua to promise him everything needed for his recovery. His illness was very severe and the pain so intense that in all the twelve days he lay there there was not an hour when he did not pray for death. When however he finally recovered, he returned to Siena; then after cheering his father, whom he never saw again, and greeting his kinsmen, he went back to Germany.

On his way, near San Casciano, he met Tommaso, Bishop of Bologna, who was going to Rome, and thanked him for remembering him when he had been ill there. They drank together and renewed their old friendship, but Tommaso did not think the reconciliation was even yet complete, for some time later, when he was going as ambassador to the Emperor, he asked his friend and relative, Piero da Noceto, who was also a loyal old friend of Aeneas, to give him a letter of recommendation to him. But this was entirely unnecessary, for Aeneas forgot nothing so quickly as a grudge. Still, when he received Piero's letter, he showed himself so much the more eager to do Tommaso every service as the bond of two friendships is stronger than one. Thus all the rust of dissension was wiped away and their friendship was renewed closer than ever.

With Tommaso was Juan de Carvajal, who had recently come from the Emperor. He brought a letter from Eugenius in which Aeneas was appointed Apostolic Secretary, a post into which he was inducted later at Rome. This seems to me an extraordinary distinction and I do not

[13] Future Pope Nicholas V.

know whether anyone else has ever had the good luck to be so exalted by fortune that he served as secretary to two popes, an emperor, and an antipope. For Aeneas held this post not only nominally but actively, first under Felix, then under the Emperor Frederick, later under Eugenius, and finally under Nicholas.

At this time the Imperial Electors in session at Frankfort, roused by Eugenius's removal of the Archbishop of Cologne, and of Jacob, Archbishop of Trier, made a secret compact that, unless Eugenius annulled the dismissals, relieved the nation of its burdens, and recognized the authority granted to their councils at Constance, they would recognize his deposition which had been voted at Basle; and they sent ambassadors to the Emperor to explain these matters to him and to six sworn counsellors only and to beg him to join in their concordat and send his representative with them to Rome. When the Emperor heard the purpose of the Electors, he said that he would send an ambassador to Eugenius and would ask him to grant their petitions; but he would have nothing to do with the concordat, saying that it was outrageous and impious to desert the Pope if he did not grant what they asked. Therefore he sent Aeneas to Eugenius to persuade him not to defy the Electors, but especially to beg him to restore the deposed archbishops to their former dignity. For he said that this would make all Germans throw off their neutrality and return to his bosom; if however he persisted in his harsh attitude, there would be danger of the scandal of a permanent schism. All the Electors' secret decisions the Emperor, who was not under oath, revealed to Aeneas and bade him tell them to the Pope; and since the Electors were to have another meeting at Frankfort on the first of September to hear the Pope's reply and to abandon their neutrality according to their compact, he instructed Aeneas to go straight to Frankfort, where he would meet the other delegates, and make known to them Eugenius's decision.

It was then spring, a season when so much rain fell that it destroyed all the bridges in Carinthia and carried them down the river. On this account they were obliged to travel for three days led by native guides over very high and pathless mountains and precipitous, snow-covered crags.

When they reached Rome, Eugenius, at Tommaso's suggestion, heard Aeneas before he heard the delegates of the Electors and he promised to do everything that the Emperor urged. He then directed Tommaso to go to Philip, Duke of Burgundy, and obtain his consent to the reinstatement of the archbishops, because, as Philip's nephew had been nominated for the post at Cologne and his natural brother for that at Trier, he thought he ought not to promise to reinstate the bishops without consulting him. Tommaso was instructed, after he had learned Philip's wishes, to proceed to Frankfort. Aeneas had planned to accompany him as far as Parma, but since Tommaso seemed somewhat dilatory *and slow* in procuring his letter, he thought he had better go on ahead. When he had reached Siena and was staying with his family, he fell ill suddenly of the stone and was still in bed the following day when Tommaso arrived. The Bishop stopped only to greet Aeneas and went on at once, since his business was urgent. But Aeneas would not be beaten by sickness and the next day, though he was not yet well, he followed and caught up with him at the Carthusian monastery of Florence. They then set out together for Pistoia and Lucca. Aeneas however entered Florence, while Tommaso was excluded *as being the legate of Eugenius, whom the Florentines then hated*. At Lucca they stayed a day with Piero da Noceto, who went with them through the valley of Garfagnana as far as the house of Tommaso's sister, Catherina, who was married to a very influential nobleman of the valley named Cesare. She received her brother, whom she had not seen for a long time, with extraordinary affection and great honor.

Leaving Piero here the others made their way to Parma over the very high and rough Silanian Alps. There Tommaso, who was exhausted by the long journey on foot and the sleepless nights spent with rustic hosts, was stricken with a very severe fever. He at once sent for Aeneas and tearfully begged him to go on immediately, that his delay might not interfere with their business; and he gave him the apostolic letter for Juan de Carvajal, saying that if he did not recover shortly, he would write Eugenius to appoint someone in his place.

Aeneas was reluctant to leave the sick man, but realizing the necessity he resumed his journey. Crossing the Po at Brescello he went on to Mantua and Verona; then going by way of the valley of Trent and the Brixian Alps, he stopped to see Sigismund, Duke of Austria, who was staying in the valley of the Inn. He went hunting with him and saw a sight worth telling: a huge stag, after a long chase by the hounds, was finally forced to plunge into the river and then to give itself up alive to grace the prince's table.

From there Aeneas went by way of Nassereit and the valley called the Vale of Hell (Höllenthal) over a high mountain ridge to Kempten, Memmingen, and Ulm, but could get no farther because brigands were blocking all the approaches to Frankfort. While he was debating in anxiety and uncertainty what he should do, presently, just as if the day had been definitely appointed for the meeting, couriers came in with the news that Peter, Bishop of Augsburg, Sylvester, Bishop of Chiemsee, and the Chancellor Caspar, "white souls" and the Emperor's envoys, were close at hand. Nothing could have been more welcome to Aeneas, not only because of his acquaintance with them but because of the increased safety of traveling. Soon they all set out together for Frankfort and were joined in a few days by Jacob, Margrave of Baden, and Albert, Margrave of Brandenburg. Tommaso, after an illness of ten days, at last began to recover and continued his journey. He passed unrecognized through Savoy to the court of the Duke of Burgundy and having obtained from him what he asked, arrived at Frankfort toward the end of the Diet. Meantime Juan de Carvajal and Nicholas of Cusa were doing their best to make the princes satisfied with the letter Aeneas had brought. But all their efforts were in vain, since the ambassadors of the princes who had been in Rome reported that Eugenius *had shown himself rude, haughty, and bitterly hostile to their nation and* had answered them very harshly. Thus Eugenius's cause seemed desperate, because the Emperor did not dare declare for him alone against all the Electors.

In this Diet Aeneas did a bold and remarkable thing which I cannot bring myself to pass over. The Archbishop of Mainz, who had affixed a seal to the concordat of the Electors both for himself and for Frederick of Brandenburg, on being asked by the Emperor's spokesman to change his vote was not unwilling to do so, provided he could be assured that he would not be considered to have broken his word. Then Aeneas bade his companions be of good courage, for he would easily satisfy the Archbishop of Mainz. He sat up all night and from the princes' rough draft, on the basis of which they wished to compose a letter to Eugenius, he constructed another, squeezing out all the venom, which Eugenius loathed, and amplifying all the motions which concerned the provision to be made for the nation, the reinstatement of the archbishops, *and the respect to be shown the authority of the General Councils.* When he had finished, he directed that this draft should be shown to the Archbishop of Mainz and that he should be told that it embodied the Emperor's wishes; that Eugenius intended to provide for the nation; and that there was no reason to doubt that they could obtain their requests from His Holiness, if they would again send ambassadors to him. The Archbishop of Mainz thought this satisfactory and just, and presently, with the imperial delegates and those from the Archbishops of Magdeburg, Bremen, and Salzburg, the Margrave Frederick, and many other princes, he entered into an agreement to affix the seals of them all to Aeneas's draft and sent it to Rome. The Electors and all the other princes were dismayed at hearing this, but did not dare oppose it, for most of the nation was in favor of the draft.

At the end of the Diet Tommaso, Bishop of Bologna, and Juan de Carvajal, as they were passing through Neustadt in Austria, stopped to thank the Emperor warmly for sending to Frankfort such powerful and loyal ambassadors. While continuing their journey to Rome they were both raised to the cardinalate in recognition of their able and successful management of affairs. A few days later the Emperor appointed Aeneas and the noble Bohemian knight, Procop von Rabstein, ambassadors to the Roman Curia. With the consent of the Archbishop of Mainz and the Margrave of Brandenburg, he empowered them, if Eugenius should accept the proposals agreed upon at Frankfort, to abandon neutrality and in the name of the nation resume their allegiance to the Holy Apostolic See.

Meantime Johann of Lysura, when he found that events were not going to his liking, changed his liking to suit events and having made his submission to the Archbishop of Mainz, obtained from him the post of ambassador to Eugenius. The Emperor's envoys found him at Siena with many other ambassadors from princes and all proceeded together to Rome. They were met at the first milestone by the households of the Pope and the cardinals and all the prelates of the Curia, who escorted them into the city like returning generals who have conquered the enemy.

Two days later they were summoned before Eugenius and given audience in a secret consistory, where Aeneas acted as spokesman for them all and was applauded loudly by both Pope and cardinals. But that very day Eugenius fell ill and was obliged to take to his bed, leaving the question to be handled by the cardinals. When Eugenius had approved the entire draft and had composed a letter in answer to it, all the ambassadors were admitted to his chamber and made their submission to the Pope as he lay in bed. He at once put the apostolic bulls into Aeneas's hands and immediately the proceedings were resumed in public consistory, where the cardinals presided and the communications of the Emperor and the other princes were made known. Then in the general rejoicing throughout the city bonfires were lighted, and there was incessant ringing of bells and blowing of horns. The next day suspension of business was proclaimed and a general thanksgiving was decreed. The cardinals and all the other prelates with the people following in procession carried the crown of Sylvester, the head of John the Baptist, and precious relics of the saints from the church of San Marco to the Lateran, where mass was celebrated and a long and elaborate eulogy of Frederick and Eugenius was delivered.

While these things were taking place, there was a rumor that Niccolò, Bishop of Trieste, had died. The first cardinal to hear this was Tommaso, Cardinal of Bologna, and he learned of it from the Deacon of Aquileia, who had asked his aid in obtaining that church for himself. But the Cardinal, as soon as he heard the news, communicated it in a short note to his colleague Giovanni, Cardinal of Sant' Angelo, adding that here was an opportunity to advance Aeneas. Aeneas happened to be dining with Giovanni and was chatting as usual on various topics, when Giovanni handed him the note to read and asked what he thought about it. Aeneas answered, "I will not seek an office beyond my deserts, but if it is offered, I will not refuse it." The next day, when Lodovico, Cardinal of Aquileia, asked for the church at Trieste for his deacon and various others proposed other candidates, Eugenius refused them all and steadily asserted that he would be willing to trust the papacy itself to Aeneas. But when inquiry was made as to whether the church was really vacant, the rumor was found to be groundless. Aeneas, however, was made Apostolic Subdeacon by Eugenius.

For sixteen days after the submission of the Germans Eugenius fought against disease and death until, beaten at last, he died on the feast of St. Peter's Chair in the year of our salvation 1447. When his funeral rites had lasted nine days, the cardinals went into conclave to elect his successor, appointing Aeneas and Procop with the other envoys of the princes to guard the door. When they had sat up for two nights, Tommaso, Cardinal of Bologna, was elected pope and assumed the name of Nicholas V, in memory, many think, of Niccolò, Cardinal of Santa Croce, who had been his master and was thought to have lost the papacy on the death of Martin because he was absent on a mission to France. As soon as he had entered the palace of St. Peter, he summoned Aeneas, confirmed him as secretary and subdeacon, and charged him with carrying the cross before him on the day of his coronation.

Twenty days after Aeneas had left Rome Nicholas received authentic news of the Bishop of Trieste's death and without consulting any cardinal or calling a consistory he came into the Sacred College in robe and miter and, at first to the amazement and then with the approval of all the members of the Holy Senate, he pronounced Aeneas Bishop of Trieste and sent him his presentation free of dues. The Emperor Frederick, too, when he heard the church had become vacant, said, "We shall get this church, which is properly under our rule, for Aeneas," and he wrote the Pope a letter on the matter, not knowing that it was already settled. So when Aeneas returned to the Emperor in complete ignorance of what had happened, he found himself appointed to the bishopric by the desire of both Pope and Emperor. Nor were the people of Trieste, who were usually hostile to foreigners, averse to Aeneas, but although the canons had elected their own deacon and their first citizen, they bade him withdraw and with one accord bestowed the post on Aeneas even before he had arrived.

While these things were going on, Filippo Maria, Duke of Milan, died of dysentery, having publicly proclaimed Alfonso, King of Aragon, his heir, *though it was not within his competence to do this*. Therefore the Emperor sent Aeneas to Milan and with him Friedrich, Bishop of Seckau; Caspar Schlick, his chancellor; Johann, his chamberlain; Jacopo Landrono, his physician; and Pancraz Riutschad (all noble knights) to lodge a claim that the dukedom had reverted to the empire. Thus at one and the same time the lordship of that powerful city was claimed by the Emperor Frederick, Alfonso, King of Aragon, and Charles, Duke of Orléans, for the last-named also asserted his right, based on the marriage contract made between his father and Filippo's. But the Milanese, eager for freedom, had chosen a senate from their foremost citizens and had elected magistrates to carry on the government. Rejecting the King and the Duke, after they heard Aeneas speak for the Emperor they acknowledged him as their lord, reserving however the right to govern their own state. Then they finally came to the point where they were ready to accept Frederick's rule on certain conditions. This, though not all that was properly due him, seemed to Aeneas in the circumstances reasonably satisfactory, but his German colleagues by insisting on too much lost everything.

Aeneas on his return to Vienna was consecrated with the Apostolic Legate, Giovanni, Cardinal of Sant' Angelo, as his sponsor and then went to Trieste, where he was enthusiastically received by the people and celebrated his first mass. After a short stay he was ordered to go to Istria, where he adjusted a dispute about boundaries between the Emperor and the Venetians, though it afterward broke out again. On his return to Trieste he learned that Rupert von Wallsee was engaged in a war with the Triestines, in which his own church was the chief sufferer. His tenants were being driven from their lands and their cattle seized; and when he went to the Emperor to complain, it was only by making the greatest haste that he escaped being waylaid by Rupert, who was very eager to take him captive.

Meantime Caspar Schlick, who had been falsely accused before the Emperor, had been compelled to give up the church of Freising, which he had obtained for his brother, and was in greater disfavor with the Emperor every day. Aeneas, because of his friendship and almost continual association with him, fell under suspicion also and his position seemed to be becoming precarious. However by steering a middle course so as not to offend his friend on the one hand or his master on the other, he was restored to favor and obtained on the Emperor's recommendation the very important parish church of Castro Vindelico.

At this time [14] Count Francesco Sforza was besieging Milan. The panic-stricken citizens implored the Emperor's aid and Aeneas was sent there a second time in company with the lawyer, Hartung, to promise help to the besieged, if they would submit to the Emperor. On that journey they encountered many difficulties. After visiting Duke Sigismund at Innsbruck and persuading him to join them in the matter of Milan, they had come down through the lofty Bormian Alps to the Valtellina. Here they found that the people were divided, some favoring the city of Milan and others Francesco Sforza; that Lake Como was largely in the hands of the enemy; and that they were in danger everywhere. Therefore they had to make their way sometimes at night by water, sometimes by day over steep and pathless mountains, and when they finally arrived at Como, they had to stay there eighteen days because all the region between Como and Milan was held by the enemy.

When Sforza learned that ambassadors from the Emperor had come, he gave orders that all the approaches should be guarded and that the ambassadors, if they could be caught, should be brought to him in chains. They however obtained a force of some two hundred cavalry and infantry and having found three trustworthy fellows called guides, who knew the roads, they set out from Como for Milan about sunset. But when they had traveled for perhaps two hours and a black night was already upon them, the cavalry took advantage of the darkness to desert. The party had been joined by the ambassadors of the Duke of Savoy and several Milanese on their way home from a business trip to Germany. When these men learned of the desertion of the cavalry, they feared an ambush and in great terror advised returning to Como.

But Aeneas summoned the captains of the infantry and when he found them loyal and recognized one of them as a Sienese by his speech,

14 1449.

he turned to the merchants and said, "Have no fear. Now that we have come through the mountain passes into the open plains we have already escaped the danger of an ambush, which is always laid in narrow places, and we have our choice of a thousand paths. Only bad luck can now lead us into the hands of the enemy and God's goodness will save us from that. Come with me and I will this very night return you safe and sound to your own homes." So they continued on their way and about the tenth hour a little after sunrise they entered Milan, where they were received by all the populace with the greatest rejoicing.

But while the ambassadors were at Como, the government of the city had passed from the people, who were devoted to Rome, into the hands of a few men who secretly favored Francesco Sforza. Therefore Aeneas asked the senate to permit him to address the people and give them the Emperor's message.

Next day the people gathered in great numbers in the senate house, and after the Emperor's letter had been produced and publicly read, Aeneas spoke to the following effect. He said that at Filippo's death the Emperor had sent ambassadors to demand for himself the government of their state; he had not been listened to, though his demands were just, but the Milanese, exulting in their new liberty, had themselves elected magistrates to administer the state and this situation had continued down to that very day. The Emperor, though he had been so unjustly rejected by them, had with his usual mildness shown no anger. In the meantime Count Francesco Sforza had appeared. Though once their friend, he had become their enemy and had brought the towns under his power; the city had been besieged and was enduring great hardships; their soldiers had deserted to Francesco; the people were suffering from lack of food; no one of the neighboring princes could aid them; the Emperor alone, forgetting all repulses, had pity on them. If they were now finally ready to submit to the Holy Empire and acknowledge the Emperor as their lord, he was ready to help them. They must take into consideration the fact that preliminaries had already been arranged with the Emperor's cousin, Duke Sigismund, a neighbor of the Lombards, and that in a short time a large force could cross the Alps and descend into their territory. They must not rely only on themselves, which would be hopeless, nor on the other hand must they think they would lose their liberty if they acknowledged the sovereignty of the Emperor, for to serve legitimate and natural lords was the only true liberty; in so-called democracies there were always found some to put a yoke on the people. Furthermore they must decide whether they preferred to have the Emperor or Sforza rule them, for things had come to such a pass that, if they did not submit to the Emperor, they could not escape the tyranny of Sforza. If the Emperor were acknowledged by them, he would show his citizens extraordinary favor and grant them important privileges; they would be able to do business freely in Germany, to make their state truly golden and the capital of all Italy.

After this speech Guarniero discoursed on the sweetness of liberty, though he said nevertheless that they must choose the chief men of the people to discuss the Emperor's message with the ambassadors. But some nights later, while the matter was still pending, three "gates" of the city (for so they call its divisions) armed and hailed the Emperor as their lord. There are six "gates" in the city and the people are distributed among them. The will of any four gates is binding on all. When therefore three were already turning to the Empire to save them, the senators hearing the tumult, before the populace could throng to the fourth gate, rode into the city and bade the people lay down their arms and go home quietly. They assured them that they too were ready to acknowledge the Emperor's sovereignty, provided the city's honor were kept inviolate, and that they were discussing the matter carefully with the ambassadors. Then representatives were chosen, who conferred with the ambassadors and agreed that if the Emperor would help them against Sforza, they would consent to the following terms: the Emperor should appoint a German to administer justice in Milan itself, and in the other towns anyone he pleased; appeals from the other governors should be heard by the one at Milan and from his decision there should be no appeal; the revenues from the states subject to Milan should belong in equal parts to the Emperor and to the Milanese; Milan should pay yearly 50,000 florins to the Emperor and he should collect the tribute due from the churches and the nobles; all vassals should swear allegiance both to the Emperor and to the state; if the Milanese should acquire any town or territory by force of arms, the Emperor was to receive its allegiance together with the payment of a fitting sum. *These terms seemed satisfactory to the ambassadors, but having been instructed to ask for more, they could not accept them.*

Meanwhile Carlo Gonzaga, a brave general who seemed to be the only hope of the Milanese, came to Aeneas in the dead of night and having summoned Hartung also, urged them to ask again for a popular assembly, promising that he would be present and would incite the people, who had the greatest confidence in him, to demand the Emperor as their lord. He said he had no doubt that they would depose the magistrates and entrust the government to the imperial ambassadors until the Emperor should come himself or send his representative, and he assured them that he had already taken steps with certain powerful citizens to bring this about. Although this plan seemed likely to succeed, Aeneas thought it extremely hazardous and although he knew that there can be no great or memorable act without some risk, still, thinking that this was by no means becoming to him as a priest, he said that he had carried out the Emperor's orders; the people had heard the Emperor's will and could now, if they chose, obey him; to employ force was not easy nor was it within his instructions; Carlo deserved the Emperor's favor for his proposal and he would report his loyalty. But after this Carlo asserted everywhere that Aeneas was for Sforza; so true it is that there is nothing which the evil minds of the malicious do not distort.

Aeneas and Hartung, when they were unable to elicit anything further from the Milanese, procured a letter to Sforza and went to him in his camp—to his complete astonishment, for he said he could not understand how they had succeeded in getting into Milan past his pickets. They talked with him at some length in the presence of the Venetian and Florentine envoys; then, after all the rest were dismissed, they remained alone with him for an hour explaining the Emperor's attitude, and finally were sent away with every mark of honor.

On their return to Germany they found the Emperor at St. Veit, a town of Carinthia. He was pleased with the promises of the Milanese, but the latter, after waiting two months for his reply, fearing that they would be overpowered by Sforza's army, proceeded to murder the Tuscan Galeotto, expel the rest of the senators, and make a treaty with the Venetians. When the Venetians also failed to give them sufficient aid, they murdered the Venetian ambassador, Leonardo Venerio, in a street riot, opened thir gates to Francesco Sforza, and conferred on him the insignia of the dukedom—such is the madness of the mob.

Aeneas meanwhile had gone to his church at Trieste, but in the jubilee year he was recalled by the Emperor and sent with Gregor Volckenstorf and Michael Pfullendorf to Alfonso, King of Aragon and Sicily, to arrange a marriage between the Emperor and Leonora, sister of the King of Portugal. The Portuguese ambassadors were already gathered at Naples. When after forty days of negotiation the matter was finally concluded, Aeneas, in the presence of the King, the Apostolic Legate, the Cardinal of Amiens, the Dukes of Clèves, Calabria, Suessa, and Silesia, and a great number of prelates and counts, delivered a speech in the senate hall of the Castelnuovo at Naples on the nobility and virtue of the contracting parties. This was afterward committed to writing by many. Going from here to the Pope toward the end of the jubilee year, he announced in a public consistory that the marriage had been arranged and that the Emperor would come the next year to be crowned.

This journey had not been without dangers. The Ligula is a river of the Volscians, deep and everywhere bordered by woods whose trees overhang the water and form numerous bridges. The boats there are very small, but Aeneas and his companions, misled by the insistence of the sailors, embarked. Being compelled to travel by night they frequently struck against the branches and finally, when the darkness was thickest, were caught on a huge trunk, where for two hours they were in danger of their lives. In that same spot a little later a boat was sunk and eleven men were drowned. Not far from Cumae, when they were about to cross another river near the coast and their attendants were already on board, the ship, which was overloaded, capsized and spilled men and horses into deep water. But the men escaped by catching hold of a rope and the horses swam to safety.

Now, since we have related the mishaps, it is only fair to tell the pleasant events. When Aeneas stopped in his journey at Ferrara, he found there his cousin, Jacopo Tolommei, a distinguished lawyer and a judge of the Ferrarese senate, whom the Emperor later created Count of the Lateran. He said that he had learned in a letter from his wife that Nerio, Bishop of Siena, had died and that Aeneas was said to have been appointed to succeed him. This was afterward confirmed by the Legate at Bologna. The facts were as follows. On the death of Nerio the Sienese earnestly recommended to the Apostolic See the Count Abbot of the monastery of San Galgano, an excellent man, one of their own citizens and approved by their government. They declared he was the only man they wanted for their bishop. Various cardinals urged other candidates, but the Pope, who alone thought of Aeneas in his absence, proposed his name to the sacred college and persuaded them to transfer him from Trieste to his native city. He told the Sienese that he had given them a distinguished bishop and when they heard that it was Aeneas, they expressed the warmest thanks to His Holiness, realizing that beyond their highest hopes a noble and learned man and their own citizen was coming back to his native city. When Aeneas passed through Siena, they were eager to install him in the episcopal palace without waiting for the apostolic letter and offered him immediate possession of all his rights and privileges. Aeneas however said they must wait for the letter.

When therefore Aeneas returned to Rome from Naples, he went to thank the Pope and he received from the camera *the very unusual honor of* a letter of appointment free of all duties. On his arrival at Siena, the home of his fathers, the clergy and the people came out in procession to meet him and he was escorted into the city under a golden canopy with greater acclamation from the citizens and greater honor, they say, than had ever been given to any bishop.

In the course of this journey also he persuaded Pope Nicholas to send that holy man, Giovanni Capistrano,[15] a disciple of St. Bernard, to Germany to plant there again the rule of St. Francis, which had been abolished in all that country. Aeneas later heard him preach at Vienna, where he was much liked by the people and believed to perform miracles.[16]

On his return to Austria Aeneas brought back not only a marriage contract [17] that pleased the Emperor but the assurance that the Pope, the Sienese, the Florentines, the Bolognese, the Marquis of Este, and the Venetians would all give safe-conduct to the Emperor when he went to be crowned; for he had negotiated the matter satisfactorily with all of them.

Meantime the Bohemians, after many vain efforts to get Ladislas for their king, had proclaimed a Council of the Realm at Prague to discuss their affairs. They threatened that unless Albert's son and the heir to the kingdom were sent to them, they would themselves choose another king. Therefore Aeneas and other nobles were dispatched to confer with them. But since the plague was raging at Prague, the Council was transferred to the village of Beneschau. When Aeneas had there publicly delivered the Emperor's message, assured them that a king who was

15 Capistrano preached in many cities of Germany, fought against the Hussite heresy in Moravia, and continued into Poland, Pastor II, 125 *sq.* Later we find him a powerful influence in rousing a crusading spirit in Hungary on the eve of the victory of Belgrade over the Turks, *ibid.,* 393 *sq.* Cristoforo da Soldo gives a vivid account of this celebrated preacher whom he heard address a great throng at Brescia in 1451. He tells of Capistrano's healing of the sick, restoring the dead to life, etc. While listening to him, da Soldo narrowly escapes being trampled to death by the crowd. Unmindful of Capistrano's powers, he tells us that he was saved only by the timely help of fellow spectators!

16 A. S. aroused the ire of the Italian Minorites by asserting that though he had heard of the wonders performed by Capistrano he had himself never witnessed any supernatural occurrences. This unwillingness to commit himself is but a thin disguise for his essentially critical, skeptical outlook. A. S.'s opinion of Capistrano underwent a change. Later, as pope, he refused to canonize him.

17 Between the Emperor Frederick and Eleanor of Portugal.

a minor and needed guidance could be in no better hands than the Emperor's, and promised that they should soon have their wish, their anger cooled and they promised not to call anyone else to the throne. After a long and shrewd conversation with the regent, George, about the blessings of peace and unity, Aeneas decided that he was a man led astray by his lust for power rather than by heresy. This is characteristic of many of the Bohemians, who would rather rule over heretics than be subject to the faithful.

In the course of this mission Aeneas twice visited the Taborites, the worst of all heretics in Bohemia, and had very spirited arguments with them about the faith. But since he sent the illustrious Cardinal of Sant' Angelo an account of the customs of the Taborites, the situation of their city, and the heresy of the people together with the text of his speech, and since this letter is extant and has been included by me among those collected in a volume, I pass over these matters here and hasten on to others.

The following year was the one when the Empress Leonora was, according to agreement, to sail from Portugal to the harbor of Telamone in Sienese territory and the Emperor Frederick was to enter Italy and be crowned at Rome. He was very eager that they should go to Rome together and together be crowned by the Pope's own hands. Therefore twelve noble matrons and maidens were chosen to receive the royal bride at the harbor and to be her attendants and two barons and two knights were appointed to accompany them. To this number were added Aeneas and the Emperor's secretary, Michael Pfullendorf, who were to discharge the duties of ambassadors. After they had received the Empress at Telamone they were all to escort her to Siena and there await the Emperor's arrival. Aeneas and Michael were further instructed to inform the communes and princes of Italy, and especially the Pope, that the Emperor, about whose coming they were beginning to have doubts, would certainly arrive at the feast of St. Martin to ask safe-conduct for him; to fix fair prices for the supplies he would need. Letters dealing with these matters were sent ahead.

At this news the powerful in Italy were filled with terror, the weak with hope; princes wavered, rumor was rife, and there was fear of uprisings such as had been known of old at the coming of emperors. But the Sienese were more frightened than anyone else, because they thought that Aeneas, a member of a great and noble family, bishop of their city, who had the ear of the Emperor and was highly esteemed by him, desired a revolution in their government.

Now Siena is considered next to Florence the chief city of Tuscany; it rules many flourishing towns and possesses a wide territory. At first the nobles were in power, but when they were divided among themselves and voluntarily withdrew, the government passed to the people. Among them also, as usually happens, some were more able than others and as one party after another became powerful, it seized the government. One party was called The Nine, another The Twelve, not because these were their actual numbers but because they appointed that number of Priors to govern together; another, because under its regime it had reformed the city's laws and rebuilt the walls, was called The Reformers. Of these the so-called Twelve (they were actually five hundred), although they are rich merchants, are nevertheless considered insignificant; they have been deprived of any part in the government and live an almost servile existence. The Nine and The Reformers share the functions of government equally with the people and allow the nobles on sufferance, as it were, a certain number of offices. Thus the Sienese thought that Aeneas, being a noble, would at the Emperor's arrival set on foot some scheme to restore his family to their old prestige and power.

When therefore he had carried out the Emperor's instructions at Venice, Ferrara, Bologna, and Florence and was on his way to Siena, they were afraid of him, watched to see what he would do, and forbade the people to go to meet him. Some, as is the way of the populace, even hurled abuse at him and the ruling party actually hated him. The way of the world is certainly absurd with nothing about it fixed or stable. During the preceding year no one could look at or praise Aeneas enough, but now when he entered the city, he was hateful to all and not a soul did him the honor of going out to meet him. At his house he was welcomed by only a few; in the public squares he heard many curse him; *it was even rumored that there was a conspiracy against his life*. But he bore everything calmly and smiled to himself at the change of fortune.

When therefore he appeared before the senate, after discharging the Emperor's mission he begged the presiding magistrate not to be suspicious of him, saying that one who had been loaded with so many favors by their government had no reason to wish to oppose it; he, who as bishop was their most honored citizen, desired peace and loathed all dissension; the Piccolomini family, to which he belonged, had like the other nobles always been treated honorably by the party now in power; Gregorio Lolli, a celebrated lawyer and one of the chief magis-

trates of the city, was his cousin, the son of his father's sister, Bartolommea; his sisters were married to members of the ruling party and their
children would be his heirs; in short there was no conceivable reason
why he should be hostile to the government. He said furthermore that
the Emperor was not coming to be king of Italy but to be crowned; he
had with him illustrious princes and powerful nobles, who were all
lovers of peace and came as friends not foes; nothing was to be feared
from them, as they desired only permission to pass; the Emperor had
never loved civil strife, his honor was to be relied on, and he carried out
faithfully what he promised. By these words he appeased them somewhat and was enabled to remain among them in safety.

Meanwhile his colleague and very dear friend, Michael Pfullendorf,
was stricken with fever and breathed out his high and noble spirit.
Aeneas gave him splendid burial in the Cathedral of the Blessed Virgin.
Then, wishing to bow yet further to his unpopularity, because there
were still some in Siena who whispered against him, he went at once
with his colleagues to Telamone to await there the arrival of the Empress and also to avoid being found at Siena, if the Emperor should in
the meantime set out for Italy. He could not go to the Pope for fear that
the Empress, with whose reception he was especially charged, might
land while he was detained in Rome.

The Pope, who knew the character of the Romans, realized that
many were eager for a change of government. Fearing a popular disturbance (for the Florentines too were saying that there was a prophecy
that he would either die on March 20 or be most foully taken prisoner),
he had already sent word to the Emperor that he should put off his
coming till summer, giving as a further excuse the scarcity of supplies.
He commanded Aeneas to come to him as soon as possible. Aeneas
however, knowing of the message sent the Emperor, wrote the Pope a
letter, in which after making his excuses he expressed his astonishment
at the Pontiff's change of heart. He said he thought it dishonorable that
the apostolic word should be recalled; he remembered very well that
the Pope had told him that, if the Emperor wished to come to Rome,
he should choose the winter, because that was a more healthful season
and provisions were more abundant then; all the preparations for his
coronation had been made; the Pope had himself of his own accord
invited him to come and it was unseemly to reverse his instructions
now, when it was well known that the Emperor was on the very eve
of starting and his bride might land in Italy any day. He added that he
had heard that the Pope was apprehensive and that the Emperor was

feared at Rome, but he assured him that these fears were groundless.
He said the Emperor was just and attached to Nicholas; there was
nothing he hated so much as disorder; he would die sooner than break
his word; the imperial retinue was composed of great nobles who were
eager for peace and devoted to religion, the Church, *and God.*

Nicholas was impressed by these words and wrote the Emperor a
letter telling him to come when he saw fit. This he sent first to Aeneas
to be forwarded to the Emperor if he thought best. Aeneas was satisfied
with the apostolic letter and at once dispatched it by courier to Frederick.

But meantime disturbances had arisen in Austria, which put off the
Emperor's journey many days, and the Empress was seriously delayed
by unfavorable winds and violent storms. Therefore Aeneas had to
spend sixty days at Telamone, days which were very dull both for him
and for his colleagues. Still he employed the interval in visiting Monte
Argentario and the famous Port' Ercole and Ansedonia, which is worth
seeing, for, though its buildings are in ruins, its walls, built of huge,
square-hewn stones fitted together with extraordinary precision without
mortar, still stand on a hill above the Tuscan Sea looking out toward
Carthage.

By a remarkable coincidence, on the very day when the Emperor,
who had crossed from Germany into Italy and was proceeding as
quickly as possible, entered Florence, the Empress, sped by some breeze
from heaven *or by sheer chance,* landed at Leghorn.[18] Aeneas too received on the same day letters from both the Emperor and the Empress
bidding him and his colleagues come at once to Pisa. Thereupon, accompanied by his colleagues and the ladies in waiting, he obediently
made haste to go thither through Grosseto, Scarlino, and the territory
of Volterra. The Emperor had already sent to meet the Empress Johann,
Bishop of Ratisbon; his kinsman Vanco, Duke of Silesia; Michael,
Count of Magdeburg; his chamberlain, Johann; Ulrich Sonnenburg,
Chancellor of Austria; Ulrich Starnberg; his physician, Jacopo Landrono; and other noble knights. But no definite arrangements had yet
been made. Therefore they debated a long time at Pisa about sending
the bride to the Emperor, till finally, after the other matters had been
arranged, the Marquis of Portugal, who had received Leonora from
her brother and was charged with bringing her to the Emperor, in the
presence of the ambassadors, the distinguished nobles of Pisa, and the
notaries, took the Empress by the hand and delivered her to Aeneas
that he might escort her to the Emperor. This was very annoying to

18 February 2, 1452.

Duke Vanco, who thought that this honor belonged to him because of his kinship with Frederick; but the Portuguese and the imperial ambassadors thought differently.

While this was going on at Pisa, the Florentines, who are harsh and tyrannical rulers of that city and suspect all Pisans, were displeased that so many foreigners had come there and were staying so long. Nevertheless they were restrained from taking any action by Aeneas, who was better known to them than the rest and from day to day kept promising that they would depart.

Meantime the Emperor had reached Siena and was awaiting his bride there. When he learned that she was coming with all possible speed, he sent to meet her first the citizens, then his brother Albert, Duke of Austria, then his cousin Ladislas, King of Hungary and Bohemia, and fourth and last the clergy carrying relics of the saints. He himself with the two Apostolic Legates, Pope Nicholas's brother, the Cardinal of Santa Susanna, and the Cardinal of Sant' Angelo, at his side awaited the bride outside the city between the second and third gates. There in a wide open space the royal couple dismounted and embraced. Heinrich Leubing, an expert in canon law, spoke for the Emperor and Aeneas for the Empress. Soon after this the Sienese erected there a marble column as a lasting memorial, that afterages might know that an Emperor from the East and an Empress from the West had first met in that place.

Meanwhile the Sienese had banished from the city all those among The Twelve and The Nobles who could bear arms, and especially Aeneas's kindred, the Piccolomini. But when they realized the Emperor's mildness and clemency and saw that Aeneas had spoken the truth, they returned to their old admiration for him, proclaimed him their good father and citizen, recalled his family, ceased to suspect them, and appointed him their ambassador to the Pope.

When the Emperor had ascended the ridge of Mt. Cimino above Viterbo, he summoned Aeneas as he rode along and said to him, "Look you, we are going to Rome. I think I can see that you are going to be cardinal. Nor will your good fortune stop there, but you will be still further exalted and the chair of St. Peter awaits you. Do not despise me when you attain that honor." Aeneas replied, "I do not aspire to be pope or cardinal." "Nevertheless," the Emperor broke in, "I see that this is to be." Aeneas took this as a jest. Proceeding with the Emperor to Rome he was foremost among his prelates and replied in his behalf to the greetings of the cardinals and chief citizens who came out to meet him.

After the Emperor had stayed one night outside the walls, Aeneas was summoned to the Pope, who was ill in bed, and made clear to him that the Emperor's attitude was friendly and to be trusted, adding that he was astonished that the honor of so great a prince could have been questioned. The Pope replied by quoting what many persons had told him and said, "To be too apprehensive is not so bad as to be too trusting."

When the Emperor finally entered the city and at the door of St. Peter's kissed the Pope's holy feet, Aeneas, by his orders was his spokesman, as he was also on the occasion of the Emperor's petition for the crown of Milan, called the Lombard Crown, and at the blessing of the bridal pair in the course of the marriage ceremony in which Leonora was united to Frederick by His Holiness himself. Finally, when Frederick was crowned emperor at the altar of St. Peter, Aeneas was charged with making the proper responses and he also handled many private matters between the Pope and the Emperor.[19]

Now there is one thing which I think ought not to be passed over, a matter concerning dreams, which seems worth recording. The day after the coronation the Emperor with three Councillors, of whom Aeneas was one, had audience with Pope Nicholas. After they had talked for some time, the Emperor said, "You remember, Father, that after the coronation I was going to tell you about my dream. It is as follows. The night after you left me at Vienna the last time, I dreamed that I had come to Rome and was being crowned by your hands. And in my sleep I marveled and thought my coronation was not valid, since it had been performed not by the Bishop of Rome but by the Bishop of Bologna. When I awoke I paid no attention to the dream, but after I learned from Aeneas's letters that you had been made cardinal and then pope, I was immediately convinced that, as has actually happened, I should be crowned by your hands." Then Nicholas said, "The dreams of rulers often come true. I myself the night before Eugenius died thought in my sleep that I was in this very room, which, as you, Aeneas, know, was then divided into two parts. Eugenius, taking off his robe and then his tunic, put them upon me and lifting from his own head a high miter such as our soldiers wear, put it on mine. Finally, taking me by the hand and pointing to this throne, he said,

[19] The royal party entered the city March 9, the marriage took place on the 16th, and the imperial coronation on the 19th.

'From this seat I shall go to St. Peter.' He died the next day. His body was carried into the church of St. Peter and perhaps his soul is even now rejoicing in communion with his glorious predecessor. Twelve days later the papacy was conferred upon me."

While these things were going on, it was the general opinion that Aeneas, who appeared to be in high favor with the Pope and the Emperor, was to be made cardinal. This was not unlikely, for Nicholas had promised Frederick that the next time he made any cardinals Aeneas should be the first named. He did not break his word, but he died without appointing anyone to that office. *Such distinction is not always open to him who deserves it but is often the prey of the unworthy. Some however deserve it first and then attain it, while others make themselves worthy after achieving it. Some carry their spoil with them to the tomb without ever having deserved it.*

After this the Emperor left for Naples, but Aeneas, who was not well, remained a few days at Rome and with the others attended on the young King Ladislas. Meantime it was reported to the Pope that the King was planning to escape and unless he were guarded, would be off home. Accordingly at the fifth hour of the night said to be chosen for the flight, he summoned Aeneas and told him to have the King's house closely guarded. Aeneas went to the palace and warned the guards not to give any opportunity for disloyal plots and to restore their charge safe and sound to the Emperor on his return. However no certain evidence of such a plan was discovered, though the King's tutor attempted a still greater crime at Florence.

When the Emperor returned and again appeared before the Pope and the Holy Senate, Aeneas in his name read two speeches in public audience: one thanking the Pope and the cardinals for the distinguished favors they had bestowed on the Emperor; the other begging that a crusade against the enemies of Christianity should be proclaimed and equipped and imploring the Pope to put a stop to the harrying of Christians in Greece and the Orient. Finally, when Aeneas left Rome with the Emperor, he was sent as spokesman of the Apostolic See with the powers of legatus de latere to Bohemia, Silesia, Austria, Moravia, Styria, Carinthia, and Carniola. Not long after, at the urgent request of the Emperor, the Pope extended his mission to include the kingdom of Hungary.

When the Emperor had returned to Siena and was afraid to go on to Florence because he thought that his stay at Naples had aroused the suspicion of the Florentines, Aeneas was sent ahead and succeeded in

restoring public confidence and making the Emperor's passage safe.
The envoys of Hungary and Austria were there, awaiting the Emperor.
They invited Caspar, King Ladislas's tutor, to a conference and persuaded him to carry off the King from the authority of the Emperor,
outlining their scheme as follows: The boy was to be instigated, after
he had followed Frederick on his departure as far as the gates of the
city, to say that he would like to stay some days longer in Florence
and then, after he had asked permission, to wheel his horse about;
they would arrange with the magistrates to have men at hand to resist
the Emperor if he should try to use force with the boy. But the Florentine senate was aghast at such an outrage. With unshaken integrity
they rebuked the intermediaries and sent the Emperor away un-
hindered and loaded with honors.

When Frederick arrived at Ferrara, he was urgently besought to
raise the Marquis Borso to the rank of Duke. He was at first unwilling,
but finally, yielding to the arguments of Aeneas and the persuasions of
his counsellors, he created a dukedom from the territory of Modena
and Reggio and made Borso Duke. All Italy said this was good policy
and a good investment. *They did not yet know the new prince's
character.*

When the new Duke was publicly invested with the insignia of
his rank in the usual fashion, the duty of delivering an oration on the
graciousness of the Emperor, the glories of the house of Este, the ability
of Borso, and the exalted rank conferred upon him was assigned to
Aeneas; and when they came to Venice, no one else was delegated to
speak for the Emperor on important matters before the Senate and the
Doge.

When the Emperor finally returned to his own country and the
Austrians had led a great army against him and besieged him for
some days near the city of Neustadt, pounding the walls with bombards
and other engines of war, Aeneas stayed undaunted at Frederick's side.
When a truce was made and King Ladislas had been sent back, Aeneas
was the chief among the numerous distinguished ambassadors sent by
the Emperor to the Congress called at Vienna to discuss peace. The
envoys of all Germany, the great prelates, illustrious counts and famous
barons met at his house. There he spoke twice for the Emperor before
the nobles of Hungary who had assembled from all parts of the kingdom, and once before the Bohemians.

During these events the Turks, who had for a long time been
masters of Asia Minor and most of Greece, laid siege with a great

army by land and sea to Constantinople, the capital of the eastern Empire and the only city in Thrace to resist the Mohammedan yoke. After a siege of thirteen days they stormed, captured,[20] and sacked it, killed the Emperor Constantine, massacred all the nobility, reduced the people to servitude, and polluted with their Moslem filth the famous church of Santa Sophia and all the basilicas of the city. This was sad news to the Christians, especially to Pope Nicholas and the Emperor Frederick III, whose reigns had been branded with no small infamy by this foul insult to the Christian religion. *For what calamity of the times is not laid at the door of princes? All troubles are ascribed to the negligence of rulers. "They might," said the populace, "have aided perishing Greece before she was captured. They were indifferent. They are not fit to rule. The Emperor, now that he knows what has happened, in his eagerness to wipe out such a stain of infamy is incurring a greater. For he has begun and has not finished. He calls Christians together to consult for the common weal and does not come to the Congress himself."*

The Emperor commanded the Germans to assemble at Ratisbon,[21] a city of Bavaria on the Danube, and he summoned thither Philip, Duke of Burgundy. This celebrated and able prince on receipt of the Emperor's letter immediately abandoned his operations against the uprising in Flanders, which he was engaged in putting down, and made the long journey to Ratisbon; for he was the one among the Christian princes who showed himself most hostile to the Turk, whether from a desire to avenge his father, whom the Turks had once taken prisoner and held for a huge ransom; or through love of religion, thinking this the surest path to eternal life; or because he sought thus to capture the applause of the populace, to which almost all mortal men are slaves. The Emperor, though he had given them good reason to count on his coming, changed his mind and stayed in Austria, fearing that the flames next door in Hungary would finally set fire to his house. The robber chiefs, Gilles and Hanchrauter, were at this time ravaging the districts of Hungary nearest to Austria and Styria and it was thought probable that John Hunyadi, the governor general of that kingdom, *who had already taken the field,* would soon fight a battle with them. Whoever came out victorious would be a source of apprehension to the Emperor. Therefore Frederick, who like most men chose to handle his private affairs himself and affairs of state through ambassadors, sent to Ratis-

[20] May 29, 1453.
[21] The meeting was called for April 23, 1454.

bon brilliant orators from his court: two barons, two bishops (Ulrich of Gurk and Aeneas of Siena), and with them Nicholas, Cardinal of St. Peter, who was then at his church in Brixen. Pope Nicholas sent Giovanni, Bishop of Pavia, to commend to the Diet the protection of the Catholic Faith and to offer his aid.

When all the delegates had assembled, at a meeting in the town hall before numerous prelates of the Church and Christian princes Aeneas made a speech for the Emperor, in which he showed clearly and lucidly the extent of the harm inflicted on all Christendom by the fall of Constantinople and the danger that threatened if no action were taken to check the Turks. He urged the necessity of all the powers arming in defense of the common weal and presented the excuses of the Emperor, who, he said, had been obliged to remain at home, though all his reasons sounded lame. The speech for the Pope was delivered by Giovanni, Bishop of Pavia, and that for Burgundy by Jean, Bishop of Toul, whom Pius II later transferred to the church at Tournai. The Cardinal of St. Peter also spoke in favor of war and a considerable number of others harangued to the best of their ability, as is usually the case in a large assembly.

When Philip heard Aeneas, he said, "What is the use of a long discussion? Aeneas has shown us our duty. Let others give their opinions; I will speak for myself. I realize the crisis in which Christianity finds itself. If we wish to keep our faith, our liberty, our lives, we must take the field against the Turks and crush their power before it becomes any stronger. I will not refuse to devote my person and my resources to this cause, if only some other prince who is fit for this enterprise will gird himself to go with me." The whole assembly applauded Philip and voted him the only one of them all qualified and deserving to govern a state. Then when all had expressed their opinions, a vote was taken on Aeneas's motion and there was no one who did not vote for a crusade against the Turks.

On the adjournment of the Diet Aeneas returned to the Emperor. He had intended to go back to Italy and spend the rest of his life in his native city, but when he asked the Emperor's permission, Frederick refused it and kept him to be his spokesman at the Diet of Frankfort, because he seemed the only man in the palace who felt any great concern about defending the Faith or could exert any influence by his speeches.

When the date for the Diet arrived, Aeneas, the Bishop of Gurk, and the Margraves of Brandenburg and Baden were appointed delegates.

On reaching Frankfort they found there only a few members and those hostile to the Emperor and the Pope. Some days later came Theodoric, Bishop of Mainz, Jacob, Archbishop of Trier, and delegates from almost all Germany. From Italy the Pope and the Marquises of Este and Mantua sent representatives. Alfonso, King of Sicily, and the Venetians were even later, their ambassadors reaching Germany only after the Diet was dismissed. The Hungarians and Burgundians were present, the former asking, the latter offering aid. There was present also Giovanni Capistrano, a Minorite monk famous for the holiness of his life and his tireless preaching of the word of God, and regarded as a prophet by the people, though he had little success in persuading them to make war on the Turks. The Germans had changed their minds and none of them was in favor of a crusade. As if their ears had been infected with some poison, they could not bear to hear the name of the Emperor or of the Pope, who, they said, *were false and greedy and* wanted to rake in gold, not make war; *this was a fine sort of trick, to proclaim a crusade against the Turks, that money might be extorted from the Germans by artful wiles as from barbarians. These two grasping lords of the world were planning to divide the profits between them.* But, they asserted, the result of the Diet would be very different from what those princes expected, for the German peoples would neither contribute money nor enlist for military service. All, won over to this opinion, cursed the Emperor and the Pope, insulted their ambassadors, jeered at the Burgundians, who seemed inclined to the expedition, and abused the Hungarians, whom they accused of wishing to involve Germany in their calamities, since they were unable to defend their own kingdom.

There seemed not the slightest prospect of favorable action, since the decision taken at Ratisbon was being summarily rejected. But when the Diet actually opened and Aeneas had made his speech, *wonderful to relate,* the old enthusiasm for the war suddenly revived in all. He spoke for almost two hours and was listened to with such absorbed attention that not once did anyone clear his throat or take his eyes from the face of the speaker. No one thought his speech long, no one but was sorry when it ended. They heard numerous other delegates, but they listened with weariness and derision, *especially to the Bishop of Pavia, the Apostolic Legate, whose speech, in which he compared the Church to a beautiful woman bewailing her misfortunes, who had appeared to him in a dream, was thought to be less dignified than befitted so grave a matter.* Aeneas's speech however was praised by all and written down by many. As a result of his arguments the vote to make war, which had been passed at Ratisbon, was reaffirmed; the Hungarians were promised aid to the extent of 10,000 cavalry and 32,000 infantry; and it was decided that the Imperial Electors and all the princes of Germany should go to the Emperor at the approaching feast of Pentecost to make the final arrangements for hastening the crusade. When the Diet adjourned after taking this action, the ambassadors of the Emperor returned to Austria.

Just when there was every reason to hope that the next summer a great host would be put into the field against the enemy, news was suddenly received of the death of Pope Nicholas V, which in an instant rent the web that had been so long in weaving and showed how vain are the designs of men and how futile their pains. For what knowledge of the future have they? What certainty on which to base their plans? All man's endeavors fail, if they are not aided by the hand of God. It was not the will of the Divine Mercy that the Turkish empire should be extended at this time, yet it was preserved a little longer for the rebuking of our sins.

Nicholas had sat on the throne of St. Peter about eight years. He owed his distinction not to his birth but to his learning and intellectual gifts. He was born in Sarzana, a town in Tuscany not far from the Magra River, but his family had originally come from Lucca. He celebrated the jubilee year, which was attended by throngs of pilgrims from all nations. He canonized Bernardino of Siena. He crowned and anointed the Emperor Frederick and the Empress Leonora of Portugal at Rome in the church of St. Peter, the chief of the apostles. He erected magnificent buildings in his city, though he began more than he finished. He created seven cardinals, among them his own brother, Filippo, Bishop of Bologna, a man of great charm and the most loyal of friends. When the Church was reunited, he recognized several of the cardinals who had been created during the schism. When Stefano Porcaro, a Roman of honorable birth, plotted to raise revolution in the city and to seize and kill the Lord's anointed himself, he thwarted his designs and had him put to death. He attained success and fame in many great undertakings but was unhappy in the fall of Constantinople, which occurred during his pontificate and was a black stain on his reputation. While he was seeking to wipe it out, he died from gout, which attacked his entire body, and at his death all the ambitious projects against the Turks collapsed.

After Nicholas's funeral the cardinals, who were concerned about his successor, entered the conclave as is the custom. There they split into divers factions and it was exceedingly difficult for two thirds of the Sacred College to agree, *since everyone wanted the papacy for himself.* After the scrutiny had been taken twice without election, certain cardinals conferred outside the place of scrutiny and decided to elect Bessarion, Cardinal of Nicaea, because he seemed the fittest to govern the state. A sufficient number were about to agree upon him and there seemed no doubt that at the next scrutiny he would be chosen pope by a two-thirds vote; indeed petitions were already being addressed to him. But when this became known to the opposite faction, Alain, Cardinal of Avignon, went round to one and another and said, "Shall we then give the Latin Church a Greek pope? Shall we put a neophyte at the head of the book? [22] Bessarion has not yet shaved his beard and shall he be our head? *Have we any assurance that his conversion is sincere? It is but a short time since he attacked the faith of the Church of Rome and because today he has had a change of heart, shall he be our master and lead the Christian army?* [23] Behold the poverty of the Latin Church which cannot find a man worthy of the papacy without having recourse to the Greeks! But do as you will senators; I and those who think with me will never agree to a Greek pope." These words influenced some of the cardinals so much that there was not the least chance of two thirds of the college acceding to Bessarion, who, after being one night definitely regarded as pope by many, found himself the next morning still cardinal with less prestige than before. Such is the common fate of those who have fallen from high hopes.

When they came again to the scrutiny and tried the method which is called "accession," two thirds agreed upon the man who had been generally regarded as the least likely candidate. This was Alfonso,[24] Cardinal of the Santi Quattro Coronati, a Spaniard from Valencia, of noble birth, an eminent jurist, a man of great and wide experience, but very old and almost decrepit, for he was over seventy. Some years before, when the Holy See was vacant, he is said to have predicted his own election to everyone he met, asserting that he would undoubtedly be

[22] I.e., at the head of the Church. *Cf.* Psalm 39:8-10 (transl. from the Vulgate, 1914): "Then said I, Behold I come. In the head of the book it is written of me that I should do thy will :...I have declared thy justice in a great church, lo, I will not restrain my lips: O lord, thou knowest it." The Messianic interpretation of this passage is shown in Hebrews 10:7, and by inference would apply to Christ's Vicar.

[23] Bessarion's conversion to the Roman obedience was quite consistent with his earnest efforts in behalf of the union of the Greek and Latin churches at the Council of Ferrara-Florence. This gifted scholar and patron of letters had been raised to the cardinalate in 1439.

[24] Alfonso Borgia, elected April 8, 1455.

pope, but no one had believed him and his words were thought an old man's babbling. Now his prophecy turned out to be true. He said he had received it from St. Vincent, a fellow countryman of his, now dead, whom he afterwards canonized.

When Alfonso was seated in St. Peter's chair, he took the name of Calixtus III and vowed to direct all his efforts against the impious Turks. Almost at once he declared war against them, gave absolution for their sins to all who enlisted, and sent ambassadors to France and Hungary to raise armies.

When this news was heard in Austria, there were not a few who tried to persuade the Emperor that the time had come to exert pressure on the Apostolic See in order to reduce its power in Germany. They said that the agreements made with Eugenius IV had been violated and that they owed no obedience to the new pope until he granted the petitions of the German nation; that Germany was regarded as a servant, while she deserved at last to be free. Jacob, Archbishop of Trier, who expected to profit from the dispute, insisted stubbornly on this policy, but Aeneas on the contrary said that it was not to the Emperor's advantage to lessen the prestige of the Pope in order to win the favor of the people, which is by its very nature extremely fickle; the reins of government must not be handed over to the populace, which he knew to be hostile to the rule of princes; among princes friendship was sometimes to be found, but between the people and a king there was undying hatred; the Pope and the Emperor needed each other's help and it was folly to injure a man whose assistance you hoped for; the beginning of a new pontificate was the time to win the favor of the Pope by benefits, but, if you began with injuries, it was then difficult to open a way to good will. He urged Frederick to send assurances of obedience, as his ancestors had done, and to make an honorable treaty with the new pope, declaring that the Germans would support the Emperor in such a compact.

Aeneas's advice prevailed and he himself together with the lawyer, Johann Hinderbach, was sent to carry out his policy. But before going to Rome they were instructed to stop at Friuli to settle a dispute about boundaries between the Venetians and the Austrian subjects. When they had spent several days at Pordenone discussing this matter and were still unable to win over the *stubborn* Venetian ambassadors, they went to Venice and had audience with the Senate. There, although the Emperor's cause was opposed by the Doge, Francesco Foscari, whose eloquence and prestige were very great, Aeneas persuaded the Senators to rescind their decree which forbade the people of Pordenone to have any dealings with the subjects of Venice. Then the two colleagues went on to Rome, where they were received with all the greater honor because they had been so long and so eagerly awaited. At their arrival a public consistory was convened, in which Aeneas, after having made his submission in the time-honored way, delivered a speech in praise of the Emperor and the Empire and discussed also the proposed war against the Turks. This was afterward written down and widely circulated.

At this time it was common report that during the season of Advent, which was approaching, Calixtus would create new cardinals and it was persistently rumored that Aeneas would be one of them. Thus, wherever he went, he was pointed at as soon to be raised to the cardinalate, and indeed Calixtus himself had said as much.

When the day arrived and a secret consistory was held for the purpose, report came from the palace that a number of cardinals had been created and that Aeneas was among them. Many came to congratulate him as he lay sick with the gout and when he heard the news, he said very calmly with no change of expression, "If this news is true, it will be generally known within two hours. Meantime I shall be prepared for either result. I shall not be shaken by fear nor deluded by vain hope." On the other hand Juan, Bishop of Zamora, when he was greeted in the same way, said, "At last I have attained that which I have been anxiously awaiting for thirty-nine years!" and, after making a present to the messenger, he knelt before the image of the Blessed Virgin and gave thanks to her and to her Son, *because they had at last answered his prayer.* So different are the natures of men! Some are ready to believe what they desire and others what they fear.

When the matter had been debated a long time in the consistory, three cardinals were created, two of whom were the Pope's nephews, Luis, Presbyter of Santi Quattro Coronati, and Rodrigo,[25] Deacon of San Niccolò. The third was Jaime, Deacon of Sant' Eustachio, of the royal house of Portugal. They were all *so* young, though of great promise, *that it was not inaptly said that the three cardinals together had not years enough for one. It was evident that men were not made cardinals because they could help the Church but because they themselves had need of her help; though it is indeed a common fault to subordinate the office to the man, not the man to the office.* The creation of the cardinals was not published immediately, but the consistory was

25 Rodrigo Borgia, the future Pope Alexander VI.

dissolved as if no action had been taken and all the senators were instructed to say nothing about it. However, some of the Pope's household guessed what had happened because writing materials had been called for and some hints were given by gestures. *Secrecy is hard to achieve.*

The cardinals' reason for wishing to conceal the election for a time was their hope that they might trick the Pope, who, they thought would probably die before the announcement was made. But *it was* the Pope *who tricked the cardinals, for* in the course of the next summer, when only one cardinal, *who did not dare raise any objection,* was present (the rest had gone away to escape the heat), he made the public announcement. *This brought discredit on the college, because, when the Pope wished to elevate together with his nephews men of ripe years who had deserved well of the Roman Curia, it had agreed to those who appeared less suitable and rejected those who were generally thought most worthy of the honor. Nor did Calixtus escape censure for having preferred the ties of the flesh to the advantage of the Church.*

About this time when all Italy was breathing more freely because of the recent peace (for all the powers had laid down their arms), a new disturbance arose, which would not let that sinful land rest. Jacopo, the son of Niccolò Piccinino, who had long been in the service of the Venetians and was a general who could not endure peace, crossed the Po with a large force of cavalry, penetrated into Romagna, and from there marched into Tuscany against the Sienese, the weakest of all Italian powers, with the intention of seizing their state and making himself tyrant of that famous city; and indeed he was already allowing himself to be styled Duke of Siena. Alfonso, King of Sicily, was bitter against the Sienese because, though they were his allies and bound to him by a treaty, they had made peace with the Duke of Milan and the Florentines without saying a word to him, and for this reason he encouraged Piccinino in ravaging their territory. *Shortly before this the Sienese had been engaged in a war with Ildebrando, Count of Pitigliani, in which they had hired two captains notorious for their perfidy, Roberto Corrigiano and Sigismondo Pandolfo Malatesta, the prince of all wickedness, both of whom promised Piccinino to desert to him. Roberto was summoned to the palace where he was murdered forthwith and flung through a window into the piazza. Sigismondo, the poison of all Italy, who was reserved for greater crimes, saved himself by flight.*

In these circumstances the Sienese must have submitted to Piccinino, who had already seized the considerable Sienese towns of Citonio and

Monte Marano with their citadels, had reinforcements not arrived in the
nick of time from Francesco Sforza, Duke of Milan, the Venetians, and
Pope Calixtus. They were commanded by distinguished generals, who
fell upon Piccinino and routed him. The latter had to yield to superior
strength and was so terrified that he did not think himself safe till he
had arrived with all speed at Castiglione, a town on the Sienese coast
which Alfonso *had taken from the Florentines and* was then holding.
Here he shut himself up and existed for several days on wild plums.
He was rescued by Luca Sclavo, who, though he was guarding Orbetello for Siena, allowed himself to be bribed. Having tricked and taken
captive the commandant of the citadel, he admitted Piccinino's troops
and the general himself, who was conveyed to Orbetello by sea. There
Piccinino was again besieged, but the town was difficult to take by
storm, especially for those who did not desire to succeed. For the Italian
mercenaries had realized that if Piccinino were overpowered and captured, they would have to go back to tilling their fields, since peace
would reign everywhere; and they worshipped him as a god because
he alone could furnish occasion for war. Therefore when he was suffering from hunger, they supplied him with bread; they reported to him
the plans of their generals and refused to obey their officers. Alfonso also
sent him supplies by sea.

The siege dragged on from day to day and all attempts to take the city
came to nothing. By this time the Sienese, whose money and grain were
exhausted, could hold out no longer. Calixtus was weary of the expense
involved. Their other allies were not so prompt as at first in sending
them aid and things had come to such a pass that the besiegers were in
as much danger as the besieged. Therefore it seemed to the people of
Siena that their one salvation was to ask Alfonso to grant them terms of
peace and to seek the aid of him whose alliance they had despised, since
he was the only one who could give orders to Piccinino. *So little do the
populace care for honor when it is opposed to expediency!*

Aeneas had already returned to Siena and was soon to leave for
Germany. The magistrates of the city, who are called Priors, and those
who presided over the balia sent for him and besought him not to refuse
to go to Alfonso in behalf of his native city and beg him to grant peace
to Tuscany. First however Aeneas was to ask Calixtus to agree to
Siena's sending ambassadors to the King. Aeneas consented in order not
to fail his country in such a crisis; for unless she obtained peace immediately, she would surely lose her independence. Therefore he returned
to Rome and with considerable difficulty persuaded the Pope to intercede

with Alfonso. *Calixtus hated Alfonso bitterly and did not think such a step would increase his prestige but even he had to obey Necessity, the mistress of the world.* He sent with Aeneas Giovanni Sogliera, a distinguished theologian whom Pius afterward appointed to the church at Barcelona, to treat for peace in his name. The Sienese sent two other ambassadors, the lawyer, Galgano Borghese, and Leonardo *inappropriately* named Benvogliente. When the time came for them to start, Aeneas had an attack of gout which kept him at Rome a week. His colleagues went on ahead and met Alfonso at Trajetto, where they show the tomb of the elder Africanus not far from the river Liris, which we now call the Garigliano.

When Alfonso had heard Galgano and Leonardo, he replied with a very harsh speech, in which he made many complaints about the Sienese. *He rehearsed the benefits he had conferred on them and recounted the ingratitude of the state to him. He declared that the people of Siena deserved no one's pity.* He could not bring himself to give the ambassadors themselves a civil look. But when Aeneas arrived, he was received with smiles and flattering words and as soon as the King saw him, he said, "Now I will talk about peace, since we have an intermediary whom I like," and negotiations began forthwith. But since there were many snags and new difficulties arose every day, the matter dragged on for several months and was discussed now at Naples, now at Puteoli, and sometimes at Torre del Greco—wherever Lucrezia was staying.

She was a beautiful woman or girl, the daughter of poor but noble Neapolitan parents (*if there is any nobility in poverty*), with whom the King was so desperately in love that in her presence he was beside himself and could neither hear nor see anything but Lucrezia. He could not take his eyes off her, praised everything she said, marveled at her wisdom, admired every gesture, thought her beauty divine. He had made her many presents, had given orders that she was to receive the honors of a queen, and at last was so completely dominated by her that no one could get a hearing without her consent. Marvelous is the power of love! A great king, lord of the noblest part of Spain, obeyed by the Balearic Islands, Corsica, Sardinia, and Sicily itself, who had subdued many provinces of Italy and defeated the most powerful generals, was finally conquered by love and like any captive of war was a slave to a weak woman! He had no intercourse with her (if report is true) and they say she used to declare, "Never with my consent shall the King ravish my maidenhood! But if he should attempt force, I shall not imitate Lucretia, the wife of Collatinus, who endured the outrage and then took her own life. I will anticipate the outrage by my death." *But noble acts are not so easy as noble words nor did her afterlife bear out her protestations. For after Alfonso's death she went into Piccinino's camp, where she had no reputation for virtue; indeed it was common talk that she was his secretary's mistress and had a child by him. But Alfonso thought there was nothing in the world more divine. Though wise in everything else, in regard to this and hunting he was stark mad.*

While Aeneas in his efforts to secure terms of peace was following Alfonso about even when he went hunting, he visited Baiae, Cumae and the ruins of ancient cities, Salerno, Amalfi, and the venerable tombs of the Apostles Andrew and Matthew, where the holy bodies are said to exude the famous manna. He saw also the source of the Sarno, which is so cold that the darker kinds of wine, when put into it, turn white in a short time. In this place not long afterward, when he was already pope, his forces and those of King Ferrante, who had shown themselves too daring, were beaten and put to flight, while Simonetta, general of the papal troops, was killed by a stone from an engine of war. There is a town here called Sarno from the river. He also visited Nola, which derives no less glory from the holy life of Paulinus, the Confessor, than from Roman history and the death of Marcellus.

On his return to Naples, when he went one day to see the King in Castelnuovo, just as he was entering the triumphal gate, Alfonso, who was walking with his courtiers in the hall opposite the gate, saw him and, turning to his nobles, said, "Do you want me to show you the pope?" When they said "Yes," he continued, "There he is. The Bishop of Siena, who is just entering the gate, is destined by God to be pope and he is the man whom the cardinals will elect to succeed Calixtus when he dies. There is no one whom they could justly prefer to him." When the courtiers reported this to Aeneas and congratulated him, he replied to them all, "But the cardinals are not accustomed to elect any but a cardinal. Do not believe this till you see me wearing the red hat, of which I know myself to be unworthy."

Meantime it was rumored that a huge Turkish force commanded by the Sultan himself and powerfully equipped with engines of war had besieged Taurunum, by land and sea. This is a town in Russia (once called Upper Moesia) between the Danube and the Save at their confluence, which is now called Belgrade or sometimes the second Alba. Alfonso, disturbed at this news, asked those who were standing around him how the besieged could be aided and Aeneas said, "It is no use to think about aid. For the wars of the Hungarians and Turks are not like Italian wars, which seldom come to a pitched battle and are aptly called by our soldiers 'negotiations.' This very moment, while we are speaking, either the enemy or the Hungarians are in flight and we shall presently have the report."

A week passed and a letter did in fact arrive from Hungary announcing that the Christians under the sign of the Cross, who were besieged in Taurunum, had made a sally against the Turks and by divine rather than human aid had won a most glorious victory, inflicting great loss on the enemy; the Sultan had been wounded in the breast; his army was scattered, all the engines of war abandoned, and he himself had fled in panic with a few followers. The information was so precise that no further evidence could be required.

Before long this good news was followed by the conclusion of peace with the Sienese on condition that Piccinino in consideration of a sum of money should return Orbetello to Siena and should withdraw from Tuscany to winter in the Abruzzi and the territory of Aquila.

After these questions were settled, Aeneas returned to Rome and, though he wished to visit his native city and then go back to the Emperor in Germany, he was kept at the capital by Pope Calixtus, who promised him the cardinalate if he would stay. Aeneas complied, *though he suspected that Calixtus would yield to the cardinals, who dreaded nothing so much as the creation of new colleagues, especially those who they feared would be rivals for the papacy.*

At Advent, which may almost be called "election time" for cardinals, *there was bitter dispute in the apostolic senate, because Calixtus wished to create cardinals and the college opposed him. Now they said there were too many cardinals already; now they heaped abuse and insults on the persons named as candidates and, as is their habit, inveighed more and more bitterly against those who were considered better and more worthy of the papacy. Nevertheless Calixtus won with the vigorous support of the three cardinals he had already created and showed himself, as was fitting, the head and master.* He created six new cardinals; Rainaldo Piscicello, Archbishop of Naples, Lucrezia's uncle, whose creation Alfonso urged as a personal favor; the Spaniard, Juan, Bishop of Zamora, eminent for his knowledge of the law, who had served in the Curia with wisdom and integrity for thirty-nine years; Giovanni of the noble Milanese house of the Castiglioni, Bishop of Pavia; Aeneas, Bishop of Siena, whose creation was urged not only by the Emperor but by King Ladislas of Hungary and almost all the German princes; Jacopo, Bishop of Montefeltro, a Roman and the brother of the physician Simone; Richard, Bishop of Coutances, a Norman priest nominated by King Charles of France. There was general approval of all these *except the Bishops of Naples and Montefeltro, who, it was said, had not been elevated for their merits nor at the request of proper sponsors, but one had been granted to a courtesan and the other to a physician.*

When the people heard that Aeneas had received the red hat, it was at once rumored that Calixtus had designated him as his successor and there was great joy throughout the city. Siena too, when it learned of the honors conferred on its bishop, made holiday amid public rejoicing, *though privately the governing party was profoundly distressed, fearing (as actually happened) that Aeneas might some day be pope and try to make them receive into the public offices the nobles of the city, whom they hated and had long ago totally excluded from the government.* But above all the Emperor Frederick was highly elated when he heard that his ambassador had been chosen into the sacred college. Alfonso, King of Aragon and Sicily, received the news with no small gratification, *seeing that the way to the fulfillment of his prophecy was now open.* All the princes of Germany sent Aeneas congratulatory letters, feeling that Germany herself had been honored in him. Nor were they mistaken, for Aeneas, not only as cardinal but as pope, always showed himself the champion and defender of the Germans and in regard to German affairs Calixtus listened to him more than to all the other cardinals.

[Meanwhile Aeneas's views prevailed on the appointments of the Bishops of Ermeland and Ratisbon.—Ed.]

This increased Aeneas's reputation among the cardinals to no small degree. *In two disputes he had defeated his opponents and restored causes that had almost been given up.*

While these things were going on, Lucrezia, whom I have mentioned above, came to Rome with as large a retinue and as much pomp as if she were queen. Calixtus received her in a consistory with the cardinals present and honored her in many ways. This displeased Aeneas and many others, who thought it unseemly that a woman whom the King loved for base reasons should be exalted in the sight of the Apostolic Majesty. Though Aeneas was devoted to Alfonso, he did not visit his mistress at Rome as did many of the cardinals, including Pietro of San

Marco, who showed himself not so much master of ceremonies as an expert seeker after worldly favors.

During this time the kingdom of Naples was racked for many days by an earthquake such as our fathers cannot remember to have seen or heard. At Naples itself many splendid buildings fell and Ariano and many other towns were completely destroyed. It was said that more than thirty thousand bodies were buried under the ruins. The people everywhere left the cities and moved into the country. There was a period of public penitence, men and women mortifying themselves by fasting and scourging. Then also there appeared in the Aegean Sea an island never seen before, small but rising forty cubits above the water. It blazed for some days till there was no more bitumen to feed the flames.

At this time King Charles of Sweden because of his cruelty to Christian priests and his complete enslavement to avarice and lust was dethroned through the efforts of the Archbishop of Upsala, who led an army against him. He was succeeded by Christopher, who is still reigning.

Aeneas, because his gout was worse than usual, went with Calixtus's permission to the baths at Viterbo, hoping for some relief but not expecting a cure, since this disease, when once it has become chronic and deeply rooted, is ended only by death. While taking the baths, he began his History of Bohemia, which he dedicated to Alfonso, King of Aragon and Sicily—*inauspiciously, as it turned out,* for the King died [26] before the work was finished. He had fallen ill of a slow fever while Aeneas was at the baths and lingered forty days between hope of life and fear of death. Finally he paid his debt to nature, having designated as his heir his illegitimate son, Ferrante, whom Popes Nicholas and Eugenius had declared eligible to rule. The King died in sanctity, for he confessed his sins like a Christian and received the sacraments before he passed to the other life. He charged his son to give the Pope 60,000 gold ducats toward the crusade against the Turks and left large legacies to pious causes. He directed that his bones should be taken to Aragon. The carrying out of these instructions however was hindered by the outbreak of war; for although at Alfonso's death all the princes and states of his realm acknowledged Ferrante as their sovereign and swore allegiance to him, Pope Calixtus *transferred the hatred he had felt for Alfonso during his life to his son and* declared that the kingdom of Sicily had reverted to the Church of Rome. *It was common talk that*

[26] June 27, 1458.

he intended to put his nephew, Borgia, on the throne. But what is more uncertain than the plans of men? While Calixtus was unduly elated at the death of his royal enemy and thought that now everything was going to be easy for him, he himself fell ill and being weakened by extreme old age died within forty days.

Giovanni Caimo, the envoy of Francesco Sforza, Duke of Milan, who was passing through Viterbo, went to see Aeneas there and in the course of conversation said he had been sent to Calixtus to tell him that it was not acceptable to Francesco that Ferrante should be deposed from his father's throne; if the Pope had any such intention, he must know that the Duke of Milan would be against him. When he heard this, Aeneas said, "In that message you are bringing Calixtus his death-blow!" And such was the case, for when the Pope heard that Francesco did not agree with him about the kingdom, he soon fell ill of the malady from which he died. His nephews buried him in the basilica of St. Peter in the place called the chapel of St. Mary of the Fevers, which used to be the temple of Apollo. He died on August 6, in the year of our Saviour 1458. The cardinals, as was customary, celebrated his funeral with magnificent rites.

When Filippo, Cardinal of Bologna, who was spending the hot days of summer at Bagnareia, received the news, he went to Viterbo and accompanied Aeneas to Rome for the election of the next pope. As they approached the city together they were met outside the walls by the entire Curia and most of the populace, who all declared that one of them would be elected pope. All other cardinals who were within a hundred miles of Rome returned also, so that there were nineteen in the city. During the funeral ceremonies, however, the Cardinal of Fermo was attacked by a slow fever and followed to the tomb Calixtus, whom he had *too passionately* aspired to succeed. He was a man who would have been a model of virtue, if he had not let *ambition and* a violent temper master him. His life was pure, his learning and experience great, *but he was too hot a partisan of the Ghibellines.*

Ten days after Calixtus's death the other eighteen cardinals entered the conclave,[27] while the whole city waited in suspense for the outcome; though indeed it was common talk that Aeneas, Cardinal of Siena, would be pope, since no one was held in higher esteem.

The conclave was held in the apostolic palace at St. Peter's, where

[27] I.e., August 16. The account which follows constitutes a unique source of information concerning these earlier conclaves. A very large part of it was suppressed in the printed editions. It is here reproduced in full.

two halls and two chapels were set apart for it. In the larger chapel were constructed cells in which the cardinals might eat and sleep; the smaller, called the chapel of San Niccolò, was reserved for discussion and the election of the pope. The halls were places where all might walk about freely.

On the day of their entrance nothing was done about the election. On the next day certain capitulations were announced, which they agreed should be observed by the new pope, and each swore that he would abide by them, should the lot fall on him. On the third day after mass, when they came to the scrutiny, it was found that Filippo, Cardinal of Bologna, and Aeneas, Cardinal of Siena, had an equal number of votes, five apiece. No one else had more than three. *On that ballot, whether from strategy or dislike, no one voted for Guillaume, Cardinal of Rouen.*

The cardinals were accustomed, after the result of the scrutiny was announced, to sit and talk together in case any wished to change his mind and transfer the vote he had given one to another (a method called "by accession"), for in this way they more easily reach an agreement. This procedure was omitted after the first scrutiny owing to the opposition of those who had received no votes and therefore could not now be candidates for accession. They adjourned for luncheon and then there were many private conferences. The richer and more influential members of the college summoned the rest and sought to gain the papacy for themselves or their friends. They begged, promised, threatened, and some, shamelessly casting aside all decency, pleaded their own causes and claimed the papacy as their right. Among these were Guillaume, Cardinal of Rouen, Pietro, Cardinal of San Marco, and Giovanni, Cardinal of Pavia; nor did the Cardinal of Lerida neglect his own interests. Each had a great deal to say for himself. Their rivalry was extraordinary, their energy unbounded. They took no rest by day or sleep by night.

Rouen, however, did not fear these men so much as he did Aeneas and the Cardinal of Bologna, toward whom he saw the majority of the votes inclining. But he was especially afraid of Aeneas, whose silence he had no doubt would prove far more effective than the barkings of the rest. Therefore he would summon now some, now others, and upbraid them as follows: "What is Aeneas to you? Why do you think him worthy of the papacy? Will you give us a lame, poverty-stricken pope? How shall a destitute pope restore a destitute church, or an ailing pope an ailing church? He has but recently come from Germany. We do not know him. Perhaps he will even transfer the Curia thither. And look at his writings! Shall we set a poet in Peter's place? Shall we govern the Church by the laws of the heathen? Or do you think Filippo of Bologna is to be preferred?—a stiff-necked fellow, who has not the wit to rule himself, and will not listen to those who show him the right course. I am the senior cardinal. You know I am not without wisdom. I am learned in pontifical law and can boast of royal blood. I am rich in friends and resources with which I can succor the impoverished Church. I hold also not a few ecclesiastical benefices, which I shall distribute among you and the others, when I resign them."

He would then add many entreaties and if they had no effect, he would resort to threats. If anyone brought up his past simony as an indication that in his hands the papacy would be for sale, he did not deny that his past life had been tainted with that stain but swore that in the future his hands should be clean. He was supported by Alain, Cardinal of Avignon, who lent him every assistance in his power, not so much because he was a Frenchman siding with a Frenchman as because, at the elevation of Guillaume, he expected to obtain his house in Rome, the church of Rouen, and the vice-chancellorship. Not a few were won over by Rouen's splendid promises and were caught like flies by their gluttony. And the tunic of Christ without Christ was being sold.

Many cardinals met in the privies as being a secluded and retired place. Here they agreed as to how they might elect Guillaume pope and they bound themselves by written pledges and by oath. Guillaume trusted them and was presently promising benefices and preferment and dividing provinces among them. A fit place for such a pope to be elected! For where could one more appropriately enter into a foul covenant than in privies? Guillaume could certainly count on the two Greeks, the Cardinals of Genoa, San Sisto, Avignon, Colonna, and Pavia. The Vice-Chancellor, the Cardinals of Bologna, Orsini, and Sant' Anastasia were doubtful and seemed likely to accede to him if pushed a little. Indeed they had almost given him definite grounds for hope. Since it now appeared that eleven were agreed, they did not doubt that they would at once get the twelfth. For when it has come to this point, some one is always at hand to say, "I too make you pope," to win the favor that utterance always brings. They thought therefore that the thing was as good as done and were only waiting for daylight to go to the scrutiny.

Some time after midnight the Cardinal of Bologna went hurriedly to Aeneas's cell and waking him said, "Look here, Aeneas! Don't you

know that we already have a pope? Some of the cardinals have met in
the privies and decided to elect Guillaume. They are only waiting for
daylight. I advise you to get up and go and offer him your vote before
he is elected, for fear that if he is elected with you against him, he will
make trouble for you. I intend to take care not to fall into the old trap.
I know what it means to have the pope your enemy. I have had experience with Calixtus, who never gave me a friendly look, because I had
not voted for him. It seems to me expedient to curry favor beforehand
with the man who is going to be pope. I offer you the advice I am
taking myself."

Aeneas answered, "Filippo, away with you and your advice! No one
shall persuade me to vote for a man I think utterly unworthy to be
the successor of St. Peter. Far from me be such a sin! I will be clean of
that crime and my conscience shall not prick me. You say it is hard not
to have the pope well-disposed to you. I have no fears on that score. I
know he will not murder me because I have not voted for him. 'But,'
you say, 'he will not love you, will not make you presents, will not help
you. You will feel the pinch of poverty.' Poverty is not hard for one
accustomed to it. I have led a life of indigence heretofore; what matter
if I die indigent? He will not take from me the Muses, who are all the
sweeter in humble fortunes.

"But I am not the man to believe that God will allow the Church, His
Bride, to perish in the hands of the Cardinal of Rouen. For what is
more alien to the profession of Christ than that His Vicar should be a
slave to simony and lewdness? The Divine Mercy will not endure that
this palace, which has been the dwelling of so many Holy Fathers, shall
become a den of thieves or a brothel of whores. The apostleship is
bestowed by God, not by men. Those who have conspired to commit
the papacy to Rouen are men; and men's schemes are vain—who does
not know it? Well has their conspiracy been made in the privies! Their
plots too will have to retire and, like the Arian heresy, their most foul
contrivings will end in a most foul place. Tomorrow will show that the
Bishop of Rome is chosen by God not by men. As for you, if you are a
Christian, you will not choose as Christ's Vicar him whom you know
to be a limb of the devil." With these words he frightened Filippo from
going over to Rouen.

Next Aeneas went at daybreak to Rodrigo, the Vice-Chancellor, and
asked whether he had sold himself to Rouen. "What would you have
me do?" he answered, "The thing is settled. Many of the cardinals have
met in the privies and decided to elect him. It is not for my advantage

to remain with a small minority out of favor with a new pope. I am
joining the majority and I have looked out for my own interests. I shall
not lose the chancellorship; I have a note from Rouen assuring me of
that. If I do not vote for him, the others will elect him anyway and I
shall be stripped of my office." Aeneas said to him, "You young fool!
Will you then put an enemy of your nation in the Apostle's chair? And
will you put faith in the note of a man who is faithless? You will have
the note; Avignon will have the chancellorship. For what has been
promised you has been promised him also and solemnly affirmed. Will
faith be kept with him or with you? Will a Frenchman be more
friendly to a Frenchman or to a Catalan? Will he be more concerned for
a foreigner or for his own countryman? Take care, you inexperienced
boy! Take care, you fool! And if you have no thought for the Church
of Rome, if you have no regard for the Christian religion and despise
God, for Whom you are preparing such a vicar, at least take thought
for yourself, for you will find yourself among the hindmost, if a Frenchman is pope."

The Vice-Chancellor listened patiently to these words of his friend
and completely abandoned his purpose.

After this Aeneas, meeting the Cardinal of Pavia, said to him, "I
hear that you too are with those who have decided to elect Rouen. Is
this true?" He replied, "You have heard correctly. I have agreed to give
him my vote so that I may not be left alone. For his victory is already
certain; so many have declared for him." Aeneas said, "I thought you
a different man from what I find you. Only see how much you have
degenerated from your ancestors! Your father's brother (or was he
your mother's?), Branda, Cardinal of Piacenza, when the papacy was
beyond the mountains in Germany (for John XXIII, when he appointed
the Council of Constance, had carried the Roman Curia across the
Alps) never rested till he brought the Holy See back to Italy. It was
owing to his diplomacy, devotion, and genius that on the withdrawal
of the contestants for the papacy, Martin V, a Roman of the house of
Colonna, was elected pope. Branda brought the Apostolic Curia back
from Germany to Italy; you, his nephew, are going to transfer it from
Italy to France. But Rouen will prefer his own nation to Italy and a
Frenchman will be off to France with the supreme office.

"You say, 'He is under oath. He will not go outside this province
without the decree of the senate and if he wishes to go, we will not
consent.' What cardinal will dare oppose him when he is once seated
on the apostolic throne? You will be the first, when you have secured

some rich benefice, to say, 'Go where you will, Holy Father.' And what
is our Italy without the Bishop of Rome? We still have the Apostleship
though we have lost the Imperium, and in this one light we see light.
Shall we be deprived of this with your sympathy, persuasion, help? A
French pope will either go to France—and then our dear country is
bereft of its splendor; or he will stay among us—and Italy, the queen
of nations, will serve a foreign master, while we shall be the slaves of
the French. The kingdom of Sicily will come into the hands of the
French. The French will possess all the cities and strongholds of the
Church. You might have taken warning from Calixtus, during whose
papacy there was nothing the Catalans did not get. After trying the
Catalans are you so eager to try the French? You will soon be sorry if
you do! You will see the college filled with Frenchmen and the papacy
will never again be wrested from them. Are you so dull that you do
not realize that this will lay a yoke upon your nation forever?

"And what shall I say of this man's life? Are you not ashamed to
entrust Christ's office to a slippery fellow who would sell his own soul?
(Fig. 3) A fine bridegroom you are planning for the bride of Christ!
You are trusting a lamb to a wolf. Where is your conscience? your zeal
for justice? your common sense? Have you so far fallen below your
true self? I suppose we have not often heard you say that it would be
the Church's ruin if it fell into Rouen's hands? and that you would
rather die than vote for this very man? What is the reason for this
change? Has he suddenly been transformed from a demon to an angel
of light? Or have you been changed from an angel of light to the devil,
that you love his lust and filth and greed? What has become of your
love for your country and your continual protestations that you preferred Italy above all other nations? I used to think that if everyone else
fell away from devotion to her, you never would. You have failed me;
nay, more, you have failed yourself and Italy, your country, unless you
come to your senses."

The Cardinal of Pavia was stunned by these words and, overcome
alike with grief and shame, he burst into tears. Then stifling his sobs
he said, "I am ashamed, Aeneas. But what am I to do? I have given my
promise. If I do not vote for Rouen, I shall be charged with treachery."
Aeneas answered, "So far as I can see, it has come to the point where
you will be guilty of treachery whichever way you turn. You now have
to choose whether you prefer to betray Italy, your country, and the
Church or the Bishop of Rouen." Convinced by these arguments Pavia
decided it was less shameful to fail Rouen.

   *When Pietro, Cardinal of San Marco, learned of the conspiracy of
the French and had lost hope of getting the papacy himself, actuated
alike by patriotism and hatred of Rouen, he began to go to the Italian
cardinals urging and warning them not to abandon their country; and
he did not rest until he had gathered all the Italians except Colonna in
the cell of the Cardinal of Genoa, revealed the conspiracy that had been
made in the privies, and showed them that the Church would be ruined
and Italy a slave forever, if Rouen should obtain the papacy. He implored them individually to show themselves men, to consult for the
good of Mother Church and unhappy Italy, to put aside their enmities
for one another and choose an Italian rather than a foreigner for pope.
If they listened to him, they would prefer Aeneas to all others. There
were present seven cardinals: Genoa, Orsini, Bologna, San Marco,
Pavia, Siena, and Sant' Anastasia. All approved Pavia's words except
Aeneas, who thought himself unworthy of so exalted an office.*
   The next day they went as usual to mass and then began the scrutiny.
A golden chalice was placed on the altar and three cardinals, the Bishop
of Ruthen, the Presbyter of Rouen, and the Deacon of Colonna, were
set to watch it and see that there should be no cheating. The other
cardinals took their seats and then, rising in order of rank and age, each
approached the altar and deposited in the chalice a ballot on which was
written the name of his choice for pope. *When Aeneas came up to put
in his ballot, Rouen, pale and trembling, said, "Look, Aeneas! I commend myself to you"—certainly a rash thing to say when it was not
allowable to change what he had written. But ambition overcame prudence. Aeneas said, "Do you commend yourself to a worm like me?"
and without another word he dropped his ballot in the cup and went
back to his place.*
   When all had voted, a table was placed in the middle of the room
and the three cardinals mentioned above turned out upon it the cupful
of votes. Then they read aloud the ballots one after another and noted
down the names written on them. And there was not a single cardinal
who did not likewise make notes of those named, that there might be
no possibility of trickery. *This proved to be to Aeneas's advantage, for
when the votes were counted and the teller, Rouen, announced that
Aeneas had eight, though the rest said nothing about another man's
loss, Aeneas did not allow himself to be defrauded. "Look more carefully at the ballots," he said to the teller, "for I have nine votes." The
others agreed with him. Rouen said nothing, as if he had merely made
a mistake.*

This was the form of the ballot: The voter wrote with his own hand, "I, Peter (or John or whatever his name was) choose for pope Aeneas, Cardinal of Siena, and Jaime, Cardinal of Lisbon"; for it is permitted to vote for one or two or more, on the understanding that the one first named is the one preferred, but if he does not have enough votes to be elected, the next is to be counted in his place, that an agreement may more easily be reached. *But a thing advantageous in itself some men pervert to base ends, as Latino Orsini did on that day. He named seven in the hope that those he named might be influenced by that good turn either to accede to him in that scrutiny or to vote for him in another; although he who has the reputation of a cheat does not gain much by tricks.*

When the result of the scrutiny was made known, it was found, *as we have said before,* that nine cardinals (Genoa, Orsini, Lerida, Bologna, San Marco, Santi Quattro Coronati, Zamora, Pavia, and Portugal) had voted for Aeneas; the Cardinal of Rouen had only six votes, and the rest were far behind. *Rouen was petrified when he saw himself so far outstripped by Aeneas and* all the rest were amazed, for never within the memory of man had anyone polled as many as nine votes by scrutiny. Since no one had received enough votes for election, they decided to resume their seats and try the method that is called "by accession," to see if perhaps it might be possible to elect a pope that day. *And here again Rouen indulged in empty hopes.* All sat pale and silent in their places as if entranced. For some time no one spoke, no one opened his lips, no one moved any part of his body except the eyes, which kept glancing all about. It was a strange silence and a strange sight, *men sitting there like their own statues;* no sound to be heard, no movement to be seen. They remained thus for some moments, those inferior in rank waiting for their superiors to begin the accession.

Then Rodrigo, the Vice-Chancellor, rose and said, "I accede to the Cardinal of Siena," *an utterance which was like a dagger in Rouen's heart, so pale did he turn.* A silence followed and each man looking at his neighbor, began to indicate his sentiments by gestures. By this time it looked as if Aeneas would be pope and some, fearing this result, left the conclave, *pretending physical needs, but really* with the purpose of escaping the fate of that day. Those who thus withdrew were the Cardinals of Ruthen and San Sisto. However, as no one followed them, they soon returned. Then Jacopo, Cardinal of Sant' Anastasia, said, "I accede to the Cardinal of Siena." *At this all appeared even more stunned, like people in a house shaken by unprecedented earthquakes, and lost the power of speech.*

Aeneas now lacked but one vote, for twelve would elect a pope. Realizing this, Cardinal Prospero Colonna thought that he must get for himself the glory of announcing the pope. *He rose and was about to pronounce his vote with the customary dignity, when he was seized by the Cardinals of Nicaea and Rouen and sharply rebuked for wishing to accede to Aeneas. When he persisted in his intention, they tried to get him out of the room by force, resorting even to such means to snatch the papacy from Aeneas.* But Prospero, *who, though he had voted for the Cardinal of Rouen on his ballot,* was nevertheless bound to Aeneas by ties of old friendship, *paid no attention to their abuse and empty threats.* Turning to the other cardinals, he said, "I too accede to the Cardinal of Siena and I make him pope." When they heard this, *the courage of the opposition failed and all their machinations were shattered.*

All the cardinals immediately fell at Aeneas's feet and saluted him as Pope. Then they resumed their seats and ratified his election without a dissenting vote. At this point Bessarion, Cardinal of Nicaea, speaking for himself and for the others who had voted for the Cardinal of Rouen, said, "Your Holiness, we approve your election, which we do not doubt is of God. We thought before and still think that you are worthy of this office. The reason we did not vote for you was your infirmity. We thought your gout the one thing against you; for the Church needs an active man who has the physical strength to take long journeys and meet the dangers which we fear threaten us from the Turks. You on the contrary need rest. It was this consideration that won us to the side of the Cardinal of Rouen. If you were physically strong, there is no one we should have preferred. But, since God is satisfied, we must needs be satisfied too. *God Himself, who has chosen you, will make good the defect in your feet and will not punish our ignorance.* We revere you as Pope, we elect you again, so far as is in our power, and we will serve you faithfully."

Aeneas answered, "Your Eminence of Nicaea, your opinion of us, as we understand it, is much higher than our own, when you attribute to us no defect except that in our feet. We are not ignorant that our imperfection is more general and we realize that our failings, which might justly have caused us to be rejected as pope, are almost innumerable. As to any virtues which might raise us to this post, we know of none; and we should declare ourselves utterly unworthy and should refuse the honor offered us, if we did not fear the judgment of Him Who has called us. For what is done by two thirds of the sacred college, that is surely of the Holy Ghost, which may not be resisted. Therefore we obey the divine summons and we praise you, Your Eminence of Nicaea, and those who voted with you. If, following the dictates of your conscience, you thought we ought not to be elected as being inadequate, you will still be welcomed by us, who attribute our calling not to this man or that but to the whole college and to God Himself, from Whom cometh every good and perfect gift."

With these words he took off the garments he was wearing and put on the white tunic of Christ. When asked by what name he wished to be called, he answered, "Pius," [28] and he was at once addressed as Pius II. Then after swearing to observe the capitulations that had been announced in the college two days before, he took his place by the altar and was again reverenced by the cardinals, who kissed his feet, hands, and cheek. After that the election of a pope was proclaimed to the people from a high window and it was announced that he who had been Cardinal of Siena was now Pope Pius II.[29]

The attendants of the cardinals in the conclave plundered Aeneas's cell and *meanly* carried off all the plate (though it was very modest), his clothes, and his books; and the infamous rabble not only pillaged his house in the city but actually demolished it, taking away even the blocks of marble. Other cardinals, too, suffered losses, for while the people were waiting in suspense, various rumors got about and as now this cardinal, now that was reported elected, the crowd would rush to their houses and plunder them. The Cardinal of Genoa, whose name was mistaken for Siena, lost part of his possessions. Though many names were mentioned, none was received with enthusiasm except that of the Cardinal of Siena. *When the cry arose that Rouen or Genoa or Lerida (for there were reports of them too) had been elected, all cast down their eyes and cursed the college. Only their personal friends were pleased; the rest shared the general sorrow. But* when it was certain that Aeneas had been seated on Peter's throne, there was no one who did not rejoice. You might have seen not men only but *the very animals and* the buildings of the city exulting. Everywhere was heard laughter and expressions of joy and the cries of men shouting, "Siena! Siena! *O happy Siena!* Viva Siena!" Though the city was under arms and no one seemed to have confidence in anything but the sword, presently,

---

[28] Inspired in this choice by Virgil's "pius Aeneas."
[29] Pius was elected August 19, 1458; his coronation took place September 3rd.

when the people were told that the papacy had fallen to Aeneas, the aspect of the capital was completely changed. What had a little time before been the city of Mars all at once became the city, *I will not say of Venus, the mother of that ancient Trojan Aeneas, but* of Peace and Quiet, and joy and tranquillity reigned everywhere.

Meantime the new Pope after taking a little refreshment was escorted to the Basilica of St. Peter and conducted to the high altar, under which lie the bodies of the blessed Apostles. Shortly after, he took his seat according to custom on the high throne and in the apostolic chair itself. There the cardinals and bishops and after them many of the people kissed his feet and reverenced him on his throne as Christ's Vicar. Then after a brief interval, when evening was coming on, they escorted him back to the palace. At nightfall fires blazed at every crossroad and on every tower; singing could be heard; neighbors called to neighbors; everywhere horns and trumpets blared and there was no spot in all the city which did not share in the general rejoicing. The older men said they had never seen such enthusiasm among the Roman populace.

The next night in a procession that reached from Hadrian's mausoleum to the Church of St. Peter the chief citizens of Rome on horseback and carrying lighted tapers went to the palace to greet the Pope.

Not only Rome but many states of Italy and many princes, when they heard of the accession of Pius, expressed the liveliest satisfaction, but the Sienese especially were elated, because their own citizen had been so exalted that he was now looked on as the first of all men on earth (*though, to be sure, many who were enemies of the nobles grieved in their hearts*). Ferrante, King of Sicily, welcomed the news because he realized that a friend of his father was now seated in the chair of St. Peter. Francesco Sforza, though he had expected a different pope, was nevertheless pleased to learn of the election of Aeneas, whom he had once received with honor in his camp, when he was attacking Milan. Borso, Duke of Modena, held military maneuvers and gave many conspicuous signs of his joy. His friendship with Aeneas dated from the time when he had received his dukedom from the Emperor Frederick, a favor in which Aeneas had had no small hand. He hoped that under the pontificate of Aeneas his fortunes and prestige would increase and therefore he saw to it that Ferrara and all his dominions should evince extravagant pleasure at the accession of the new pope. *How many ways men have to get interest on their money!* The Marquises of Mantua, Monferrato, and Saluzzo were equally delighted, for they all knew Aeneas and were his friends.

Only the Venetians and Florentines *among the Italians were sorry to
hear the news; the Venetians because Aeneas, when he was the Emperor's ambassador, had often seemed to them to speak overharshly in
their Senate and to accuse them of tyranny; the Florentines because, as
is the way of mankind with their neighbors, they hated the Sienese.
They were so vexed at Aeneas's accession that when they were greeted
by persons they met on the road with the customary words, "May God
aid you," they answered indignantly, "He is busy with the Sienese,
whom He is trying to bless!" Nevertheless the Venetians and the Florentines concealed their sentiments and* like the other Italian powers sent
to Rome very distinguished ambassadors to congratulate the new Pope
and pledge him their obedience.

Among the Transalpine princes the Emperor Frederick was especially
gratified, since it was from his service that Aeneas had been called to
the cardinalate and had finally ascended the throne of St. Peter. All the
Christian princes of Spain showed their satisfaction, but Scotland, Denmark, Poland, France, Hungary, and Cyprus were not pleased to hear
that a friend of the Emperor had become Christ's Vicar. The King of
Bohemia was particularly distressed, for he realized that the Pope knew
him for a heretic. Philip of Burgundy and Lodovico of Savoy were delighted with the elevation of their old friend Aeneas.

BOOK II

POPE PIUS II was crowned at Rome in St. Peter's September 3, in the year of our salvation 1458, and the same day he went in solemn procession to the Lateran, where he narrowly escaped death in the mob who fought with swords for the horse on which he had ridden. He was saved by the mercy of Heaven and after celebrating mass gave a royal banquet not only to the cardinals but to all the ambassadors of princes and all the nobles and chief men of the city who were present. The same night he returned to his palace in the Vatican.

Among all the purposes he had at heart none was dearer than that of rousing Christians against the Turks and declaring war upon them. This race, which had once migrated from eastern Scythia, had subdued Cappadocia, Pontus, Bithynia, and almost all Asia Minor. Soon after, they had crossed the Hellespont, seized most of Greece, and advanced their arms as far as the famous rivers Save and Danube. There still stood in mid-Thrace the royal city of Byzantium, which Constantine the Great, who had rebuilt and greatly enlarged it, called New Rome. The populace, however, insisted that it should be named Constantinople after its second founder. During the pontificate of Nicholas V, Mahomet, Sultan of the Turks (Fig. 25), besieged this city and having made a breach in the walls, as has been previously described, took it by storm and sacked it. Constantine, the last emperor of that name, was murdered, or, it is rumored, trampled to death by the cavalry. Mahomet, elated with this victory, began to aspire to the sovereignty of all Europe and, having collected a huge army, planned to cross into Hungary through Upper Moesia; but in the pontificate of Calixtus III he was stopped at Alba (a town at the confluence of the Save and the Danube, which was called Taurunum in antiquity) by a Christian army under the sign of the cross led by Giovanni Capistrano, a Minorite friar renowned for his sanctity, and John Hunyadi, governor of the kingdom of Hungary. He was defeated with great loss, driven from the field, and forced to a humiliating and hasty retreat. Nevertheless he did not lose courage nor relax his hatred of the Christians, but recruiting fresh forces day by day, he proceeded to harry now the Albanians, now the Rascians, now other neighboring Christian peoples, resolved to trample down and utterly annihilate the Holy Scriptures and the Divine Law of Christ.

As a nation the Turks are foes of the Trinity. They follow a certain false prophet called Mahomet, an Arab imbued with Gentile error and Jewish perfidy, who listened to Christians infected with Nestorianism and Arianism. He advanced his fortunes by seducing an influential widow and became notorious for his intrigues; he collected a band of brigands with which he made himself lord over the Arabs. Acquainted as he was with the Old and the New Testament he perverted them both; he had the effrontery to say that he was a prophet and talked with angels and he cast such a spell over ignorant peoples that he was able to give them a new law and persuade them to abandon Christ, the Savior. For he made use of incantations and magic and by permitting lust and incest he easily won over to him the common people, who are prone to sensual pleasure. Except wine there was nothing he did not allow them, in order to persuade them to worship according to his law, which, though it admits that Christ was inspired of God, born of a Virgin, and able to perform miracles, yet denies that He was divine and that He suffered the agony of death for our redemption. It does not acknowledge the Prophets or heed the precepts of the Apostles or the Evangelists. The influence of this monstrous doctrine increased to such an extent that almost all Asia and Africa was infected with its poison; it made its way with the Turks into Greece and through the Moors took possession of Baetica in Spain; and although the Bishops of Rome have tried in many ways to combat this plague, nevertheless it has continued to gain strength gradually to this day and has penetrated to our very vitals.

Pope Pius was afraid of this poison and decided to take steps to prevent its worming its way further, but he did not rely on himself alone (that is, on the power of the Apostolic See), for the conquest of the Turks seemed to him a task not for this or that realm but for all Christendom. Thinking therefore that he must ask the advice of those whose aid he needed, he determined to call a congress of princes and free peoples to discuss together the common weal. First however they had to consider where the congress should be held. It seemed better to him to call the congress near the Alps in some place midway between the Pope and the transalpine sovereigns. The question was debated for a long time in council with the cardinals and though many of them,

entirely satisfied with the present state of things and liking their easy
life in the capital, were against him, the Pope's firmness prevailed and
his plan was adopted.

Then the bishops, abbots, notaries, royal ambassadors, and all the
officials of the Curia were assembled in the palace chapel that their
advice also might be heard. There the Pope made public the project he
had long cherished. He told them what disasters the Turks had inflicted
upon Christians and how they were striving to overthrow the Gospel.
He declared that nothing was more bitter to him than to behold the
ruin of a Christian nation, that he was charged with the care of their
most holy religion, and that he had decided to take the offensive against
the Turks. But since this could not be done without the aid of Christian
sovereigns, he had determined to hold a congress at Udine or Mantua
to hear the advice of those whose aid he meant to implore. It was hard
for him to leave Rome, the seat of St. Peter the Apostle and the stronghold of the Christian faith, but it was still harder that in his pontificate
the holy Gospel should be overthrown and, to save it, he was resolved
to stake not only the city and the patrimony of St. Peter but his own
person and his life. Therefore, though he was old [1] and ill, he proposed
to cross the ridges of the Apennines and the waters of the Po to consult
with Christian potentates about the salvation of the Christian religion.
And he continued speaking in this vein earnestly and at length.

All applauded his courage and his purpose and extolled him to the
skies as the only man who had at heart the safety of the Faith. Then the
usual public consistory was held and an apostolic letter was read, in
which a day was set [2] for the congress and the princes were summoned
to one or the other of the two cities.

When they learned of this decision, the Romans were greatly distressed because they realized that they were going to be deprived of the
emoluments from the Curia. They had no expectation that the Pope,
afflicted as he was with sickness and old age, would ever return. Some
said his real objective was not Mantua but Siena and that he pretended
the congress was to be at Mantua that he might stop at Siena on the
way and thus enrich his native city; others asserted that the Pope would
go not only to Mantua but to Germany, since, having spent his youth
among the Germans, he would gladly return to them and would see no
impropriety in establishing the Apostolic See across the Alps. All des-

---

[1] Pius was fifty-three years old at this time but prematurely aged as a result of ill
health.

[2] June 1, 1459.

paired of his return to Rome. Women went wailing through the streets, children blasphemed, and men cursed. The elder men who had more sense went in throngs to the pontiff; they opposed his departure and besought him to remain in their city, holding out many inducements if he would stay. The Pope tried to console them, explaining the necessity for his going and promising a speedy return, but he could not speak to his people without tears. There was universal mourning and there had not been such rejoicing at the accession of Pius as there was now sorrow when his decision to depart was known among the populace; so true it is that there is no joy that is not speedily followed by grief.

The Pope's journey was made more difficult and dangerous by the fact that the affairs of the kingdom of Sicily had not yet been settled. This kingdom belongs legally to the Church of Rome. For a long time the French held it in fief, paying an annual tribute of 8,000 gold ounces to the Bishop of Rome; but when Queen Joanna II had come to despise Louis of Anjou, whom she had adopted as her son, and had summoned Alfonso, King of Aragon, from Spain to be her successor, conditions were changed and instead of the French, the Catalans or Aragonese came in. Numerous battles were fought between Louis and Alfonso, in which Fortune, as is her habit, exalted now one and now the other. When Louis died of a fever, his rights were transferred to his brother René. The Queen sometimes loved Alfonso and sometimes hated him. At her death René made his entrance into the kingdom where many welcomed him with enthusiasm and did homage to him as king, but though he continued for many years to contend with Alfonso for the throne, he was finally conquered and forced to withdraw. Alfonso remained in the kingdom, but he was not recognized as vassal by Pope Eugenius IV, who had favored René, until it was proved that the latter had disregarded his promises and broken his oath. Alfonso was then crowned by Eugenius.

Alfonso had one son, Ferrante, by a lady who was noble but the wife of another man. Eugenius declared him eligible to succeed and so did the next pope, Nicholas V, who also confirmed Alfonso as king. As long therefore as Eugenius and Nicholas lived Alfonso reigned in peace and quiet without opposition. Nicholas was succeeded by Calixtus III *of Valencia,* who had been for a long time at Alfonso's court and was under particular obligation to him, because it was owing to the King's entreaties that he had obtained the cardinalate. For these reasons Alfonso thought that no request of his would be refused by a pope who had once been his subject and had owed his elevation to his favor, and he was led by this confidence to demand that not only the fief of the kingdom but also the Marches of Ancona and various other places belonging to the Church should be handed over to him. This was far from the intention of the Pope, who, finding himself the Vicar of Christ, saw no reason to yield to the King or to alienate the Church's rightful possessions. Thus there was bitter enmity between them which lasted to the end of their lives, *although some, especially those who were the admiration of Florence and whose great wealth was imputed to them for wisdom, thought this was a pretense. For these men believed that the two aged foreigners pretended to hate each other so that they, who already held nearly two thirds of Italy, might more easily gain the rest of it. But in fact the enmity was entirely genuine and implacable and it went with them to the grave.* Alfonso died first by forty days. When Calixtus learned of his death, *he restrained neither his tears nor his laughter.* He wept for mortal frailty; he laughed *because his enemy had been removed,* saying with the Prophet, "The snare is broken and we are escaped."

When Ferrante claimed his father's throne, the Pope refused to listen, asserting that the princes and peoples who had acknowledged him as their king had been wrong, and summoning the cardinals and the pre- lates of the Roman Curia who had a reputation for learning, he declared that the kingdom of Sicily had reverted to the Church of Rome. He intended to take it by force *and hand it over to his nephew* and he had already collected a considerable army. Death however prevented him from satisfying *alike* his own schemes *and his nephew.*[3]

Meantime Ferrante's ambassadors approached the Pope. They dwelt on the memory of Alfonso, who had been very fond of Pius when as Bishop of Siena he had been the Emperor's ambassador at Alfonso's court, and they begged the Pope not to reject the son of his old friend nor refuse his father's throne to one who was the choice of all. Pius replied, "We loved and admired Alfonso for his noble character and this shall be greatly to Ferrante's advantage, if he does his duty toward the Church of Rome." When they asked him what Ferrante must do, he said, "The assessment due the Apostolic Camera he shall pay each year; whenever the Pope asks for aid, he shall cheerfully furnish it; he shall not encroach on the rights of the churches; he shall order Piccinino to withdraw from the Church's territory and if he does not obey, he shall compel him by armed force; he shall grant peace to Sigismondo Malatesta on the terms dictated by the Pope; he shall restore Benevento

---

[3] Rodrigo Borgia who later became Pope Alexander VI.

to the Church; Terracina he shall hold for ten years with payment of
a tribute and shall then hand it over to the Roman pontiff."

These terms seemed harsh to Ferrante, who sent back his ambassadors
again and again to try to persuade the Pope to make fewer demands.
The answer was that Pius was no trader to demand much with a view
to getting at least a little; that he must take his kingdom on these conditions or do without it. At last Ferrante was beaten, since the Pope's
meaning and words were always the same. The question was brought
before the sacred college and the cardinals, except the French, who were
less loyal to the See than to their king, assented to the Pope. Even the
French were at last won over by argument and agreed with the rest
that it was expedient that the kingdom be given to Ferrante. They
asked however not to be compelled to sign the decree. The request was
granted. The kingdom was granted to Ferrante by decree of the senate
and Cardinal Latino Orsini was sent to Apulia to crown the King and
receive his oath of allegiance to Pius and his successors.

Next the barons of the Roman territory were summoned to Rome
and enjoined that no one should stir up dissension during the Pope's
absence. They bound themselves by an oath to keep the peace; if anyone
broke it he was to be punished severely. And since the Romans were
desperately afraid that when the Pope went away they would lose forever the Roman Curia, Pius announced with the approval of the senate
that if he should die outside the city, the election of his successor might
not take place elsewhere than in Rome; and he set a time limit beyond
which the cardinals who were at Rome should not wait for those who
were absent. Furthermore, since he was leaving in the capital during
the entire time of his absence some of the cardinals and auditors of the
Rota as well as advocates and litigators, he declared that the Roman
Curia was with them as much as with him.

*One of the influential men at Calixtus's court had been the Venetian
Francesco Venerio, who, in order to amass as much money as possible
for the Pope, asked to inspect the books of the bankers and then, seizing
his opportunity, fined them heavily because, he said, they had mis-
managed the business of the Apostolic Camera. At Calixtus's death they
appealed to Pius and recovered all their fines, Cosimo dei Medici receiving back 1,500 ducats and Ambrogio Spannocchi as large a sum. The
same procedure was followed in regard to the others who reported
themselves unjustly fined. Calixtus during the last days of his life had
imprisoned Francesco in the Castle of Sant' Angelo. Pius removed him
from there and put him in charge of a senator, that he might satisfy his*

creditors on the Capitol, but he died before his affairs could be thoroughly investigated.

When matters were thus arranged in the city and Niccolò, Cardinal of St. Peter, had been put in charge there, on the 20th of January, the day set for his departure, the Pope went in the dead of night from the papal palace at St. Peter's in the Vatican to Santa Maria Maggiore on the Esquiline. He remained there the next day and blessed a throng of weeping citizens, unable himself to restrain his tears. The following day he descended by way of the baths of Diocletian and the hill of the Subura to the Flaminian Gate, which is now called Porta del Popolo, and thence to the Ponte Molle, escorted thus far by the cardinals and most of the nobles and the populace of Rome. There troops of armed cavalry were waiting to be the Pope's bodyguard. The people were sent back and six cardinals were chosen to attend the Pope on his journey. The other cardinals, some of whom were infirm, were bidden to remain permanently in Rome or to wait for spring, when the weather would be milder, before following Pius. But the Pope, who made allowances for the ailments of others, had no mercy on his own and, though suffering from gout and various other complaints, preferred to risk his life rather than defer the day set for his departure. His friends argued with him and tried by many devices to delay him, urging the frightful winter, the frozen Apennines, the thousand perils of the journey. When none of these objections produced any effect, there were some who said, "Think, your Holiness; if no considerations for your own safety will make you stay, at least have some regard for the Roman Church, which is entrusted to your care, and see how many plots are being laid against it. Who will protect the patrimony of St. Peter in your absence? The instant you have crossed the Po, ravening wolves will fall upon your kingdom; for what land breeds more usurpers, not to say brigands, than yours? Some will mangle Picenum, others Umbria, and so on, and they will strip bare your bride. When you return you will find no place you can call your own to lay your head."

To this the Pope answered, "Surely God, Whose cause we go to plead, will grant us a better lot. But if the Divine Compassion permits that which you fear to come about, I should rather see the Church spoiled of these temporal goods than of her honor. If we do not keep our promise, our honor is lost and who will ever trust us again? The Faith too is at stake, assailed by the Turks against whom this congress has been called. If we go on, it is true that the temporal power may totter; but this has often been lost and often recovered. If we once abandon our spiritual

kingdom, it is uncertain whether it can ever be won back. Let these tran-
sient things go, provided we keep those that are more substantial." And
without further ado he set out on his journey.

The first night was spent at a Campanian villa belonging to the
Orsini sixteen miles from the capital. Here the Archbishop of Trani,
brother of Cardinal Latino, received Pope Pius and all the Curia with
great magnificence. When he learned that Assisi had been recovered
without recourse to arms, he continued his journey in a much happier
frame of mind, realizing that God, Who had thus furthered his undertakings, was his sure ally and that things had begun most auspiciously.
Nevertheless he thought best not to go straight through Tuscany, because he did not wish to enter Siena till he was reconciled with his
fellow citizens; for he was somewhat annoyed that they had refused to
admit to a share in the government those who are called the nobility,
though he had repeatedly asked them to do so.

Siena is a very famous city of Tuscany and possesses wide lands.
Many strange stories are told about its founders, but the stock originated
at Rome and took from there the device of the she-wolf with the twins
hanging on her teats. Some think they have been mixed with Gallic
stock since the time when the Senonese Gauls invaded Rome and were
defeated and routed by Camillus. For they say that the remnants of both
armies settled where Siena now is and built two towns which afterwards, at the time of Charlemagne, were united in one great city. For
our part we neither affirm nor deny these ancient tales, but we can assert
that in this city there were many nobles and very powerful men who
erected lofty palaces, high towers, and very splendid churches while
they administered the state. When however the nobler families began
to quarrel about the government and sometimes appealed even to armed
force, the nobility decided to resign the management of affairs to the
people, reserving for themselves only a few offices; but when the people
became accustomed to rule and had once tasted the sweets of office and
the fruits of power, in their increased wealth and splendor they disdained the nobility, banished certain noble families, and sent the rest
under the yoke like slaves, although they shared with them a few minor
offices. The whole city was so torn with civil discord that it was the
universal opinion that she would soon lose her liberty.

But the great God looked with loving eyes on a state dedicated to His
Mother, the Virgin Mary; for when Pope Pius succeeded to the papacy
on the death of Calixtus, he at once took thought for his dearly loved
country. He disrupted the schemes set on foot against her and frightened off her enemies by his authority. Moreover he thought it greatly

concerned the city's welfare that the places of citizens who had been removed from the government should be filled from the nobles and that it did not befit her dignity that the nobles, to whom he himself belonged by birth, should be regarded as slaves in his native city. The Sienese, suspecting this would happen, in order to forestall any complaint, elected to office Pius's own family, the Piccolomini, thinking that he would demand nothing further. But Pius, who was concerned not for his own house but for the whole state, thought that nothing had been accomplished unless all the nobles were returned to power, and he sent ambassadors to demand that all the rest of that order should be made equal to the Piccolomini. The people were violently excited by this demand; they declared that the Pope's request was outrageous and that the state would never consent, even if they were compelled to stand a siege and starved into eating their own children. Pius on the other hand insisted and swore that, if they did not obey, he would withdraw his favor from a city which refused to comply with just demands.

It was for this reason therefore that he now changed his route and leaving Tuscany proceeded through Umbria, threatening that if the Sienese did not do as he wished, he would disregard his own city and go on to Mantua through Perugia, Arezzo, and Florence. Therefore he went to Cività Castellana. From here Pius crossed the Tiber by a wooden bridge, recently constructed and decked with ivy and green boughs, not far from Magliano, a Sabine town subject to the Romans. All along his route the people poured out to greet him; the priests bearing holy relics offered prayers for his happiness as he passed; boys and girls wearing wreaths of laurel and carrying olive branches wished the great Bishop long life and felicity. Those who could touch the edge of his garments thought themselves blessed. Everywhere the road was thronged with people and strewn with fresh grasses; the squares in the towns and cities were carpeted with precious fabrics; the houses of the citizens and the churches of God were splendidly decorated. So he passed through Narni and Terni (*where he was almost in danger of his life while the citizens fought with swords for his horse*) to Spoleto.

No less honor was shown the Pope here. It is a city built on a mountain whose summit is crowned by a very famous citadel, the work of a former cardinal, Egidius, strongly fortified by the nature of the place as well as by the height of the walls and the work of men's hands. From here there is a view of the entire valley, which is called the Valley of Spoleto and is certainly a charming and healthful spot. From it rises a high and steep mountain on which as in a wilderness many anchorites worship God with devotion. There are also several monasteries whose monks are famous for their holiness. When the Goths ruled Italy and later when the Lombards were masters and later still when the French were in power, Spoleto was very important, the capital of Umbria and the residence of dukes, and the title "Duchy of Spoleto" survives even today. Here the Pope stayed two days and gave a dinner to the cardinals who accompanied him, at which he himself was present in excellent spirits.

From here Pius went to Assisi and stood in the citadel which had been betrayed to Piccinino for a price. Assisi was made famous by St. Francis, the founder of the Minorites, to whom poverty seemed the greatest wealth. A splendid church was erected to him in which they say his bones are buried. It is in fact two churches, one above the other, decorated with frescoes by the Florentine Giotto, who is agreed to have been the greatest painter of his time. The monastery which is attached to the church of St. Francis is considered the head of the entire order and there is no building of this order in the whole world which surpasses it.

When Pius had surveyed the citadel and observed that there was only one place where it could be stormed, he ordered a tower to be erected there. This was later built at great expense and rendered the fortifications impregnable.

Then crossing the Tiber again, Pius continued his journey to Perugia, where he was shown every honor that the mind of man could invent. For although it was the bitterest winter weather, the city was adorned as if it were spring. The whole place was gay with greenery; men and women were eager to gaze on the Pope (for it was eighty years since anyone there had seen a Vicar of Christ); along every street hung the papal arms and the gold crescent moons; there were military maneuvers; there was every sign of extravagant delight; the cardinals and all the members of the Curia were received with gracious and lavish hospitality.

Perugia is very old and is one of the twelve chief cities of Etruria mentioned by ancient writers. Part of the walls built by the Emperor Augustus is still to be seen. It has long been famous in arms and letters and especially in law, in which Bartolo was distinguished and after him Baldo and Angelo.

Pope Pius arrived at this city on the eve of the Purification of the Blessed Virgin Mary, Mother of our Lord, and on the feast day offered her the customary candles. A few days later he dedicated the large and splendid cathedral of San Domenico. Federigo of Urbino came here to see the Pope and was very graciously received. Ambassadors from Lodovico, Duke of Savoy, also came to make submission to the Bishop of Rome according to ancient custom. There came to meet him too the ambassadors from Siena begging him to come to their city. The Pope was glad to see them and was rejoiced to be invited and entreated to go to his beloved birthplace. He wished however to find the city unarmed and desired that when he entered Siena he should be at liberty to consult with the senate about their form of government. This they conceded, though much against their will.

The Pope remained at Perugia three weeks and then, to the grief of the citizens, who hoped that their lord would stay longer, he set out for Siena and came to Lake Trasimeno, made famous by the disaster to the Romans and the victory of Hannibal. For several days before the Pope's arrival the lake had been stirred up by a severe storm so that it was impossible to sail upon it, but now, as if in obedience to Divine Will, the violence of the winds subsided. When the Pope stepped on board ship, the sea submitted to him like a tamed beast and with the cessation of the wind the lake became so extraordinarily calm that they took a huge catch of fish. While he was crossing to the island, where he spent the night with the monks of St. Francis, the waves were still and they remained quiet all that evening and night and the following morning till his boat reached the shore. Then again violent winds began to rage and to wrestle together, so that those who were following the Pope barely escaped drowning. The inhabitants of the region were struck with amazement that Trasimeno, which all winter is wind-swept and unmanageable, submitted to be crossed by the Pope.

Next Pius came to the river, or rather swamp, called Chiana, which separates the territory of Siena from that of Perugia. Here ambassadors from the Sienese received the Pope with a large company and great rejoicing and escorted him to the ancient city of Chiusi, the birthplace of King Porsenna, which was once rich and famous but now *is a mean hamlet and* has very few inhabitants. Pliny says there was a labyrinth here which was not the least among the wonders of the world. That there is no trace of it left may seem itself a wonder. From here Pius proceeded to Sarteano, a town *allied rather than* subject to Siena and once the property of Orvieto. When Ladislas, King of Sicily, was leading a great army against the Florentines and the Sienese refused to let him pass, he halted here thirteen days and every day made an attack on the city. But all his efforts were in vain, partly because of the courage of its defenders and partly because of the treachery of Paolo Orsini, who sent messengers to report all the king's plans to the townspeople.

From Sarteano the Pope went on to Corsignano. A high mountain rises from the valley of the Orcia River, crowned by a plateau a mile long and much less broad. In the corner which in winter looks toward the rising sun there is a town of little repute but possessed of a healthful climate, excellent wine, and everything else that goes to sustain life. Travelers to Rome from Siena, after leaving the Castle of San Quirico and going straight ahead to Radicofani, pass Corsignano on a gently sloping hill at their left three miles from the main road. The greater part of the town once belonged to the Piccolomini, and Pius's father, Silvio, had his ancestral estates there. Here Pius was born and here he passed his childhood. Returning to it at this time he hoped to have some pleasure in talking with those with whom he had grown up and to feel delight in seeing again his native soil; but he was disappointed, for most of those of his own generation had died and those who were left kept their houses, bowed down with old age and illness, or, if they showed themselves, were so changed as to be hardly recognizable, for they were feeble and crippled *and like harbingers of death. At every step the Pope met with proofs of his own age and could not fail to realize that he was an old man who would soon drop,* since he found that those whom he had left as children had sons who were already well along in years. The town was wonderfully decorated. The people were excited and in holiday mood over the presence of the Pope, who they boasted had been born among them, and they could not look at or cheer him enough.

Pius stayed at Corsignano for the feast of St. Peter's Chair and said mass. He decided to build there a new church and a palace and he hired architects and workmen at no small expense, that he might leave as lasting as possible a memorial of his birth.

The Pope slept that night [4] in the hospice of Santa Maria which is called Cuna, six miles from Siena, and the following day with a great crowd of citizens amid incredible enthusiasm on the part of the populace he entered his own city which was beautifully decorated and making holiday. Nowhere had he seen greater evidence of rejoicing. Nevertheless among the chief men were not a few who hated the sight of the Pope, *who they knew had favored the nobles.* They held their peace however in fear of the people and smothered their anger while they simulated pleasure by their expressions, knowing very well that they would rouse the fury of the populace against them if they should seem to fail in welcoming the Pope at his entrance.

After this Pius brought up the question of recalling the nobles. He

[4] After leaving Corsignano.

summoned the senate and spoke as follows: "We are deeply grateful to you, men of Siena, for having admitted our noble Piccolomini to a share in the government. If you are wise, you will welcome to a share in the government the nobles who, now that all fear of their wealth has been removed, are like yourselves or humbler, and you will not allow them to be inferior to you. This is the one effective measure to keep your liberty and preserve your city. This is the advice we give to our dearly beloved country. If you reject our exhortations, we cannot cherish any good hope for this state. For a state divided is threatened with ruin, and peace does not dwell where justice is an exile. If you grant the nobles their due, then, if any adversity threatens, not only will our aid be prompt and ready but you will be helped by the omnipotent hand of God Himself, Who is ever on the side of the righteous."

When the Pope had spoken thus, the cardinals who were with him spoke to the same effect, each according to his ability. The answer of Siena was that the Priors of the city would convene the senate according to custom and report its decision to the Pope. The senators found it hard to deny the Pope what he asked, harder still to grant it. His request was rendered more difficult of attainment because the law required that three hundred senators must be present and that two thirds of the votes cast should be necessary for a decision. Moreover the populace, *corrupted by hate, avarice, and ambition,* could not realize what was for their own good.

The council was recalled repeatedly; a vote was taken again and again, but still it was impossible to get two thirds of the senators to accept the Pope's terms. When however he grew more insistent and demanded a reply before he left, *and it appeared that he would be furious if he did not prevail,* the senate finally voted to admit the nobles to all offices and to grant them a fourth of some privileges and an eighth of *the* others. The announcement of this vote soon filled the whole city with rejoicing. The entire senate and all the magistrates went to acquaint the Pope with what had been done. Pius, though he realized that his wishes had not been fully met, still, in order not to cast gloom on the city, appeared pleased and thanked the senate, praising what they had done and saying that he hoped for something more when he returned from Mantua.

At nightfall evidences of rejoicing were seen everywhere. Bonfires blazed throughout the city, bells and trumpets made a joyful din, people and nobles exchanged greetings, invitations, and embraces.

As a mark of gratitude to his fellow townsmen the Pope on the advice of the brethren granted Siena the fortified town of Radicofani on Monte Amiata, to be held by them forever on condition of the yearly payment of a fixed sum to the Apostolic Camera. A time limit to their tenure had been set by his predecessors, which was on the point of expiring. This town Nanni Piccolomini, a general of no small reputation, had once wrested from a certain bandit and handed over to Siena. Thus it came about that both possession and title to the place were conferred by the house of Piccolomini on their native city.

At this time too the church of Siena was raised to metropolitan rank and by putting under its control the churches of Grosseto, Massa, Suana, and Chiusi the Pope did his best to confer high honor on his city. The first archbishop was Antonio Piccolomini, whom Pius had designated as his successor in this church when he had himself ascended the throne of St. Peter.

The Pope's mother had died four years earlier, his father eight. The latter was buried at Corsignano, the former at Siena, both in Franciscan monasteries. Long ago a certain knight of the Piccolomini family named Piero had erected at the Minorite convent before the city gates a sumptuous marble tomb for himself and his descendants, in which many of his family now lie. In this tomb the brethren of the order buried the mother of Pius (then Bishop of Siena and absent in Germany), who had fallen asleep at Creula, a fortified stronghold of the diocese, and had desired to be buried in a Franciscan monastery. This angered Piero, grandson of the first Piero, who thought it an outrage that the dust of one of alien blood should mingle with the bones of his ancestors; for Vittoria, Pius's mother, though married into the Piccolomini family, was by birth a Fortiguerra. Therefore Piero gave orders that the next night the body should be exhumed and interred elsewhere. The monks then laid the noble lady inside the church by the high altar, but in the earth without any marble, hoping that her son would some day do honor to his mother. Nor were their hopes vain; for when Pius, who had some time before learned of the details of his mother's death and burial, returned to his own city, he had the bones of his father Silvio moved from Corsignano to Siena and a noble tomb of white marble from the Ligurian mountains built for both his parents. (Fig. 4) He himself composed the following couplet for their epitaph:

Here I, Silvio, lie, my wife Vittoria by my side.
Our son, Pope Pius, laid us in this marble tomb.

When Pius entered the Florentine territory, he was met at the town of Poggibonsi by ambassadors, the chief men of the city, who did honor to the Vicar of Christ in glowing words. This town is in our time of slight importance and lies in the valley of the Elsa River, but was once built on the lofty mountain which overlooks its present site. It was large and populous and difficult to storm. But since it took the side of the Ghibellines and often gave the Florentines a great deal of trouble, they first destroyed its walls, then razed it and moved it to the site just described. Here the Pope spent the night and the next day was met at San Casciano by new ambassadors, more numerous and more distinguished, who escorted him to the beautiful estate of a private citizen not far from the town, where he passed that night. The following day on his way to the Carthusian monastery he was met by the lords of Faenza, Forlì, and Imola and soon after by Galeazzo Sforza, the eldest son of Francesco Sforza, Duke of Milan. This handsome youth was not yet sixteen, but his character, eloquence, and ability were such that he exhibited a wisdom greater than that of a grown man. In his expression and bearing there was the dignity befitting a prince; his extemporaneous speeches could hardly have been equaled by another after long preparation; there was nothing childish or trivial in his conduct. It was astounding to hear the sentiments of an old man issuing from the lips of a lad and to listen to a beardless boy giving utterance to the ideas of a graybeard. His father had sent him with a splendid and magnificently accoutered escort of five hundred horsemen from Milan to Florence and thence to meet the Pope. Encountering Pius at the third milestone a little beyond the Certosa, Galeazzo dismounted and kissed the holy feet according to custom.

Luncheon was laid for the Pope in the monastery and after it he made haste toward the city, where he was met about two stades outside the gate by the chiefs of the Guelfs and at the gate itself by the Gonfalonier and many other magistrates, called the Lord Priors, who greeted the Pope humbly, kissed his feet, and commended to him the city and the people. The Pope because of his gout could not ride on horseback but was carried in a gold chair on the shoulders of his attendants. Just as he entered the city, after the priests carrying the sacred relics had received his blessing and had advanced to take their places at the head of the procession, Sigismondo Malatesta and the other vicars of the Church, whom I have mentioned above, raised the Pope's chair on their shoulders and carried their master some distance, *Sigismondo exclaiming indignantly, "See to what we lords of cities have been brought!"*

Galeazzo, who was too short and somewhat weak in the legs, though he could not help with the weight, yet laid his hand on the chair as desiring to appear to be one of the bearers. The chief men of the city walked on either side. The bearers were changed at fixed intervals and the most distinguished citizens claimed a part in this service. When Galeazzo had walked a short distance, he remounted at the Pope's command and, soon after, the vicars of the Church did likewise. The city was full of people, both citizens and outsiders. (Fig. 7) From the neighboring towns and from the country they had gathered from all sides to see the new Pope. The women were richly dressed and there was a marvelous variety of costumes in both domestic and foreign style, *but their whitened faces clearly betrayed the use of cosmetics.* The Pope visited the church of the Reparata and the baptistery of San Giovanni and at both blessed the people. He was lodged at Santa Maria Novella, where Martin and Eugenius had been entertained before him.

Florence, *once called Fluentia from the river Arno which "flows" through it,* is now the capital of Tuscany. It was built on the ruins of Faesulae, which was destroyed by Totila, King of the Goths. The city subjugated Volterra, Pistoia, Arezzo, Cortona, and Pisa; deprived Lucca of much of her territory; inflicted great disasters on the Sienese, at whose hands she herself sometimes suffered. She often opposed the German emperors. Henry VII pitched his camp before her walls and laid strenuous siege to the city, which he would certainly have taken had he not been called to Naples to fight King Robert and on his way there with part of his forces died from poison at Buonconvento, as I have before related. Charles IV advanced with an army up to the gates of Florence and restored the Ghibellines who had been expelled. The Dukes of Milan have cherished the bitterest hatred against the Florentines and have inflicted heavy losses upon them, though not without damage to themselves. Francesco Sforza made himself Duke of Milan with their help and was their fast friend. The kings of Naples were regarded by them now as friends, now as foes, and at one time were masters of the city, which was also once ruled by the Duke of Athens. When the latter was finally expelled, the people asserted their independence, though they first began to know real slavery when they believed themselves free, having driven out one master only to admit many. The city has often been racked by civil war, while the upper classes fought together for the mastery.

The most distinguished Florentines of our time have been thought to be Palla Strozzi, Niccolò Uzzano, and Rodolfo Peruzzi. Palla surpassed all others in wealth, Niccolò in wisdom, Rodolfo in military prowess. Against these men Cosimo dei Medici stirred up a faction and as a result he was banished and remained for some time in exile. Uzzano was already dead. Then when Pope Eugenius was residing in Florence, amid the strife of the various parties Cosimo returned and in the general confusion cowed his opponents and regained his old prestige. He drove into exile Rodolfo and Palla together with numerous other citizens and they never returned, though Rodolfo, enlisting the services of Niccolò Piccinino against his country, raided and plundered the district of Mugellana. He afterward died in exile. Palla endured adversity cheerfully, occupying himself till he was very old in the study of philosophy at Padua, where he died when nearly ninety, a man who had not deserved banishment at the hands of his countrymen.

Cosimo, having thus disposed of his rivals, proceeded to administer the state at his pleasure and amassed such wealth as I should think Croesus could hardly have possessed. In Florence he built a palace fit for a king; he restored some churches and erected others; he founded the splendid monastery of San Marco and stocked its library richly with Greek and Latin manuscripts; he decorated his villas magnificently. It was beginning to look as if by these noble works he had overcome envy, but the people always hate superior worth and there were some who asserted that Cosimo's tyranny was intolerable and tried in every way to thwart his projects; *some also hurled insults at him.*

The time was now at hand for making a valuation of the property of each citizen. The Florentines call this process catasto; the Sienese, libra. By it the magistrates learn the resources of the citizens and can thus apportion the burdens fairly among them. Cosimo urged a new catasto; his opponents were against it. Therefore it was decided to call a parlamento. While it was assembling, armed men, gathered from all quarters at Cosimo's orders, surrounded the piazza and made it clear that any who objected to his plans would do so at their peril. The catasto was voted under fear of armed force and some of the citizens who had opposed it were banished, others fined.[5] After this Cosimo was refused nothing. He was regarded as the arbiter of war and peace, the regulator of law; not so much a citizen as the master of his city. Political councils were held at his house; the magistrates he nominated were

---

[5] Such was the impression given. It is not wholly correct. The decision in regard to a new *catasto* was the work of the Signoria which had been chosen by lot and was therefore no longer a "packed" Medicean body. The new *catasto* would have struck at all the rich and still further weakened Medicean control.

elected; he was king in all but name and state. *Therefore when Pius once asked the Bishop of Orta what he thought about Florence and he replied that it was a pity so beautiful a woman had not a husband, the Pope said, "Yes, but she has a paramour," meaning that she had a tyrant instead of a king and referring to Cosimo, who like an unlawful lord of the city was grinding the people with cruel slavery.* During Pius's stay in Florence Cosimo was ill *or perhaps, as many believed, he pretended to be ill that he might not have to wait on the Pope.*

Cosimo's ancestors came to Florence from Mugello. His father Giovanni, *who became a client of the Medici, took the name of that family. He* had left a great fortune to his sons, Cosimo and Lorenzo, and Cosimo had increased it to an incredible degree, extending his business transactions over all Europe and *trading* even as far as Egypt. He was of fine physique and more than average height; his expression and manner of speech were mild; he was *more* cultured *than merchants usually are* (Fig. 5) and had some knowledge of Greek; his mind was keen and always alert; his spirit was neither cowardly nor brave; he easily endured toil and hunger and he often passed whole nights without sleep. Nothing went on in Italy that he did not know; indeed it was his advice that guided the policy of many cities and princes. Nor were foreign events a secret to him, for he had correspondents among his business connections all over the world, who kept him informed by frequent letters of what was going on around them. Toward the end of his life he suffered from gout, a disease which he lived to see passed on to his sons and grandsons. At the time the Pope was in Florence he was more than seventy years old.

At this time there passed away in the Lord, Antonino, Archbishop of Florence, a member of the Order of Preaching Friars and a man whose memory deserves to live. He conquered avarice, trampled on pride, was utterly unacquainted with lust and most abstemious in food and drink; he did not yield to anger or envy or any other passion. He was a brilliant theologian; he wrote several books which are praised by scholars; he was a popular preacher, though he inveighed against sin with the utmost violence; he reformed the morals of clergy and laity; he strove earnestly to settle quarrels; he did his best to clear the city of feuds; the revenues of his church he distributed among Christ's poor; to his relatives and connections, unless they were very needy, he gave nothing. He used only glass and clay dishes; he wished his household (which was very small) to be contented with little and to live according to the precepts of philosophy. When he died he was given a splendid public funeral. At his house nothing was found except the mule on which he used to ride and some cheap furniture; the poor had had everything else. The whole state believed that he had passed to a life of bliss—nor can we think their belief unfounded.

In former ages there have been many illustrious Florentines whose names are known even today, but most illustrious of all was Dante Alighieri, whose great poem with its noble description of Heaven, Hell, and Purgatory breathes a wisdom almost divine, though, being but mortal, he sometimes erred. Next to him was Francesco Petrarca, whose equal would be hard to find if his Latin works were comparable to those he wrote in Italian. The third place I should not go wrong in assigning to Giovanni Boccaccio, though he was *a little* more frivolous and his style was not highly polished. After him comes Coluccio, whose prose and verse suited his own age but seem rough to ours. He was Chancellor of Florence, and Galeazzo, Duke of Milan, used to say that Coluccio's pen did him more harm than thirty troops of the cavalry of the Florentines, who were then the enemies of Milan. For Coluccio was a shrewd man and, though his style lacked elegance, yet he had a thorough understanding of the general truths by which men are stirred and in his writing he handled them most skillfully. After several years he was succeeded in office by Leonardo, who was born in Arezzo but had been made a Florentine citizen. He was deeply versed in Greek and Latin *and his eloquence was almost Ciceronian.* He made a brilliant reputation by his many translations from Greek into Latin. Almost his equal in prose and his superior in verse was Carlo, who was also an Aretine by birth but a Florentine by courtesy. Poggio too was a famous citizen of Florence. After he had served for some time as papal secretary and had written several distinguished works, he finally returned to his native city, where he was made Chancellor and ended his days among his own kinsmen. A great many more men might be mentioned by whose abilities the power and prestige of Florence have been increased.

The admirers of Florence call attention not only to her illustrious citizens but to the size of the city (*which is surpassed in all Italy by Rome alone*), the lofty and extraordinarily thick walls which encircle it, the elegance of the streets and squares which are not only wide but straight, the magnificent churches, and the splendid towering palaces, both public and private. But among all the buildings none is more deserving of mention than the church of the Reparata, the dome of which is nearly as large as that which we admire at Rome in the temple of Agrippa called the Pantheon. Next comes the palace of the Priors and third that built by Cosimo. They admire too the sanctuary of St. John the Baptist and the church of San Lorenzo (also built by Cosimo). They mention the bridges which unite the city cut in two by the Arno and the numerous population and the costumes of both men and women and the shops of all sorts and the great estates and the splendid luxurious villas near the city erected at no less expense than the city itself, and finally the quick wits of the citizens, though they most excel in trade, *which philosophers think sordid. They seem too bent on making money, and therefore when the chief men of the city had collected 14,000 ducats from the people to honor the Pope, they kept the greater part for the city and used part to support Galeazzo and his retinue.* They spent very little on entertaining the Pope nor did they lay out much on lavish spectacles, though they brought lions into the piazza to fight with horses and other animals and arranged tournaments in which much more wine was drunk than blood spilled.

The Pope remained a week, in the course of which Sigismondo Malatesta earnestly besought him to arbitrate between him and Ferrante, King of Sicily, who was making war against him.

Sigismondo, of the noble family of the Malatesta but illegitimate, was very vigorous in body and mind, eloquent, and gifted with great military ability. He had a thorough knowledge of history and no slight acquaintance with philosophy. Whatever he attempted he seemed born for, but the evil part of his character had the upper hand. *He was such a slave to avarice that he was ready not only to plunder but to steal. His lust was so unbridled that he violated his daughters and his sons-in-law. He outdid all barbarians in cruelty. His bloody hand inflicted terrible punishments on innocent and guilty alike.* He oppressed the poor, plundered the rich, spared neither widows nor orphans. No one felt safe under his rule. Wealth or a beautiful wife or handsome children were enough to cause a man to be accused of crime. *He hated priests and despised religion.* He had no belief in another world and thought the soul died with the body. Nevertheless he built at Rimini a splendid church dedicated to St. Francis, though he filled it so full of pagan works of art that it seemed less a Christian sanctuary than a temple of heathen devil-worshippers. In it he erected for his mistress a tomb of magnificent marble and exquisite workmanship with an inscription in the pagan style as follows, "Sacred to the deified Isotta." *The two wives he had married before he took Isotta for his mistress he killed one after the other with the sword or poison.*

*He showed himself a perjurer and traitor to Alfonso, King of Sicily,
and his son Ferrante. He broke his word to Francesco, Duke of Milan,
to the Venetians, the Florentines and the Sienese. Repeatedly too he
tricked the Church of Rome. Finally when there was no one left in
Italy for him to betray, he went on to the French, who allied themselves
with him out of hatred for Pope Pius but fared no better than the other
princes.* When his subjects once begged him to retire at last to a peaceful
life and spare his country, which had so often been exposed to pillage
on his account, he replied, "Go and be of good courage; never while I
live shall you have peace."

Such was Sigismondo, intolerant of peace, a devotee of pleasure, able
to endure any hardship, and greedy for war. *Of all men who have ever
lived or ever will live he was the worst scoundrel, the disgrace of Italy
and the infamy of our times.* (Fig. 6) Alfonso hired him for a large sum to
fight for him in the war he was waging with the Florentines. Sigismondo
however, attracted by a new price, went over to the Florentines and
turned his arms against Alfonso, alleging as a reason for his perfidy
that his stipend had not all been paid on time. This was a heavy blow
to the King, who now had to face an enemy whom he had hired to be
his champion. There is no doubt that the treachery of Sigismondo was
the salvation of the Florentine cause and so, on the conclusion of a
general peace and an alliance among the princes of Italy, Sigismondo
as well as the Genoese and Astorre of Faenza was excluded, the King
reserving the right to declare war on those who had broken their oaths
and betrayed him. Alfonso therefore equipped a powerful fleet against
the Genoese and in the last year of his life (which was also Pope Calixtus's last) he sent against Sigismondo a large army commanded by
Piccinino, the son of Niccolò, a step enthusiastically supported by
Federigo of Urbino, who had his own reasons for hating Sigismondo.
The war dragged on for some time, not only during Alfonso's life but
after his death, since his son was as enraged at Sigismondo as his father
had been. The tyrant's subjects suffered for their master's guilt and the
poor had their houses burned over their heads because of the arrogance
of an impious scoundrel. A region famous through all Italy, which,
though subject to the tyrant, belonged legally to the Church of Rome,
was being ravaged and laid waste. Pope Pius, deploring this fact,
included among the conditions imposed on Ferrante when he was
invested with the kingdom of Sicily, that he should make peace with
Sigismondo on terms dictated by the Pope himself. But after Pius had
recovered Assisi, his freedom to dictate was restricted and it was decided

that peace should be made on certain specific conditions; or, if Sigismondo would not consent to this, they should annul the mutual agreement made when the Pope was a free agent. It was settled that this should not continue in force later than the month of February, but afterward the time was extended to include March and then April.

When Pius was at Florence only four days of this period were left and the King's agents were not there to state his case. There were present however ambassadors from Federigo of Urbino and Jacopo Piccinino, to whom the King had delegated the matter. The Pope directed four cardinals to hear the two parties and to reconcile them, but they were unsuccessful. Then the Pope in person heard the arguments and claims of both sides and there was no doubt that Sigismondo was guilty of treachery. It was therefore decided that he should pay for his offense with money or, if he had none, should pledge his castles. But since much was demanded in the King's name and Sigismondo offered little, the case seemed to be almost desperate. The ambassadors asserted that victory was theirs; Sigismondo declared he was not yet beaten and that he would suffer anything rather than surrender what was demanded. In the midst of his insolent blustering the Pope said to him, "Be quiet. We are concerned for your house, not for you. It is not you but your subjects whom we pity, since your actions give you no claim to consideration *and no punishment is adequate for your crimes. Your life heretofore has been such that no penalty too severe for your wickedness could be devised.* No matter how long you talk in your own defense, *there is no one who does not think you a traitor to Alfonso.*" Sigismondo, terrified at hearing this, consented to terms that seemed likely to be acceptable, but the other side with the insolence of the victor objected and would consent to no compromise.

The Pope, though he had the power to make any decision he pleased about Sigismondo, nevertheless thought it disgraceful to consider victory rather than justice and for a long time strove to settle the quarrel to the satisfaction of both sides. When he failed, he released both the King and Sigismondo from their agreement, uncertain whether a war of this kind or peace was more advantageous for the Church, since it was common knowledge that Piccinino could not keep quiet and if he were freed from the war with Sigismondo, he would probably turn his arms against the Church. Pius therefore came to the conclusion that it was God's will that the peace could not be arranged. The Florentines agreed with him and rejoiced that the day had come when a scoundrel should at last be punished as he deserved.

The Pope slept the first night after leaving Florence in a very beautiful villa in the Mugello[6] belonging to Cosimo. The next day he crossed the summit of the Apennines and spent the night in the town of Firenzuola. On leaving Firenzuola the Pope crossed another ridge of the Apennines with considerable toil and difficulty and arrived at Pianoro, having met the Bolognese envoys a little beyond Caprenno, which is on the boundary between the Florentine and Bolognese territories.

Pius entered Bologna amid great enthusiasm of the populace and the chief men of the city carried his chair. The next day, after mass at San Petronio, he publicly blessed the people and then, returning to his palace, gave the citizens who thronged about it an opportunity to say whatever they desired; for they had come to thank the Pope for not disdaining to visit his own city. The role of orator had been entrusted to the jurist Bornio, a man of wide reading with a melodious voice. He delivered a long speech in which he said not what he had been instructed to say but what he chose. For after he had eulogized the Pope as much as he thought sufficient, he spoke finely and at length of the fertility of the Bolognese land, the mildness of the climate, the enthusiasm of the people for letters, their churches, walls, public and private buildings. He inveighed *bitterly* against the citizens, *calling them enemies of law, foes of goodness and equity, men who could be restrained by no reins; greedy for the property of others, wasteful of their own, observing neither the rights of marriage nor the bonds of hospitality. Nothing was holy to them, who had no regard for honor or any respect for oaths. Some of them were tyrants, others slaves. Some plundered, others robbed; some killed their enemies with the sword, others with poison; some were adulterers, others panders. All crimes and vileness had made this their chosen home and no city showed so foul a countenance as Bologna.* He begged the Pope, since by the grace of Heaven he was there in safety, to set himself to root out vice and reform the city.

As Bornio poured out all this boldly and intrepidly in a torrent of oratory, he roused the enmity of the citizens present but the admiration of the foreigners. For who would have thought that anyone would speak thus about his own country? All men make excuses for their country, whose disgrace they think is theirs. *But Bornio's speech was thought to be true and he himself was looked on not so much as an orator as a philosopher.* The Pope praised his eloquence and learning

[6] Caffagiuolo.

and promised his aid in reforming the state, on condition however that
he found the people capable of being restrained by laws.

The University of Bologna is very celebrated not only among the
Italians but among foreigners and it has trained many scholars, citizens
of other states, as well as Bolognese, who later defended the very citadel
of political science, so that their opinions have almost the force of
actual laws. Nor was philosophy barren here, for her students have
become so proficient that they have afterward held professorships in
many places.

*The Bolognese have won no great glory in arms; it is generally con-
ceded that they are cruel rather than brave at home and cowardly
abroad.*

The Pope left Bologna and proceeded along the Reno ånd the Po to
Ferrara.[7] Borso, who was the Vicar of the Church of Rome there, met
him at the boundaries of his lands with a large company of nobles.

Borso was a man of fine physique and more than average height with
beautiful hair and a pleasing countenance. He was eloquent *and gar-
rulous and listened to himself talking as if he pleased himself more
than his hearers. His talk was full of blandishments mingled with lies.
He desired to seem rather than to be* magnificent and generous, though
when the Emperor Frederick passed through Ferrara on his way to
and from Rome, Borso loaded him with honors and gifts and thus persuaded him to raise the earldom of Modena to a duchy and create him
duke, as we have told before. During his lifetime the people erected in
the square a statue representing him seated administering justice. It
bore an inscription composed in flattery and adulation, for Borso loved
nothing so much as praise. He bought as many precious stones as he
could and never appeared in public without jewels. He collected rich
household furnishings: even in the country he used gold and silver
dishes.

When Pius was elected pope, Borso gave many evidences of his delight; he arranged military contests and offered prizes for the victors;
he gave presents to the couriers who brought the news; he ordered
bonfires to be lighted throughout his domains and gave a banquet to
his friends, to whom he boasted that Pius was a connection of his, since
his mother had been a Sienese of the Ptolomei family which is kin to
the Piccolomini. He also gave thanks to God that He had vouchsafed
him a pope who would deny him nothing. And indeed he would not
have been mistaken in this conviction if he had asked for favors more

[7] After six days.

proper to grant; *but when he made improper requests, he found that honor was stronger in Pope Pius than benevolence.* He did however obtain very important concessions and hoped every day for greater ones.

For this reason and also because he bore in mind the experience of others, he received the Pope with the highest honors and endeavored to outdo those through whose lands he had already passed. At the gate he presented him with the keys of the city and walked beside his chair between the bearers till he was bidden to mount his horse. All the road to the cathedral was covered with carpets and strewn with flowers; the houses were decorated; there was singing and cheering everywhere and the people kept up a continuous cry of "Long live Pope Pius!" The cardinals and the entire Curia were served meals from the palace. There were all sorts of shows and a number of speeches were delivered by very eloquent orators. It was the time of the celebration of the feast of the Most Holy Body of Our Lord and there was a solemn procession through the piazza with the Pope blessing the people and carrying the Host.

Pius remained at Ferrara a week. In private audiences Borso continued to complain bitterly that his requests had been refused, but the Pope easily confuted his arguments. The Duke promised on no account to absent himself from the congress at Mantua, alleging that it was his dearest wish to establish Christianity among all mankind.

Guarino of Verona, then an aged and venerable man, who had been the teacher of almost all who have attained distinction in the humanities in our day, presented himself before the Pope and delivered a speech worthy of his reputation and character. There came to him also the Sicilian Giovanni Aurispa, a distinguished Greek and Latin scholar, who was then almost ninety and died soon after. This year was marked by the death of three very eloquent men, for Poggio, whom we have mentioned above, departed this life at Florence and Giannozzo Manetti at Naples. Giannozzo also was a Florentine, a very learned man who was at home in Hebrew as well as in Greek and Latin. No one of them could complain of the laws of nature, for all were over seventy and had lived beyond the common lot. He who thinks more is due him is unreasonable.

After leaving Ferrara Pius sailed up the Po to Revere, a town belonging to the Marquis of Mantua. The Po rises in the Cottian Alps, flows through Cisalpine Gaul receiving into itself many rivers, most of them navigable, and empties through three mouths into the Adriatic. The Greeks called it the Eridanus, which figures in the myths of the daugh-

ters of the Sun and the burning of Phaëthon, which it is said to have
opposed. It is inferior to no river of Europe, though the Rhine and the
Danube are longer and have more tributaries. While the Pope was
sailing on it, two fleets met, those of the Duke and the Marquis. The
former was carrying Pius, the latter hoped to carry him. On both, trumpeters filled all the surrounding valley with an extraordinary din. They
displayed a whole forest of banners tossing in the wind. The inhabitants,
seated along the banks, implored the Pope's benediction and when he
blessed them, they shouted, "Viva!"

After they had sailed into the Marquis's domain and the Pope had
boarded the ship of his new host, Borso went back, having first greeted
the Marquis and obtained the Pope's permission to depart.

The next night was spent at Revere, where there is a royal palace
only half completed, which shows by its plan and workmanship the
consummate genius of the architect. The following day the Pope
reached the mouth of the Mincio and sailed up the river as far as the
lake on whose left bank is pointed out a hill held sacred by the Man-
tuans where they say *the divine* Vergil lived. Around it lies the little
village where the great poet was born. The Pope spent the night on an
estate belonging to the Duke about two miles from here, that he might
enter the city the next morning.

The Mincio rises in Lake Garda and spreads into a fen which surrounds most of Mantua. The city itself lies in a swamp and can be
reached only by bridges or boats. (Fig. 8) It is large and can accommodate a numerous population. In it are many splendid houses and palaces
fit for kings, but in summer the dust and in winter the mud are very
annoying to the inhabitants. The people are most kindly and hospitable.
There are many convents for both men and women where saintly souls
dwell.

Pius entered Mantua on May 27, five days before the appointed date.
The city was full of guests and thronged with the people of the neighboring towns. Among them was Bianca, Duchess of Milan, daughter of
the late Duke Filippo Maria and wife of Francesco Sforza, a woman of
high spirit and extraordinary wisdom. She had with her a most noble
brood of children of both sexes, four boys beautiful as angels from
heaven and a girl named Ippolita, lovely in face and character, who was
betrothed to the son of the King of Sicily. Many other noble maids and
matrons and illustrious men were in her retinue.

Bianca and Barbara awaited the Pope's arrival on a platform erected
in front of the cathedral. He entered the city in a procession arranged

as follows. First came the servants of the Curia and the attendants of the cardinals; then the minor officials of the Curia; then twelve white horses, riderless and decked out with gold saddles and bridles; then three banners, on the first of which shone the sign of the Cross, on the second the keys of the Church, and on the third the five crescents which are the arms of the Piccolomini. These were carried by nobles in armor mounted on richly caparisoned horses. Next came a red and yellow canopy and after that the priests of the city in splendid robes carrying the sacred relics. They were followed by the ambassadors of kings and princes, the subdeacons, the auditors, scribes, and advocates of the Apostolic palace under a golden cross. Then came a golden tabernacle borne on a white horse under a silk canopy and surrounded by many tapers, in which was the Eucharist, that is, the sacred Host of our Savior. Next rode Galeazzo of Milan and the Marquis Lodovico, then the venerable order of cardinals, and finally the Pope himself raised high on his throne, wearing the papal robes and the miter blazing with precious gems. He was carried on the shoulders of nobles and blessed the people as he proceeded. Behind him came the gentlemen of his bedchamber and his personal attendants, then the bishops, notaries, abbots, and a great throng of prelates. At the city gates Lodovico dismounted and presented the Pope with the keys of the city. This was done by all those whom the Pope visited on his journey except the Sienese and the Florentines, *who, though under the heel of popular tyranny, wished to make a show of freedom by keeping the keys.*

From the gate all the way to the church of San Pietro, which is the cathedral, not a foot of ground but was covered with carpets and the walls on both sides were adorned with flowers and tapestries. Women, boys, and girls crowded the windows and roofs, but still there was a great press and all the approaches were thronged with people. In many places were altars smoking with incense. No voice was heard except the shouts of the populace crying, "Long live Pope Pius!"

When they reached the church, there was prayer and the singing of a hymn and the announcement of plenary remission of sins to all present, after which the Pope was received in a splendid palace and everyone went home to his own house.

The next day Bianca and Barbara had audience with the Pope, kissed his holy feet, and obtained the spiritual grace they begged. Bianca's daughter Ippolita delivered a speech before the Pope in such elegant Latin that all present were lost in wonder and admiration.

BOOK III

O N June 1,[1] the day fixed for the opening of the Congress, the Pope
descended from his palace to the church accompanied by the
cardinals, bishops, and all the clergy. The monks of every order in the city
had also been bidden to assemble and mass was celebrated with solemn
pomp and with profound reverence on the part of all present. Then the
Bishop of Coron, a man distinguished for his learning as well as for his
probity, delivered a speech in which he explained the Pope's purpose,
the reason for the Congress, and the need for action and exhorted all
who had gathered there to further the Pope's desire with ready and
willing hearts. When all were on the point of rising, Pius made a gesture for silence and from his throne spoke as follows:

"Our brethren and our sons, we hoped on arriving at this city to find
that a throng of royal ambassadors had preceded us. We see that only a
few are here. We have been mistaken. Christians are not so concerned
about religion as we believed. We fixed the day for the Congress very
far ahead. No one can say the time was too short; no one can plead the
difficulties of travel. We who are old and ill have defied the Apennines
and winter. Not even mother Rome could delay us, although, beset as
she is with brigands, she sorely needed our presence. Not without
danger we left the patrimony of the Church to come to the rescue of
the Catholic Faith which the Turks are doing their utmost to destroy.

"We saw their power increasing every day, their armies, which had
already occupied Greece and Illyricum, overrunning Hungary, and the
loyal Hungarians suffering many disasters. We feared (and this will
surely happen if we do not take care) that once the Hungarians were
conquered, the Germans, Italians, and indeed all Europe would be
subdued, a calamity that must bring with it the destruction of our Faith.
We took thought to avert this evil; we called a Congress in this place;
we summoned princes and peoples that we might together take counsel
to defend Christendom. We came full of hope and we grieve to find it

[1] 1459.

vain. We are ashamed that Christians are so indifferent. Some are given over to luxury and pleasure; others are kept away by avarice. The Turks do not hesitate to die for their most vile faith, but we cannot incur the least expense nor endure the smallest hardship for the sake of Christ's Gospel. If we continue thus, it will be all over with us. We shall soon perish unless we can summon up a different spirit.

"Therefore we urge you, who are holy men, to pray God without ceasing that He may change the temper of the Christian kings, rouse the spirit of His people, and kindle the hearts of the faithful, so that now at least we may take arms and avenge the wrongs which the Turks day after day are inflicting on our religion. Up, brethren! Up, sons! Turn to God with all your hearts. Watch and pray; atone for your sins by fasting and giving alms; bring forth works meet for repentance; for thus God will be appeased and have mercy on us and if we show ourselves brave, He will deliver our enemies into our hands. We shall remain here till we have learned the disposition of the princes. If they intend to come, we will together take counsel for our state. If not, we must go home again and endure the lot God has given us. But so long as life and strength last we shall never abandon the purpose of defending our religion nor shall we think it hard, if need be, to risk our life for our sheep."

The cardinals and bishops listened with rapt attention to the Pope's words and praised his purpose to the skies. They thought he had made a noble beginning by granting pardon for their sins to all who had duly cleared their conscience by confession.

After some days, since only a few delegates had gathered and there were no reports that more were coming, people began to disparage the wisdom of a pope who had undertaken so much toil for nothing. Everywhere the members of the Curia were murmuring. *The Cardinals attacked him and accused him of obstinacy and lack of judgment.* Nor did they restrain their pens. To Italy and to all the regions on both sides of the Alps they kept dispatching *abusive* letters. Those who did not dare write themselves delegated this office to friends or servants. They said that Pius had been foolish to come to Mantua, that very few representatives of princes had assembled there and still fewer were likely to come; the place was marshy and unhealthy; the heat was intense; they did not like the flat wine or any of the other things necessary to sustain life; most of them were sickening; very many were catching the fever; nothing was to be heard except the frogs. Some too sent a letter to the King of France in which they asserted that the Congress ought to be transferred to another place and some reported that the day of the Congress had been postponed.

No one, however, was said to speak more contemptuously of the Pope than Lodovico,[2] *Cardinal of Aquileia* (Fig. 10), *who kept asserting in his household or even in a group of prelates that the Pope's projects had been childish. He declared repeatedly that Pius showed inexperience and lack of foresight in abandoning Rome to lodge with one stranger after another and thinking by his exhortations to draw kings into war and exterminate the Turks, whose strength was unconquerable. He would have done better to stay at home and look after his Church. He urged the Venetians not to send ambassadors to a congress which was destined to have no results.*

Jacopo, Cardinal of Sant' Anastasia, also indulged in venomous talk to his friends, openly accusing the Pope of folly in coming to Mantua to enrich foreign peoples and leaving his own in poverty. The common saying is true, "Of four wheels the worst one squeaks." Jacopo owed his cardinalate to the merits of his brother, who had been Calixtus's physician, rather than to his own. His stature was small and his wisdom smaller. He had no experience of affairs, no distinction of learning or character. He was of low birth and came to Rome from Umbria. He was born in a mean village called Colliscipoli, a word which some say means "Scipio's hill," others "Onion hill."

Some of the cardinals went to the Pope and said: "What is your object? It is no use to keep us here unless you mean to kill us with this pestilential climate. Why do you not leave? You were here on the appointed day; you have remained here a sufficient time. The princes stay at home and insult you and us. All realize that you were concerned to defend the Faith. That is enough for your honor. Who can blame you if you cannot conquer the Turks by yourself? Let us go back to our homes. If there are any who wish to further the cause of Christianity, they will not refuse to follow wherever you go."

Amid all these voices the Pope stood firm and unshakable and he did not put men's talk above salvation, since he sought to find favor with God, not with the majority. But there were also among the cardinals some of better judgment who urged him to persevere: for example Bessarion of Nicaea and Juan of San Sisto, one a Greek, the other a Spaniard. Some, although they cherished other thoughts in their hearts, tried to curry favor with the Pope by pretending they were not averse

[2] Lodovico Trevisano has been known erroneously since the sixteenth century as Scarampo-Mezzarota.

to staying. Those who urged departure, when they could not persuade him to agree, scattered among the neighboring castles to escape the heat of the city. The Cardinal of Aquileia went to Padua, on the pretext of taking the baths, and then to Venice. In both places he set on foot many schemes against the Cardinal of San Marco to prevent his obtaining the church at Padua. He talked outrageously about the Congress of Mantua and disparaged everything that was being done there.

While this was going on, ambassadors from Thomas, Tyrant of Morea, came to the Pope. This province used to be called Peloponnese and was considered the stronghold of Greece. It is shaped like a chersonese[3] and is washed by the Aegean and Ionian seas. Here was famous Corinth and Elis so celebrated for its games and Sparta, the ancient seat of Agamemnon and Menelaus who destroyed Ilion to avenge the rape of Helen, and the still older Argos and Nestor's Pylus. Once they were splendid cities, but now they lie nameless—except Corinth, some remains of which are to be seen at the Isthmus. When Constantinople was taken by the Turks, as we have said, and the Emperor Constantine Palaeologus was killed, his brothers, Thomas and Demetrius, took refuge here. Sometimes they paid the Turks tribute, sometimes they attacked them, relying on Italian auxiliaries and the natural defenses of the country. Then when dissension arose between them, Demetrius took the side of the Turks and betrothed his daughter to Mahomet; Thomas with the help of the Albanians, of whom there are a great number in the Peloponnese, deprived his brother of a large part of the kingdom, routed the Turks who had attacked him, and took many prisoners. He sent sixteen of these by the ambassadors mentioned above as a gift to Pius, begging him to aid a winning cause and saying that he did not need a large army, for a small force of Italians would be enough to expel the Turks from the peninsula.

Meantime ambassadors had arrived at Mantua from Cyprus, Rhodes, Lesbos, and Asia. At this time too the Albanians, Epirotes, and Bosnians and the whole coast of Illyricum had sent envoys to implore aid and the entire city was by now thronged with men from the East, who were there to ask help against the Turks. Hence arose the saying that Orientals, whom they call Levantes, are quick and clever; Occidentals, whom they call Ponentes, are dull and sluggish—which is as much as to say that those who give aid are difficult and captious, those who ask it are energetic. For aid was looked for from the West and from that direction few came. The embassies from the East all came to complain.

[3] I.e., a peninsula.

Only the Ragusans promised aid against the Turk to the extent of their ability. The King of Bosnia, though he had secretly come to terms with the Turks, sent ambassadors to the Pope to ask aid against them.

The mountain kingdom of Bosnia adjoins the Rascians and the Hungarians. In it there are many Manichaeans, who, although they wish to be thought Christians, are nevertheless very far from observing the law of Christ. They are blasphemous and heretical. Aurelius Augustinus wrote a book against them. The Ragusans and Trigurians, who live along the shore of the Adriatic, are neighbors to the Bosnians, who undoubtedly were originally an Illyrian people. To the west and south lie the Croats, who are also Dalmatians. As the Romans once called their princes Caesar or Augustus and the Egyptians theirs Pharaoh or Ptolemy, so the Bosnians called their kings Stephen. The Stephen who sent ambassadors to Mantua was crafty and shifty. Shortly before this, through the intervention of the papal Legate, Giovanni, Cardinal of Sant' Angelo, he had gone to Matthias, King of Hungary, and concluded a treaty with him, making many promises of aid against the Turks and telling even more lies. At that time the Rascians were having difficulty in resisting the attacks of the Turks and therefore the King of Hungary allowed Stephen's son to take over the defense of the strongly fortified town of Senderovia on the Danube. A few months after he entered it he called in the Turks and sold them the town for a great weight of gold. This was as crushing a blow to the spirits of the Hungarians as the loss of Constantinople had been. For Senderovia is, as it were, the gate from Rascia to Wallachia, a most convenient base for making war against the Hungarians. It has many ships for crossing the river and landing on the other bank is very easy. The Bosnian envoys however had left Mantua before the betrayal was generally known and it was reported first to the Hungarian ambassadors. They were the Bishops of Csanad and Zengg; Stephen, Count of Croatia, a Roman of the Frangipani family which once had produced the most holy Pope Gregory, the glory and model of all popes; and a certain learned doctor of Treviso afterward appointed by Pius to a bishopric in Dalmatia.

When now the envoys of kings and princes had begun to assemble at Mantua, there was a heated argument as to how they should be seated. Kings would not give place to kings nor dukes to dukes, but each claimed first place for himself, disputing and gesticulating till finally, that this might not interfere with the business in hand, the Pope laid down the rule that a back seat should imply no loss and a front seat no increase of honor or privilege. But even this did not appease them all, as we shall tell later. The bishops, for their part, did not like the custom of the Roman Curia of giving precedence to the Apostolic notaries. On the other hand many thought the usage of the Curia was a sacred law that ought by no means to be changed and they asserted that it would be a great scandal and the world would practically go to pieces if any decision against the notaries should be made. But Pius, considering the lofty eminence of the episcopacy, than which there is nothing in the Church more exalted, and that the Pope himself, the Vicar of Christ, is content with the title of bishop, decided that the notaries had come to take precedence of the bishops through some mis-understanding rather than by regular usage and he forbade this to be the case in the future, thus laying down a principle which almost the whole world received with approval. Although the notaries strenuously opposed this action, canvassing *the cardinals* and making many attacks on the Pope, still they were obliged unwillingly to accept his ruling.

Not many days earlier there had departed this life Theodoric, Arch-bishop of Mainz, an ignorant man *debauched by lust and dissipation.* Still he deserves honorable mention for this *one thing,* that at the time of the schism at the Council of Basle he had taken the side of the Apostolic See, *though indeed in extreme old age he lost this virtue too by being disloyal and running after heresies.*

Mainz is a very famous city on the left bank of the great Rhine at its confluence with the Main, from which it takes its name. It was once French but is now German *and this proverb is current about it: "Mainz wicked* (nequam) *from antiquity."* * Men of old founded there a rich church whose archbishop ranks first among the imperial electors. It has thirteen suffragans, who administer parishes all the way from Italy to Saxony. Therefore when it became vacant, many powerful men aspired to it, of whom the most eager was Diether von Isenburg, a man of noble birth though less conspicuous for his rank than for his faithlessness and ambition. When during the pontificate of Calixtus he had failed in his attempt to buy the church of Trier, for which he had offered a very large sum in gold, he turned his attention to the church of Mainz, of which he was canon, and since he knew very well that he could not secure a majority of votes in the chapter (for it is difficult to bribe a large number) he bent his efforts to getting the matter entrusted to the decision of a few. Seven men were named and these were empowered

---

* A pun upon the word *nequam* which was also the name of its legendary founder—a prince of magicians.

to elect the bishop. Three, who had been bribed long ahead, voted for Diether; three for Adolf of Nassau, distinguished alike for his family and his probity, who counted emperors among his ancestors; the seventh voted for another candidate, but was finally bribed with 3,000 florins to accede to Diether, who was thereupon declared elected and by a mischievous precedent installed in possession of the property of the church. He sent ambassadors to Mantua demanding with excessive arrogance and pride that his election be confirmed. Pius, who did not know what had happened, said, "We are here holding a congress in regard to the Christian religion. We summoned hither Theodoric, who was then archbishop, that as priest of a great church he might give counsel and aid to the Catholic Faith, which the impiety and ferocity of the Turks is trying to destroy. Now that he is dead it is proper that the man chosen in his place should come and we will confirm him at once."

The ambassadors replied that Diether was ill of a fever and besides had no money; furthermore that the journey would be long and dangerous. The Pope answered that he could wait for him to recover but he refused to accept the excuses of poverty and the inconvenience of the roads. The envoys were sent back but returned once more. Piety was worsted by impiety and clemency by obstinacy. Diether could not be persuaded to come to that great congress called for so holy a purpose. The Pope, on the motion of the Cardinal of San Marco, confirmed him in absentia with the proviso that he should be bound to present himself within a year before the Holy Apostolic See, should receive from it a rule of conduct, and should affirm under oath that which he had promised and sworn by the mouths of his authorized ambassadors. However, as we shall relate in its proper place, his honor was that of a barbarian, he did not keep his word, and he had no regard for the sanctity of an oath.

The Emperor Frederick meantime dispatched three ambassadors to the Congress: Antonio, Bishop of Trieste; Johann Hinderbach, Provost of Trent; and Heinrich Senftleben, Dean of Breslau. Though these men were eminent enough, personally acceptable to the Pope, and invested with full powers, still they did not give that impression of prestige which so august and awe-inspiring a congress seemed to demand. Therefore the Pope sent Heinrich back to the Emperor with the following message: "The Congress in session at Mantua is profoundly concerned as to the defense of religion against very powerful enemies, whose destruction touches you most nearly after the Hungarians. Pope Pius left the kingdom of the Church of Rome to come here; he weighed neither danger nor expense if only he might further the common weal. He hoped that you would meet him here, since you would have to make no longer journey than he. You however have neither come nor sent ambassadors worthy of such an occasion or of yourself. Those who observe this think that you are either stingy and trying to economize or careless of the defense of the orthodox Faith; and they do not consider you fit to rule over Christians.

"For how can you be called the protector and advocate of the Church when you not only desert the Church but slight the very religion and faith of Christ? Perhaps you have a grudge against Pius because you think he has usurped an honor that belonged to you and on this account are unwilling to meet him. You are mistaken, for Pius is not seeking his own honor so much as yours and he holds you dearer than his own soul. It is of your glory he is thinking and it is to guard this that he urges you to come to confer with him about the safety of all. If you cannot do this, at least send ambassadors of distinguished rank and prestige and do not let the Church of God perish through this indifference (or must we say avarice?) of yours."

After Heinrich had departed with this message, Philip, Duke of Burgundy, who had written that he would attend the Congress and was considered the most zealous of all who had at heart the destruction of the Turkish nation, changed his mind and decided to stay at home, not so much of his own will as because of the advice of his friends, who feared that an uprising was brewing in France. The King of France was angry with Philip because he had taken in his eldest son Louis, Dauphin of Vienne, when he fled to him for refuge, and had made no effort to reconcile him to his father. Philip on his side asserted that the King had acted dishonorably in seizing certain towns in the duchy of Luxemburg (i.e., within the jurisdiction of the empire) in violation of an ancient treaty made at Toul between the French kings and the Roman emperors, by which the Emperor was forbidden to claim any sovereignty in the kingdom of France and the King in the empire, even though a people might voluntarily surrender to them. It was unjust, he repeated, that the King should violate the treaty and dare to molest the duchy of Luxemburg which was Philip's fief.

This was the correspondence that was going on between the King and the Duke and neither showed signs of yielding to the other. On the contrary their complaints grew more bitter every day and their disagreements had become open enmity. For these reasons the Burgundians thought the Duke would be very ill-advised to leave home. Some said that there was danger of ambushes on the way, others that the hardships were too much for an old man, others that the Italian climate and the summer heat were to be feared, while others raised objections to still other difficulties of travel.

When Philip, convinced by these arguments, had made up his mind to stay at home, he decided to send his sister's son, Jean, Duke of Clèves, and Jean of Croy, who had won many battles and was considered the most illustrious man in all France. With them went many knights and celebrated experts in both canon and civil law and also Jean, Bishop of Arras,[4] Papal Referendarius, a man of almost unbounded learning *and acceptable to Pius*. Clèves's road from Philip's court lay through Flanders, Picardy, Paris, the rest of France, and Savoy. The French, when they beheld the most splendid embassy they had ever seen, went to the King and gave an exaggerated report of what was actually great enough. They praised Burgundy for his devotion to the Faith and blamed the French King for his neglect of it. They said the Pope had called a congress on important matters and in spite of his age had left Rome to come to it; and they asserted that it was unbecoming the royal dignity to be absent from such a gathering. Roused by this outcry Charles also decided to send a large and distinguished embassy.

The Duke of Clèves and his train proceeded by way of Savoy and Mont Giove (which today has the better name of St. Bernard) to Aosta; then through Ivrea, Vercelli, and Novara to Milan, the capital of Lombardy. Here he stayed some days and was loaded with the highest honors by Duke Francesco. Then he continued his journey by Lodi and Cremona to the Congress.

The next day[5] there was a public consistory in which the Bishop of Arras delivered a speech before Pius seated in all his papal majesty. He praised to the skies the Pope's purpose of protecting religion, Philip's ardor, the prestige of the embassy, the family of the prince himself, and the ancestral as well as the more recent exploits of the Burgundians. He explained why Philip had not come himself to the Congress and finally assured the Pope that he would do everything which could be expected of him to defend Christianity. He was heard with eager attention and all the assembly applauded Philip's attitude.

The Pope from his lofty throne answered to this effect: There was

[4] Jean Jouffroy.
[5] After the arrival of the Duke of Clèves.

no one, he said, who did not know of Philip's illustrious lineage, in which shone the blood of both Burgundians and French, and that both these nations had extended their fame by their deeds—although, to be sure, Philip had no need of a gallery of ancestors, seeing that his own virtue was the light of his age. He praised highly also the Duke of Clèves, who had taken a very long and difficult journey to attend a congress which was to discuss the protection of the religion which the Turks were everywhere trying to rend in pieces. He had done his duty and discharged his obligations as became a Christian prince. If the rest were animated by a like zeal, Turks would not now be insulting Christians nor would Saracens be guarding the sepulcher of our Lord. Perhaps God would have pity on His people and cause other Christians to be moved by the example of Duke Philip and the Duke of Clèves and would give the lie to those who had despised the Congress of Mantua and belittled with mocking words all that went on there. Other matters must be put off to other days.

With these words he closed the session. As a mark of respect the Cardinal of Autun escorted the Duke of Clèves to his lodgings.

When Clèves and his colleagues were asked what counsel or aid Philip offered, they said they had been sent by their prince to hear the Pope's intentions and to report his plans to Philip. When they were a second time called on to speak, they said that Philip had often discussed with his friends the Pope's project and that, holy as it was, it appeared to him so difficult as to be almost impossible. A crusade against the Turks demanded very great strength, since, having been victorious for so many years, they inspired terror in Christians by their mere fame and prestige. Whenever our ancestors had led an army against the East they had raised forces from France, Germany, and England; now these provinces either had trouble at home and were engaged in civil war or they were quarreling with their neighbors for the possession of territory; they must first be reconciled and then war might be declared on the Turks; it was ill for those who were at variance with their own citizens to draw the sword against foreigners; Philip would do whatever the Pope commanded to bring about a declaration of war by united and harmonious princes.

The Pope replied that you could not deal with God as with men. Philip must consider what gifts God had heaped upon him, who was lord of so many rich provinces, lived in such luxury, had so long enjoyed unimpaired health, had a son to succeed him, and was held to be the happiest of all Christian princes. Unless he showed himself grateful to God, of Whom he had received all things, he need no longer look for divine mercy, since God was against those whom He found ungrateful for the benefits they received.

Both the envoys and the Pope spoke at length on these matters and many days passed in fruitless argument. Nor did it do any good to call in the cardinals, for nothing could be got out of the envoys until they had twice had private audience with the Pope. Only then did they give in and promise that Philip, when he was required in the Pope's name, would send to Hungary or hire there at his own expense 2,000 cavalry and twice as many infantry, who should continue to fight the Turks as long as there was a Christian army in the field.

After this promise Clèves at once began to talk of returning home. The Pope however desired him to await the arrival of the Dukes of Milan and Modena, who were expected very soon. On that account Clèves stayed eight days longer than he had intended, but when one of them, Borso, revoked his promise and the other put off fulfilling his, he received the Pope's permission to withdraw. It is hard to bring about an agreement among great princes who have no love for one another and will not compromise. Harmony among sovereigns is rare and good faith rarer. Envy spares nothing.

Clèves departed somewhat ailing. Jean of Croy, who had been stricken with a very severe fever, was given up by the physicians, but he disregarded their advice and recovered; for though suffering from the intense heat and very weak, he started on his journey and after a few days of travel by coach was restored to his former vigor. Some of Philip's ambassadors however waited till the end of the Congress. Two went to the Emperor.

A few days later Francesco, Duke of Milan, arrived. He was a prince celebrated alike in peace and war. His father, Sforza Attendolo, was born in the village of Cotignola in Emilia of poor and humble parents. He soon left their farm to become a soldier and joined Broglio Brandolino [6] of Forlì, a distinguished captain of that time. Since however he had neither horses nor arms, he served his first campaign in the mean capacity of mule driver. Before long he was made a squire and having done valiant service in battle was rewarded by being enrolled among the cavalry. He was a man of splendid physique with such eloquence as

---

[6] A curious slip. Broglio of Alessandria and Brandolino of Forlì were two persons, colleagues in arms, as Pius himself says in his *Decades Blondi*.

befits a soldier. He was quick to act and had great presence of mind as well as a versatile genius. Since he was conspicuous among the horsemen of the time and had performed many feats of military prowess, at Broglio's death he was put in command of a considerable army.

His young son Francesco, who had already displayed great ability, was then with the army and by the unanimous vote of the soldiers soon succeeded to his father's command. It is said that he was the son of a concubine; *that astrologers and those who are called genethliacs* [7] *often commended him to his father as destined to become a most brilliant general;* and that Sforza often said, "If Francesco lives, he will surpass me in courage and good fortune. *In the opinion of those who measure the courses of the stars the constellations at his birth were so auspicious that they portend a throne and the height of glory for him."* Human destiny delights to change the highest to the lowest, the lowest to the highest, but rarely has any man climbed from a cottage to a throne without ability. Empires are won by perseverance, courage, and wisdom; by idleness, cowardice, and ignorance they are lost.

Francesco owed his dukedom to his own and his father's merits. When he came to Mantua he was sixty years old.[8] His mother was still alive but died two years later. He sat his horse like a young man; (Fig. 9) he was very tall and bore himself with great dignity; his expression was serious, his way of speaking quiet, his manner gracious, his character in general such as became a prince. He appeared the only man of our time *whom Fortune loved.* He had great physical and intellectual gifts. Unconquered in war he came from a humble family to a throne. He married a lady of great beauty, rank, and virtue, by whom he had a family of very handsome children. He was rarely ill. There was nothing he greatly desired which he did not obtain, *and did not allow the stars which at birth (they say) he had found so propitious to be found false.* Some misfortunes however did befall him. His mistress, whom he loved passionately, was murdered by his *madly* jealous wife; his comrades in arms and old friends, Troilo and Brunoro, deserted him for Alfonso; another friend and comrade, Ciarpellone, he convicted of treason and hanged; he had to bear the treachery of his brother Alessandro, who went to France and tried to rouse the French against him; he had to imprison his son Sforza for plotting against him; he lost in war the Picene territory which he had won in war. No man lives whose

---

[7] I.e., those who, at the birth of a child, foretell his future from the stars.

[8] Authorities incline to accept 1401 as the year of Francesco Sforza's birth, in which case he was fifty-eight, not sixty years old at this time.

felicity is so untroubled that he does not have to quarrel in some respect with the fluctuations of his fortune. He is happy whose troubles are few.

Francesco was met on his entrance to Mantua by two cardinals. He came from Cremona by boat down the Po and the Mincio, the sluggish stream which surrounds Mantua. Everywhere skiffs and other craft were plying up and down and a great crowd came out of the city to see this famous duke. They could not gaze enough at his handsome face and his princely bearing *nor praise them enough*. All thought him worthy to rule. He was accompanied by a numerous and noble retinue among whom no one could be seen whose garments did not glitter with gold or shine with silver. When he entered the city there was much talk about the dignity and glory of the Apostolic See and men everywhere were heard saying, "See how lofty and exalted is the authority and majesty of the Bishop of Rome when so great a prince has come to kiss his feet!"

The next day the Pope gave Francesco audience in public consistory. After he had kissed the holy feet and made a short address he was bidden to seat himself in the place assigned to cardinal deacons. He then presented Francesco Filelfo, a distinguished author *of satires* and a poet learned in Greek and Latin, to plead his cause. Filelfo, after eulogizing Francesco and the Pope, spoke at length of the Turks and at still greater length of the Greeks, showing how necessary was the crusade against the former, how warmly Francesco favored it, and what aid he promised the Christians.

When he had ended, the Pope praised his speech in glowing terms and called him "the Attic Muse." Then turning to Francesco he said that he had justified his reputation and all their hopes. He had followed in the footsteps of his illustrious father, who had exposed himself to great dangers for the Church of Rome, the mother of the faithful. He had been indeed a noble man and the most distinguished soldier of his time, a second Ajax in battle, a second Nestor in counsel. He had feared no man but inspired fear in all. All living men honored his exploits. Pius himself as a youth had heard of them from his uncle Giovanni Tolommei, who had served under Sforza both as common soldier and as commander, and he had marveled at the courage and the glory of such a hero. The son had surpassed his unsurpassable sire. He had been victorious over all with whom he had ever contended. He had won the name bestowed by the ancients on the bravest Romans and most highly honored among the Italians. The dukedom of Milan had come to him not by succession from his father, *which would have been due to fortune,* but by popular election, which was due to his virtues.

In one respect only was his father his superior; for the father had always defended the cause of the Church, while the son had sometimes attacked it. Yet not even in this respect was he hopelessly inferior to his father, since from a Saul he had become a Paul, had aided Pius's predecessor Calixtus against Piccinino, during Pius's own pontificate had often lent his support to the Church, and even now had come to this Congress where he was nobly promising to use all his resources to defend against the impious Turks not only the Church of Rome but religion itself, the Catholic Faith, and the very name of Christ. He indeed was acting as became a Christian prince; if the others were found to be like him, Christians not only need have no fear of Turkish arms but they might actually take the offensive and easily regain Greece and Asia, which had been lost through the indifference of their ancestors. He hoped that Francesco's example would rouse many Christian princes who appeared to be asleep and that when they at last realized the danger that threatened Christianity, they would take up arms against the enemy. If this happened, as he hoped, Francesco would be among the foremost to whom the Church of Rome and the entire Christian religion would owe the profoundest gratitude.

With these words the Pope adjourned the meeting for the day amid enthusiastic applause.

Borso, Duke of Modena, who was governing Ferrara for the Church of Rome, had promised to go to Mantua when Pius should summon him. When however he was actually summoned, he wrote that *he would come in a few days. When summoned yet again he had changed his mind and refused, giving as an excuse the evidence of the astrologers, who said that the stars foretold his death if he went to Mantua. The Pope rebuked him for heeding pagan nonsense and for saying that he could know the future by inspection of the stars and he accused him of inventing all this to avoid coming to the Congress. He said Borso was afraid to show himself among good men, that he preferred to live with beasts rather than with human beings, that he was ungrateful to God and unworthy of such an abundance of blessings, since he was unwilling to endure the fatigue of a single day's travel by water in the cause of the Faith, and that he who stayed away from a congress called to defend the name of Christ was neither devout nor a Christian. The pronouncement of the astrologers, which had been given in March, had*

been known to him before he had promised the Pope to come; nothing
was more unbecoming a prince than to go back on his word.

Borso replied with many excuses, but they were childish and un-
worthy to vex the Pope's ears; and though he was beaten by argument,
he would not own himself beaten. Finally he said he was sick of a fever
and needed rest. But he left Ferrara for Emilia, where in the midst of
the summer heat he went hawking, (Fig. 11) *jeered at by all who heard*
the story.

But when Borso had been summoned from his hunting to the Con-
gress by numerous letters and messengers, he was finally abashed and
wrote that he would come when August was over, as that was the
fateful month. But he proved as false as before. Deceit is easy for a
man accustomed to it and lips that have got the habit of lying are not
easily shut against a lie.

Ambassadors had now arrived from Florence, Siena, Lucca, and
Bologna, the chief men of these states, to offer their share in defense of
the common weal. King Ferrante of Sicily had sent the Archbishop of
Benevento (*who was later removed on account of his crimes*) and the
Duke of Andria to represent him.

Ferrante's letter was much more satisfactory than his envoys' speeches.
Whereas they said little about championing religion, the letter revealed
the King's high and noble purpose to defend the Faith. When the instructions of all the ambassadors present were read before the assembly,
none were found to be more comprehensive than those sent by Ferrante;
for his contained a vow and an oath as to making war on the Turk.
But though he had resolved to take the field, he was distracted by the
plots of the Prince of Taranto and involved in great disasters, of which
we shall tell in their proper place.

While these things were going on, Sigismondo Malatesta, who was
every day more sorely beset by the forces of Piccinino, appealed now to
Francesco, Duke of Milan, and now to Pope Pius for peace. With the
same purpose Ferrante had sent to Mantua the Bishop of Bitonto, a
man as shrewd as he was delightful, and Antonio Cincinello, one of his
court officials, and these men constantly besought Pius to make peace
between the opposing powers. Pius said that he would do nothing unless
he were given a free hand in fixing the terms of peace, for their former
agreement had long since expired and now it was the Pope's purpose to
settle the quarrel in accordance with right and justice. Ferrante, Federigo of Urbino, and Jacopo Piccinino consented to make peace on
certain conditions which seemed overharsh. The matter was debated

many days. Finally all agreed that the Pope should arrange a peace at his own discretion.

It was uncertain whether peace or war was more for the Pope's advantage. Everybody knew that even if Piccinino should be reconciled to Sigismondo, he would keep his army and engage in new enterprises and that he would certainly attack either the Church's subjects or the Sienese. For he would not dare attack the Venetians, the Florentines, the Duke of Milan, or the King of Sicily, since they were stronger than he, or the Duke of Modena to whom he was attached. In the Church's domain there were many factions which in the Pope's absence might call in Piccinino. On the other hand if he allowed the war to continue, one of two things would happen: either Malatesta with the help of the Venetians would successfully defend his cause or he would be conquered and leave Piccinino in possession of the field. Either would be disastrous. If the Venetians should take up arms for Sigismondo, all Italy would again be split into factions and the crusade against the Turks would be forgotten. If Malatesta should be defeated, Piccinino would be undisputed master, the Church would find herself faced with a most dangerous neighbor and would be fostering a mouse in her wallet or a serpent in her bosom. There was also a third possibility, that Piccinino and Sigismondo might join forces and with their combined armies ravage the lands of the Church and divide the provinces—so fickle and ambitious are men in arms, so inconstant in their aims, so eager for power.

The Pope therefore, although he was not without fears for his own fortunes, decided for the present to have regard to the losing side; for the future he put his hope in the grace of God, Who has the power to guide all things to the best issue. Taking on himself therefore the responsibility for the decision, he ordered the two sides to lay down their arms immediately and to release their prisoners. He commanded Pergola and numerous other places to surrender to Federigo of Urbino. Sinigaglia and Mondavio, together with the vicariate and Montemarciano, were to remain as pledges in his own possession till the terms he should impose were fulfilled. As to the rest he promised that he would pronounce judgment within two months, reserving the right, if he saw fit, to advance the time limit as often as he pleased. He added also that Sigismondo for his sins was to be required to pay not more than 60,000 or less than 50,000 ducats before the expiration of a year; otherwise the towns held as pledges should go to the King in payment. Furthermore he was not to engage in hostilities against the King for two years.

Those who were sent to carry out this decision were heard with dissatisfaction. The terms seemed harsh to both sides, especially to Piccinino, who saw clearly that he was going to be stripped of the prizes of victory. Nevertheless they soon laid down their arms according to the Pope's edict and surrendered their cities—all except Pietra Robbia, where by a trick of Sigismondo's the inhabitants pretended to rebel. Piccinino turned over a number of the towns he had captured to the soldiers to plunder. In other respects the terms were complied with and Sigismondo had now the advantage of an alliance with Italy, which had never been his before, so that he was able to enjoy leisure—though indeed his restless spirit and evil mind always preferred war to peace.

Meantime the ambassador of Casimir, King of Poland, entered Mantua with a splendid retinue. He was a learned man, nephew of that Sbignew who had been cardinal and Bishop of Cracow. He had a great number of attendants, all dressed alike in their national costume, wearing plumed hats, carrying quivers and slings, and mounted on very sleek horses. There came also spokesmen for Lodovico, Duke of Savoy: the Bishop of Turin, the Marshal of Savoy, and other nobles and learned men of that province. Of all Italy only the Venetians were missing. Although they had assured the Pope before he left Rome by many messages and letters that they would be among the first to send envoys, nevertheless when they were summoned they failed to obey. Two reasons deterred them: first they had not secured the church of Padua as they desired, and second they were terrified that they would be left to fight the Turks singlehanded if on their arrival at Mantua they should find that the Christian princes hung back from defending religion. Furthermore the Venetians at the Curia kept writing to their friends at home many things that made the populace in general averse to this noble project. For as a rule the members of the Curia are *perverse and* inclined to slander, since nearly all of them are slaves to *avarice and* ambition. The Pope naturally can advance and enrich only a few out of so many, and those who are passed over, thinking they have been unjustly treated, *hate him and* talk and write against him. *They backbite and slander him and praise no one less than the Pope* while he lives, though when he is dead they sometimes approve of him; the acts of his successor are his vindication. Therefore any Venetians in the Curia who did not realize their ambitions wrote to their friends letters which the latter interpreted as opposed to the Pope's purpose. *The state (democracy being prone to suspicion) put the worst interpretation on everything,* especially the merchants, for whom it was advantageous to have peace with the Turks.

We wish at this point to speak more fully of the Venetians, since they are today the most powerful state on both land and sea and seem not unfitted for the larger empire to which they aspire.

Venice is the name of both the city and the province. The ancients gave the name Veneti to all who lived in the marshes between Grado and the mouth of the Po, the region which is called Fornaci. This extends eighty miles north and south and runs as far back from the Adriatic as the sea ebbs and flows. Some include Ravenna also in Venetia. Strabo appears to be of this opinion, for in speaking of the marshes and the great harbor made by the Brenta River he says: "In the marshes is the great city of Ravenna, built entirely of wood and intersected by canals, where men go about by means of bridges and boats. When there are floods it is completely inundated and the slimy mud deposited everywhere by the sea on one side and the rivers on the other emits a most foul stench." But as Adria, which used to be on the mainland, is now surrounded by marshes and the sea, so Ravenna, which was formerly in the water, is now high and dry.

Venetia originally occupied almost all the islands between Grado and Loredo which constituted one body politic composed of a number of towns. Today the buildings are continuous, forming one city divided by canals flooded with salt water which serve as streets. The large canals are broad enough to permit a galley to be rowed in them. There are paths paved with brick for pedestrians. Merchandise is shipped here from almost the entire world and there is no more famous trading center in all Europe. Merchants from all over the West bring their wares here and carry away the wares of the East. They have an armory and a magnificent dockyard called the Arsenal protected by all sorts of engines where they are ceaselessly building galleys and other craft. It is thought that at a moment's notice they could at pleasure equip 100 galleys and as a matter of fact they have sometimes done so.

The entire city is constructed of brick, but if their empire continues to flourish, it will soon be of marble, and indeed at the present time the palaces of the nobles are veneered with marble and glitter with gold. The celebrated church of St. Mark the Evangelist is constructed *of eastern marble,* its many gilded domes adorned with the work called mosaic. They say that in this church there is a treasury which surpasses the wealth of kings, containing rubies, diamonds, and all kinds of precious stones. All this splendor was stolen in our day by a worthless

Greek by a most ingenious method.[9] He was however caught at last and put to death, though the Doge Francesco Foscari advised against it, saying that a man so bold as that ought to be preserved. The gilding on the top of the campanile is said to have cost sixty thousand ducats. The doges' palace which, as we have said above, was burned and rebuilt, is enormous, raised on marble columns and splendidly decorated. Other sumptuous and beautiful churches *and monasteries* are scattered through the city, which grows in size from day to day. It has no walls, their place being taken by the water, as the mainland is three miles distant at the nearest point. In our time it has had citizens illustrious in letters: the Augustinian friar Paolo,[10] a professor whose books on logic are today regarded as authoritative; Francesco Barbaro, a Greek and Latin scholar, who has made translations from Greek into Latin.

So much for the Venetians. Though they long refused to send their ambassadors to the Congress of Mantua, finally on learning that the Duke of Clèves had arrived, that the French envoys were expected soon, that Francesco Sforza, Duke of Milan, himself was present, *and that they alone of all Italy were missing, fearing public infamy* they sent two envoys with a picked company of young nobles, accompanied as a mark of honor by some 500 knights. Francesco Sforza out of respect to the city of Venice met them outside the walls and entered the city riding between the two envoys. One of them, Lodovico, delivered a brilliant speech in a public consistory, for he was not only a jurist but an eloquent orator. The purport of the speech was as follows: The Venetians execrated the insolence of the Turks in invading the lands of others, but they accused the Christians of cowardice in not defending their own possessions or daring to take arms for their religion. They had only praise for the Pope, who in his anxiety for the common weal had come to Mantua at the cost of toil and money. They urged a crusade against the Turks if it could be undertaken by the united forces of all Christians and they promised to do great things to bring that about.

In answer Pius, after some preliminary words about the origin of the Venetians and their glorious history, praised their offers in defense of

[9] Sanudo tells the story of a certain Stamati Carsioti di Retino who hid himself nightly in the baptistry chapel of San Giovanni and dug pieces of stone from the wall separating the chapel from the sanctuary of the church. When he had made a hole big enough to admit him he crawled into the sanctuary and stole a great array of jewels, including the ducal beretta. The crime was betrayed to the doge by a fellow Greek whom Stamati had taken into his confidence.

[10] Probably Paolo Veneto, a fourteenth-century writer whose book on logic was printed in Venice in 1491.

religion even though they were made on a condition very difficult to fulfill. He rebuked the lateness of the ambassadors, who had been the last to arrive though they were nearest the place of the Congress. He recalled the great affection of Pope Alexander III for the Venetians and assured them that he himself would hold them in no less regard if they stoutly did their part, as they should, to defend the Faith.

Since the Congress was now complete (though the French had not yet arrived), the Pope decided that before Francesco, Duke of Milan, who could not be kept there long, should leave, he would address all who were present and urge them to declare war. Therefore after mass in the cathedral all the princes and envoys were summoned to an assembly. There were many quarrels about the seating, but none sharper than that between the Venetians and the Savoyards. The former urged the power and antiquity of their empire, the latter their noble lineage and precedent. Since there seemed no other way to settle the question, as the disputes were gradually growing hotter and Ursato,[11] who displayed more arrogance than wisdom, seemed ready to come to blows, the Pope seated the Venetians behind the ambassadors of the Duke of Burgundy and directed the Savoyards to sit on the footstool of his throne. Then after commanding silence he spoke for three hours amid such close attention that not a word was lost and although he had been for some days suffering from a severe cough, the Divine Mercy came to his aid so that he did not cough once during his speech or betray the least hoarseness. He spoke long and eloquently about making war on the Turks and showed conclusively that it was not only expedient but righteous, easy, and necessary. His speech was afterward published in a volume with others.

When the Pope ended, the Greek cardinal Bessarion replied for the College in a speech as long as the Pope's, showing what a blow the Christians had suffered in the loss of Constantinople and what evils were upon them unless the attempts of the Turks were thwarted. He reminded them that victory was easy for the bold and with many arguments pleaded the necessity of war. He declared that the sacred college praised and approved everything the Pope had said in his speech, though it showed how far Latin eloquence surpassed Greek.

There were present also ambassadors from Hungary who had an opportunity to speak in their turn, coming last because they were there to ask aid. After they had applauded the Pope for his concern for the common weal, they attacked the Emperor at length for having caused

[11] Ursato Giustiniani, the Venetian envoy.

the Hungarians still more trouble when they were in difficulties with
the Turks and having involved their kingdom in fresh dissensions. On
this the whole assembly began to murmur against the Emperor, but his
envoy still did not dare to refute the accusations in so large a gathering,
not being used to speaking in a public meeting.

Then the Pope said, "Hungarians, what you have said is irrelevant
and against your own interests. We are now debating about war with
the Turks and with your cause at heart we are trying to arm the Emperor and all other Christians to aid you. Do you come to seek help
and yet attack with abusive words those who have the power to give
that help? This is not the way to benefit your kingdom nor is this the
place to bandy reproaches. Misery and arrogance are poor housemates.
As for us, we have found the Emperor a lover of justice and we do not
think your King fails in honor, though they are indeed at variance
about your kingdom. No one however thinks his own cause unjust.
When they come to know the truth they will obey the truth and we
must try to make them friends. We have already sent to them one ambassador; we will send still another if need be, that nothing may be left
undone to reconcile these sovereigns. Meanwhile let us settle the matter
in hand; let us have no quarreling here nor any word of abuse."

The Hungarians on hearing this sat silent while all the rest applauded
the Pope's words and unanimously voted for war against the Turks.
Then the Congress was adjourned for that day.

The following day all the ambassadors and princes from Italy who
were present were summoned before the Pope. The Genoese were not
as yet officially present but had secretly promised their aid. The cardinals sat to the right and left of the Pope; the princes and the ambassadors were seated by districts. When they were ready to listen, the Pope
said, "My sons, on your advice we have determined to declare war
against the Turks and we have no doubt that if Christians come to the
defense of their own salvation there will be horses, men, ships, and
money in abundance. Now we must consider whether we are to attack
the enemy by land or sea or both together; how large a fleet and land
army is needed; from what nations soldiers are to be levied: whether
we desire to aid the Hungarians with money or with men. Take counsel
for the good of all and state openly what help you can promise." [12]

After this there was a long argument with the Venetian ambassadors,

[12] Then follow the proposals by various delegates for recruiting forces and raising
money. The Pope outlines his own plan. This is all summarized in the concluding
speech of Book II.

*whose words were very different from their feelings. They favored the
war against the Turks with their lips but condemned it in their hearts.
They are not people who embrace splendid projects. They are mostly
merchants whose nature, intent on gain, usually shrinks from noble
aims which cannot be achieved without expense. The Venetians thought
that if war were declared against the Turks, all their trade with the
East, on which their livelihood depended, would cease and that after
Greece was freed the western princes would not allow the Venetian
republic to have sovereignty in Dalmatia and the East. They feared too
that while they were occupied with a war with the Turks, the Duke of
Milan would attack them; for men always suspect others of their own
designs. They had therefore instructed their ambassadors to prolong
the discussion and hold out fair hopes, but to promise nothing definite
or binding.* When however they were pressed more insistently they said
that the Venetians would join *in the war* only on condition that they
be allowed the sole conduct of naval matters; that they should have the
spoils taken from the enemy; that a large fleet be raised; that an army
of 50,000 cavalry and 20,000 infantry should march from Hungary
against the Turks. They said a fleet of sixty galleys and twenty saette
was needed and 8,000 soldiers besides rowers and other sailors to man
them *though before they had said that a much smaller number would
suffice.* They promised only that they would furnish the ships themselves and their equipment. For everything else they expected pay and
for this purpose they demanded the tenths, twentieths, and thirtieths
raised within their jurisdiction, which they thought would amount to
150,000 ducats. Not satisfied even with this they demanded from the
general treasury 1,500,000 more. Such was the liberality of the Venetians.

The Pope answered them as follows: "Ambassadors of the Venetians,
we see that it is not your purpose to defend religion, since you ask an
almost impossible price. It is a matter for sorrow that your state *has so
degenerated that she* who in the past has gladly armed great fleets for
the defense of the Faith is now unwilling, *if we take everything into
account,* to arm even a single ship. Against the Pisans and the Genoese,
against kings and emperors you have often waged great wars at your
own expense in behalf of your allies and subjects. You now demand a
price to fight for Christ against the impious Turks, *but even if it were
given you you would not arm. Alas! Venetian race, how much of your
ancient character have you lost! Too much intercourse with the Turks
has made you the friends of the Mohammedans and you care no more
for religion."*

Much was said to this same effect and often *more severely*. The envoys being cautious made answers *more* specious *than true. Nothing on their lips matched what was in their hearts.*

They opened one line of argument after another, exaggerating the strength of the enemy and belittling ours and trying to take up time till the Congress should be dissolved. *Nor did they come to the palace except by appointment. Their bearing was full of pomp and pride. They knelt reluctantly in the Pope's presence and though they saw the ambassadors of kings and of the Emperor himself and mighty princes lie prostrate long after kissing the Pope's feet, they themselves, either from their inveterate pride or the rudeness inherited from their fishermen ancestors, rose immediately. If they were kept waiting a single minute in the Pope's anteroom they at once complained as if insulted and wrote to their senate that they were no more honored by the Pope than if they had been ambassadors from Ancona. This made the Venetians (who were already embittered on account of the church of Padua) more and more violent against the Pope. But as a matter of fact he was excessive and lavish in the honors shown the Venetians rather than remiss. They made these and countless other misrepresentations, in order to pile trouble on trouble.*[13]

Some days later the French approached Pius and said there were some things they wished to say about the kingdom of Sicily which they were unwilling to reveal in the presence of the ambassadors of certain princes. The Pope allowed them to invite whom they pleased. They made the Bailli of Rouen their spokesman. When there was silence he proceeded to make a long speech about the great exploits of the French (whom he called Liliati) in defense of religion and the many benefits they had conferred on the Apostolic See. He explained how the kingdom of Sicily had come to them and how much blood it had cost. Alfonso, he said, had had no justification for ejecting them by force of arms. The Pope had acted unfairly in setting over so great a kingdom Alfonso's bastard son, who was unworthy of the crown, and rejecting René, the rightful king. Calixtus, Aragonese though he was, would never have done such a thing. The French had been unjustly treated by the Pope. They begged Pius, who had *foolishly and rashly* deposed the best blood of the Liliati and preferred the Aragonese, to revoke in wis-

---

[13] The attitude of Venice was to refuse to associate itself with any move hostile to Mahomet II until the Christian powers of Europe gave evidence of a willingness to unite in a common effort against the Turk. Venice did not wish to bear the onus of such an enterprise alone and had ample reason to doubt the likelihood of a united European front.

dom what he had done in folly, to proclaim René king, to reject Ferrante. In this way the French would be compensated for the insults put upon them.

This was the gist of the speech *but the words were bombastic and pretentious and there was no lack of characteristic French threats and boasts.* When they heard them, all the friends of France reared their crests and exulted like conquerors thinking the Pope would not dare to reply. He indeed for the time being made only the following brief answer: "Royal ambassadors, we have listened to your defense of René's cause and your accusation of ourself. Our policy in regard to the kingdom of Sicily was determined on the advice of the cardinals. If now it is demanded that it be revoked as unjust, it is proper that we ask the advice of these same men. When that has been done, we will answer your complaints and requests." Then he dismissed the meeting.

After this the Pope had a serious attack of stomach trouble and was so racked by a dry cough that both he and his physicians had doubts whether he would live. The French, when they heard of this, said it was a pretense, not a real sickness; demanded their answer; grew pressing and insistent. They thought the Pope was beaten by their arguments and was trying to avoid replying to them. When Pius learned of this he said, "Even if I must die in the midst of the assembly, I will answer *this insolent embassy* and pain shall not conquer my spirit nor shall sickness make me appear a coward."

Therefore after summoning the cardinals and informing them of the reply he meant to make, though some urged him to deliver it before a small gathering, he gave orders that all the ambassadors of princes should be summoned together with the chief men of the Curia. When they had gathered in great numbers the Pope, who was weak and in great pain, emerged from his chamber and entered his audience hall. When silence had been proclaimed, at first he sat pale and distressed on his lofty throne and could hardly speak. But as his emotion mastered him, words came flooding to his lips and, fired with the power of his own eloquence and rising above his pain, he spoke for three hours without the slightest effort and was listened to by all with the most profound attention.

In his speech the Pope admitted that the glory of the French was far greater than it had been described by the Bailli. They had indeed conferred many benefits on the Church of Rome but had received no less in return. The measures taken in regard to the kingdom of Sicily were neither unjust nor unreasonable. It was the complaints of the French which were unjust, since their rights had in no way been interfered with. Indeed that they themselves were in the wrong could not be denied, since in their own kingdom they had passed a law in opposition to the Apostolic See which would be the damnation of many souls.

This speech is published with others, so that there is no reason why parts of it should be inserted here. If anyone wishes to see how conclusively the arrogance of the French was answered. he must look it up in the volume of orations.

When Pius had ended, the French declared that their king had been insulted and they demanded to be heard, that they might not seem to leave the honor of their sovereign undefended. The Pope replied: "I will hear you when and as often as you please, *but understand that I shall have the last word and do not be surprised if you who have stung are stung yourselves. This See does not yield to any, even the mightiest king."*

The ambassadors left the palace with indignation and threats. The Pope left the hall to return to his chamber entirely free from weariness and pain, for the heat of speaking had dispelled all the chill from his stomach. The delighted cardinals went in to thank him for saving the honor of the See. The members of the Curia, who had begun to seem to despise the Pope, now admired him, applauding especially what he had said about the Pragmatic Sanction and asserting that never within the memory of our fathers had there been a pope who had uttered words more truly papal.

After this the French, on being asked what aid they would furnish against the Turks, replied that it was useless to think about the Turks unless French and English relations were settled, since no one was willing to leave his country defenseless against the enemy. They must first find a way to make peace at home and then consider war against foreign foes. The Pope answered: "Before the French and English are reconciled the Turks will exterminate the Hungarians. Your aid will come too late. *You call your king 'most Christian' yet you care not to come to the help of the Christian religion.* You might have aided the Christian cause with money at least if not with soldiers; and yet we cannot see why you and the English could not also send the soldiers required of you. For if both send proportionately the same number you will be no less strong against the enemy at home than now."

The French were beaten at every point and when they could not meet his arguments, they said they had been instructed to make no promises in the matter unless the English should be present and agree to terms of peace. Since they had not come, they could say nothing. The matter was dropped and there were no more negotiations with the French.

During these days Francesco Sforza, who had returned to Milan, sent the Pope three very fat steers which had been fed on turnips and were used to being washed with warm water, combed every day, and bedded on clean straw. Pius gave one of these to Sigismund,[14] one he divided among the ambassadors of princes, and the third he kept for himself and the cardinals. All liked the meat so much that they vowed they had never tasted anything sweeter; *but it was not bought cheaply, for those who brought the oxen were presented with 100 gold ducats.*

A few days later in the church of St. Andrew before the senators and all the ambassadors of princes, after mass had been celebrated the Pope commanded silence and from his throne spoke as follows: "My brothers and sons, we have for eight months awaited those who have been summoned to the Congress. You know who have come. To hope longer for the arrival of anyone who could contribute anything to our cause is vain and therefore we may now disperse. We have done what had to be done here. We pray that God's cause has been well pleaded. Though we dreamed of more than we have found, nevertheless we cannot think that nothing has been accomplished nor is all our hope gone. We must now expound the present situation that all may know what prospects we have and what kings and peoples have been ready to protect the Faith or indifferent. If the Hungarians receive aid, they will attack the Turks energetically with all their forces. The Germans promise an army of 42,000 fighting men, Burgundy 6,000. The Italian clergy with the exception of the Venetians and the Genoese will contribute a tenth and the laity a thirtieth of their income; the Jews a twentieth of their possessions. With this sum naval forces can be maintained. John, King of Aragon, promises like aid. The Ragusans will furnish two galleys, the Rhodians four. So much has been promised by princes and ambassadors in solemn and explicit agreement.

"The Venetians, although they have promised nothing publicly, when they see the crusade actually ready will surely not fail us nor endure to seem inferior to their ancestors. We can say the same of the French, the Castilians, and the Portuguese. England, now racked with civil war, holds out no hope nor does Scotland, remote as it is at Ocean's farthest bounds. Denmark, Sweden, and Norway also are too far away to be able to send soldiers and they have no money to contribute, as they are

[14] Duke of Austria.

content with fish alone. The Poles, who border the Turks along Moldavia, will not dare to desert their own cause. The Bohemians we shall be able to hire; they will not fight outside their country at their own expense. Such is the situation of the Christian cause. Italian money will equip a fleet, if not at Venice then at Genoa or in Aragon, and it will not be smaller than the occasion requires. The Hungarians will arm 20,000 cavalry and as many infantry. These with the Germans and Burgundians will make 88,000 soldiers in the field. Does anyone think the Turks will not be conquered with these forces? They will be joined by Georg Skanderbeg and a very strong force of Albanians and many all over Greece will desert from the enemy. In Asia Charamanus and the Armenians will attack the Turks in the rear. We have no reason to despair if only God Himself will favor our undertaking. Go and tell those at home what has been done here; admonish your masters to fulfill their promises promptly; and by your words and works strive that the Divine Mercy may be propitious to us."

At these words all present confirmed their promises; those who had offered nothing sat silent and confused. Borso's ambassadors, that they might seem to have done somewhat more than the rest, promised 300,000 ducats for the crusade—to the derision of their hearers *who knew how empty were the promises of a man whose mean soul would do least when it promised most.*

After everyone had spoken the Pope bade all the cardinals, bishops, abbots, and priests present don their sacred robes. He himself came down from his throne and knelt at the steps of the high altar. There with sighs and tears for a long time he intoned in a voice of supplication verses of the Psalms appropriate to the occasion, while the prelates and all the clergy made the responses. Then he spoke to the people and blessed them. Thus he brought to an end the Congress of Mantua.

BOOK IV

THE Pope, having dismissed the embassies of Germany and the other provinces, left Mantua and with four cardinals went to Revere by boat. The rest made the journey by land. The Cardinal of San Pietro set out for his church *against the Pope's advice* and met with a scandalous reception there. Colonna decided to visit Venice. On his arrival he was presented with citizenship and enrolled among the patricians of the city, *as if it were more important to be a Venetian noble than a Roman prince.* The Cardinal of Ruthen, who had collected a quantity of arms for the aid of his people, intended to cross over into Greece, but he got no further than Ancona; for the winter was very cold and by this time (toward the end of January) ice and snow were everywhere.

The members of the Curia were amazed that the aged Pope should travel in such bitter weather, but he who had not quailed at the cold when he went was not dismayed by the cold when he returned. He spent a night in Revere and the next day was met on the Po by Borso in the Bucentaur, surrounded by such a throng of smaller craft that there was no part of the river that was not churned by their oars, and the many-colored standards fluttering in the breeze were a marvelous sight. Trumpets, pipes, and all sorts of instruments made sweet music from the lofty sterns. There were impersonations of various gods and goddesses, giants and virtues; on the dikes which prevent the river from overflowing, boys and girls were singing and men and women sat there as if at a show. Some shouted "Viva" to the Pope and some to Borso.

Now that they had met Borso, Lodovico of Mantua took leave of the Pope, commending himself repeatedly to his favor, and returned home. Pius boarded the Bucentaur and was conveyed to Ferrara, where he was met by priests carrying sacred relics and by a great throng of people and was lodged in the citadel which is situated above the riverbank. Although they entreated him to stay over the next day, he refused. On the ship Borso signed the decree providing for the contributions of tenths, twentieths, and thirtieths. He was the last to sign *and later the first after the Florentines to violate it.*

Crossing the Po, Pius proceeded by water through the marshes to the Reno, which has been mentioned above. It was a very difficult journey, for a clear winter had frozen over all the water and a channel had to be opened with axes. But when they came to the Reno they encountered ice so thick that it could not be broken and the Bolognese had provided no means of transport. Therefore the Pope had to be carried in a chair while his attendants had to walk. Thus darkness overtook them and they were forced at some inconvenience to pass the night in any peasants' huts they could find. The Pope with a few of his companions stayed at the country house of Xante Bentivoglio. The next day he entered Bologna where he slept in the apostolic palace; but in spite of the entreaties of the Bolognese he would not consent to remain another day.

Next the Pope came to a place called "unloading of asses," [1] on the summit of the Apennines. The journey was made with great difficulty on a snowy, rainy day and he had to ride sometimes in a carriage, sometimes in a chair. When he reached Firenzuola he had an attack of stomach trouble and the next day went to Caffagiuolo, Cosimo's magnificent country place in the Val Mugellana, where he had spent a night on his way to Mantua. Here he found a messenger from Federigo of Urbino, a shrewd man who confirmed what Pius had already heard of Piccinino. He said that Piccinino intended to march into the Abruzzi against Ferrante and that Federigo would, if the Pope so ordered, close the road to him. This matter was referred to Francesco *Sforza.*

When the Pope entered Florence he was loaded with extraordinary honors by the state. The most distinguished citizens came out to greet him; the magistrates received him at the gate. After speaking *at length* of the Congress of Mantua in a manner highly flattering to the Pope, they begged him to spend the next day with them and he did not refuse their request.

Cosimo, who had been too indifferent to wait on the Pope when he was on his way into Gaul, *by no means slighted him on his return. He* came to him late at night and in the course of their conversation expressed surprise that he was committed to a war with the French for the sake of Ferrante. The Pope replied that it was intolerable that a king whom he had himself confirmed should be ejected by force of arms; nor would this make for the freedom of Italy; if the French should once get

[1] Scarcagliasini.

possession of Ferrante's kingdom, they would undoubtedly proceed to subdue Siena; the Florentines, *being French in their sympathies,* would not raise a finger against "the lilies"; Borso, Duke of Modena, appeared to be more French than the French themselves; the princelings of Romagna inclined toward the French; Genoa was already subject to them and so was the state of Asti; if the Pope should come to be their friend, there was nothing in Italy that would not go over to them. In protecting Ferrante he was protecting Italy and his honor demanded this course in accordance with the treaties that had originally been made with Alfonso. He could not break his word as could the Florentines and Venetians, who suited their compacts to expediency.

Cosimo applauded the Pope's spirit and admitted he was right, but he declared that the populace would act honorably only when forced by self-interest or fear. With some diffidence he asked a number of favors, among them that his grandson, if he appeared worthy, might be made cardinal. Finally, when on taking his leave he tried to kiss the Pope's foot, but because he was crippled with gout, was unable to bend, *he laughed and said, "Two Florentines named Papo and Lupo returning from the country met in the piazza and offered each other their hands and a kiss. But they were both very fat and there was such corporosity (if I may use that word) on both sides that they could touch only their stomachs. Gout now denies me what corpulence refused them."* The Pope *laughingly* dismissed him and gave instructions that on the next day some of the cardinals should take up with the Florentines the question of the tenths, twentieths, and thirtieths, so that when it came time to raise a fleet, it would not be necessary to treat the subject as if it were quite new to them.

A delegation from the citizens now waited on the Pope and he reminded them of the promise made by their ambassadors at Mantua and of the surety given for them by the Duke of Milan. The Florentines admitted everything, but they said the envoys who had pledged the state had had their instructions from the priors and certain senators; this was the customary procedure but was not valid unless afterward ratified by the great Council of State. It was very seldom that it refused to ratify what ambassadors so instructed had promised, but in this matter, which was of the utmost gravity, there was not the slightest hope of the people's consent; for there were only a handful who could be persuaded to pay the thirtieth, though perhaps the clergy would not refuse their tithe.

The Pope was amazed at such impudence on the part of the Florentines and inveighed at length against the injustice of those *who in dis-*

cussing the cause of the Faith could employ fraud and trickery. He
declared that it was shameful to give instructions that had no authority
and still more shameful to take advantage of them; if in other matters
they were used to be confirmed, most especially ought they to be ratified
in this matter of supreme importance. Since however he was merely
wasting his time, he took what he could get, dismissed the state *which
was acting like a haggler not to say a courtesan,* without further delay,
and on the third day returned to Siena where his fellow citizens were
awaiting his coming with the greatest eagerness. His entrance to the
city was like a triumph and he was received with splendid and incredible honors, for the citizens, who were beginning to think they
should never see their father again, now, revived by his sudden and
unexpected return, evinced the most extravagant joy, especially the
women, who are naturally more inclined to religion and more devoted
to the priesthood. Though it was the usual cold February weather,
greenery was everywhere. Not a square but was decorated with flowers
and carpeted with fragrant herbs. Everywhere evergreen trees had been
planted, everywhere was heard the singing and shouting of the exultant
populace.

The Pope returned to Siena on the twelfth day after leaving Mantua [2]
and two days before the feast of the Purification of the Supreme Mother
and Immaculate Virgin. The feast was celebrated amid great rejoicing
on the part of the citizens and the Pope himself distributed the consecrated tapers.

Shortly before this Antonio, Archbishop of the city, had died while
he was visiting the baths for his health. The Pope appointed to his duties
and office his sister's son, Francesco,[3] then twenty-three years old.

At this time Federigo of Urbino waited on the Pope. He was an able
and eloquent man, but blind in one eye, which he had lost in a tourna-
ment. (Fig. 14) The Pope listened to his lavish promises and gave him
funds with which to get Piccinino's soldiers away from him and prevent
Ferrante's enemy from invading the kingdom; for the rumor was
abroad that the celebrated general Piccinino, who had deserted Ferrante,
would shortly march against his kingdom and there was no friend of
Ferrante in all his realm who did not tremble before so great a name.
Therefore the Duke of Milan and Pope Pius decided that Sforza's son [4]

[2] January 31, 1460.
[3] Francesco de' Todeschini, son of Pius's sister Laudomia, later Pius III. He was adopted
by the Pope and assumed the name of Piccolomini.
[4] *Sic.* Alessandro was Francesco Sforza's brother.

Alessandro with the Duke's forces, Federigo with the King's troops, and Giovanni Malavolta with those of the Church should meet Piccinino in the Picene territory and prevent his crossing it. After this plan had been agreed upon, Federigo returned home.

The season of Lent was approaching which is regarded as the regular election time for cardinals and it was already common talk that the new pope desired to create new cardinals, as if he would not be considered a pope complete in all respects unless he did so. At this time many persons presented petitions: the Emperor urged one candidate, to whom the Pope enthusiastically assented; the King of France presented two names; the King of Aragon one; Ferrante, King of Sicily, and Francesco, Duke of Milan, several each; the Duke of Savoy one; the Duke of Burgundy one; the Marquis of Monteferrato one; the Florentines and Cosimo one. The Pope favored very few of these candidates and himself had others whom he considered worthier and thought likely to be loyal to him. He began therefore to speak to individual cardinals with a view to finding out their attitudes in advance. *From some he exacted a written statement; from others he accepted their word.* As soon as he found that he was going to get practically what he wanted he called a sacred consistory on the Wednesday when the creation of cardinals is commonly discussed and began as follows:

"The harvest indeed is great but the workers are few. Our harvest, my brethren, is the salvation of souls; the field in which we reap is the Church, which we are charged to govern with your counsel. This it is our duty to defend against the Turks and other infidels; from this we are bound to uproot the tares and noxious weeds, that is, heresies and vicious practices, if we wish to bring a bounteous harvest to God's threshing floor and finally store an abundance of clean, well-threshed wheat in the granary. You have been appointed our co-workers to this end, but you are few and some we cannot use because of your age or sickness. Therefore we must increase your number and add others to supplement the strength of the weak. We must however take care, difficult though it is, to choose those worthy of so high an office, that no man may say, 'Thou hast multiplied the nation and not increased the joy.' But if this dignity is to be given only to those who really deserve it, we must look in Heaven for those on whom to confer the red hat. We however, as being but men, shall elect men, since it is not Heaven and angels but the earth and men that we are to govern.

"We are surprised that there is such a throng of aspirants; for what cleric does not think himself worthy to be cardinal? does not ask? is not insistent? does not wish, so to speak, both to be and to be thought to be among the candidates? This dignity is become cheap indeed when even children think they have a claim to it. *This is the fault of our predecessors, who created certain persons manifestly unworthy. We may speak of those who are dead. You know for instance the Cardinal of San Marco whom some called the buffoon of your order. You too are to blame, who do not preserve the dignity and sanctity becoming this eminence; for you live so that you seem not chosen to govern the state but invited to enjoy pleasures. You do not abstain from hunting or games or intercourse with women. You give dinners of unseemly magnificence. You wear too costly clothing. You have abundance of gold and silver plate. You keep more horses and servants than you need. All men desire these luxuries and there is no one who is not naturally inclined to pursue pleasure. But if sobriety, dignity, temperance, learning, sanctity bestowed nothing but this office, fewer would seek it.* Such however are the times on which we have fallen. We cannot prevent their asking nor can we easily admit them. Do you consider who are suitable. As to the number we will ourselves decide, taking care that too many shall not cheapen this dignity or too few fail to satisfy the requirements of the state."

After this he disclosed the names of those who were seeking the cardinalate either on their own initiative or through others. *When he ended, Lodovico, Cardinal of Aquileia, said, "I am shamed to sit in this place which every man thinks due him. The path to this eminence used to be open only to the most illustrious. A man who attains the cardinalate should be without spot or blemish. This supreme dignity admits of no stain. Your predecessors have been used to elevate men of noble birth, eminent for learning and holiness. You have named a number whom I would not have as servants in my kitchen or stable. Nor do I see the necessity for the creation of new cardinals. There are enough of us already, whether you wish to send ambassadors or to hold a council at home. We are cheapened by too great numbers. We have not enough resources for ourselves and you wish to add others to take the bread out of our mouths. Further, you have not yet mentioned anyone whom I consider worthy of the red hat."*

When he had spoken those who knew him smiled, but the Pope said, "Your Eminence of Aquileia, if Eugenius and Nicholas and my predecessor Calixtus had observed your rule in creating cardinals, you would either not now be a cardinal or would be sitting here with fewer colleagues."

Filippo of Bologna said, "Your Holiness, you have mentioned many names, but left out your nephew. Why do you not think he too ought to be elevated?" and Pius answered, "Our nephew is too young and has not all the qualifications which the cardinalate demands."

With these words he bade the cardinals confer together while he himself went into another room and took a little food, for the day was already far gone and the business required a long time.

The Pope then rejoined the college and after many arguments on both sides the cardinals agreed that five should be chosen, with the proviso that one should be the Pope's nephew. When Pius had made sure of these, he said, "You will not, I am sure, refuse me a sixth to whom no exception can be taken and whom you will undoubtedly approve when you hear his name." They asked to know the name before agreeing, but the Pope desired their consent first and at last won his point. Having got their approval he named as the sixth Alessandro da Sassoferrato, General of the order of St. Augustine, a man celebrated for his knowledge of theology and illustrious for the purity of his life. When he was named no one opposed him, for true virtue, though it is often assailed covertly, is safe from open attack. The list of the new cardinals was as follows: Angelo, Bishop of Reati, was named first. He was the brother of the late Cardinal of Fermo, a holy and upright man whom the Pope, before leaving Rome, had made his Legatus at Bologna. After him came Eberardo, Bishop of Spoleto, distinguished for character and learning and reputed a champion of justice. He was a native of Narni and at that time referendarius and a member of Pius's private household. Next came Niccolò of Pistoia, Bishop-elect of Teano, a member of the papal court celebrated for his legal knowledge. Fourth was Burchard, Provost of Salzburg, whose election it was decided should not be made public till others should be chosen from the nations across the Alps. Fifth was Alessandro, whom we have just mentioned, and sixth Francesco, the Pope's nephew,[5] who was then studying pontifical law at the University of Perugia and had already taken his doctorate. He received the rank of deacon in the college of cardinals on account of his youth, the others that of presbyter. Since they were all agreed, Pius did not wait for Friday when it was customary to announce and publish the cardinals, but that same day, contrary to the expectation of all, he made the announcement and publication. This relieved the old

[5] Although a youth of twenty-three at this time, his record in a quick succession of important offices is remarkable. He became Archbishop of Siena in January 1460, Cardinal in March, and was assigned to the post of legate to the March of Ancona (Picenum).

cardinals of considerable annoyance, since the various aspirants had been giving them no peace.

It was thought that the Pope had done extremely well by Italy in creating five cardinals from that country. On the other hand he had done an unprecedented thing in elevating to the cardinalate at the same consistory two members of his household and his nephew. One point however was universally approved, that none of those named seemed undeserving of so high a dignity. No one could remember a creation when so short a list included so many men of the highest distinction, and furthermore these illustrious persons had been chosen without the intercession of princes.

Everyone was astonished at the election of Alessandro, which was announced before anyone had even thought of it, since no one expected a poor monk from a narrow cell, however eminent a preacher of the word of God and however holy and distinguished a man, to be chosen among the cardinals; for the cardinalate aims at the heights. But it was Pius's opinion that virtue should be honored even in a poor man, for he knew well that the first princes of the Church had been poor and lowly as the world judges. He sought even in remote monasteries for noble souls and did not despise lack of gold in one who was made illustrious by riches of character. Everyone saw that Pope Pius loved virtue and therefore many after this strove more ardently after righteousness. Nothing is such a spur to virtue as the hope of its reward in honor.

Pius, having appointed Saturday [6] for the consistory in the cathedral, commanded that the three new cardinals already at Rome should be summoned and before they arrived he spoke at length about the election and the merits of each, proving that the creation of all had been just and necessary. Then when they entered, he bade them take their places at the chancel and addressed them as follows: "My sons, you have received a most high and exalted dignity. In being called to the Apostolic College you will become our counsellors and co-judges of the world. It will be your duty to decide between cause and cause, blood and blood, leprosy and leprosy. As successors of the Apostles you will sit around our throne; you will be senators of the city and the equals of kings, in very truth the hinges of the world, which must turn and regulate the gate of the Church Militant. Consider what men, what minds, what integrity this dignity demands. This office calls for humility, not pride; generosity, not greed; temperance, not drunkenness; self-control, not lust; knowledge, not ignorance; every virtue, no vice. If heretofore you have been

[6] March 8, 1460.

vigilant, you must now practice vigilance against a malignant foe who never sleeps for thinking whom he may devour. If you have been generous, pour out now your wealth in noble causes and especially in succoring the poor. If temperate in food and drink, now especially shun luxury. Refrain from avarice, do away with cruelty, banish arrogance. Have holy books ever in your hands. Day and night be learning something or teaching others. So act that your light shall shine before all men and, finally, be such as you thought cardinals ought to be before you yourselves rose to this eminence."

After these words he summoned them to kiss his foot and then offered them his hand and cheek. The old cardinals also kissed them and made room for them to sit. Then the advocates pleaded a number of cases and when these had been settled, the old cardinals stood in a ring around the Pope and the new ones kneeling took their oath according to the ancient formula. Then the Pope placed the red hat, the badge of the cardinalate, on the head of each and a chorus sang a hymn giving thanks to God. The old cardinals, except two who remained with the Pope, escorted the new cardinals in procession to the altar of the Blessed Virgin and there the senior cardinal made them an eloquent discourse, invoking many blessings on them and on Holy Church. After this they returned to the Pope, who dissolved the consistory and returned to his palace.

A like ceremony was held a few days later on the arrival of the Cardinals of Rieti and Siena, one coming to Siena from Bologna and the other from Perugia. The Pope praised the Cardinal of Rieti as became his merits; the Cardinal of Siena, since he was his own nephew and overyoung, he said he should never have elevated if he had not been persuaded by the entreaties of the cardinals.

After this Pius went into seclusion with the Minorites who are called Observantists not far from Siena. The monastery is called Capriola. It was built by St. Bernardino, in whose memory it has been enlarged and beautified, and its brethren are among the most saintly of the order. The Pope accompanied by the Cardinals of Spoleto and Teano remained here two weeks to get some little rest from business. He did not however discontinue the signatura or secret consistories nor did he refuse audience to any who approached him. He set up an audience chamber in a sunny spot at the foot of a mountain in a grove always green with many laurel and ilex trees, and the fact that in his search for seclusion he found spring before it was due added greatly to his pleasure.

Returning to Siena before Palm Sunday Pius performed with due

devotion all the ceremonies which are yearly celebrated in memory of
Christ's passion and to the glory of the Resurrection. Then he fell ill of
gout and suffered also from neuralgia. When he was somewhat recovered, he went on the advice of certain of his physicians to the baths
at Macereto, though many less competent tried to dissuade him. This
was the reason for his staying so long at Siena, though he also desired
to favor and benefit his birthplace, so that, beset as it was by war, pestilence, and civil strife and oppressed by poverty, it might gain some small
relief through the emoluments of the Curia. Reflecting on the weakness
of his city, which could not last long on account of the continued and
numerous dissensions among the citizens, before he went to the baths
he summoned the wiser members of the government and those who
seemed free of personal prejudice and asked what possible way there
could be to reform and unite the state. They answered that they ought
to invite into the government those who are called the Twelve, about
four hundred in number, among whom were many rich merchants.

The Pope approved this plan, though it seemed difficult of accom-
plishment, and delegated the Cardinals of Santa Cecilia and Santa
Susanna to find out the attitude of the leading citizens. After they had
talked with a considerable number, they reported that while many were
favorable more were opposed. When the matter became generally
known, the magistrates of the city, at the instance of the Captain of the
People (for such is the title of the chief magistrate), and a great throng
of citizens came and besought the Pope not to bring up the subject of
the Twelve. *They declared them to be a class of men reckless, seditious,
poisonous, bloodthirsty, and hostile to those ruling; they themselves
would rather eat their sons than share the government with the Twelve.*
If he had any further wishes concerning the Nobles, he would find the
Sienese ready and willing to carry them out. This influenced the Pope
to refrain from asking more, for fear that further insistence would
annoy the state and get him nothing but hatred. In regard to the Nobles,
however, he urged them to follow the course which the Cardinal of
Santa Susanna would lay before them. The magistrates withdrew with
many promises, exultant that they had shelved the cause of the Twelve
and had time to consider about the Nobles.

The Pope then carried out his intention of going to the baths. It was
the sweet season of early spring. All the hills about Siena were smiling
in their vesture of foliage and flowers, and luxuriant crops were growing up in the fields. The Sienese country immediately around the city
is indescribably lovely with its gently sloping hills planted with culti-

vated trees and vines or plowed for grain, overlooking delightful valleys green with pasture land or sown fields, and watered by never-failing streams. There are also thick forests planted by nature or man where birds sing most sweetly and on every hill the citizens of Siena have built splendid country seats. Here are noble monasteries where holy men live; there private palaces built like fortresses. Through this region the Pope traveled in a happy mood nor did he find the baths less pleasant. They lie ten miles from the city in a valley two or three stades wide and quite eight miles long. It is watered by the Mersa River, a tributary of the Ombrone. This never dries up and is full of eels which, though small, are very white and sweet. The valley at its entrance is highly cultivated and thickly dotted with castles and villas; near the baths where it ends, it is wilder. It is closed by a substantial stone bridge and by dark wooded cliffs. The mountains which ring the valley on the right are almost all covered with the evergreen ilex; those on the left with the acorn-bearing oak and the cork tree. Around the baths are simple houses used as inns. Here the Pope passed a month and though he bathed twice every day, he never omitted the signatura or other state business. About the twenty-second hour he was accustomed to go into the meadows and, sitting on the riverbank where it was greenest and grassiest, he heard embassies and petitioners. Every day the wives of the peasants brought flowers and strewed the path by which the Pope went to the baths; and the only reward they expected was permission to kiss his feet.

As a mark of favor to his fellow citizens the Pope had granted plenary indulgence to all who visited the cathedral of Siena on the day of Pentecost. Though his cure was not complete, he returned to Siena to inaugurate the feast and was present at the ceremonies, which were thronged by a great multitude from Tuscany, Liguria, Gaul, Umbria, and Picenum. As a result of this exertion he grew worse and was obliged to stay at Siena longer than he had intended. Finally he left the city late one night and went back to Macereto. After a few days there he went on to the baths at Petriolo, which are believed to contain more sulphur and to be more efficacious. This place is five miles from Macereto on the road to Grosseto and the sea in a deep valley made by the Farma River. It is famous for its trout. All around it rise lofty mountains, rocky but wooded and grassy too. Around the baths are houses, few in number but able to accommodate many guests. These the Sienese within our fathers' memory surrounded with a wall, that brigands might not lie in wait for the bathers as had sometimes happened in the past. Here for twenty days the Pope had the warm waters poured through a pipe onto the crown of his head; for the physicians said this would be beneficial, since his brain was too moist.[7]

While this was going on, Ferrante, King of Sicily, encouraged by the arrival of Simonetto and other captains of the Church, took the field and offered battle to the enemy. When they refused, he assumed the offensive and drove them from their position, never halting till all were routed and penned up in the town of Sarno. This is about thirty miles from Naples. Part of it lies on a high hill and part in the plain below. Its defense is not so much in its walls as in its water. From the base of the mountain crystal springs gush out to form the Sarno River mentioned above, which is so icy that it kills grass and trees and no fish but crabs can live in it. In this town King René's son Jean, the Prince of Taranto, all the nobles of their party, and all the infantry and cavalry had taken refuge after their rout, since they had been unable to withstand King Ferrante's charge. There was no doubt that in a short time hunger would force them to surrender or to disperse and leave the field to the enemy, for penned up as they were, they could bring in no supplies and they had already begun to consider the best route for flight.

Nothing contributed to their escape so much as the rashness of Ferrante, who was made overbold not only by his own temperament but by necessity. His soldiers excelled the enemy in bravery rather than in strength. But they were ugly and dissatisfied, demanded their pay, and made threats if the money were not forthcoming. The King had nothing to give them and already two hundred foreign mercenaries, called musketeers (scoppeterii), had deserted to the enemy because they were not paid. Ferrante feared that if any more deserted, he should have to raise the siege and without money he could not make the soldiers do anything. In these straits he thought it advisable to make a sudden assault on the city in the hope of storming it and satisfying his army from the spoils of the enemy. When this plan was discussed in council, the majority agreed, but Simonetto was against it, because he thought that the enemy could not easily be dislodged from a fortified position and that they could be conquered by hunger better than by the sword. Nevertheless he advised attacking a certain tower near the town, for if they took this, it would be impossible for the enemy to get out to forage. Simonetto's motion prevailed, but when the tower was taken at the first assault, the maddened and victorious soldiers in their wild elation could

---

[7] It was assumed that the treatment would induce sweating and so dry up the affected area.

not be restrained. The rash troops disregarded the commands of their officers and entered the city gates on the heels of the fleeing enemy. There was a fierce battle within the walls in which many fell. The papal forces suffered most, being massacred by the fusiliers, who, as we have said, had deserted the King.

The musket (scoppetum) is a weapon invented in Germany in our time. It is of iron or copper as long as a man, as thick as the fist, almost entirely hollow. Powder made of charcoal from the fig or willow mixed with sulphur and niter is poured into it; then a small ball of lead the size of a filbert is inserted in the front end. The fire is applied through a small hole in the back part and this explodes the powder with such force that it shoots out the ball like lightning with a report like a clap of thunder. This report is popularly called a scoppium, hence the name of the scoppeterii. No armor can withstand the force of this engine and it penetrates wood also. Therefore the royal and papal forces, though they had entered the town and had taken some prisoners, were repulsed by the scoppeterii with a considerable number of killed and wounded and pursued by the enemy a long distance from the town. While Simonetto was charging the enemy and trying to rally his own men, he was struck by a bullet. He was thrown from his horse and died without speaking a word. Though he would have chosen a longer life, yet this was the end he desired, for he used often to say to his friends, "May God grant me to die in the exercise of my profession and the service of the Church!" His body was found by the enemy and given honorable burial attended by Prince Jean and all the nobles.

When the news of Ferrante's defeat at Sarno was received at Siena, the French, of whom there were many in the Curia, cheered, danced about the city, lighted bonfires, abused the Catalans, jeered at the Aragonese, insulted even the Pope's household, taunted the Lombards and Florentines, and struck with their fists or swords any who they thought did not sufficiently applaud their madness. They gouged out the eye of a Burgundian and killed a citizen of Siena who showed some slight disapproval of their clamor. The Pope endured all this calmly, saying to himself, *"How would they treat us in their country, should we come to them, when in our country they insult us so shamelessly? Behold, O Italian race! will you be able to endure as masters these men who are so insolent as servants? They are servants in the Roman Curia and they put on the countenance of a ruler.* What would they do if they should *some day secure the papacy* or come to rule Italy? *Woe to thee, Italy! if thou art forced to go under their yoke!* I will help thee, with all my might that thou mayst not have to endure such cruel masters, although neither Venetians nor Florentines give any aid and their people, while they are trying to subdue thee and care not to agree among themselves, are preparing the way for foreign sovereignty over thee."

Meantime another calamity occurred. Misfortunes rarely come singly. At Rome (Fig. 17) the brothers Tiburzio and Valeriano disturbed the peace of the city in many ways. *Their mother was a sister of Stefano Porcari whom Nicholas V had arrested for treason and hanged in Hadrian's tomb. His father had been executed on the Capitol for the same crime and many others of their kinsmen had perished in the same way. These two were no better than their forebears.* When they saw that in the Pope's absence the city was governed less strictly and that the magistrates had not the courage to punish crimes, they thought it was an opportunity to corrupt the youth of Rome and finally to destroy the power of the papacy by causing a revolution. They had as their accomplices a very bold and energetic youth named Bonanno, Giovanni Filippo, who was versed in all manner of wickedness, and a number of others notorious for their crimes. Conspiring with these men they at first ventured on insignificant pilfering of *hens and* cheap trifles; then they proceeded to rape and to the theft of precious objects; and finally did not refrain from abducting girls or from murder and arson. The magistrates were unable to control them by armed force, since they were about 300 wild youths, all experienced fighters ready to come to one another's help on the instant. Citizens did not dare lift their hands against the sons of citizens. All waited to see what the governor, what the Senator would do, and both of them stayed at home panic-stricken.

The governor, since his own splendid house, built on the site of Pompey's Theater, was in the Campo dei Fiori where he could hear the threats of the conspirators daily, moved to the apostolic palace. At that, the conspirators, thinking themselves victorious, became even more insolent. They rioted more wildly through the city, flogged and plundered the citizens, robbed the poor of their substance, outraged women, and strangled or drowned in the Tiber girls who resisted assault. They would have preferred to attack the houses of the nobles, but feared to call down upon themselves the might of the city. They were content therefore to take advantage of the forbearance and indifference of the rich in order to rob the poor of their meager possessions and satisfy their lust on their women until increased numbers and greater strength should enable them to fall upon the fortunes of the wealthy also.

There was one of their number whom they had nicknamed Ina-

morato because of his passion. He was desperately in love with a Tras-
teverine girl who was promised to another and she, it was said, returned
his love. On the very day of the wedding, as she was going to her
bridegroom, Inamorato carried her off in the open street. This outrage
was more than the magistrates, who are called ward captains (capita
regionum), could endure. By a surprise attack they captured Inamorato
and handed him over in bonds to the Senator to deal with him officially.
When the conspirators learned of this, they were afraid that the culprit
would be punished and therefore, scattering armed through the city,
they seized and carried off a member of the Senator's household named
Caro. The citizens, roused by this unprecedented act, went in a body to
the governor. They urged him to pluck up courage and employ armed
force. They offered their assistance and declared that it would be an easy
matter to round up the conspirators if the governor and the Senator
would only be bold and follow the advice of the citizens. The conspirators, in terror of an armed populace, took refuge in the temple which
M. Agrippa dedicated to all the gods, or, to put it better, all the demons.
The ancients called it the Pantheon; now it is consecrated to the Blessed
Virgin and takes its name from her. The magistrates did not dare risk
fighting citizens with citizens for fear that if the people were armed,
the state would throw off the yoke of the priests and assert its freedom.

The conspirators remained some days in the temple, supplied with
food by the citizens who lived near and feared that otherwise they might
be attacked in the night. At last they were persuaded to leave the temple
on condition that they should surrender Caro in return for Inamorato.
But not even this restored peace to the state. A few days later Bonanno,
one of the conspirators, was walking armed in the city when he fell in
with the members of the Senator's household. He was ordered to lay
down his arms and his refusal was followed by a scrimmage in which
he killed one of the marshals and triumphantly routed and dispersed all
the Senator's party.

After this the youths roved fearlessly through the city with or without weapons and there was no crime they did not commit with impunity. When Antonio, the Pope's nephew, heard that they had seized a
tower on the outskirts of the city not far from San Lorenzo in Lucina,
he at once went with a company of horse from the Vatican to the Ponte
Molle and entering the city by the Porta del Popolo, hastened to the
tower to capture the conspirators there. But when they learned of his
approach, they abandoned the tower and made for the heart of the city,
where they entrenched themselves in the magnificent palace built by

Cardinal Fermo. It was not Antonio's intention to take foreign horsemen into the crowded quarters of the city, since he was not yet certain
of the temper of the people, who would not be likely to do violence to
their own kinsmen, and the governor did not think it for the good of
the state to employ some citizens to capture others. The conspirators,
meeting in the palace of the Cardinal as in a town hall, laid their plans
for robbery and outrage and banqueted together, giving up the days to
brigandage and the nights to revelry. Tiburzio was regarded as their
lord and master and everything hung on his decision. When anyone
asked how Lord Tiburzio did, they would answer, "Tiburzio does thus
and so."

The good citizens were ashamed that things had come to such a pass
that the city seemed to be in Tiburzio's power and they were eager to
wipe out such disgrace by arms. When this proved impossible because
of the governor's cowardice, the nobles went in a body to Tiburzio and
urged him to leave the city and not make his native place a den of robbers. If he persisted in rioting about the city, the nobles would not
continue to tolerate it; it would be a simple matter to raise a troop of
soldiers who would throw these headstrong lads into prison; the youths,
who would be easily routed for lack of any fixed plan, would afford
them little protection; if the Senate once took up arms, it would not
rest till it had destroyed all the conspirators and completely freed the
state from such wretched slavery; the Pope, though he was now absent,
would soon return and would pardon neither Tiburzio nor his accomplices if he found them pillaging the city; they had better submit to
their fellow citizens and go now; in that case it might be possible that
at the request of the state the Pope would finally forgive them.

Persuaded by these arguments, Tiburzio decided to withdraw and,
leaving the palace, proceeded through the city to the gate like some
great prince escorted on either side by the conservators and the apostolic
notary, Giorgio Cesarini, and followed by a great crowd which had assembled to see him as if he were some captain of a mighty host.
Tiburzio, in high spirits, after saluting the citizens at the gate, withdrew
with his fellow conspirators to the towns of the Savelli, never doubting
that he could return when he would.

Meantime nine of the conspirators had committed a horrible crime.
Going by night to the monastery of Sant' Agnese outside the Porta
Salaria, they forced the bars of the gates, burst into the cells and closets
of the nuns, and not only assaulted them but plundered the belongings
of their victims and carried off the holy vessels. When the Pope heard of

this and realized that there was no way to save the city except to return to his See, he at once announced that within twenty days he would set out for Rome and directed the members of the Curia to assemble there during that time. When this news reached Rome there was as much rejoicing as if some great victory had been reported or as if they thought the city was being founded and built for the first time. There was a solemn procession through the streets, bonfires were lighted, prayers were offered in all the churches for the Pope's safe and swift return.

After settling affairs at Siena the Pope left the city on September 10, the day that had been set for his departure. The whole city wept nor could the members of the Curia keep back their tears on leaving that delightful spot and that charming people. The Pope, though he was grieved to the heart to leave his beloved birthplace not knowing whether he should ever return, nevertheless restrained his tears and did not weaken even when he was met by his weeping sisters. The magistrates of the city escorted him outside the walls as far as the monastery of the Angeli. There, when he had blessed the citizens and was asked if he had any commands, he said, "My sons, I bid you live in harmony, which alone can preserve a state. Lay aside the enmities that are consuming your hearts. Have done with dissensions, factions, cabals. Consult together for the common good. Love justice and hate iniquity. Oppress no one. Protect widows and orphans. Honor priests. Do not violate the immunity of churches. Punish the wicked. Retain such laws as are good and just; repeal the rest. Find brides for your young men. Exclude the unmarried and the weak from office. Set a limit to dowries and expenditures. Keep an account of your exports and imports; a state is badly off that buys more than it sells. These timely precepts I leave *with you* now. If you observe them, they will not prove unserviceable." With these words he set out on his journey.

The next day he came to Corsignano where he fell seriously ill, moisture spreading downward from his head and so weakening his chest, arms, and entire body that he could not stir without assistance and seemed on the point of death. The illness lasted twelve days. When he was restored to health, he was highly delighted to see rising in his native place buildings which seemed likely to equal any in Italy. Here the Pope was waited on by Roberto of the Counts of San Severino, a distinguished captain whom Francesco, Duke of Milan, was sending into the Kingdom with a large force to help Ferrante prevent the enemy from following up their victory at the Sarno. On the news of the Pope's illness Piccinino, who was in the Abruzzi, was summoned by some of the nobles and leaving his baggage behind, marched rapidly with his entire army over the rough mountains to the contado of Albi with the intention of making a swift descent on Roman territory.

The Pope also cut short his stay at Corsignano and went on to Radicofani. Then he crossed by way of Abbatia and the town of Piano to the boundaries of the Church, which are about midway between Proceno and Piano. There in a green meadow near a never-failing stream the people of Proceno had made shelters of brushwood in which they received their lord on his return from abroad with loud cheers and great rejoicing and prepared a meal for him. After this he went on to Proceno, once a famous and almost impregnable town surrounded by lofty cliffs. It has often fallen into the hands of brigands, often changed masters, and has suffered many calamities, sometimes sacked, sometimes burned. Under Eugenius IV after being held for a time by Francesco Sforza's garrison it returned to the Church. Now under Pope Pius it is reviving and increasing in wealth and population. After giving it his blessing the Pope went on to Acquapendente, a place as large as a city, which the Sienese Antonio Petrucci, who was governing it for Francesco, sold back to Eugenius, from whom it had been taken by force of arms. Pius spent the night there and the next day came to Bolsena, one of the twelve cities of Etruria and renowned in antiquity. Even within the memory of our fathers it was a large and populous town. It was destroyed by the English [8] and today is but an insignificant fortress. Only the richness of the soil, the convenience of the lake nearby, and its position on the road to Rome save it from complete annihilation. The nobles of the ancient family of Cervari of Orvieto were long masters here but under Pope Nicholas V they were deposed by the rebellious townspeople and the place returned to the Church. Long afterward under Calixtus III civil strife broke out with bloodshed on both sides.

Pius stayed at Bolsena one day and reconciled their differences. Then he set out for Orvieto, where there arose a dangerous quarrel over boundaries, since both the people of Orvieto and those of Bolsena wished to carry the Pope while he was in their territory and the boundary line is uncertain. They fought with fists and swords and a number on both sides were wounded. At last the fighting was with difficulty stopped by the arrival of the Pope's cavalry, who attacked both parties with arrows and lances. When the Pope was approaching the city and came in sight of the walls, he was met by ambassadors who said, "In

[8] This incident may well belong to the period of John Hawkwood's activities with English mercenaries during the latter half of the 14th century.

this spot a pope of Rome, when he had been driven from our city, once cursed our people. Since that day we have been torn by civil strife and have had no respite. Our city, which once envied none in Tuscany, is now pitied by all men. This is divine vengeance. We are feeling the effects of the apostolic curse. Bless the state; lift the ban. With your blessing the divine favor will return." The Pope consented and having made the sign of the Cross over the city, he entered it amid great rejoicing of the people.

A rocky mountain about six stades high rises in the middle of the valley. On its summit is a plateau three miles in circumference. Precipitous cliffs nowhere less than twenty ells high take the place of walls. Here were once splendid private houses and great palaces built of hewn stone. Age has destroyed much, civil strife has burned and ravaged more. Half-ruined towers and crumbling churches are still to be seen, but the church of the Blessed Virgin, which is inferior to no church in Italy, stands intact in the middle of the city. It is remarkable for size, material, workmanship, and design. The walls and floor are of varicolored marble; the façade is very high and wide and filled with statues by the best sculptors, chiefly Sienese, who are not inferior to Phidias and Praxiteles. The faces stand out from the white marble as if alive and the bodies of men and beasts are so well rendered that art seems to have equaled nature. Only speech is lacking to make them live. You may see the Resurrection of the dead, the Last Judgment of our Savior, the punishment of the damned, and the rewards of the elect as vividly as if they were taking place before your eyes.

When Pius had left Orvieto and come into the territory of Bagnarea, he again found himself in danger the moment he reached the boundary. His chair was surrounded by an excited mob of the people of Orvieto and Reggio; for these cities were involved in a dispute about their boundaries and had no intention of letting Pius be carried in their territory by any but their own people. They fought with weapons or without and finally some were wounded with arrows and some with swords. The Pope's bodyguard put an end to the fight and seizing the Pope's chair carried it and him well beyond the place in dispute. There the men of Reggio with their women and children came running out, offered him presents, and refreshed all his retinue with food and drink.

Next the Pope came to Montefiascone, which some assert was the city of the Faliscans, an error which Leonardo Aretino is said to have held. The city lies on a high mountain above the lake of Bolsena and looks toward Monte Cimino on the east. Here the French, when the popes were of that nation, built a splendid palace for a summer residence, for they find the heat of Italy very trying. The palace was built like a fortress with halls, dining rooms, and chambers such as befitted the dignity of the Pope, but now most of it is in ruins owing to age and neglect. Pius was lodged here, but not being able to bear the violence of the winds (for it is a regular palace of Aeolus), he went the next day over open country to Viturvium, which nowadays we call Viterbo and take to mean "vita inermium," i.e., "life of the unarmed," on the theory that under the Roman empire veteran soldiers used to retire to pass their old age near the warm springs which bubble up there in profusion. The Pope was met on the way by the Roman ambassadors who came to implore him to return to the capital. They were four eloquent speakers, of whom two, Antonio Caffarelli and Andrea of Santa Croce, were jurisconsults and advocates of the Sacred Consistory, and the other two prominent members of the Roman nobility. They were accompanied by a band of handsome youths magnificently dressed and mounted on splendidly caparisoned horses.

In this city the Pope gave audience to the Roman envoys in the presence of the sacred college. Since they were almost equally eloquent they spoke individually, that it might not appear that one was superior to another. They described the grief of Rome at Pius's absence, the many troubles that had arisen, the reluctance with which the Romans had seen him depart, their resentment at his stay in the houses of strangers, the joy with which they now looked forward to his return. The very walls of the houses, the very walls of the city, were exulting at the report that Pius was coming back. They applauded the Pope's acts at the Congress of Mantua; his speeches, arguments, plans, and replies. They commended to him the city, which was the capital of the world, and its citizens; they begged him not to remember the sins which the youth had committed. The state would lead a better life and be at peace as soon as their father Pius returned to his sons.

To this the Pope answered, "With tears and bitter grief on both sides we left the city which is our country no less than is Siena; for the house of Piccolomini which bore us migrated of old to Siena from Rome as the names Enea and Silvio, so common in our family, show. It was therefore most grievous to us to leave a city that had deserved so well of us and our heart already foreboded the troubles that later arose among you. But pondering on the necessity of the Church and of the Catholic Faith, which the Turks are bent on trampling underfoot, and reflecting that the only salvation for Christianity lay in our meeting with the princes and undertaking to defend religion with our united power and wisdom, we set out, reluctant and willing at the same time. Reluctantly we were leaving our beloved spouse, willingly we were striving to succor our most loving mother.

"If we have not succeeded as we hoped, nevertheless we do not regret our purpose and our toil. The whole world understands that strength, not courage has failed us. Now no one can accuse us of leaving the true Faith to perish while we lived in luxury at Rome, seeing that, though weighed down with age and infirmity, we have not shrunk from cold or rain or snow, have made a long journey, lodged among strangers, summoned princes, admonished peoples, waited patiently, done everything in our power, that we might consult together for the common good. Very few came; fewer still put religion before pleasure. And what blame can now be imputed to us?

"Our soul is vexed by that which we hear has happened among you. We are grieved indeed that robberies, murders, adultery, acts of sacrilege in such numbers (so we are told) have been committed by your young men. We do not accuse you, who were ready to punish these crimes if only our magistrates had been alert; rather we accuse those who through cowardice and sloth allowed the youth to riot so wantonly. We commend your loyalty, who in the face of so many temptations have not failed in your duty. You are truly wise and upright men who serve your master faithfully, though indeed your servitude is sovereignty.

"What state can be found more free than Rome? You pay no taxes; no burdens are imposed upon you; you hold most honorable offices in the city; you sell your wine and grain at your own prices; your houses bring you in high rents. And furthermore, who is your master? A count perhaps? Or a marquis, duke, king, emperor? A greater than all these is he whom you obey, the Bishop of Rome, the Vicar of Jesus Christ, whose feet all men desire to kiss. Truly is he called King of Kings and Lord of Lords in reverence for Christ whose representative he is on earth. You are indeed wise, men of Rome, to obey, honor, and revere this lord of yours. For it is he who gives you fame and riches, who brings to you the wealth of all the world; and the Roman Curia, which you maintain, itself maintains you and brings you gold from every land. We rejoice that you know and guard your good fortune. We rejoice that a joyful city awaits us, since with joy we ourselves are hastening thither. We shall decide on the day of departure with the advice of our brethren and as soon as it is fixed, you shall know."

The envoys enthusiastically applauded the Pope's answer and communicated it to the conservators of the city. The Roman people were wild with delight at the thought that the Curia would be with them any moment.

Pius [9] replied to this, "You all urge us to stay here, but we think we ought to go. Unless we enter Rome before Piccinino, our kingdom is vanquished and we do not know whether Rome can be regained in our day. Eugenius lost it and for nine years he wandered about from one strange lodging to another. And what glory is left the Pope if Rome is lost? *His letters seem to have no weight unless they are dated from St. Peter's at Rome.* You say that Piccinino holds the surrounding country. That is true. You say that Everso is in arms on both sides of the Tiber. We admit it. But he will not be able to prevent our crossing. We will avoid his territory and shall not have to fear his ambush. Our escort will be larger than his army. You say that our soldiers, even if they succeed in crossing the Tiber unseen, will find themselves face to face with Piccinino. If we consider and are afraid of every danger which may conceivably happen, what in heaven's name shall we dare to do? This very moment the roof may fall and crush us. Wherever you turn there are always hazards. No great and memorable deed is done without risk. We may be shut up in the city as you say; we may be captured; we may be killed. We do not deny it. But what more honorable place for a pope to die than Rome? What tomb more fitting than the Vatican? As for us, we have faith that God will aid the righteous cause. But if by some inscrutable divine judgment it is decreed that we fall into the enemy's hands or die by an impious sword, we do not shrink. To die for Rome and in Rome, to meet death for the patrimony of St. Peter is glorious; to flee from it is pitiful. Go therefore and tell the cardinals that we shall at once set out for our city."

When they heard this, the entire Curia was in an uproar, some carried away by joy, others by fear. The Pope set out about the twentieth hour, going through the middle of the city, though some thought that he ought to take a secret path outside the walls.

By evening they had arrived at Canapina, where they spent the night. This palace is near the foot of Monte Cimino on its eastern side, but it is in a dark and very deep valley so that it gets little sun. A stream running down the mountain washes the walls of the town. The hills are thickly covered with chestnut trees which in summer make the place even darker. There is hardly any other tree except walnuts and a few

[9] Having been advised not to go to Rome because of the danger threatening the city from Piccinino.

apples. The people have built huts of wood and live packed into them like bees in hives. Even the smallest holds several families. This promiscuous living tends to multiply the race. The thick smoke inside dries up noxious moisture. The Pope was put in a small chamber just large enough for a bed and, to avoid smoke, had no fire.

The Pope lunched at Nepi and left immediately after. The wife of Napoleone Orsini had prepared one of her "puzzling dinners" [10] for him in Campagnano, but he went on to Formello where he found no preparations at all, no food or drink or bed. They had to go to the peasants for bread and onions to satisfy their hunger and they quenched their thirst with wine just pressed which was not so good as water. *The Cardinal of Avignon, who could not endure any inconvenience, went to Campagnano, where he was received with honor in the Pope's place and devoured the Pope's dinner. Pius avoiding the Colonnas and the Orsini as enemies, went to the Savelli. Formello is fourteen miles from Rome. It is a place belonging to the Orsini, not very well fortified, though its citadel is not to be despised.*

The next day before dawn the Pope left for Rome and because their dinner the night before had been somewhat meager, he ordered lunch to be prepared on the way beside a clear stream of living water which gushes from an ancient grotto under a shady grove in a secluded valley. While he was lunching here, the governor and the senator of Rome and many nobles came joyfully to meet him, as did the Cardinal of Sant' Anastasia and his brother, the physician Simone. They all shared the Pope's meal and after it resumed their journey. The fields were full of people coming to meet and greet the Pope. The conservators with the chief citizens met him at about the sixth milestone with young men on foot to carry the Pope's litter. Most of them were youths who had been eager for a revolution, accomplices of the mad Tiburzio, and therefore the Pope's friends urged him not to trust himself to these young miscreants but to be carried rather by his own bodyguard. The Pope laughed at their advice and bidding the Romans approach and take up his chair, he said, "Thou shalt tread on the adder and the basilisk; the lion and the dragon thou shalt trample under foot. This prophecy has often been fulfilled before now and shall be fulfilled today. For what beast is more savage than man? What animal does worse harm than man? But man is a changeable animal and the fiercest hearts often grow gentle. These youths were ready, if they had been able, to despoil us of

[10] Terence, *Phormio*, 342, *cena dubia*, i.e., a dinner where you are puzzled as to what dish to try first.

our city and our life. They were not able. They have realized their error. Now grown gentle they will carry on their shoulders him whom they wished to trample under foot."

Pius was not mistaken. The youths took up his chair with the greatest eagerness and joyfully carried their lord to the Porta Flaminia, now called the Porta del Popolo. He passed the night in the monastery dedicated to the Blessed Virgin adjoining the gate within the walls. They say Nero was murdered here *and this was considered a good omen because* with the help of the Holy Virgin *Pius too was going to kill his Neros.* The next day, October 7, the Pope made a kind of triumphal progress through the city to St. Peter's amid extraordinary acclamation from the populace. Houses all along his way were decorated, the squares were covered with carpets, and all the streets were strewn with flowers and grass. Inside the church the pallium which the Pope had been wearing over his head was torn to shreds *and in the struggle to seize it many were injured.* The Pope knelt at the high altar and weeping did reverence to the relics of the holy apostles. Then he withdrew to the palace and his own chamber. At nightfall all the populace on horseback and carrying torches thronged to the papal palace and winding about in procession before the door, with loud shouts and great rejoicing they wished the Pope long life and happiness.

BOOK V

BOOK V

MEANWHILE a certain Roman went to the Pope and told him that Bonanno, the boldest of the youthful conspirators, who after being explicitly condemned had chosen voluntary exile, had returned to Rome and might be taken prisoner. He specified the place where Bonanno could be found, adding that he was in hiding at his brother's house and had returned to the city for love of his mistress. The Pope put the matter in the hands of Niccolò Soldano. Men were sent to take this brigand, but they misguidedly attacked the house with a great din and neglected to guard the rear. Bonanno, who knew he was being hunted, when he heard the noise escaped half naked by leaping from a back window jeering at Soldano as he fled. Then for some days he lay hid with friends. The informer returned to Soldano and again said that if he would listen to him, Bonanno could be taken and with him Tiburzio's brother Valeriano, a young man of desperate boldness, and some five others of the conspirators who were planning to escape the next day at dawn by the Porta Appia which leads to San Sebastiano. *Cavalry and infantry must be sent by night into the theatre near the catacombs of Calixtus; he himself would accompany the conspirators and give the signal for bursting out of ambush.*

Soldano reported this to the Senator and both went to the Pope and explained the scheme. The Pope did not approve the plan. He said the theatre was two miles from the city and there was danger of treachery. Deifobo's and Silvestro's soldiers might be there and he who had promised to betray the traitors might betray the Senator's troops. They must however take measures to meet the situation. It would be safer to set a trap in the city by stationing a guard at the gate and soldiers could be posted in ambush at San Sisto to fall upon the conspirators as they went by. They would flee toward the gate, since there was no other way of escape, and being hemmed in on both sides by the hedges and walls of vineyards, these wicked youths would be caught as in a blind alley.

This scheme was approved, but the conspirators did not attempt to go out and they had their work for nothing. The same man came back yet again and explained the reasons for the delay; but he said that the next day the youths would surely go, this time by the Porta San Paolo; they must set an ambush near the triumphal arch of Constantine, from which the road is enclosed as far as San Gregorio; soldiers must be posted in the Colosseum and in the street leading to Santi Giovanni and Paolo. His advice was taken and before dawn all the preparations had been made.

Just after sunrise Bonanno with his companions and the Roman informer came to the Colosseum and while he was hesitating which road to take, the informer said, "What are you waiting for? This is our safest road"—and pointing to the arch of Constantine himself rode through it followed by his companions. At once soldiers burst out of the Colosseum and gave the signal for the rest to make haste. (Fig. 13) They fell upon the conspirators who, attacked both in front and rear and not knowing where to turn, trusted to their own strength and with drawn swords joined battle. The informer began to cry out and lament, flinging himself on the ground and shouting, "What do you want of me? What have I done? Why do you set upon me as if I were a malefactor? If I am guilty, kill me. If I have committed no crime, why do you rob me of my property? Give back an innocent man's goods, I implore you do not carry off my poor little bags!" (He had filled small bags called "bolge" with flints and had carefully closed and sealed them to make the conspirators think that he was carrying his money out of the city never to return and therefore he kept screaming for help at the top of his lungs like a woman.)

But Bonanno, when he saw he was surrounded, put all his trust in his own prowess. Courageously brandishing his sword and wheeling his horse hither and thither he wounded one adversary after another and for a long time withstood their attack. When he was finally unhorsed by a lance thrust, though dashed to the ground he would not surrender or own himself beaten. He was captured by a fierce onset of the soldiers, bound flat on his horse's back like a corpse, and taken to the Capitol. His splendid courage availed him nothing, but it did advantage Valeriano, who escaped unrecognized among the maddened soldiers while the battle was raging around Bonanno. The other conspirators also escaped. Two innocent men were captured and soon released. The informer, who was also taken prisoner, was held for some time on the charge of being a malefactor and traitor and was guarded up to the last as closely as if he were still under suspicion and were to be put to the torture. However at the request of a number of citizens who went surety for him he was finally released.

Bonanno, though there was no doubt about his crimes, his adultery, thefts, and murders, was nevertheless put to the torture and kept some time in prison in the hope that this might put an end to the traitorous designs of the conspirators. When this was known at Palombara, Tiburzio, supposing that his brother Valeriano had been taken with Bonanno, summoned the conspirators and decided to return to Rome in order to sound his friends as to the possibility of bringing about a revolution and thus freeing all captives. If this scheme were not successful, he planned to seize some citizen of Siena for whom the captives might be exchanged.

When Savello was asked to send Tiburzio infantry to help start a revolution in the city, he said he could not spare it *and that the city could not be taken with a small force.* Deifobo and Antonello held out the hope that if they should learn that a revolution was actually taking place in the city, they would immediately be at the gates with troops. Tiburzio was joined ill-advisedly by some fourteen of the conspirators, who thought the city was open to them as before and that the youth of Rome favored their designs, since the Pope's army was far off and the Capitol had only a small garrison. They entered the city near the baths of Diocletian where part of the wall had collapsed and when they reached the thickly built quarters, they called on all the citizens they met to take arms. They declared that the time had come to free the city from the *foul* yoke of the priests and that Deifobo and Silvestro were at hand with a large force to help the Romans if they would assert their liberty. Only let the citizens awake at last, let them dare to strike a blow for freedom and no longer endure to seem less valiant than their ancestors *to whom death was not so hard as servitude.* When no one responded and the conspirators saw that the people were orderly and quiet, they gave up hope of taking the city and proceeded to carry out their second plan.

After traversing a large part of the city, they came about an hour after noon to the church of Sant' Eustachio, near which are the buildings where goods are deposited and duty levied. Here they seized the young Sienese who was sitting at the receipt of customs and ordered him to go with them, threatening with drawn swords to kill him if he did not make haste. The youth dazed with terror obeyed and they had got as far as the Palazzo Colonna when the cry was raised all over the

city that Tiburzio had entered with the conspirators; that he was armed
and rushing about in every direction; that he had many supporters, was
looting houses and taking prisoners; and that the power of the priests
was seriously threatened. A mob gathered at the papal palace demanding counsel and help.

The Pope *had just risen from his noonday nap and* on hearing the
uproar asked what all the commotion meant. He was told that the
citizens were in arms, the conspirators had entered the city and seized a
young Sienese, everything was in confusion and everyone in terror for
his own safety. Pius replied, "Nonsense! There is no danger. We know
the temper of the citizens. The Romans desire the Pope, not brigands,
for their lord. Tiburzio is captured unless he saves himself by flight or
hiding. He has woven a rope for himself. The prey has now fallen into
the snare. This day will be the doom of the conspirators." With these
words he ordered the Cardinals of St. Peter and Santa Sabina to mount
their horses and urge the citizens to take arms against the scoundrels.
Those who first laid hands upon them should be rewarded.

Already however Alessandro Piccolomini,[1] the Senator of the city,
the Vice-Chamberlain, and many others had armed and put themselves
at the head of the troops from the Capitol. They were joined by a number of citizens, friends of peace and of the papacy. The most fiery of
them seemed to be Rustico, the brother of Agapito and Marcello, but
all charged fiercely on the conspirators, who when they saw no other
hope, abandoned the youth whom they had seized and took to flight,
leaving the city at the point where they had entered it. There outside its
walls they fell in with a Lombard horseman, who had galloped down
from the Capitol far ahead of the others, and brutally murdered him.
Giovanni Filippo, a spirited youth notorious for many murders,
mounted the Lombard's horse, which carried him to safety and with
him another of the conspirators no better than he. The rest, when they
saw flight was impossible (for a large force under Alessandro was at
hand), scattered into hiding places to wait the advantage night would
bring them. In a valley nearby were thick beds of reeds mixed with
brambles and taller plants, where they thought they could hide, but
Alessandro, knowing which way they had gone, let loose the dogs and
sending all the foot soldiers after them searched every possible hiding
place. They found Tiburzio's hand ballista, which he had thrown away
in his exhaustion, and this showed he could not be far off. After a long

[1] Alessandro Miraballi-Piccolomini, an old friend of Pius from Naples, one of several
favorites upon whom the name of Piccolomini had been conferred.

search they found and captured him and nearby they came on five others with their heads buried in the grass like pheasants and dragged them out by the heels. The rest were saved by the approach of night and by the elation of the searchers, which made them less thorough after they had found Tiburzio, since their object seemed to be attained with the capture of the man who was considered the leader and head of the conspirators.

The glory of this achievement went mainly to three men: Alessandro, who was the first to mount and never stopped following the fugitives till they were taken prisoners, heartening his men into courage by his own presence and by promises, with a daring that sometimes seemed excessive; the Senator, who dashed up fully armed and did the work of a brave soldier; and Tommaso Piccolomini. Tommaso had been ordered by the Pope to be present as an observer, but finding not only the citizens but the members of the Curia hesitating at the gate and refusing to go to the help of the soldiers (for they feared an ambush), he courageously forced them to make a sally. Later he was responsible for having the captives led through the city to the Capitol, though the others thought they ought to be hurried outside the walls to the Ponte Molle and then to Hadrian's Tomb for fear the populace should set them free. The following day the Romans thanked Tommaso in the presence of the Pope for having had so good an opinion of the Roman people.

When the conspirators were dragged through the streets with their hands bound behind their backs, some of the citizens contemptuously and derisively hailed Tiburzio as their lord, others as their king; some called him Tribune of the Roman People, some the champion of ancient liberty and bringer of peace. He made no answer but walked in silence with his eyes cast down. The joy not only of the citizens but of the Curia on that day was incredible: "For the first time now the city is safe." "Now our women can be chaste." "Now our property will be our own." "Now we can sleep soundly." "Blessed be Pius who has freed us from such danger!" Men and women, boys and girls shouted, cheered and embraced the members of the palace, congratulated the Church, declaring that now the city was truly the Pope's. The conservators with the foremost citizens went to Pius and begged him to punish the captives, since it was a case of their safety or that of the city. The Pope commended the conduct of those who had obeyed the Senator and Alessandro. As to the culprits, he said the law must take its course.

When Tiburzio was put to the torture, before revealing his schemes

and the names of his accomplices in crime, he begged that his body
should not be mangled. He knew he must die but he entreated that it
might be as quickly as possible, so that one who had deservedly lost his
body should not lose his soul also in torment. When one of the by-
standers taunted him with folly, he replied, "Well said! *The Fates
would never have brought me to this if I had been wise.*" When he was
asked what hope had led him to conspire against the Church, he said
that he had been convinced by those who were considered prophets
that the papal power would fall that year. Finally when he was bidden
to confess everything he had done and planned, he said that seeing the
Romans were disaffected in the absence of the Pope he had thought
that since he had influence with many of the young men he could free
his country from the ecclesiastical yoke *and avenge his father and uncle
whom Pope Nicholas had put to death when they asserted their liberty.*

Tiburzio said the letter [2] *had procured him an interview with Jean
and that at the advice of the Prince of Taranto he had been ordered to
go to Jacopo Piccinino and had said to him, "Jacopo, from what I hear,
you are in league with the Savelli and the Colonnas and Count Everso;
you have promised them aid in order to exterminate the Orsini. If you
do this, the contado of Albi and Taglicozzo is to be yours.* These are
mountainous districts which cannot possibly feed your soldiers unless
they eat stones. I offer you a far richer prize. If you will listen to me,
I promise you Rome, the mother of cities, the capital of the world. I am
a Roman citizen *of no mean birth.* All the youth of Rome follow me;
five hundred bold and energetic young men have sworn allegiance to
me; the citizens are ashamed and sick of the papal power. If you give
me your word to lead an army into the Roman territory at once, I will
go ahead and when I have encouraged the conspirators, who desire
nothing so much as a revolution, I will open the gates to you. The
members of the Curia and the merchants will afford us rich booty. The
Patriarch is there and his fortune will provide for your soldiers for a
year. There will also be some wealthy citizens whose possessions you
may plunder, since they are on the side of the Church." He said that
Piccinino had listened to him eagerly, had commended his courage and
his purpose, and promised all he asked, but he had been intercepted by
the Church's captains and prevented from entering Roman territory on
the appointed day. Meantime Bonanno had been captured and with
him, it was said, Valeriano. He had wished to help his brother and his
friends and therefore misguidedly entered Rome.

[2] Procured from Everso of Anguillara.

Such was Tiburzio's confession. Bonanno had before told the same story and the rest confirmed it. When Tiburzio was asked whether he had meant to kill the Pope, he answered that he had once planned to, if he could enter the palace, but he had given up hope of that possibility because the Pope could easily have taken refuge in the Castle of Sant' Angelo. (Fig. 12)

When the Senator had learned everything, he was planning to punish these frightful crimes with specially devised punishments. The Pope however restrained his severity, saying that death was sufficient punishment for even the worst crime. Therefore Bonanno (who had been kept till that day), Tiburzio, and six others ended their unhappy lives by hanging. *They were attended according to Christian custom by priests reminding them of the salvation of the soul and the mercy of the Pope, who during the execution of the sentence tearfully repeated psalms and poured out this prayer: "O Lord God, Thou hast freed Thy servant from the hands of his enemies. Thou hast given peace to the city and bruised the heads of the serpents. Blessed be Thy name forever and may all the people sing Thy praises. Thou hast honored me, O Lord, this day and made me secure on Thy throne. They who persecuted me have fallen into the pit. They now pay the penalty for their iniquity and are soon to depart from this light. They repent, I believe, of their impiety. Thou knowest their hearts and dost search their reins. O most merciful God, grant them forgiveness in their misery and open to them the bosom of Thy mercy. Grant them in this their last hour a brave spirit and true contrition for their sins. For I too, the unworthy Vicar of Thy blessed Son and the humble successor of St. Peter, by the authority which Thou hast divinely bestowed upon me and with the invisible keys which I bear in Thy name, grant to Tiburzio and those condemned with him, inasmuch as they are truly repentant and have confessed their sins, full absolution for all their crimes and I open to them the gates of Paradise. I pray that Thou, O gracious Lord, Father of Mercies and God of all comfort, ratify and accept this my concession."*

Such was the fate of Tiburzio, Bonanno, and the conspirators taken with them. Valeriano, Giovanni Filippo, and many others went into voluntary exile.

While the siege [3] was still going on, there was all sorts of talk in the city about the Pope's course of action. Many blamed him for going to war for Ferrante, and the French cardinals were sowing damaging rumors broadcast. Pius, in order to win over the people, summoned the

[3] Of Donadei.

cardinals, magistrates, and chief citizens and addressed them as follows: "We are exceedingly grateful to you, our citizens, because, while we were looking after the interests of the state abroad, you remained steadfast in your duty, though on one hand insolent youths were rioting in the streets and on the other the greed of the nobles was devastating the fields and stirring up revolution, and also because on our return you at length restored to us the city safe and sound.

"But we have not sent for you today to praise your merits. You have been summoned for another reason. There are some, we hear, who are filling your ears with pernicious and false rumors, who accuse us of loving war, saying that when we might have peace we prefer arms and are supporting an unjust cause in the Kingdom of Sicily; that as a result war has broken out at home and around our walls and you are punished for our guilt. Therefore we have thought it necessary to call you together and discuss frankly the grounds for this war; for thus you will see that we hate war and desire peace and quiet and that this war is not only righteous but was forced upon us. We shall not rehearse fancies and empty nonsense which are the delight and sustenance of our enemies. We shall put before you the plain and naked truth, whose countenance, if it could be seen, shines brighter than Lucifer or Hesperus and which is always victorious in the end. God alone knows the hearts of men.

"When some years ago the Sultan Mahomet seized the royal city of Constantinople and swollen with conquest threatened utter ruin not only to the Greeks but to the Hungarians, Italians, Teutons, and the other worshippers of Christ, Italy was aflame with fierce wars. Through the efforts of our predecessor, Pope Nicholas, the princes of Italy met and laid down their arms and furthermore, that it might be easier to march against the Turk, the enemy of religion, they not only made peace among themselves but entered into a compact providing that they should come to one another's aid if any of the parties to the compact should be injured.[4] The Pope was appointed head, protector, and director of the compact. Alfonso, King of Aragon and Sicily, was then alive, an illustrious prince powerful because of his resources and his wisdom. He was designated as head of the league next to the Pope, both in his own name and in that of his son and heir, Ferrante, who, though born out of wedlock, had been declared by Apostolic dispensation eligible to rule. Nicholas persuaded them to make this compact, his

---

[4] Peace of Lodi, 1454.

successor Calixtus approved it, and we on the advice of the brethren confirmed it.

"But when Alfonso died while Calixtus was still pope and his son demanded his kingdom, the Pope refused, asserting that the kingdom reverted to the Church, and he determined to back his claim by arms—whether rightly or not does not concern us here. His plans were interrupted by his sudden death, which occurred forty days after Alfonso's. On our accession we found the Church in confusion and assailed from all sides. Piccinino had been admitted by treachery to Assisi, Gualdo, and Nocera. The commandants of strongly fortified citadels belonging to the Church, who had been appointed by Calixtus's nephew Borgia, refused to restore them. Ferrante was demanding possession of his throne and threatening war if he did not obtain it. We had no soldiers; he had Piccinino in his service and the Duke of Milan was his friend. Realizing that a great crisis threatened the Church we laid the matter before the senate. All the cardinals, even the French, voted to invest Ferrante. Cardinal Latino Orsini was sent into the Kingdom to invest and crown him. No just claim of René's was thereby denied.

"The princes, dukes, barons, counts, and commoners of the realm were all obedient to Ferrante, had asked that he should be proclaimed king, and had sworn allegiance to him. Either the kingdom belonged to Ferrante by his father's will and was justly granted to him or it belonged to René, who had in that case been deprived of nothing, since the Apostolic letter specified that the rights of others should not be infringed. But since the question of 'rights' was doubtful and the claim presented by each was plausible, it was allowable to prefer the one already in possession. If neither had a right, then he who had no right suffered no wrong. If a reversion was justifiable and Calixtus's pronouncement was valid, what complaint had René or anyone else if with the consent of our brethren we granted to Ferrante the kingdom that had reverted to the Church? Here at Rome before we left, at the Congress of Mantua, and at Siena, whenever we were approached on the subject of the Kingdom by René's ambassadors, we always offered to proceed according to law. But René trusted more to arms than to law and while we were preoccupied at Mantua with plans against the Turks, he sent a strong fleet commanded by his son against the Kingdom, a fleet raised with the money which the Cardinal of Avignon had collected three years earlier from the tithes promised by the French clergy for a crusade against the Turks. He incited the barons of the Kingdom to rebellion, disturbed the peace of those districts, ravaged the land everywhere with rapine, murder, and arson, hindered the crusade against the Turk, and did all in his power to destroy the Christian religion, though we still hope that the labors we have undergone for the common weal will not be wholly wasted.

"When Ferrante saw his danger and realized that with his subjects revolting and the enemy growing stronger every day he was faced with ruin, he sought aid from us, his immediate overlord. He reminded us of the compact we have mentioned above and besought us not to fail him in his extremity, not to turn our back on our pledged word. We promised aid and bade him be of good courage. But before sending troops into the Kingdom we sent the Archbishop of Ravenna, a just and influential man, to command both sides to lay down their arms and seek a road to peace either through the arbitration of their friends or by the course of law. Since his way lay through country already submissive to René, he asked René's son for safe conduct.

"It seemed to us shameful that a man whom we had recognized as king should be thrust out of his father's kingdom by force of arms without trial or benefit of law or a hearing of his cause. We sent aid, not to deprive René of his throne, but to protect Ferrante in possession of it, as we were bound to do not only by the compact but in accordance with the direct lordship over the Kingdom which is vested in the Church of Rome.

"You know now in full, citizens, the righteousness of our cause and that we have left our adversaries no just ground of complaint against us. *Now hear what injuries they have inflicted on us.* We say nothing of the many writings with which they have tried to besmirch our name and of the embassies which they have sent to stir up princes against us. We are silent as to the hindrances they have put in the way of arming a crusade against the Turk. We pass over the fact that Jacopo Piccinino had surrendered to them without our orders and tried to take from us by trickery the city of Ascoli. For the sake of brevity, we forbear to mention many other things, but about one thing we cannot keep silence. This same Piccinino has but lately informed us that he is (God save us!) in the service of the Duke of Calabria and is commanded to attack in armed force not only the Orsini but us, our subjects, the Romans, Rome, and all the patrimony of St. Peter; that he has heretofore done less than he was bidden, but henceforth he will carry out his orders to ravage all the country with fire and sword. We have ourselves learned not only from those who have been arrested but from letters of the conspirators which have marvelously and by some divine aid fallen

into our hands, that Jacopo Piccinino conspired with Tiburzio and some
of the nobles, who were lingering around the city walls, to plunder the
Roman territory, sack Tivoli, enter Rome (where the youths were to
open the gates to him), give over the houses of the members of the
Curia, merchants, and rich citizens to be plundered, seize the chamberlain and divide his wealth, murder our nephew, outrage your daughters
and wives, carry off our boys to fight, and commit many other unspeakable crimes—in all of which he would undoubtedly have succeeded if
our army had not been rushed from the Abruzzi to meet Jacopo's rapid
march and if we had not made all haste back to Rome. We thank the
everlasting God that we anticipated such accursed schemes and averted
such dire calamity.

"We do not then love war nor do we of our own will take up arms
nor do we fight for a trifling cause. To keep the faith, to preserve the
authority of the Church, to defend the peace of our subjects, the safety
of the citizens, your hearths, your altars, your wives, your children, O
people of Rome, we have gone to war. We are not the first who have
taken arms for the Kingdom of Sicily, which belongs to the Church.
Almost all of you can remember Eugenius IV and Martin V. Your
fathers have seen Clements and Bonifaces and Nicholases. Who of them
did not involve himself in war, that for the glory of the Roman See they
might maintain in possession of their thrones the kings whom they had
set up? Away with empty rumors! If any pope ever loved peace and
desired tranquillity in the city, it is we who, loving Rome as our own
country, regard and cherish you all as sons in respect to the dignity of
the See, as brothers in our affection for our country, as fathers as regards
the glory of your ancestors. For we too are originally Roman. The
house of Piccolomini, to which we belong, moved to Siena from this
city, *as the names Enea and Silvio so frequent in our family show.*

"This, citizens, is what we wished to say to you. It is a leaf of the
Sibyl we have read. He who tells you otherwise is false and a liar. Do
not listen to liars nor let yourselves be broken because you are buffeted
by a few annoyances. After the storm will come calm weather. Endure
for a little. Soon this war will be over and most fair peace will again
appear, to your glory and ours."

With these words Pius ended. The Romans were overjoyed to know
that their lord was so amply provided not only with courage but with
right and justice. They thanked him warmly for making clear to them
the origin and course of the war and its reasons, of which many had
been in ignorance. They offered to give their fortunes at the Pope's

pleasure and were ready to expose themselves, their wives and children to any dangers, since the enemy had set on foot so unjust and impious a war.

On December 29, in the fourteen hundred and sixtieth year from the incarnation of the Word, the Pope received news of the death of the celebrated Guarino of Verona, who fell asleep in the Lord having made his peace as becomes a Christian. His passing was mourned by scholars, especially his pupils, who had flocked to him from all Europe, for he taught both Greek and Latin and translated into Latin many Greek works. It is owing to his labors that we can read Strabo. He left learned sons. Many epitaphs were written for him. No scholar of our age has left a higher reputation. Ferrara keeps his body.

Meanwhile the Cardinal of Nicaea,[5] who had gone from Mantua to Germany as Legatus, on his arrival at the Emperor's court found war ablaze everywhere.

The Cardinal, though he was now almost hopeless of success, nevertheless summoned the German princes to Austria to claim the fulfillment of their promises made at Mantua. Not the princes themselves but their ambassadors came, and even they came to offer words, not deeds. All temporized, gave farfetched reasons for objecting, pointed out the disagreement among the princes, would listen to none of Nicaea's arguments. Bessarion, that he might seem to leave undone nothing which might further his purpose, started for Nuremberg and got as far as Mainz, imploring all the princes and peoples on the way not to fail the Faith in its need, not to allow the strength of the Turk to increase, but to go to meet the enemy while he could be conquered. All stopped their ears and received his words as if they were so much empty talk. There was not a man who would promise to help religion.

Meantime Diether, because he had not reimbursed the merchants who had paid the Apostolic Camera the sum of 14,000 ducats for him, on the expiration of the allotted time was excommunicated. Outraged that anyone should have the insolence to [forbid him to] touch Christ's blood, he began to persecute the Church of Rome publicly as he had before done secretly, and in the German diets, which he called for that purpose, he was often heard to say, "There are two things that torment me especially. If I could accomplish them successfully, I would gladly die. One is to depose the cowardly Emperor who rules us and enthrone a good man in his place; the other to throw off at last the yoke of the Apostolic See, so that while free in temporal matters, we may no longer

_____
[5] Bessarion.

*be enslaved spiritually." At Mainz he spat out all his poison. "What are
we doing, Germans?" he cried. "Are we to be bondsmen forever? Shall
we accept as law whatever the Roman See commands? Shall we send
our gold, our substance there? Shall we never realize what deceits it
practices? What is the meaning of this pretended crusade against the
Turks? Why are tithes demanded, why are indulgences issued, except
to raise money? Gold is what both the Emperor and the Pope of Rome
are after. We are giving our wealth to enrich Italy and Hungary's
neighbor, Austria. A man can get nothing at the Apostolic Curia unless
gold intercedes for him.*

*"I am learning that from my own experience, for the price for con-
firmation of my election was 20,000 ducats and because I could not pay
it at once I have been excommunicated. The Archbishop of Trier had
to pay twice as much for his church. The French are much wiser, for
they do not apply to the Pope either for their pontifical churches or for
the lesser ones. Why do we not adopt their Pragmatic Sanction and look
out for our own interests? Pluck up heart, my brothers, and at last
claim that liberty which is most dear to your race. For myself, I hereby
appeal to a future council, that I may not be crushed under injustice.
You, if you so decide, will join my appeal in the name of the nation
which the Apostolic Legate, who is going to exact the tithes, is loading
with censures too heavy to endure."*

*When he had spoken, most thought him sacrilegious and mad, but
many held him to be wise and good and believed that he had the
nation's best interests at heart. Nevertheless only a few dared to join in
his appeal, for they were afraid of the censure of the decree of Mantua
and not entirely without fear of God. Diether's perfidy thwarted all the
Cardinal of Nicaea's efforts.[6]*

At the beginning of his pontificate Pius had sent a professor of the
Minorite brethren named Lodovico to the East to arouse the Christian
kings of Iberia, Armenia, and Mesopotamia to take up arms against the
Turks in Asia in the fortunate event of Christians organizing a crusade
against the same enemy in Europe. Lodovico said he had been in Persia
during Calixtus's reign and had found there many Christians and
friends of Christians who hated the Turks. Shortly after the Pope's
return from Mantua this man landed at Rome accompanied by many
ambassadors of eastern princes, as follows: David, Emperor of Treb-
izond, sent Michael Aldighiere; George, King of Persia, Armenia
Major, and Iberia Minor, the son of Alexander, sent Nicholas Telephus;

[6] The narrative of this important episode is continued in Book VI.

Hasan, King of Mesopotamia, son-in-law of the Emperor and son of Carailucas Trucomannus, a friend of the Christians though not a Christian himself, sent Mahomet Trucomannus; Gorgora, Duke of Iberia Major, the son of Gazabecch, sent Casadas Carcecchas; Urtebek, lord of Armenia Minor, sent the Armenian Moratus.

The ambassadors differed not only in their ways but in their dress, so that everybody marveled at them. Wherever they went the populace stared and a crowd of children followed them. The Persian envoy had his head shaved except for a small ring of hair like our monks. The envoy of Mesopotamia the same, except that on the very crown of his head was a little tuft of hair such as they say the heathen flamens used to wear on their caps. They had traveled through Colchis and Scythia across the Don and the Danube into Hungary and thence to Germany, where they paid their respects to the Emperor Frederick. From there they went to Venice, where they were received with distinguished honors by the Senate. This caused them to be accepted as genuine ambassadors, for Venice had commercial relations with the East. When they arrived in Rome they found themselves no less welcome. They were received as royal ambassadors, met by the order of prelates, and entertained with food and lodging at the public expense. It was said that some of them ate every day as much as twenty pounds of meat apiece.

When the Pope gave these ambassadors audience in a consistory, they spoke as follows: "You sent to us the Minorite friar, Lodovico of Bologna, who said that you had gone to Mantua to hold a congress of Christians and declare war against Mahomet, Sultan of the Turks; that you desired our princes, while you attacked him in Europe, to stir up revolt in Asia. His words were well received. Our princes hate the Turks. They love you and revere you as Christ's Vicar. They profess obedience to you and therefore, though they had bitter feuds among themselves and were at war, nevertheless at the bidding of your envoy they laid down their arms and are ready to take them up again against the Turk when you shall so command. A hundred and twenty thousand fighting men will be ready in Asia to invade Mahomet's empire as far as the Hellespont and the Thracian Bosporus whenever you desire, provided that you and the western nations likewise attack the Turks. We have been sent to tell you this and to kiss your feet as being God's representative on earth. In league with us are Bendias, King of Mangrelia and Arabia; Panchratius, King of the Iberians who are now called Georgians; Mania, Marquis of Gori; Ismail, the son of Spediar, lord of Sinope and Casatimena; Fabia, Duke of Anagasia; Charamannus, lord of Cilicia. They will give us the greatest assistance. The one thing we ask of you now is that you will appoint Lodovico, who has brought us here, patriarch over those who observe the ritual of the Roman church in the East and are loyal to your See."

When they ended, the Pope applauded the desires of the princes and made it clear that he considered their offers of great importance. He recounted what had taken place at Mantua, saying that he had done his best but that the Christian princes had not assembled there. Nevertheless he hoped they would assemble if they learned of the purpose of the eastern nations. He thought it would be helpful if the ambassadors themselves should proceed through Italy across the Alps into France and tell the King of France and the Duke of Burgundy what they had told him. Without the French it would be hard to make any crusade that would be worth while. That was the nation that had often fought gloriously against the heathen on land and sea and now it would be the one most dreaded by the Turks. The ambassadors consented but asked for their traveling expenses and the appointment of Lodovico as patriarch. The Pope granted both requests, only stipulating that Lodovico should not sign or style himself patriarch till he returned and should not carry the credentials of that office with him but leave them in the keeping of the Cardinal of St. Peter so that meantime they might get more information about the territory to be included in the patriarchate.

The ambassadors traveled through Italy and France and visited the courts of the King of France and the Duke of Burgundy, but they found no support. All shifted the responsibility for the cause for which they pleaded to the Pope, as if it were his duty to conquer the Turk even without the help of kings. Nevertheless by begging they scraped together a considerable sum of money. They were present at the funeral of King Charles, who died at this time, and saw the coronation of Louis, but got no more from the son than from the father. After some days spent in discussion they returned at last empty-handed.

In the meantime many reports had come to the Pope which made him suspicious of this embassy. It was said that Lodovico was a liar and a deceiver; that men from the East had come with him for the sake of gain pretending to be royal ambassadors and bringing forged letters from princes. Furthermore Lodovico had already disregarded the Pope's instructions by having himself addressed as patriarch wherever he went and accepting greedily the honors shown him as such. It was a matter of general knowledge too that in Hungary and Germany he had granted dispensations which even legates de latere would not have dared to grant without special instructions. For all these reasons, when he returned from France he did not find the same favor for himself or the ambassadors that they had been shown before. When the Pope reproved him for disregarding the Apostolic commands, he had no answer, but the only punishment he received was that he could not obtain his credentials as patriarch and narrowly escaped imprisonment. The Pope's forbearance was not so much for him as for the companions he had brought with him, since it was still a question whether they were genuine or pretended ambassadors, and on this account he gave them money for their return journey. Lodovico went with them and, putting in at Venice, he managed to get himself consecrated priest and patriarch by certain bishops who were ignorant of the facts. When the Pope learned of this, he wrote to the Patriarch of Venice to put the cheat in prison, but Lodovico was warned by the Doge and fled precipitately. Where he or his companions went or what they did afterwards has never been learned from that day to this. In matters carried on from a distance there is abundant opportunity for deception and the truth can seldom be discovered. From that time the Pope was suspicious of any communications from the East, especially when they were brought by men who were poor and unknown.

After the storming and sack of Donidei which was reported to the Pope on Oct. 31 when he was celebrating vespers for All Saints, the army went into winter quarters, Alessandro at Nepi and Federigo of Urbino among the Sabines. Both went to Rome to see the Pope during the feast of the Nativity and attended him as he was drinking with the cardinals after vespers according to the time-honored custom. A few days later there was a public consistory at which they were present. At this Andrea Benzi, fiscal advocate, at the Pope's bidding delivered a long and brilliant speech in which he execrated the crimes of Sigismondo Malatesta: his robberies, arson, massacres, debauchery, adultery, incest, murders, sacrilege, betrayals, treason, and heresy. He implored the Pope to rise in vengeance on them, to give ear to the prayers of suppliants who could no longer endure the cruel yoke of the tyrant, to cleanse Italy at last of that foul and abominable monster, during whose life no good man in any of his domains could live.

When the Pope heard this accusation, he said, "There are two states to which men go when they depart this life. One is the heavenly city of Jerusalem, the country of the blest; the other is in Hell, where is the abode of Lucifer and the prison of the damned. Our ancestors declared that in the former were enrolled many whom we revere as saints and worship with the adoration called dulia.[7] In doing this we observe the ceremony which we call canonization. Our predecessor Eugenius IV canonized Nicholas of Tolentino; Nicholas V Bernardino of Siena; Calixtus III Vincenzo of Valencia and the Englishman Osmund. We have been petitioned to enroll Catherine of Siena, Rose of Viterbo, and Frances of Rome among the maids or widows who are the saints of Christ and to declare that they have been received into the heavenly city. And this is just, for we believe that their virtues have earned this honor. *But no one of them has been so extolled by the most eloquent advocates, who have in these last days spoken in their praise, as Sigismondo Malatesta has today been cursed. Furthermore what has been said about the maidens requires proof; Sigismondo's crimes are manifest and evident, and not to one or two individuals only, but they are notorious to almost all the world. Let him then take precedence and before they are canonized in Heaven, let him be enrolled a citizen of Hell. Sigismondo's crimes, unprecedented in our age, call for new and unprecedented procedure. No mortal heretofore has descended into Hell with the ceremony of canonization. Sigismondo shall be the first to be deemed worthy of such honor. By an edict of the Pope, he shall be enrolled in the company of Hell as comrade of the devils and the damned. Nor shall we wait for his death, if haply he may come to his senses, since he has left no hope of his conversion. While still living he shall be condemned to Orcus and perhaps while still living he shall be hurled into the flames.* We might at this moment pass sentence on him, since the crimes of which he is accused can be concealed by no evasions; but we will be more merciful. We will summon the accused; if he comes in will hear him; we will observe the customary procedure of the courts. To you, then, our dear son, Cardinal of St. Peter in Vincoli, who have heard the accusations against Sigismondo, we entrust this case to be heard, investigated, and decided sine debito." With these words he dissolved the consistory. Thereafter the Cardinal from the beginning of the case followed his own procedure.

Meantime Thomas Palaeologus, brother of the last Greek emperor, Constantine, had been deprived of his empire by the Turks and came to Rome, leaving at Ancona the precious head of St. Andrew, of which we shall speak hereafter in the proper place.[8] The Pope received the exile kindly and out of pity for a prince of such noble lineage lodged him in the palace of San Spirito near his own and allotted him three hundred

[7] In distinction to the worship (*latria*) rendered to God.
[8] Bk. VIII.

ducats a month for his support. The cardinals contributed two hundred more and he was also presented with the golden rose (an honor given only to the noblest) on the Sunday named for it.

Meantime Ferrante, to show his gratitude to the Pope for recognizing and defending his claim to the Kingdom, conferred the duchy of Sessa on the Pope's nephew Antonio. He assumed that this had reverted to the Kingdom because Marino, by reason of his treason and betrayal, had forfeited it. But Marino has not to this day lost actual possession and though often attacked, he defends himself stoutly. The loser in court is not always the loser in battle. Fortune is the mistress in one case, reason in the other; though there are times when justice limps.

Under Pope Calixtus the marble staircase leading up to the church of St. Peter had fallen into decay; the marble itself was corroded with age and worn away by the trampling of many feet. So powerless are all things to resist time! The Pope rebuilt it at great expense. The staircase itself was made easier and handsomer and adorned with statues of gleaming white marble from the mountains of Liguria.

During the third Lent of his reign Pius fell critically ill, his feet, hands, knees, shoulders, and almost all his members suffering from gout. This greatly distressed his friends, *but delighted his enemies, especially those who hoped the succession would fall to them (so vain and empty are man's delusions!)*. Contrary to general expectation, he recovered and on Thursday of Holy Week he appeared in public to excommunicate the two Sigismunds: Sigismund of Austria because of the violence done the Cardinal of St. Peter, and Sigismondo Malatesta for neglecting to pay the tribute due the Church of Rome. The excommunication was repeated the next year on the arrival of the head of St. Andrew, as we shall relate in its place.

While these things were happening, Alessandro Sforza [9] and Federigo of Urbino, now that the spring [10] had come and their troops were equipped and ready, declared themselves prepared to go wherever the Pope ordered. But the Duke of Milan and the Pope were not agreed. The former thought the best plan would be to grant peace to Savello on whatever terms he asked and then at once send an army into the Kingdom against Ferrante's enemies; this would be the quickest way to end the war. Cosimo dei Medici was also of this opinion. The Pope thought they should first of all attack Savello, who had rejected honor-

[9] Brother of the Duke of Milan.
[10] 1461.

able terms of peace, and that they should not fight abroad unless there were peace at home.

Pius's opinion prevailed. The two captains marched into the Sabine country and *ravaged all Jacopo Savello's territory like a hurricane, Federigo invading the upper portion and Alessandro the lower. Urbino remained in the Sabine country and after joining the Cardinal of Teano decided to attack Montorio. This town, which was situated on a very rough mountain, was strongly fortified by walls and towers and defended by mercenaries. There was no expectation that bombards could be carried over the steep and precipitous approaches. But unremitting labor conquers all obstacles. The perseverance of the Cardinal brought up one of the bombards* which had shortly before at the Pope's orders been cast by Agostino of Piacenza, a celebrated artisan in that kind of work. *He made three bombards.* The first was called Silvia after the Pope; the second Vittoria after his mother; the third, which had not yet been brought into battle, was called Enea because this had been the Pope's name before his elevation. This was larger than the others, hurling a stone of three hundred pounds, while they hurled stones of only two hundred. Their force was so great that no walls, however massive, could resist them. *This was the first time they learned in Roman territory what bombards could do, for whereas the earlier ones had shattered walls scarcely four feet thick, these demolished masses of masonry twenty feet thick. Silvia was brought up to Montorio and as soon as she began to fire, the townsmen were panic-stricken. There was only one place where the engines could be moved up and this was closed by a massive wall and rampart. Silvia demolished everything and laid the town open to the army, which at once burst in, took the men captive, plundered such property as fell in the way of their first onset, and then set fires which reduced to ashes not only the fortunes and houses of the townsmen but the very walls of the town. Poggio Moiano opened its gates to the army without waiting for a battle and so escaped destruction.*

There remained to Savello only Aspra and Palombara. The former, at a distance from Rome, did not seem likely to cause much difficulty; the latter was near and was giving a great deal of trouble, being only fourteen miles from Rome and close to Tivoli. Here Savello himself was lingering and with him Silvestro of Piacenza and Corrado Alviano, who were making numerous raids on Roman territory in company with Everso's son Deifobo who held the neighboring fort of Monticelio. It was decided therefore to move the papal forces against Palombara with a view to ending the war at last. But to storm a town so strongly fortified and bravely defended required preparation. While they were taking energetic measures for this, Savello lost courage and through friends besought the Pope's indulgence, saying that he would submit and carry out all his orders if Palombara and Aspra were left to him and Cretone and Donumdei restored. The Pope would hear of no conditions, knowing well that a siege once begun could not last long, not only because of lack of supplies but because the townspeople were hostile to Savello, who had ruthlessly murdered their parents and kinsmen.

On this account the Pope thought that if the camp were moved to Palombara, the townspeople, who were said to be about 500, remembering their wrongs, would not long endure the hardships of a siege for the sake of so cruel a master. Savello, who feared the same result, besought Ottone Caretto, the Duke of Milan's ambassador at Rome, to plead his cause and not allow a friend of the Duke to be in jeopardy. He begged that he would obtain for him the Pope's pardon and three or even two of the towns that had been his, that he might have means of support. Ottone approached the Pope, but having accomplished nothing he went to Palombara and in a private interview urged Savello to submit to the Pope's will and not try further the fortune of war now that he was deserted by all. From a pope who was pious in fact as well as in name more could be got without a compact than with one. He urged him to abandon finally the evil counsels of Silvestro and Deifobo, who had repeatedly deceived him, and not to trust Piccinino, in whose promises he had found nothing substantial.

Savello, convinced at last and realizing the magnitude of his danger, put himself and his fortunes in the Pope's hands. Following the Cardinal of Teano through Rome like a captive led in triumph he made his way to the Pope, women and children shouting insults at him in all the squares and streets and hardly keeping their hands off him in their indignation. When he was admitted to the Pope's presence, he prostrated himself and with streaming eyes and quavering voice said, "I have sinned, Holy Father, against thee and against the Church of God in rejecting thy counsels. My enemies goading me by repeated wrongs drove me to it, and my unbridled lust for vengeance. Now I come to thee as a suppliant. I lie conquered and a prisoner at thy feet. Victory has put my person and all my fortunes in thy hands. My sins are numberless, but the greatest is that I have not long since done what I do now. In my folly I have delayed making trial of thy mercy. But the

*more grievously I have sinned, the more opportunity I have given for
the dignity of thy name to shine forth. Behold me here subject to thy
judgment." When he would have said more, sobs and groans choked
him.*

*The Pope himself could not restrain his tears and it was indeed a
pitiable thing that a man of noble birth, clad in mourning garments,
stripped of all his fortunes, unkempt and in distress, should be pleading
for his life before that tribunal by which his ancestors had been loaded
with rank and wealth. What is more changeable than the present?
How varied are the turns of Fortune! How uncertain and shifting is
power, which oftenest wanes and falls when it hastens over much to
increase and knows not how to rest contented with itself!*

*The Pope's answer was as follows: "We have desired, Savello, to keep
you safe and the proof is in the letters written to you by our own hand.
It irked us to make war against you whose ancestors had been placed
by the Apostolic See among the chief nobles of the city. You have not
listened to our voice; you have called to your side the enemies of the
Church; you have plundered Roman territory. Evil counsels have deceived you. Now at last you know your errors. If you had done so
earlier, you would not have involved us in the gravest dangers nor
would you have met defeat in war. You have come to see in disgrace
what you never saw in a state of grace. You have submitted to us that
there might be room for pardon and you beg forgiveness. We cannot
refuse to pardon the humbled. Our mercy shall be greater than your
folly. Take from our hand the life of which your perfidy made you
unworthy. Go free. Keep by our gift Aspra and Palombara and hope
for greater benefits if you live a good life."*

*With these words the Pope sent Savello away relieved and happy. All
approved this act except those who loved pity less than vengeance.*

Meantime the Pope, who had been asked by his fellow citizens to
enroll the blessed Catherine of Siena [11] among the holy virgins of
Christ, called a council of the bishops then in Rome, to which three

[11] St. Catherine of Siena (1347–1380), mystic, reformer, writer, was one of the most
powerful influences in the political no less than the religious life of her day. Living the
life of an anchorite in her father's home, St. Catherine's activities ranged all the way from
humble service of the poor in her own city to direct participation in shaping the course
of papal politics. Her mission to Avignon in 1376 to persuade Gregory XI to return to
Rome is well known. Though possessed of little education, her letters are among the
masterpieces of early Italian literature. It is of interest to note that Catherine's family
belonged to the lower middle class represented by the so-called Party of the Twelve which
ruled Siena from 1355 to 1368. The canonization of St. Catherine took place on the Feast
of SS. Peter and Paul, 1461.

cardinals who had investigated her life and miracles reported all that they had learned. When the meeting, on being asked its pleasure, approved with one voice the maiden's canonization, Pius ordered a tribune to be raised in the basilica of St. Peter, from which after celebrating mass he delivered an oration on the merits of the girl. This we will not insert here, since it is included in a volume with his other speeches. At the end, with the warm approval of the cardinals, bishops, abbots, and other prelates present, he directed that Catherine should be enrolled with the usual ceremonies in the catalogue of sainted maidens and ordained an annual commemoration of her. He granted indulgence for seven years to all who visited the tomb which contains her bones and himself dictated the bull of canonization which is included in the volume with his other letters.

Rome had by now begun to swelter in a blazing July. The cardinals fled from the heat, the Curia was reluctant to stay, and everyone was afraid of the summer climate. The Pope thought it unsafe to go far from the city while the enemy were so near. The people of Sora, Aquila, and many throughout the Abruzzi were still plotting against the Church. Therefore he decided to spend the rest of the summer at Tivoli. Thus he could hold a wavering state to its allegiance and at the same time escape the noxious atmosphere of the city.

A few days later the Pope left Rome in the dead of night and reached the Aniene before sunrise. On the farther bank he was met by Federigo and the Cardinal of Teano with ten squadrons of cavalry who accompanied him as a bodyguard as far as Ponte Lucano. The Pope was delighted with the brightness of their arms and the equipment of horses and men. For what fairer sight than troops in battle array? The sun flashed on their shields and from their helmets and crests were reflected a dazzling light. Every armed company seemed a forest of lances. The youth dashed hither and thither making their horses caracole, brandishing their swords, whirling their spears, and making a show of fighting. Federigo, who was well read, asked the Pope whether the captains of antiquity had been armed as ours were. The Pope answered that in Homer and Vergil could be found descriptions of every kind of weapon which our age used and of many others which had gone out of fashion. He said that although poets invented some things, still as a rule they described things which have at some time been in use and do not depart entirely from the truth. The talk then turned on the Trojan War and when Federigo tried to belittle it utterly, the Pope proved that it was a great war and that its fame was justified. Since they mentioned Asia

Minor also and did not agree about its boundaries, the Pope later, when he got a little leisure at Tivoli, wrote a description of Asia itself, quoting from Ptolemy, Strabo, Pliny, Q. Curtius, Julius Solinus, Pomponius Mela, and other ancient authors passages that seemed to him relevant to an understanding of the subject. They carried on a pleasant and animated conversation about ancient history all the way to Ponte Lucano. There the Pope dismissed the guard and again crossed the Aniene.

At the second milestone Pius was met by the populace of Tivoli carrying olive branches and singing. With them came the chiefs of the factions, the rebellious youths, and peace-loving citizens, who took up the Pope's litter and with mingled apprehension and affection carried their lord into the city. Some of the worst offenders, thinking more of their own guilt than of the Pope's mercy, went into voluntary exile. The property of these men was confiscated but all the others were pardoned. Then in an assembly of the citizens he rehearsed the mistakes and folly of the people and showed in what danger the state had been. Finally he urged them to submit calmly to the building of a fortress, pointing out that for many reasons this would be for the city's advantage. He easily won their consent, since the good citizens realized that a fortress was necessary to quell the headstrong, and the rebellious, having received pardon for their sins, did not dare oppose the Pope who had shown them such mercy. He therefore proceeded *at once* to lay the foundations at the highest point in the city where ruins still extant showed that the old citadel had been. He erected two towers with walls 20 feet thick, one 130 feet high, the other 100. The other walls were of the appropriate measurements. He surrounded them with a broad, deep moat, dug two cisterns, and adorned the gate with marble (Fig. 15), on which he had the following verses carved:

I am dear to the good, hated by the evil, hostile to the proud, for lo!
I am Tivoli! Thus Pius ordained.

Though the work was very elaborate and costly, it was nevertheless completed within a year except for the double wall which Pius proposed to build from the citadel to the city gate, and to this they will next bend their efforts. The cost of construction would have exceeded 40,000 ducats had not the Tiburtines and other subjects of the Church furnished laborers free of charge. All approved this work and thought it imperative in order to control the insolence of their neighbors and the hotheads within their own city. The Arx Pia in Tivoli was regarded as no less important

than the Tomb of Hadrian in Rome, since the city of Tivoli is rated as
a second fortification of Rome.

Tivoli, so famous in antiquity, lies in a fold of a lofty mountain not
far from its foot, about 1,000 feet above the plain. The part of the city
where the fortress is situated is separated from the rest of the mountain,
which towers above it by a broad, deep moat. From the gate leading to
the olive groves and Palestrina to a second near the Aniene, which leads
to the meadows, and from the gate first mentioned to a third which
commands the direct road to Ponte Lucano and looks toward Rome,
the city is defended by precipitous cliffs and by the wall hastily built by
King Alfonso while he was living there. The other parts of the city are
completely protected by the Aniene, which falls to such a depth that
the eye can scarcely follow it. This river rises in the mountains not far
from the monastery of Subiaco and winds gently through a shady valley
as far as the monastery itself. There it encounters the cliff, where it
plunges with a crash into the abyss, and it does not become calm again
till it leaves the rocks and barriers of massive stone and descends to level
ground. They say that under the cave where Benedict lived was once a
wall which dammed the river and made a lake in the valley above,
whence the monastery was called Sublacense [12] but later, when this wall
collapsed, the lake disappeared.

The river then flows through a lovely valley delightful in summer,
between meadows, fields, and many castles as far as the monastery of
San Clemente, where it is again narrowed by mountain barriers and
with roaring and clamor foams its course to Vicovaro. Though from
there on it is quieter, its waters are never really calm till it reaches
the meadows of Tivoli, where it glides somewhat more gently. But
when it reaches the walls of Tivoli, after flowing some 200 feet with
the city on its left, unable any longer to find a pathway among the jutting crags it hurls itself headlong into the deep valley below with
increased noise and uproar—*and that not* with a single leap, *but rent
and torn by numerous cataracts before it reaches the bottom and rushes
on its foaming and complaining course with a din* that drowns the
human voice. Its complaining does not cease till near Ponte Lucano,
where it becomes smooth and would be navigable if the trees which
block it were removed. It empties into the Tiber near the Ponte Molle.
We call it today the Teverone. Beyond Tivoli it is crossed by four
bridges: the first under Tivoli itself is called Ponticolo; the second is
Ponte Lucano, where a marble pile, once erected as the tomb of the

[12] I.e., Subiaco.

noble family of the Plautii, now serves as a fort; the third is the Ponte Mammolo, said to have been built by Mammaea, mother of the Emperor Alexander; the fourth is the Ponte Salaro, built by the eunuch Narses. Its waters throughout its course are clear and very cold and there are many trout in it.

The part of Tivoli which lies across the Aniene is small and sparsely inhabited because of civil dissensions. It is connected with the main city by a wooden bridge. Above the river the houses of the city and the lofty cliffs serve as walls. In the city itself there is nothing especially remarkable except an old building with high and broad arches called today the Porta Obscura. It was formerly the entrance to the city where merchandise was deposited and duty paid. What were once spacious and handsome lodgings for merchants or publicans or distinguished men are now all open stabling for cattle and on the high vaulted roofs vegetable gardens are cultivated. Remains of a temple of Vesta or some other god with lofty columns are to be seen on the cliffs above the Aniene and not far from the citadel were traces of a splendid amphitheatre, but the citadel has destroyed them all. Part of the Aniene has been diverted to the city, where it serves mills, workshops, and fountains and adds greatly to the beauty of the place.

About three miles from Tivoli the Emperor Hadrian built a magnificent villa like a big town. Lofty vaults of great temples still stand and the half-ruined structures of halls and chambers are to be seen. There are also remains of peristyles and huge columned porticoes and swimming pools and baths, into which part of the Aniene was once turned to cool the summer heat. Time has marred everything. The walls once covered with embroidered tapestries and hangings threaded with gold are now clothed with ivy. Briers and brambles have sprung up where purple-robed tribunes sat and queens' chambers are the lairs of serpents. So fleeting are mortal things! Between this villa and Tivoli are most beautiful vineyards and olive groves and among the vineyards you may find all sorts of trees, including a great number of pomegranates, which bear enormous fruit of delicious flavor.

All about Tivoli in summer are the most delightful green fields where the Pope used often to go with the cardinals for refreshment of mind, sometimes sitting in a grassy nook under the olives, sometimes in a green meadow on the edge of the Aniene where they could look down into the translucent water. Two miles from the city in a secluded valley are meadows watered by many springs through which a powerful stream of water drawn off from the Aniene used to be carried on lofty

arches to the mountains which overlook Rome. Thence it was brought
by subterranean courses to Hadrian's villa and to Rome. Of the aque-
ducts themselves huge and towering masses still stand but they are not
continuous. How costly their construction must have been is evident
even today from the ruins.

Pius often rested in these meadows by bubbling springs or under the
shade of trees, talking with the cardinals about state matters or hearing
the embassies which followed him everywhere he went. In Tivoli he
lodged with the Minorites high up where there was a view of Rome,
the plain below, the Aniene, and beautiful green orchards, but no other
attraction. The house was old and tumble-down, full of rats as big as
rabbits, which disturbed the night with their scuttling up and down.
The winds too, of which the city has great wealth, were annoying and
it was impossible to keep the rain out of the leaky old building which
the careless monks had not taken the trouble to repair. These monks,
since they were Conventuals and their way of life was unseemly, the
Pope removed and replaced with Observantists.

The Pope stayed here a little less than three months, enjoying the
natural beauty of the place, though he was beset by continual anxieties,
not only those caused by war but those that even a peaceful pontificate
brings with it.

Meantime Niccolò, Cardinal of Teano, and Federigo of Urbino advanced with their army into the contado of Albi and Tagliacozzo. After
bringing part of the region under the control of the Orsini and driving
out Piccinino's garrison, they decided to march into the territory of
Aquila. In one onslaught they laid waste all the plain below the city,
drove off more than two hundred captives as well as oxen, beasts of burden, mules, and almost innumerable flocks and herds of all kinds (for
it is a great grazing country), and carried off all the corn that was lying
already threshed on the threshing floors as well as what had just been
cut or was still standing in the fields. *They carried off also more than
20,000 hens.* When the booty had been collected and heaped together,
they encamped at San Vittorino, a village four miles from Aquila, but
near enough for their banners and tents to be seen from the city. This
was a great mortification to the citizens, who had previously despised
the forces of the Church as insignificant but had now been forced to
see them ravage their fields and loot the surrounding country under
their very eyes, not daring to go out to meet them and relying solely on
their walls for safety. Now they realized the power of the Church and
they who had boasted in self-confidence and high spirits were punished

by ruin and shame. It was the righteous vengeance of God. In the pontificate of Martin V the people of Aquila were defended against Braccio by a papal garrison and they afterward joined the Bracceschi against Pope Pius. It was an ungrateful state unworthy to have the body of San Bernardino, a state that had presumed to rear its horns against the Church of Rome, its mother and liberator. But their sin was not unpunished. First their fields were ravaged, then most of the city walls, many of the houses of the citizens, and their great churches were ruined by an earthquake. It may be that God will exact still heavier penalties.

BOOK VI

WHILE these things were going on in Italy, frequent congresses were held in Germany at the instance of Diether, Bishop-elect of Mainz. He had been excommunicated because of his failure to repay the bankers from whom he had long ago borrowed money for the tithes and he now appealed to a future council as if he were the injured party. Numerous German diets were convened in which he implored the princes to support his appeal and, *as we have said before,*[1] he devised many schemes against the Church of Rome and the Emperor. Nor did he hesitate to rear his horns and kick against these supreme heads of all the world. In defiance of the Church's censures, although excommunicated, he entered the sanctuary (thus polluting by his presence the holy rites) and brazenly attended mass.

When the Pope heard of this, he sent Rudolf, Dean of Worms, and Francesco, Canon of Toledo, one an authority on civil law and the other a teacher of theology, to examine into German affairs and either quiet Diether or take steps to thwart his mad folly. Representatives of the German princes were gathered at Mainz.[2] Diether himself spoke, to this effect: "How the Pope has persecuted me heretofore I think no one of you, brethren, does not know, *since the injuries he has publicly put upon me are manifest.* Still, in case some one is in ignorance, I will repeat briefly what is common knowledge.

"In the first place, when I was elected *by the canons* to this church of Mainz and according to ancient custom had sent deputies to Mantua, where the Roman Curia then was, to obtain confirmation, he put off and slighted my request for a long time and finally sent my deputies away empty-handed because they refused to agree to his unjust demands. He demanded as the price of my confirmation an enormous sum of money *which I could never have paid,* required me to take an

---

[1] Bk. V.

[2] Convened June 4, 1461. Only two princes were present in person at this time, *viz.,* Diether and his ally Frederick Count Palatine, and a few others had sent representatives.

unprecedented oath, and (most outrageous of all) forbade me *ever to
agree to holding a general council or* to call a national congress without
his orders. I pass over many other demands most oppressive to the
German nation in regard to tithes and indulgences, to which I was
commanded to assent. *All this interfered with my confirmation.* I endured the delay with what resignation I could muster. I sent back my
delegates. I renewed my entreaties. I offered the amount of money
which my predecessors had been used to pay into the Apostolic treasury
for confirmation. The matter dragged on for a long time. Finally since
I could in no other way secure confirmation *I promised the sum demanded and* I swore, contrary to all precedent, that before the year was
out I would appear before the Pope. On the request of my agents the
bankers assumed the burden of making the payment and put on record
my obligation to them in the formula called Camerae.

"Time passed. I was unable to pay within the period appointed. I was
excommunicated and publicly denounced. *The bankers say they paid
the money to the Apostolic Camera. That is nonsense and Italian
trickery. The Pope and the bankers were in collusion. They pretend a
payment that was never made. The Italians are living up to their own
saying, that money can be extorted from barbarians by subtlety. We are
the 'barbarians.' And* what do you think is the object of these tithes
they demand, of these indulgences they offer? They say there must be
a crusade against the Turk and money is needed for that. *On the contrary, it is we on whom they have declared war, whose substance they
seek to get. It is for our wealth they are spreading their nets. The
Italians do not hate the Turks so much as they hate us.* This is a trap,
but, if you listen to me, their plot will not succeed. I have appealed to a
future council, not so much because I have been unjustly excommunicated as to prevent the people of my province from being burdened
with tithes. This is the one remedy left us against the tyranny of the
Apostolic See. If you are wise you will follow my example and seize
this opportunity of protecting the interests of your subjects."

When he had spoken and the congress seemed almost persuaded,
Rudolf rose and in his native tongue (for Diether also had spoken in
German) he said: "You must excuse me, Diether, if, when I rise in this
congress of most eminent men to defend the Pope, I refute your slan-
ders; and do you, sirs, lend me your gracious attention when I speak
for the father, lord, and master of us all. Diether insults Christ's Vicar;
he brings false accusations against him. His speech was far from the
truth; he has committed, not suffered a wrong. Listen to the facts. If I

lie, the deputies who handled Diether's business at Mantua are here; they themselves shall testify.

"The Pope, when he was asked to confirm Diether in the church of Mainz, said he would grant the request as soon as the Bishop-elect presented himself before the Curia; a congress was being held at Mantua to discuss the defense of religion; Diether's predecessor had been summoned thither and it was fitting that the man who was to succeed him should come to the congress to represent his province, which was very large and important. Who could find fault with this? Who could blame a pope for being concerned about the defense of the true Faith? Diether misinterprets the Pope's pious wish, his pious purpose. The rules of canon law require a bishop-elect to go to Rome and ask for confirmation in the pope's presence. Where is the offense in requiring an appearance which is a legal obligation? Bishops, when summoned to a synod, must obey, and what synod in our times has been held for a more important reason than that of Mantua? If bishops already consecrated might be summoned thither, might not bishops-elect? If the summons was regular, who could approve its refusal? In dishonor, Diether, you have entered upon your episcopate. The first fruits of your office are disobedience. You have begun with rebellion. You say an enormous sum of money was demanded of you. What are you thinking of, my good sir? Can you thus fling aside the truth? Beware of listening to falsehoods. Any man who says that a single penny beyond the sum regularly fixed by the Camera was demanded of you is a liar. The principal tax is at least 10,000 ducats; the servitia minuta, as they are called, and the issuance of letters amount to about 4,000. Nothing further was either exacted or demanded [3] of you nor has the church of Mainz ever within our memory paid less. The church of Trier, which is much smaller, paid under Calixtus III 30,000. What grounds for complaint have you? The Pope's too great kindness has made you insolent.

"And now as to your assertions about a general council and national diets. They are intolerable. Such things have never been thought of, much less demanded. For what concern of yours is *a general council? What concern of the Pope's is* a German diet? The Germans are free to convene when the Emperor wishes. The convocation of a general council is the business of the Bishop of Rome, not of the Bishop of Mainz.

[3] The fiscal records of the papal treasury show on the contrary that a total of over 20,000 gold florins had been paid by bankers on behalf of Diether. His agents were Piero and Giovanni de' Medici and Alessandro Miraballo. Thus Diether was not in error concerning the amount.

It is his right to command, your duty to obey. You think the word 'council' is hateful to the Pope. You are mistaken; nothing would give him so much satisfaction as to come before a congress of all Christendom, in which at last your disobedience and that of other rebels might be punished. In the event of a general synod he will preside; he will be recognized as the head, the leader, the moderator. Many will take precedence of you, though indeed you have not enough learning to dare to appear in a great church. For what could you say? You who scarcely know how to stammer a word or two of Latin? See what a champion of a general council we have found! The Church is in a fine state indeed when it has come to the point that a council is dependent on your will!

"As regards the tithes and indulgences—you seem to have forgotten your own voluntary offer: that you would authorize them in your province but wanted part of them yourself. You wished to sell your services and at that time you were not troubled by any anxiety about the provincials or any pity for your subjects or any grief at the spoliation of the Germans, provided you got your share. But the Pope thought it impious to divide with you the money destined for the use of the Faith and it never entered his head to keep it for himself. *And you call him a conniver! and you charge him with deceit and falsehood because, you say, he induced the bankers to allege a payment that was never made! You think nothing of accusing the supreme pontiff of lying and of impeaching the honor of Christ's Vicar. And where shall we look for honor if not in the Holy See? Who will prove to be true if Truth's Vicar is false? You presume too much, Diether. You measure the Pope by your own vice. Because it is your habit to connive and lie, you judge others by yourself.* I know the banking house that advanced the money and there was no secrecy about the transaction. The Pope received his share, the cardinals theirs, the other officials theirs. There are the books of the Camera, there are the public records, there are competent witnesses. The banker, who on your account is being reduced to beggary, would be only too glad if you were speaking the truth; your lies are ruinous to his purse as well as to your conscience. The Pope requires nothing of the unwilling. He declared war against the Turks. He hoped that the promises of your delegates at Mantua would be ratified. On their advice he decreed tithes and indulgences as a means of raising the money necessary for the war. If you do not wish to succor religion, you are free not to. But think of the common good. The Turks are as near to you as to Italy. We are all alike in danger. Do not think the Pope is looking for aid from the reluctant. My colleague and I pledge our word that the German nation shall contribute nothing unless of its own free will and, if necessary, we will give you a decree to this effect. You shall judge from your own investigation the state of the Church and of religion, the growing power of the Turks, the danger hanging over our heads, and the measures by which the ruin that threatens us may be averted."

This is the speech some say Rudolf made in the diet of Mainz, though most authorities state that his actual speech, though fine, was shorter and more restrained. All agree that the diet was convinced by his speech and acceded to none of Diether's demands.

Convinced by these words Diether sent for a notary and before a few witnesses withdrew privately the appeal he had put forward publicly, as if more ashamed of withdrawing than of making it. The same thing had been done a few days earlier by Friedrich, Count Palatine of the Rhine, when he learned from Rudolf that he had been misguided in supporting Diether's appeal. Neither of them kept to the path; both returned to their vomit. Diether, snapping his fingers at both divine and human laws, while still under excommunication continued to profane the holy offices and neglected to be consecrated bishop within the time fixed by law. He never satisfied his creditors; he shamelessly broke the oath by which he had bound himself to appear before the Curia; he did his best to stir up new dissension against the Pope; he ignominiously dismissed the canons of his church; he embroiled himself in most bloody wars; he burned farms and churches; he imposed crushing burdens on his subjects; he robbed some of their wives and others of their substance; he sold priesthoods for money; he showed no interest in administering justice. The whole situation was revolting. The citizens of Mainz had no respect for the chapter; the people lamented; the clergy complained; no one had a good word for the Bishop.

When the Pope heard this, since everyone who came from the region of the Rhine denounced Diether's administration and declared his life was a scandal, he thought the insolence and wickedness of the man should not be tolerated any longer, if only he could find some powerful candidate to set up as bishop in the church of Mainz in opposition to Diether so that the sentence against him might not be without effect. He found such a man in Adolf of the old and noble house of Nassau, who was beloved by both the clergy and the people and would undoubtedly have been preferred to Diether by the canons if the election had been open to the entire chapter instead of being handed over to a few and thus exposed to bribery and corruption. Diether was at once deposed and Adolf appointed in his place. The vassals were released from the oath they had taken and bidden to swear allegiance to the ncwly appointed bishop. The letters of provision were prepared and given to the Chamberlain Johann to carry to Germany in absolute secrecy.

Diether, stunned at this unprecedented act, was for some time at a loss what to do, but at last he said he appealed from the Pope, who was misinformed, to the same Pope when he should be better informed. The canons declared themselves only too eager to obey Pope Pius and embracing Adolf they set him on the episcopal throne and vowed obedience to him. The entire state was jubilant and the clergy drank one another's health, hailing the coming of the day when they had shaken off the yoke of cruel tyranny.[4]

The two allies met. Palatine promised Diether a strong army; Diether handed over to Palatine on the spot certain strongly fortified and rich castles estimated to be worth 200,000 ducats, over which they had formerly been at war. Palatine was influenced by two things, avarice and his feud with the people of Baden, whom he desired to injure. Furthermore it would gratify his ambition if he might see the church of Mainz, with which he had often been in conflict, racked with fire and sword. When Diether had allied himself with this man, the forces of the opposing parties were nearly equal. Then farms were burned, fields laid waste, towns destroyed. Very many bloody and cruel battles were fought; there was wholesale slaughter; many were taken prisoner; maids and matrons were ravished; no mercy was shown age or youth; no churches, no monasteries, were spared; both sides defiled alike the property of God and man. Diether's father, who had repeatedly warned his son not to defy the church of Rome for fear of bringing ruin upon Mainz, seeing that his efforts were vain, died suddenly of a broken heart. He was a noble man whose counsel was most highly valued by the archbishops of Mainz.

Now when the cause of France[5] was almost desperate, a sixteen-year-old girl named Jeanne, the daughter of a poor farmer, who was watching pigs in the country near Toul, was inspired by the Holy Spirit, as her later acts prove. Abandoning her herds and disregarding her parents, she went to the prefect of the nearest town, which was the only,

[4] At this point, while terms were being drawn up, Frederick, Count Palatine, urged Diether not to yield and offered an alliance.

[5] After the English victory of Agincourt in 1415 in the Hundred Years' War. The narrative of that war precedes and is omitted here.

one in that region that had remained loyal to the French, and asked for guides to take her to the Dauphin. When the prefect asked her reason for going, she said she had a divine message to deliver, which would be the salvation of him and his kingdom. The prefect laughed and thinking her crazy paid no attention. When she persisted, he tested her in many ways. He waited some days to see whether she would change her purpose or whether he could find any fault in her. But when he found her firm and unshakable and innocent of any guilt, he said, "How do I know that this is not the will of God? The kingdom of France has often been saved by divine aid; perhaps in our time too something has been ordained in Heaven for our salvation, which is to be revealed through a woman," and choosing three servants of proved loyalty he put the girl in their charge to be taken to the Dauphin.

It was a journey of some ten days and all the intervening country was in the hands of the enemy or the enemy's friends. The girl, dressed in men's clothing, passed unharmed through all difficulties and came to the Dauphin who was then at Bourges. Disheartened by so many reverses he was by now not so much concerned about defending his kingdom as about finding a place where he could live in safety as a private individual. In Spain the King of Castile and Leon, who was bound to him by ties of blood and friendship, was regarded as the most powerful prince. The Dauphin had resolved to ask him to take over the crown and the government of France and to give him a little corner of the earth where he could hide and be safe. While he was making such plans the Maid came into his presence and giving him the prefect's letter begged for a hearing. The Dauphin, disturbed at this strange occurrence and fearing a trick, sent her to be examined by his own confessor, the Bishop of Castres, a most eminent theologian, and put her in charge of noble matrons.

When Jeanne was questioned about her faith, she answered in conformity with the Christian religion.[6] When examined as to her character she was found to be chaste and scrupulously honest. The examination lasted several days. They found in her no trace of deceit or guile or evil

[6] The account which follows is a very uneven, impressionistic one, inaccurate in certain details. It enlarges upon some episodes and omits or condenses others. Pius writes with a critical detachment mixed with admiration and wonder. It will be recalled that the events here recorded took place only a few years before he himself went to France as a secretary of Cardinal Albergati; the rehabilitation of Joan after an exhaustive re-examination of the case occurred in the pontificate of his predecessor, Calixtus III. Thus it is curious that Pius does not write more accurately and more authoritatively of a case that so interested him.

intent. The only difficulty was her dress. When asked why she wore men's garments, which were forbidden to women, she replied that she was a maid and either dress was proper for a maid; she had been instructed by God to wear men's dress since she was also to wield men's arms.

After she had been thus tested she was again sent before the Dauphin. "I have come to you, O son of kings," she said, "not of my own purpose but at the command of God. He bids you follow me. If you obey, I will restore to you your throne and before long I will crown you at Rheims." The Dauphin told her she was promising something very difficult to perform; the city of Rheims, where kings were crowned, was a long way off; it was in the enemy's hands and there was no safe road; Orléans, which lay between, was besieged by the English; the French had no resources with which to aid the unhappy beleaguered townsmen, much less could they bestir themselves about his coronation.

The Maid was unmoved by these arguments. "I make no empty promises," she said. "If you trust in God, trust in me also. I have come as His messenger. I will furnish you with arms by divine aid, and with an invisible sword I will open a path. Wherever you go the people shall obey you and the nobles of their own will shall follow your standard. Do not talk to me of the siege of Orléans! First of all I will raise the siege and hand over to you a free city. Only let me have these knights whom you have here."

The matter was discussed in council for some time with various opinions. Some said the girl was crazy, others that she was bewitched, others that she was inspired by the Holy Ghost, and these last recalled the fact that Bethulia and other cities had in the past been saved by women; the kingdom of France had often been aided by Heaven; it might be that now too it was defended by a maid sent by God and that the task had been committed to the weaker sex that the French with their accustomed pride might not be overconfident of their own powers; in any case a girl whose advice was so sensible could not be called mad.

This opinion prevailed and they entrusted the matter of Orléans to the Maid. A woman was put in command of the war. Arms were brought, horses led up. The girl mounted the most spirited steed; then in her gleaming armor brandishing her spear like Camilla in the tale she made him leap, run, and curvet. When the nobles saw this, none of them scorned to be commanded by a woman. All the noblest took arms and eagerly followed the Maid, who, when all was ready, set out on the march.

The approach to Orléans by land was very difficult. All the roads were blocked by the English and at each of the three gates they had a camp fortified with a moat and a rampart. The Maid, knowing that the river Loire flows by the walls of the city, loaded ships with grain in a secluded place and embarked with her troops, sending word to the besieged that she had started. By rowing quickly and taking advantage of the swift current she appeared in sight of the city before the enemy knew she was coming. Armed English troops rushed up and putting out in small boats tried in vain to prevent her landing. They were forced to retreat with many wounds.

The Maid entered the city, where she was received with great rejoicing by the people, and brought supplies of all kinds to a populace near starvation. The next day at dawn she at once furiously attacked the camp of the enemy which was besieging the main gate. Filling the moats and shattering the mound and rampart she routed the English in confusion, captured their fortifications, and set fire to the towers and bulwarks which they had built. Having thus heartened the townsmen, she made sallies through the other gates and did the same in the other camps.

Since the English forces were stationed in several different places and one camp could not come to the help of another, the siege of Orléans was weakened by these tactics and then utterly broken. All the enemy who had fought against the Maid fell so that there was hardly anyone left to carry news of the disaster. The glory of this exploit was credited to the Maid alone, though very brave and experienced soldiers who had often commanded troops took part in it.

Such a massacre of his men and such humiliation was unbearable to Talbot, the most celebrated of the English commanders, and with 4,000 horsemen picked from the entire army he marched against Orléans to fight the Maid if she dared meet him, never doubting that when she came through the gate he could either capture or kill her. But the event proved quite otherwise. The Maid led out her troops and as soon as she saw the enemy, with loud shouts and terrific force she charged the English lines. Not a man dared to stand fast or show his face; sudden panic and horror seized them all. Although they were superior in numbers they had supposed they would be fewer and thought countless forces were fighting for the Maid. Some even thought angels were fighting on the opposite side and had no hope of victory if they found themselves battling against God. Their drawn swords fell from their hands; everyone threw away shield and helmet to be unencumbered for flight.

Talbot's shouts of encouragement were unheard and his threats unheeded. It was a most shameful rout. They presented only their backs
to the Maid, who followed up the fugitives and took or killed every man
except a very few—including the commander, who when he saw that
his men could not be rallied, made his escape on a swift horse.

The report of these things, carried to the neighboring peoples and
by them to those farther off and always increasing as it traveled, filled
all with amazement. The Dauphin, now trusting the advice of the Maid
who had confirmed her words by deeds, decreed thanksgivings to God
in all the churches and prepared to be crowned. The nobles of the entire
kingdom, when they heard of the miraculous exploits of the Maid and
learned that preparations were being made for the coronation ceremonies, gathered in arms from all France in their intense eagerness to
see her and within a month more than 30,000 horsemen ready to serve
at their own expense joined the Dauphin.

More and more exultant at the accession of such a large force, Charles,
preceded by the Maid dressed in armor and carrying his standard, set
out from Bourges, where he usually made his headquarters, and marched
toward Rheims. All the towns between were in the power of the enemy
and all the peoples, sworn to a new allegiance, had intended to keep
faith with the English and receive the Dauphin as an enemy. But when
they heard that he and the Maid were at hand, marvelous to tell! no
one met them in arms, no one closed a gate, no one cursed them as they
passed. Wherever they went the populace poured out to meet them and
saluted the Dauphin as their lord, vying with one another as to how
they might show their prince greatest honor.

When the army was about forty stades from Rheims, panic seized the
city. There seemed no safety for the English. The nobles were wavering; the populace were attracted by the prospect of a change of government. Some among the English advised removing elsewhere the sacred
oil with which the king is anointed, so that even if the city were lost,
the enemy could not be properly crowned. The French believe that once
upon a time a white dove sent from Heaven brought to St. Rémi, Bishop
of Rheims, the sacred oil for the anointing of kings, and they guard
it with the greatest reverence and think that it never grows less, though
from Clovis to our day a long line of sovereigns has used it. They say
that he who is not anointed with this oil is no true king. Though the
English had for this reason repeatedly discussed removing it, it is
thought their plan was frustrated by the Divine Will.

The Dauphin on approaching the city dispatched heralds to demand

its surrender and to announce his coronation to the people of Rheims.
The city sent eminent citizens to request time for consideration, but the
Maid gave orders that the envoys should receive no answer; there must
be no delay; everything must be done at the time God had appointed.
The Dauphin obeyed the Maid. He detained the envoys and sending
ahead some companies of cavalry advanced swiftly on the city. Then
an extraordinary thing happened which after-generations will not believe. Not a single armed man was to be found at the gate or in the city.
The citizens in civil dress met them outside the walls. The Dauphin
without conditions, without terms, without the least opposition, passed
through wide-open gates. No one protested, no one showed any sign of
resentment. Everyone admits that it was a miracle of Heaven.

While the French were entering by one gate the English were fleeing
by the other. A peaceful and quiet city welcomed its lord graciously and
he who a little time before was despised as an enemy was now revered
as a father with extraordinary affection and the highest honors. They
crowded around the Dauphin to hail him and in even greater numbers
around the Maid, whom they gazed upon as a kind of divinity. This
happened on a Saturday, the day before the feast of St. Mary Magdalene, and on the feast itself [7] in the convent of St. Rémi before a
great throng of the populace in the presence of many nobles and prelates
the Dauphin was anointed with the sacred oil after the manner of his
ancestors and received the crown of France, while the crowd shouted
"Long life and victory to King Charles!" (for that was the Dauphin's
name).

The King remained in the city four days, which was contrary to
custom, for it is usual for the kings of France the day after their coronation to make a pilgrimage to the church of St. Marcoul and heal the sick
there. The belief is current among the French that there is a disease of
the throat which can be cured only by the King's touch and certain
mystic words and that the cure takes place in this church after a coronation. The new king did not make this pilgrimage on the regular day
because he was detained by the Burgundian envoys, who had come to
salute him and brought proposals for peace. He gave them audience and
four days later set out on his pilgrimage. I have no actual evidence as
to any cures performed during it, though the French think that anything
that can conceivably happen, even by a miracle, does happen.

After this the Maid escorted the new king to Laon. Here too they
found no resistance. The whole city was open to the King. It was the

7 July 17, 1429.

same in all the towns between Paris and Laon. The citizens and all the populace poured out to meet them with the wildest rejoicing. The King was even encouraged to hope that he might take Paris, but when he had entered its territory and no one came to meet him, he realized that he had been misled and withdrew. But the Maid with a braver spirit advanced with a body of troops to the gate leading to the Marché aux Pourceaux, attacked it fiercely, and set it on fire in the hope of capturing the city. While she was fighting there with more courage than prudence and meeting with stubborn resistance from within, she was wounded by a random arrow. As soon as she knew she was hurt, she retired from the field and her men ceased the assault. It was then that the Maid's prestige began to wane, since she who had been thought inviolable was shown to be vulnerable. Thereafter her name was regarded by the English with less terror and by the French with less reverence. However her wound soon healed and she was back in camp; but though she bore arms as usual, she accomplished nothing memorable.

The Maid, when she knew that the King was crowned and safely on his throne, impatient of inaction returned to attack the enemy. She stormed many towns and received the surrender of many; some which were besieged by the enemy she saved by her prompt aid. Finally when the English were besieging the strongly fortified town of Compiègne which was hostile to Paris, she marched with her troops to aid the besieged. The enemy learned of her coming and laid an ambush for her. She had to pass through vineyards and narrow paths and when she had entered them she was attacked both in front and in the rear. There was a fierce battle in a confined space. The Maid was completely surrounded and since she could not deploy her forces and was outnumbered and had no possible chance of retreat, she surrendered. Jean of Luxemburg, the noble Count of Ligny, who was then in the service of the English, took her captive and kept her for some time in one of his fortresses.

Some say she was taken in a different way. They say that Philip, Duke of Burgundy, who had marched against the enemy then ravaging Picardy, was in the habit of hunting near the river Aisne. The Maid, who was not far off, learned of this and thinking to take him off his guard charged on the huntsmen with 6,000 picked cavalry. Philip, who was warned of the attack, quickly marshaled his men and at once engaged the Maid in a battle in which Jean took her prisoner. Philip forbade his captive being brought to him, since he thought it inglorious to have fought even a victorious fight with a woman.

However that may be, it is generally agreed that she was captured in battle, sold to the English for 10,000 crowns, and taken to Rouen, where she was rigorously examined as to whether she had dealings with diviners or the devil and whether she was guilty of any heresy. They could find nothing to correct except the man's dress she wore and this they did not think deserved the extreme penalty. She was thrust back into prison with the warning that she would suffer death if she should again put on men's clothes. She who had learned to bear arms, and delighted in military exercises was tempted by her guards, who would offer her now a military cloak, now a cuirass, now a breastplate or other armor, and sometimes she would unthinkingly put on men's garments or arms, not knowing that she was putting on death. It is possible that the English, who had been vanquished by the Maid in so many battles, never felt really safe while she lived, even though she was a prisoner; that they feared she might escape or work some magic and therefore tried to find a pretext for her death.

When the judges learned that she had put on men's dress, they condemned her to be burned as having "relapsed." *She bore the flames with unshakable and gallant courage.* Her ashes were thrown into the Seine that they might never receive any honor.

Thus died Jeanne, that astonishing and marvelous maid, who restored the kingdom of France when it was fallen and almost torn asunder; who inflicted so many heavy defeats upon the English; who being made general over men kept her purity unstained among companies of soldiers; of whom no breath of scandal was ever heard. Whether her career was a miracle of Heaven or a device of men I should find it hard to say. Some think that when the English cause was prospering and the French nobles at variance among themselves thought no one fit to be commander, one shrewder than the rest evolved the cunning scheme of declaring that the Maid had been sent by Heaven and of giving her the command she asked for, since there was no man alive who would refuse to have God for his leader. Thus it came about that the conduct of the war and the high command were entrusted to a girl. *Nor would this have been difficult to manage with the French, who think hearsay is the same as knowledge.* This at any rate is beyond question that it was the Maid under whose command the siege of Orléans was raised, by whose arms all the country between Bourges and Paris was subdued, by whose advice Rheims was recovered and the coronation celebrated there, by whose charge Talbot was routed and his army cut to pieces, by whose daring the gate of Paris was fired, by whose quick wit and untiring effort the French cause was saved. It is a phenomenon that deserves to be recorded, although afterages are likely to regard it with more wonder than credulity.

Charles, though he grieved bitterly for the Maid's death, did not desert his cause, but in person and by his captains fought many battles not only against the English but against the Burgundians—battles which are worth recording and will perhaps be included in this work.

France, wasted by such disasters, presented the appearance of a vast desert rather than a kingdom. Cities lay ruined and stripped of their inhabitants; farms were in ashes; the country everywhere was laid waste; nowhere could a small party travel in safety; if a man escaped brigands he fell among wild beasts. Martin V of the Colonna family, who was then pope, pitying these sore afflictions of the French sent Niccolò, Cardinal of Santa Croce, a man famed for his saintly life and quick wit (*whom you would hardly believe born at Bologna*) to France to try to reconcile the kings. But *the French had not yet sufficiently repented of their sins*. There still remained considerable traces of the pride inborn in that people, which made peace impossible.

This is the appropriate place to explain what is meant by the Pragmatic Sanction and how it came to exist among the French. Some say it means a rescript of a prince. We more correctly call it "sanction in regard to causes"; for causa is Latin for the Greek $\pi\varrho\tilde{a}\gamma\mu a$. Among the French however the Pragmatic Sanction was a law in regard to ecclesiastical matters confirmed by consent of the bishops and by a royal edict. It originated in the Council of Basle in the following manner: Between the Fathers assembled there and Pope Eugenius there were numerous violent dissensions which were the nursery of many evils for the Christian religion. Since each side insisted that it possessed the supreme authority, one excommunicated the other and only after many years and the greatest difficulty were they reunited during the pontificate of Nicholas V and God's flock gathered at peace under one shepherd in one fold. But while the schism lasted and the Council was in session, since the authority which had once belonged to bishops was now shared not only by abbots but by provosts, priors, canons, simple priests, and lowly monks, many of its decrees were promulgated contrary to virtue and justice in order to weaken the eminence of the Roman and Supreme See, as is often the case in a mixed crowd, which is always hostile to a prince and champions popular liberty. There were present from France and Germany many ecclesiastics of the lower ranks who through their own fault had failed to rise in the Roman Curia and so had come to the Council imbued with bitter hatred against the Apostolic See. There were also certain bishops who had been removed from their sees for their crimes. These represented the populace in the Council and sponsored laws which appeared likely to be most acceptable to the common people and would restrict the power and dignity of the Pope.

At this time a law was passed in regard to holding a council every ten years and it was declared that the Bishop of Rome was subject to a general synod in matters concerning the Faith or the ending of schism or the reformation of the Church Universal. A regulation was passed as to the number and qualifications of cardinals; the annates were abolished; reservation of benefices except such as were provided for in the corpus juris were forbidden; elections of bishops, which had largely fallen out of use, were restored; the confirmation of bishops, which all over the world had been referred to the pope, was transferred to metropolitans and their prelates; expectative graces were abolished; direct appeals, even those to the Apostolic See, were forbidden. And to all these measures was appended an irritating clause providing for the contingency of the pope's making any move or attempt against them. They passed many other measures which, though they appeared innocent on the surface, yet were full of venom. If you should read through the enormous volume of these decrees, you would find very few that do not appear to have been passed out of hatred for the Holy See or a desire for unbridled license.

When the bishops of France received these decrees, they called a synod of the church of their kingdom at Bourges and when they had examined the volume they accepted those that appeared to be to their own advantage and rejected the rest. They accepted very few measures in the precise form in which they had been passed in the Council. Some they shortened, others they expanded, as if the authority to make laws were vested in them. They produced to suit themselves a new volume of decrees containing all that had been ratified at Constance or Basle in contempt or detraction of the Apostolic See. Nor did they hesitate themselves to lay down the law for the pope and to fix the bounds beyond which he might not step.

It was the sixteenth year of Charles's reign and the 1438th of the Incarnation of our Lord, when the prelates of France on July 7 presented the completed volume of the Pragmatic Sanction to this same Charles for his approval. Charles, apparently forgetting the divine grace which he had experienced through the Maid as well as the many benefits heaped upon him by the Apostolic See in sending the Cardinal of Santa Croce to reconcile the Burgundians with him, approved these impious and unjust enactments and commanded that they should be observed throughout his dominions on pain of most severe punishment.

This decree of the King together with the constitutions of the prelates received the name of the Pragmatic Sanction. The numerous envoys sent to France by the Apostolic See during the lives of Eugenius, Nicholas, and Calixtus to obtain its annulment accomplished nothing. It was twenty-four years before it was completely wiped out under Pius II. As a result of this law the prelates of France, who thought they were going to be free, were reduced to the most abject servitude and became practically slaves of the laity. They were forced to give evidence in the French parliament in individual cases; to confer benefices at the pleasure of the king or other princes and powerful nobles; to advance to the priesthood minors, ignoramuses, monsters, and libertines; to remit the punishment of those they had condemned for misdeeds and to absolve the excommunicated without their making atonement. No independent right of censure was left them. Anyone who brought to France an apostolic letter opposing the Pragmatic Sanction was condemned to death. Cases concerning bishops, metropolitan churches, marriages, and heresy were investigated in parliament and the insolence of the laity ran riot in France to such an extent that the most holy Body of Christ, when, as often happened, it was being carried in procession to be worshipped by the people or taken as viaticum for the sick, was ordered to halt by the supreme authority of the king. Bishops and other prelates and priests deserving of respect were haled off to public prisons; estates of the Church and all property of the clergy were confiscated on flimsy pretexts of the decision of a secular judge and given over to the laity. Thus many acts of folly were brought about by the Pragmatic Sanction and either enforced or permitted by an ungrateful king.

Meantime, when the summer was over, Pius, who had been invited by Giovanni, Cardinal of San Sisto, to visit the monastery of Subiaco over which he presided, set out with four cardinals on a trip for pleasure and refreshment. They crossed the Aniene at Tivoli, followed along its left bank, and spent the first night at Vicovaro, which some think means Varro's town and some Varus's. It lies on a high cliff and is triangular in shape. Two sides are protected by precipitous rocks divided on one side by a never-failing stream and on the other jutting out into the current of the Aniene. The third side is defended by a lofty tower, a strongly fortified citadel, and an artificial moat. It still retains traces of its early splendor. A good part of the wall constructed of huge square blocks of stone such as we see in ancient works is still standing; lying

about are numerous columns and broken statues that yet give evidence
of the talent of their sculptors. Francesco Orsini, when prefect of the
city, began a noble chapel [8] of gleaming white marble and adorned it
with fine statues and flowers, works of art by no means despicable for
our times. Death prevented his completing his work and his successors,
who are contesting their inheritance by force of arms, have not yet put
the finishing touches to it.

Pius granted the town indulgence that the chapel might be completed.
He lodged in a house overlooking the Aniene which commanded a most
delightful view, as did also the mountain on the other side of the river
which was covered with forests still green and leafy. The land down by
the river was either meadows or vineyards; the hills were clothed halfway up with vines and the rest of the way with acorn-bearing oaks.

From here they went to San Clemente some two miles distant. The
people worship there with the greatest reverence and the monks are
celebrated for their sanctity. The ground where the monastery stands is
level but behind it the cliffs above the Aniene fall to such a depth that
the eye can hardly see the water at their base. The Pope entered the
chapel and prayed. Then after blessing the monks he continued his
journey, never going far from the riverbank.

There were many castles on the high hills on either side from which
everywhere men and women, old people, boys and girls ran down in
crowds to meet the Pope and receive his blessing. Some offered him
wine, others food. He ordered lunch to be prepared on the road beside a
bubbling crystal spring. It is incredible how many clear brooks run into
the Aniene, how many unfailing springs gush out on both banks, but
under the town of Agosta such a head of water bursts forth from the
living rock that it furnishes enough power to keep four mills or even
more going all the time. Its source among the rocks spreads out into a
space as broad as a courtyard, but the water is not over a man's head.
The bottom is covered with shining gravel which in many places is
spattered up with a pleasant sound by the bubbling water. The water
itself is cold, sweet, and so crystal clear that you can see to the very
bottom. By this spring the Pope lunched with the cardinals. He took
long draughts of the fresh water and the cardinals did the same, enjoying the cold water more than the sweet wine. All the populace in the
meadows beyond the spring were given food, though the crowds that
had hurried down from the neighboring castles to see the Pope were

[8] The octagonal chapel of San Giacomo known as "Il Tempietto," completed about
1464.

very large. After lunch the peasants of the region, to please the Pope, waded into the river and began to fish upstream. The Pope, proceeding along the bank (for it was field and meadowland), watched the fishers, who every time they caught a fish shouted to him and gave the trout (for there is hardly any other kind of fish in the river) to his attendants. Thus he accomplished a great part of the journey most delightfully.

When they entered the vineyards of the town of Subiaco, they were met by the Cardinal and a little later by a procession of priests and monks. The Pope was received by the people with the greatest delight, for never within the memory of man had a pope come there before. The town is densely populated. The houses are built on the side of the cliff, one above another. On the summit is the citadel, which would be almost impregnable if it were not commanded by a higher cliff across the valley. The Aniene encircles most of the town. From the town to the monastery of Subiaco is a distance of two miles over steep rocks and difficult paths which an enemy could easily cut off.

When they reached the monastery they found there enough level space for a church, cloister, and the offices necessary for a monastery. All these had been built at great expense by earlier monks. The Pope noticed a new vineyard heavy with ruddy grapes which had been quarried out of the rock. It was walled all round and encircled by a green olive grove. In the middle was a press and a white dwelling house. He asked who was responsible for this new project and was told that it was a certain Bishop of Silves, a Spaniard of Lusitania, who had grown weary of ecclesiastical pomp and hated the cares of this world. He had therefore resigned his church, keeping only an annual income sufficient to live on decently, and had come here. He lived among the brethren wearing his former dress, attended and, on occasion, celebrated mass. Except for his dress and his independence he was no different from a monk. He had built this house and planted this vineyard, which would bring the monks a large income.

The Pope sent for the Bishop and when he learned the reason for his resigning his church and for his love of solitude, he approved the purpose of a man who had learned how to exchange the things of this world for those of Heaven. The bishop died soon after this. He was blessed indeed if, as we may believe, his contempt of the world was sincere and if he did not reject a high dignity in this world in hope of gaining a higher.

Praises most acceptable to God are sung both day and night in this monastery by some of the monks and by others in another monastery

called Il Speco. This is approached by a flight of steps a mile long cut
in the rock, a very difficult path and so steep that it is terrifying to follow.
On one side a deep precipice drops to the Aniene and on the other is
a towering overhanging cliff. The path would not be practicable at all
except that it winds about like a snake now to the right, now to the left,
from the foot to the summit and is protected in many places by a wall.

The monastery is built into the base of a lofty cliff so that a part of
the roof is formed by the great crag and part of it is built to extend outside. The sacred house itself and many of the cells of the monks extend
within the rock. Benedict, that great father of the monks, inspired by
God, in whom Nursia poured out all the virtue she possessed, before
there was any building here or any man lived here, chose this spot for
a place of solitary penitence, far from the life of men, known only to
God. He made his bed on the hard stone. Here he mortified himself
with vigils and fasting; here he offered a most acceptable service to God.
Disciples followed him and the cave began to be inhabited. As in a high
cliff we see nests of swallows on the ledges of the rock, so we may see
this monastery clinging to the lofty crag from which fragments often
fall, killing monks or carrying away parts of the building. Many
miracles are reported to have been done here by the Saint and they
show the bell with which the devil tried to mock his good works.

About twenty monks live here. They are, we may well believe, dear
to God. They never eat meat; they dilute their wine with a large
quantity of water; they keep long fasts; to eat two eggs is luxury; they
live on cabbage and bread with the addition of legumes. Such are the
feasts with which they load their tables. Only the briefest time is devoted to eating and but little more to sleep; the rest they spend in
prayer. They celebrate mass with the most profound devotion and
trustingly sing hymns to God. The greater number are old men, most
of whom have lived in perfect health to eighty. Their faces are animated; their conversation worthy of reverence. Their one desire is to
be dissolved and be with Christ.

When Pius had ordered mass to be celebrated before him in both
the upper and the lower monastery and had kissed all the places which
tradition says the body of Benedict touched, he vouchsafed the spiritual
grace which the monks asked and having set at rest the consciences of
all, he went down to the town for the night.

The next day he crossed the bridge over the Aniene and climbed a
very high and difficult mountain, from which he descended to a
wooded valley where converging streams, not finding an outlet, made

a pool and marshy ground attractive to wild boars. Nearby are meadows and all around are hills covered with very high forests. Here
lunch was prepared for the Pope, at which the Cardinal of Teano was
his guest. Federigo of Urbino was following with his army to march
against the Duke of Sora and do those things which we have already
described. For our narrative is not composed in strict chronological
order; we try to assign an event merely to the year or month when it
occurred, unless we have ourselves secured fuller information in regard
to it. Perhaps some one else will undertake the task of putting each
detail in its proper order. We have not had the time.

The Cardinal of Teano after lunching with the Pope went back to
his army. The Pope, when he had blessed the people who had assembled in great numbers in the meadow, descended over rough and
wooded mountains into Campania near the town of Palliano, *which
Calixtus is said to have given Cardinal Prospero Colonna to induce him
to vote for him for pope.* Nicholas V took this town from the Contis as
punishment for a crime.

Cardinal Prospero with his brother, the prefect of the town, and his
nephews came to meet the Pope, putting himself and all he had at his
service. When they came within sight of Genazzano, the prefect leapt
from his horse, knelt before Pius, and pointing to the splendid and
lofty palace which Pope Martin V built for himself and his kinsmen,
he said, "Yonder is my house. I beg you, Father, descend to it and do
not scorn to lodge where your predecessor often dwelt. Your presence,
if you will come, will do honor to both the place and the owner." The
Pope was very eager to see this place of which he had heard much as a
lad and to find out whether Martin's buildings were superior to his,
but since the prefect the year before had disregarded all his commands,
he thought he did not deserve the chance to boast of having so exalted a
guest. *The scorner was scorned.*

The prefect's brother, Adoardo, Duke of Marsi, received the Pope in
the town of Cave and loaded him with honors. Here was seen a strange
thing which no one would believe who had not seen it with his own
eyes. In front of the town is a little pit of clay. If you plunge into it a
staff or a sword and let it stay even the briefest time, you cannot with
any force pull it out. This story was told to the Pope. He thought it a
fairy tale and refused to believe it till he sent his chamberlains and
physicians to see it tested. When the Pope's barber could not by any
strength or skill pull out a sword which had become embedded there,
he left the sword and went back dumfounded to the Pope, saying that a

place was bewitched that could hold iron or wood plunged into the bowels of the earth. This miracle was not unknown to Pliny, who says, "At Arae Muciae in the territory of Veii, near Tusculum, and in the Ciminian forest there are places where objects embedded in the earth cannot be drawn out." [9]

From Cave they went to Praeneste,[10] an ancient and famous town celebrated for great defeats of the Romans. Its ruins today attest its splendor in antiquity. All about lie ruined palaces, broken pieces of temples, squared stones of almost incredible size from the walls. It is inhabited only by a few peasants, kept there merely by the fertility of the soil. Under Eugenius it was more flourishing, but when the tyrant of the city rebelled against him, the Patriarch of Alexandria, a native of Corneto, invested the city with his army, though it was thought to be impregnable since it was situated on a high mountain and was not without defenders. He conquered it by cutting off the only aqueduct which supplied the city with water. The city was sacked and burned; the walls were razed and it was left desolate. The bells of the church were taken to Corneto. Under Nicholas V Stefano Colonna rebuilt the walls, brought back the inhabitants, and built a citadel on top of the mountain. *Would that it had been without hurt to the Church!*

After leaving Praeneste the Pope reached Passarano about noon. Below the town issues a copious and very clear spring, which is said to supply the water which the prefect of the city has drawn up by ropes from a very deep well. By this spring dinner was prepared for the Pope and the cardinals in shelters hastily built of branches. Fish from the lake *of Nemi* nearby satisfied the multitude (for it was a fast day).

From here they returned to Tivoli and from there a little later, October 6, to Rome, taking with them as hostages all who had seemed most mutinous, chief among them Giovanni, Tozio, and Clemente.

The Pope was met on his return by the college of cardinals, Thomas, tyrant of Morea, and a great throng of ambassadors from various peoples and kings. They were a marvelous sight with their foreign dress and ways, but all eyes were turned especially on the embassy from the King of Poland. It was preceded by a large body of handsome young nobles dressed in green, mounted on tall, stocky horses, their *curly* yellow hair floating behind them in the wind. They carried in one hand, as is the national custom, ballistas and in the other a sword; they wore quivers of the hide of the Libyan bear filled with arrows; on their heads

[9] *Natural History*, II, 211.
[10] I.e., Palestrina.

they wore light plumed green hats or garlands of flowers. The beauty of these lads seemed more than human. As the Pope approached they leapt from their horses and prostrating themselves together with the chiefs of the embassy they made obeisance to the Savior's Vicar, whom they had never seen before.

The Pope on his entrance into the city was greeted by the citizens with the greatest enthusiasm. After doing reverence to the blessed apostles in the Basilica of St. Peter he retired to the apostolic palace. He had been away less than three months.

BOOK VII

MEANTIME Carlotta, Queen of Cyprus, came to Pius to ask aid in her difficulties. Sending ahead couriers to ask for an audience, she sailed up the river and landed near the church of St. Paul. The Pope gave orders that the cardinals and the entire Curia should meet her and on her arrival he received her publicly in the hall of consistory. He then assigned her lodgings in a retired part of the palace where she and her retinue were magnificently entertained. She appeared to be about twenty-four years old, was of medium height with sparkling eyes and complexion between blond and brunet, *and not without charm*. Her conversation was engaging and in true Greek fashion came pouring out like a torrent. She dressed in the French mode. Her manners were such as became a lady of royal station. At their first meeting, after she had kissed Pius's feet, she said little but the next day when she had audience with the Pope in the presence of only a few, she delivered through an interpreter the following speech:

"Your Holiness, I cannot think that the misfortunes of my house are unknown to you, for what region of the world is not full of our trouble? Who does not know of the woes of the Cypriotes and the wretched lot of that kingdom? For myself, I have twice been unfortunately married. The husband I took from Portugal I lost by a sudden and untimely death. The husband I summoned from Savoy I have left besieged by the enemy. Whether he is *alive and* free or captive I know not. As the only daughter of their marriage my parents brought me up in the expectation of ruling. I succeeded my father and having been proclaimed queen ascended the throne together with my husband. My illegitimate brother (if he who persecutes his own kin is a brother) with the aid of Egypt has usurped my inheritance. He now sits on the throne and is seeking to take me and my husband to kill us. Our one remaining refuge was Cerines. There we escaped from the bloody hands of my hostile brother. The rest of the island except Famagusta and Colossus is in the possession of the enemy.

"And what enemies! Do you think perhaps that Christians or friends of our religion are opposing us? Dismiss that idea. We are waging war with the enemies of the Cross of Christ. The Egyptians, the most bitter foes of our faith and the adherents of Mohammedan madness, hold Cyprus. They have been given permission to deport from the kingdom any children they please, to destroy the temples of our God, to introduce the worship of Mahomet. My pseudo-Christian brother has bound himself to the Sultan by a most vile oath in order to gain the throne. But he is bitterly deceived. He has the name of king. The power belongs to the Sultan's admiral. I tried as long as I could to keep the kingdom for myself and for Christ. Mahomet has conquered. We have both been expelled. Our last faint hope is in my husband at Cerines, if indeed even that still remains. On my way to beg your help I fell in with Venetian ships whose captains robbed me of all my possessions. With difficulty I obtained their permission to continue my voyage keeping only a single garment and scanty rations. Driven from my kingdom, poor and naked, I have fled straight to you. Succor, I beseech you, one who has twice been as good as widowed. Pity royal blood, pity an unhappy kingdom, that it may not abjure the true faith, that the Egyptians may not come there in the place of Christians. You are the father of our religon and the Head of our faith. It behooves you to see first of all that the Christian worship does not lose ground. If Cyprus is lost, Rhodes will be lost too; nor will Crete be safe. Barbarian fleets will sail even to Sicily and the shores of Italy. From Egypt, Africa, Syria, Asia, and Greece Italy will be threatened unless you go to meet them in time, unless you lend aid before the eastern islands are in the enemy's hands. If you will help me I do not lack the courage to recover my father's throne in a very short time. A small force of western troops will give me the victory. The Egyptians cannot withstand the armies of the west. Nor do I ask aid of you only. I purpose to hasten on to my father-in-law, my aunt, and mother-in-law, and my kindred sovereigns of the French; from them I hope to raise a sufficient army. Do you furnish me with wheat and wine for my besieged supporters. But I cannot go to Savoy without your help. After being racked by storms I can no longer endure the sea, nor have I any food on my ships. The way by land is also closed to me since I have neither horses nor money. I am in your power, your Holiness. I die unless you stretch out your hand."

With these words she burst into tears and was silent. Pius answered: "Dry your tears, my daughter, and have faith. We will not abandon you. Your nobility is known to us, and your affliction. Your experience is unjust but not uncommon. A throne is an unstable thing. No power is of long duration. Fortune delights to exalt some and bring down others. Now your house *is the object of her sport*. She has given the throne to your brother and sent you into exile. In our opinion you are paying the penalty for the sins of your father-in-law and your husband. Your father-in-law, when asked in the Congress of Mantua to promise for the defense of the Faith against the Turks what the other Italian princes promised, could not by any means be persuaded to hold out the least hope of aid. Your husband, when he sailed out to you, did not deign to come to us at Mantua, as he might very easily have done since he sailed up the Po past the confluence of the Mincio. Both father and son slighted us, wherefore we said to the cardinals, 'The house of Savoy despises the Church and does not deign to promise aid to our religion.

" 'This youth who is now voyaging to Cyprus will be punished. He thinks he is going to have a kingdom as a dowry; he is wrong; he will be ejected. I pray he may escape the hands of his enemies. His father who has *insolently* refused us aid against the Turks will come to us as a suppliant to beg aid for his son. God grant that we may be able to succor him!' Our prophecy has come true. Would that it had been false: It has pleased God to punish the stubbornness of your house and of the house of Savoy. All that you have asked you shall receive from us. We will give you horses with which to go to your father-in-law and money for the journey. When you return to Ancona you will find corn and wine there for you to carry in your ships to the besieged. The army with which to regain your kingdom you will yourself raise in Savoy and France."

The Queen in reply expressed her thanks. She remained some ten days in Rome till she had visited the chief churches of the martyrs. She had four or five audiences with the Pope and then, having obtained the grace she desired for herself and her companions, she set out on her journey. The Pope directed every cardinal to give her a horse and he himself made up the necessary number. He furnished her also with a steward to supply her with funds for the journey even outside the lands of the Church if the need should arise. Her escort consisted of about fifty horsemen. The Sienese following the Pope's example supplied them abundantly with food while they were in their territory. The Florentines and the Bolognese did likewise, as did the others through whose domains they had to pass on the way to Savoy. All received her with the honors due a queen.

Nowhere was she made less welcome than in Savoy. Here she was received with grim looks, sour expressions, bitter and harsh words. "Why," her father-in-law said, "do you come to us at this time? How is it decent for a young woman to leave her husband and sail from the east to the west? to ask hospitality from so many strangers? 'I came,' you say, 'to seek aid.' But it was more fitting for a husband to seek to do that. How often have we sent aid! How often have we helped you! Even now we are supplying men, arms, corn, money. What is going to be the limit of all this? Cyprus has *already* drained Savoy; all our fatness has gone to you. The province is empty. You have lost a kingdom in Cyprus and we shall soon have no empire in Savoy, since it has come to the point where for your sake we have had to alienate our taxes and all our income." Her mother-in-law, who was also her aunt, had no kinder words for her. Therefore the unhappy queen in grief and despair sailed back by way of Mantua and Venice to Rhodes without daring to proceed to France, since she had had a taste in Savoy of the liberality and magnificence of Transalpine princes.

At this point, since the subject of Savoy has come up, we should like to mention a few important matters in regard to the princes of that country in our time.

Savoy is situated in the Alps which separate France from Italy and extends from the Gulf of Genoa to the Swiss. Part of Savoy is bordered by the province of Arles, part by Dauphiny. The Rhone flows through a large part of it. The most important part is about Lake Geneva, on which are situated the noble cities of Geneva and Lausanne. The first duke was Amadeo, whose dominion extended for a long distance on each side of the Alps. There were twelve pontifical churches under his authority. He married the sister of Philip, Duke of Burgundy. Of his two daughters he married one to Filippo, Duke of Milan, and the other to Louis, King of Sicily, whom we have mentioned above. His eldest son, Louis, he married to a bride from Cyprus. He was related by marriage with almost all Christian kings. The misfortunes of his neighbors were his great good fortune. In France there was hot dissension between Burgundians and Armagnacs. England too was torn with mad passions. In Italy the Venetians and Florentines were fighting against the Duke of Milan with implacable hatred. Amadeo in his mountain kingdom far from war was constantly being chosen as arbiter by one party or the other and he was considered the only one of them all who knew how to give good counsel to himself and others. *The folly of others made him seem wise.* For a long time the Italians on one hand and the French on the other came to him as to a second Solomon for advice on difficult

matters. Finally he too *fell and* proved that the wisdom of this world
is vain and fleeting.

In his old age there began the Council of Basle, with which from the
very first Pope Eugenius was at variance. Amadeo's wife (he had married only once) had died. They say that witches, who *are very numerous
in Savoy, and* predict the future *by tricks and the art of demons,* went
to Amadeo and prophesied that he would be pope because Eugenius
would be deposed by the Council and Amadeo would be elected in his
place. Amadeo, whether influenced by this hope or by his own nature,
abdicated his ducal throne, cast away all the pomp of the world, and
withdrew to a hermitage leaving the governing of his subjects to his
eldest son. On the shores of Lake Geneva near Lausanne were lofty
forests and beneath them meadows watered by running streams. A great
tract of these he walled in and stocked with stags and does and wild
animals that do not attack man. Nearby on the shore of the lake he
built a church. He inducted priests, instituted prebends and other dignities, and built houses where the canons could live in comfort. Not far
off he erected a great palace adequately fortified with a moat and
ramparts. In it were seven suites of apartments. Six, all alike, were
suitable for cardinals. Each had its hall, chamber, antechamber, and
secret closets or storehouses for valuables. The seventh, intended for the
Duke, no one would have thought unfit for a king or pope.

Here Amadeo lived with six nobles who had followed him. They
were all elderly and of almost the same age. Their wives were long since
dead. Not one was under sixty. Since they were knights and soldiers
who had often commanded in wars and had fought with distinction,
when they put off the garb of the world under Amadeo as their dean
and master they assumed a new service and desired to be called soldiers
of St. Maurice; nearby St. Maurice with his Theban Legion suffered
martyrdom for the name of Christ. All assumed the cloak and robe,
the girdle and crooked staff of hermits; they wore their beards long
and their hair uncut. The place was called Ripaille and is about five
miles from Thonon. The Cardinal of Santa Croce on his way to France
the second time to treat for peace put in here with his ships. Amadeo
came to meet him through the woods, which we have said were surrounded with a wall, to the gate on the shore.

It was a sight worth seeing which posterity will hardly believe. The
most powerful prince of the age, who was an object of fear to the French
and Italians alike, who had worn robes of gold and been surrounded by
throngs of courtiers, who had been preceded by axes and followed by

troops of armed men and a throng of the powerful, now received the Apostolic Legate clad in mean and humble garments, preceded by only six hermits and followed by a few priests. They seemed a company deserving of reverence. The hermits wore on their breasts a gold cross, the only sign of noble rank they retained. Everything else indicated scorn of the world. The Cardinal and Amadeo embraced and kissed with warm affection. The Cardinal could not sufficiently admire and praise the altered life of the prince, though he was suspicious of the change and feared *what was common talk,* that Amadeo forsooth hoped to be pope and for that reason had become a hermit. Amadeo remained in the hermitage wearing this garb for about eight years. Although he had delegated the cares of government to his son, he had the more important matters referred to himself. He did not resign the title of duke nor did he trust money matters to anyone else.

Meantime the delegates at Basle, thoroughly angry at Eugenius, decided to depose him. When they were unable to do this, because there were not enough bishops present, Amadeo sent to the Council all the bishops, abbots, and distinguished clergy of his domain. By their efforts the deposition of Eugenius was finally extorted from the Council and shortly afterwards by the decree of the Council (which Eugenius had already dissolved) Amadeo himself was called to the papacy. Eugenius, before he was deposed, had transferred the Council from Basle to Ferrara that it might meet there with the Greeks whose union with the Roman Church was then under discussion. But this change of place did not please all nor was Eugenius's deposition acceptable to kings and princes. Most of the world stood by him. The Germans declared themselves neutral. Only Savoy, the Swiss, and some few dioceses recognized the deposition of Eugenius and the elevation of Amadeo.

Distinguished envoys were sent from Basle to Savoy headed by Louis, Cardinal of Arles. They sought out Amadeo at Ripaille and delivered to him the decree of election. Amadeo after calling a council of his nobles (for all the nobility of Savoy had gathered there) said that he would obey the decrees of the Fathers of the holy synod. Thereupon he was received in conclave, from which he returned with his beard shaved and also his head except for a narrow circle of hair, and he was robed in the pontifical garments, *though indeed the splendor of his robes only made him more insignificant. For the barber's razor had removed what had been a real and becoming ornament, that is a long full beard which covered all the blemishes on his face and appeared to lend him a kind of dignity, and when he appeared without it, with his insignificant face, slanting eyes (for he squinted) and flabby cheeks he looked like a very ugly monkey.* Then sitting in front of the tribunal, wearing the papal robe and miter, he created Louis, the elder of his sons, Duke of Savoy and the younger, Philip, Count of Geneva.

He then went to Thonon where he held court for many days and finally at the approach of summer went with great pomp by way of Lausanne and Soloturn to Basle. There, raised on a dais before the cathedral in the presence of his sons with the Fathers standing beside him, in the midst of a great crowd of the populace who had thronged there from the neighboring districts to see this strange and unusual event, he was ordained bishop by the Cardinal of Arles and crowned with the apostolic tiara, while the scribes and advocates shouted, "Long life to Felix V (for that was the name he had taken), elected and crowned by God!" The ceremony was attended by crowds from all directions, though because only one cardinal was present, it appeared poor and mean. All the usual forms were observed. A procession of marvelous splendor passed through the city. There was a sumptuous banquet at which all the Curia were present.[1]

Felix remained many months in Basle. He presided over the Council, settled cases, created bishops, made cardinals. He received the Emperor Frederick, who was passing that way, in secret audience; and indeed the Emperor for his part did not wish publicly to acknowledge Amadeo as pope.

When Amadeo had spent the summer and the following winter at Basle without his pontificate being recognized by the Christian kings, he finally returned to Savoy the next spring and soon after summoned the Council to come to him from Basle since the Fathers were expelled from there by imperial edict. Finally when he realized he was despised by all and had no hope of commanding obedience, when Eugenius was long since dead and Nicholas V had been elected in his place, he decided, on the mediation of Charles, King of France, to give peace to the Church. He renounced the papacy, was reconciled with Nicholas, whom he acknowledged as the true pope, and received from him the cardinalate and post of Apostolic Legate *in Philip's dominions* so long as he should live, taking the title of Cardinal of Santa Sabina. In this dignity he finally died and was buried at Ripaille. He would have been deemed both fortunate and wise had he not been a fool in his old age.

Meanwhile Louis, King of France, had publicly sworn on the sacred Gospels to the Bishop of Arras and Antonio da Noceto, whom the Pope

[1] It will be recalled that Pius was in the service of Felix V at that time.

had sent to France, that he would soon abrogate the Pragmatic Sanction, since he had vowed to God to do so. He wrote the same to Pope Pius and begged him to bestow the cardinalate on the Bishop of Arras and the protonotary d'Albret, thinking that to obtain two cardinals for one letter was no more than he deserved. If he had to give up one, it could not be the Bishop. Philip, Duke of Burgundy, also wrote urgently demanding the creation of Arras. Pius for many days before the election considered the matter with the cardinals. *He regarded it as a hateful thing to do and utterly alien to the college.*

The cardinals met and pledged themselves by the most solemn promises and oaths not to allow the senate to be increased except by those whom Pius himself had created. They urged one another to resist and there was not one of the old cardinals who showed any signs that he could be influenced. They said the number was already larger than it should be and there was no need of a new creation. The Pope replied that the Transalpine nations had been neglected and some cardinals ought to be created from them. They need not now discuss the question of a creation, which had long ago been promised, but only the number and the individuals to be elected. *All attempts to persuade the cardinals as a body were fruitless. All were aghast at the Pope's words and like adders stopped their ears against persuasion, making only ambiguous and confused answers. The Pope then proceeded to speak with individuals alone. He made use of exhortation, flattery, promises, terror, and threats, whichever he thought suited to the character of his listener.*

Orsini and Avignon and many others were strongly in favor of the Bishop of Corneto, but loathed the Bishop of Arras like the devil. Among these was the Cardinal of Spoleto, who though he dared not oppose the Pope's wish, humbly entreated him not to bring a pernicious and stubborn fellow into the sacred college. The Cardinal of San Marco did likewise and one after another the cardinals kept coming to the Pope with new charges against Arras. Avignon indeed said, "I hear that you mean to make Arras cardinal. He is a heedless, pernicious fellow who makes light of any disgrace. He is venal and never holds to a purpose. He can be influenced as easily as a child and always inclines to the worse side. He is incapable of considered judgment, will yield to no one, regards himself as superior to all the world. He thinks there is nothing he does not know and that he has as thorough an acquaintance with divine and human laws as if he had established them. He has enrolled himself among poets and orators. If military science is being discussed he talks like Phormio in Hannibal's presence. He is a mer-

chant with merchants, a hunter with hunters, a sailor with sailors, a monk with monks, always teaching, never learning. What will he do in the college, this jack of all trades? Do you think he will keep silence or let anyone else speak or refrain from insulting everyone? You will be flinging a firebrand into the senate and a worm to gnaw you continually. He will be an enemy to us and to you. From this moment there will be no peace in the college. He will sow discord and nurture faction. He is a restless spirit and unless I am mistaken the son of an incubus. For myself I foresee continuous warfare with this man if he is given the red hat, and you will not be free of trouble either. I know well that you will be sorry when you have done this and will often say, 'If I had only believed Alain!' If you are wise you will not take a step that brings regret with it."

To this the Pope replied, "What you say, Alain, is perfectly true. We know the man. You have painted him as he is. But what are we to do? On every side are difficulties. If we make him cardinal we involve you and your order in a bitter war and ourselves in one still more bitter. We shall have to fight him continually; we shall never satisfy him; he will never stop seeking disgraceful ends; he will bring up disastrous subjects and be shamelessly demanding and insistent. We shall not have a moment's peace. You say we shall be sorry after doing this. Say rather we are sorry before doing it; and still we are afraid not to do it. With our eyes open we are digging a ditch for ourselves to fall into. But what would you do? Arras is a learned man and eloquent and (as you say) bold. He is Legate to the King of France. His king wants the cardinalate for him. So does Burgundy. We are promised abrogation of the Pragmatic Sanction than which nothing is more hostile to the authority of the Apostolic See. The season for creating cardinals is at hand. If we do not listen to the King's request, the Pragmatic Sanction will not be abolished in the kingdom of France. If Arras knows he has been rejected he will rage like a serpent and spit out all his venom at this See. You know the fellow's temerity and madness and his skill in persuasion, equipped as he is with wide learning which he uses more readily in a bad cause than in a good one. He will pervert the King and though he has said and even written much against the Pragmatic Sanction, so fickle is he that he will not hesitate to support the opposite side and he will find plenty of passages from the Scriptures to cite in favor of it. There is no heresy so damnable that it cannot find fuel in Holy Writ. You know the attitude of the French clergy toward the Church of Rome and how reluctant they are to give up the Pragmatic Sanction. If

Arras changes his position, no one of the King's party will be a foe to it. The King too will change. He is angry with us anyway on account of the kingdom of Sicily. It has often been heard that great fires have been kindled against the Church by those who have not been honored as they thought they deserved and that on this account went over to Mahomet and turned all Arabia, Egypt, and Syria from the true worship of Christ. We admit it is dangerous to make Arras cardinal but, if we are not mistaken, it is more dangerous to slight him. Both courses are bad but of two evils we must choose the less harmful. Resign yourself, Alain. Arras is going to be cardinal—to your and our great annoyance. We are preparing to shoulder the burden; you must do likewise."

Avignon agreed with the Pope and admitted that he was faced with an actual necessity.

Orsini remained to be persuaded. The Pope summoned him and reminded him of the honors he had heaped on his house and asked him not to oppose him in the matter of creating cardinals. If he refrained from doing so, the Bishop of Corneto, his personal friend and the foremost champion of the Guelfs, should be made cardinal. When Orsini remained firm and could not be won over, the Pope said, "You are too wise in your own conceit. You are deceived by your genius and keen intellect which sees more than it should. You think you can change our plans. You are wrong. Plans that are too deep or too subtle come to nothing. Even without you we shall create cardinals. You will find that too keen intellect of yours will not plan for the best advantage of yourself or your friends." Thus he sent Orsini away in disgrace.

Then Pius sent for Colonna and the Camerlengo and told them that if they agreed to the creation of the other cardinals, it would be found necessary to postpone the Bishop of Corneto. When they were relieved of this apprehension (for they feared nothing more than the Bishop of Corneto), they readily agreed to the others and thanked the Pope for saving them from an enemy.

Next the Cardinal of St. Anastasia was summoned. When the Pope could make no impression on him by arguments (he is so dull as to be incapable of reasoning) he disregarded him as being weakminded.

Then he approached the Cardinal of St. Peter [2] as follows: "You know, brother, the agreement made last Lent between us and the sacred college as to the creation of cardinals. The four tempora of our Lord's Advent, which we set as the extreme limit, are almost here. A creation of cardinals was promised and decreed. Now we have to discuss the

[2] Nicholas of Cusa.

number and the individuals to be created. We rely especially on you and if all the others fail us we shall never believe you will do so. Long ago you agreed to our wishes. We named the persons and you objected to none of them. Now you must maintain stoutly what you promised in secret consistory and show yourself one of those who are concerned for our honor. Six cardinals have been created, all Italians. Now foreign nations must be honored. The King of France and the Duke of Burgundy ask for Arras and other kings put forward other candidates. We cannot refuse what they ask without the greatest dishonor to ourselves and perhaps not without harm to the Church. Among the cardinals many are opposed to us. They are stiff-necked; we cannot bend them. We implore you not to join those who are of that mind. It is of the greatest importance to us that when we have shown that it is our wish to create cardinals we should not have to give in nor seem to have less power than the college. Nothing would be more harmful to the business of the kingdom of Sicily than this. Do you who love us, aid us."

The Cardinal of St. Peter listened to these words with a grim expression and finally answered as follows: "I have long suspected, Your Holiness, that I was hateful to you. Now I am certain of it since you ask of me what I cannot grant without incurring Heaven's reproach. You are preparing to create new cardinals without any pressing reason merely at your own whim and you have no regard for the oath you swore to the sacred college in the conclave both before and after your elevation, namely that you would on no account create cardinals unless with the consent of the majority of the college and according to the decrees of the Council of Constance. Now you ignore the ordinance of the synod and do not ask the consent of the college and you wish to make me a tool of your ambition. I cannot do it. I do not know how to flatter. I hate adulation. If you can bear to hear the truth, I like nothing which goes on in this Curia (Fig. 2). Everything is corrupt. No one does his duty. Neither you nor the cardinals have any care for the Church. What observance of the canons is there? What reverence for laws? What assiduity in divine worship? All are bent on ambition and avarice. If I ever speak in a consistory about reform, I am laughed at. I do no good here. Allow me to withdraw. I cannot endure these ways. I am an old man and need rest. I will return into seclusion and since I cannot live for the common weal, I live for myself." With these words he burst into tears.

The Pope answered: "You are wrong, Niccolò, when you think you are hateful to us. Since we came to know you in Basle there has never been a time when we have not loved you for your learning and your blameless character. Nor do we now ask of you what you cannot honorably do. The creation of cardinals is as necessary to the Apostolic See as the abolition of the Pragmatic Sanction is useful. If we do not create cardinals at this time, the Pragmatic Sanction will not be abolished in France and if Arras is slighted he will stir up some grievous trouble. We must also satisfy foreign nations, which were put off at the last creation. You mention the oath we swore in conclave and you reproach us for contempt of religion. You yourself are impious when behind our back also you foist this same charge on your listeners and have no thought for your prince's honor. Far be it from us to violate an oath! There is nothing we abhor so much. You say we make no effort to get the consent of the sacred college in creating cardinals. If this were so there would have been no need of our speaking to you. We have tried to persuade the entire college to agree with our wishes. But if that is not possible it will be enough for the fulfillment of our oath that the majority should assent and already we are assured of the requisite number. We should have liked to have the votes of all and especially yours which we value highly, but if we cannot bend you, we shall have to disregard you and we shall be able to create cardinals without you.

"This however we find most reprehensible of all in you, that you wish to leave the Curia because your advice is not taken. This is pride and intolerable arrogance. You have too high an opinion of yourself. It looks as if you were going to follow the example of Achitophel who hanged himself because his advice was rejected. You think your responses are going to be regarded as if they were Apollo's or the Sibyl's, you hold that your advice ought under no conditions to be rejected, and you prefer to give no counsel at all rather than counsel that is not taken. You say there is no one who does his duty and you do not realize that you are straying far from your own duty and are raving crazy when you think you must flee the Curia because your counsel is not always found acceptable. You are not acting the part of a good or a wise man. It is for a cardinal to give the advice he thinks for the common good. If his advice is heeded, he should thank God that he has given good advice; if it is rejected he should accuse his own ignorance rather than that of his chief and always approve and aid the final decision. He is ill-advised to prefer his own judgment to that of his chief or the majority of the senate.

"You find fault with everything that goes on in the Curia. Neither do we approve everything. Nevertheless it is not yours to censure. To us,

*not to you, St. Peter's skiff has been entrusted. You are bound to give
good counsel, but we are not constrained to follow your advice unless it
seems the best. At our peril the Church stands or falls. You will have to
give an account of your advice, we of our rule. Take thought for what
is yours and let the affairs of others alone. Know that you are a cardinal,
not a pope. Heretofore we have thought you wise. Today you act unlike
yourself, inconstant and grasping. You ask permission to go away. We
do not grant it. Go home and tomorrow talk to me of withdrawing, if
you see fit."*

*While the Pope spoke Niccolò was weeping and sobbing bitterly.
When Pius ended he rose silently overcome with grief and shame, and
making his way through the cardinals in the anteroom without a word
and apparently still in tears went home. Thereafter he put on a meeker
spirit and lost much of his foolish stubbornness showing that the Pope's
rebuke had not been fruitless.*

When the Pope saw that he had won over the majority of the cardinals to agree with him and was sure that his partisans whom he had sent
for would not fail him, he disregarded the rest and convened the college
on the Monday [3] before the four times of Advent.[4] He discoursed on the
creation of cardinals, stated the number, and named the individuals.
The cardinals looked at one another in silence and as they saw from
their expressions that the Pope would have to be obeyed, *since the
greater number were already persuaded,* no one dared to oppose him.
All approved the nominees and agreed to their creation.

The new Italian cardinals were Bartolommeo, Archbishop of
Ravenna, who had long been Legatus in Sicily, a man conspicuous for
learning, wisdom, and integrity; Jacopo, Bishop of Pavia, a Lucchese
by birth but a Sienese by courtesy, adopted into the Piccolomini family
by the Pope himself, who had been charmed by his cleverness; Francesco,[5] son of the prince of Mantua, who was not yet twenty years old
but looked much older (Fig. 16) and had almost the dignity and wisdom of an old man. Francesco was made deacon, the others presbyters.
The French were represented by Jean, Bishop of Arras, whose dis-

[3] Dec. 18, 1461.

[4] The "four times" are the four series of Ember Days—Wednesday, Friday, and Saturday—in the Church calendar, occurring in the first week of Lent, the week after Pentecost, the week after the Feast of Holy Cross (Sept. 14), and the week after the third
Sunday in Advent. In 1461 the Ember Days of Advent were Dec. 16, 18 and 19. The
earlier date given here by Pius has been shown by Pastor to be incorrect.

[5] Francesco Gonzaga, a youth of seventeen years who was called from his studies at
Pavia to receive the red hat.

tinguished gifts of learning, intellect, and almost superhuman memory *were sullied by avarice (now first realized), ambition, and inconstancy,* and Louis d'Albret of the French royal house, a man of quiet manner who lived as befitted his rank; the Spaniards by Jaime of Cardona, Bishop of Urgel, distinguished for his culture and his character, whose ancestors had once sat on the throne. All these were given the title of presbyter.

The Pope had already begun to be troubled with almost incredibly violent attacks of gout. On this account the announcement of the cardinals in open consistory was made without him. The Cardinal of Nicaea spoke in praise of them. The creation was considered satisfactory since all were excellent men capable of being of use to the Church either by their own talents or the help of their friends. They applauded likewise the wisdom of the Pope *in crushing the attempts of the cardinals who opposed him and triumphantly subduing the college to his purpose. Nor could there hereafter be any doubt that he would guide at will a senate of which he himself had created about half.*

Of the new cardinals only Jacopo of Lucca was present. The Pope lying in bed put the red hat on his head with his own hand, gouty though it was. The Pope's officials carried the red hats to Ravenna and Urgel; the others later came to the Curia and were duly invested with the same badge of office.

Meantime a letter arrived from King Louis of France announcing the condemnation and complete abrogation of the Pragmatic Sanction. When the Pope read it in the council he could not keep back tears of joy, seeing that at last during his pontificate this mortal poison had been removed from the Church and it had been granted to his time that the French should once more return to obedience to the Church of Rome. Antonio da Noceto also came back bringing a second letter which confirmed the first and urged that the Bishop of Arras should be made cardinal. The pontiff wrote in reply that he had already been created and with him likewise d'Albret, so that the King's joy might be full, since he had obtained two cardinals in return for his piety. He also sent Antonio to present to the King the sword consecrated on the holy night of our Lord's nativity. It was encased in a gold and jeweled scabbard and inscribed with these verses:

Let your hand, Louis, draw me against the mad Turks. I shall be the avenger of the blood of the Greeks. The empire of Mahomet shall fall in ruins and the renowned valor of the French shall again soar to the stars under your leadership.

Meantime Pius called a consistory and ordered the Cardinal of St. Peter in Vincoli to report what he had learned about Sigismondo Malatesta. The Cardinal said that an examination of the evidence in the case made it clear that Sigismondo was a heretic who denied the resurrection of the dead, asserted that the souls of men were mortal, and had no hope of a future kingdom. Murders, outrage, adultery, incest, sacrilege, perjury, treachery, and almost countless crimes of the most degrading and frightful nature had been proved against him. There was no doubt that he deserved the severest punishment.

The cardinals were asked their opinions and voted unanimously for his condemnation. In a public trial the accused was found guilty of treason against the Pope, of presuming to make impious assertions in regard to the Christian religion, of living a life foul with every crime and infamy. He was deprived of the vicariate and all his dignities and honors and was subjected to those punishments which the laws of men have decreed for heretics and traitors.

Meantime in front of the steps of St. Peter's there was built a great pyre of dry wood, on top of which was placed an effigy of Sigismondo imitating the *wicked and accursed* man's features and dress so exactly that it seemed a real person rather than an image. But that no one should make any mistake about it, an inscription issued from the figure's mouth, which read, "Sigismondo Malatesta, son of Pandolfo, king of traitors, hated of God and man, condemned to the flames by vote of the holy senate." This writing was read by many. Then, while the populace stood by, fire was applied to the pyre and the image, which at once blazed up. *Such was the mark branded on the impious house of Malatesta by Pius.*

Shortly before this there had come to Rome Giovanni da Castro, whom the Pope had known long ago when he had business at Basle and who had held the post of depositarius under Pope Eugenius. His father was Paolo, the most famous jurisconsult of his day, who for many years held a chair at Padua. All Italy was full of his decisions, for many litigants crowded to him and judges valued his opinion since his learning was sound and free from guile. At his death he left a large fortune and two sons already well along in years, the elder of whom followed his father's profession and won considerable reputation as a jurist. *The other devoted himself to trade in which (so deceitful is fortune) he contracted large debts which forced him, since he could find safety nowhere else, to take refuge with Pope Pius, whose godson he was. He obtained from him a letter enabling him to live unmolested by his creditors in the lands of the Church. He was a talented man who would better have devoted himself to letters than to trade. He had studied grammar and read history but applied himself to nothing so diligently as to astrology, interpretation of prophets, and prospecting for minerals, as if he thought by these arts he could someday recoup his losses in trade.*

Nor was he mistaken. While he was scouring all the mountains and hills *in the Church's patrimony,* he pried into the secrets of nature in the bowels of the earth, and left no sod or stone unturned. Finally in the territory of Tolfa he found alum stone. Tolfa is an old town belonging to two brothers, subjects of the Church of Rome, not far from Centocelle and Orvieto. Here high mountains rich in forests and springs run back from the sea. While Giovanni was walking through them, he came on a strange kind of herb. He was surprised and on making inquiries learned that similar herbs grew on the mountains of Asia which enrich the Turkish treasury with aluminum. He also observed white stones which appeared to have mineral in them. He bit on them and found them salt. He smelted them, experimented, produced alum.

Then he went to the Pope and said, "Today I bring you victory over the Turk. Every year they wring from the Christians more than 300,000 ducats for the alum with which we dye wool various colors. For this is not found among the Latins except a very small quantity in the island of Ischia (once called Aenaria) near Puteoli, and in Vulcan's Liparean cave; and this supply was in ancient times depleted by the Romans and is almost exhausted. But I have found seven mountains so rich in this material that they could supply seven worlds. If you will give orders to engage workmen, build furnaces, and smelt the ore, you will provide all Europe with aluminum and the Turk will lose all his profits. They will accrue to you and thus he will suffer a double loss. There is abundance of wood and water there. You have a harbor nearby in Città Vecchia where ships may be loaded to sail to the east. Now you may equip a war against the Turks. This mine will supply you with the sinews of war, i.e. money, and take them from the Turks."

Giovanni's words sounded like raving. Pius thought them dreams and empty tales of astrologers and so did all the cardinals. Giovanni, though he was often *ridiculed and* repulsed *as a babbler and a braggart,* did not give up. He managed to induce now one, now another to get him repeated audiences with the Pope that he might experiment in his presence on the stone he had found. The Pope called in experts and they attested the genuineness of the alum. They investigated to see whether there was any trickery as to the stone. They sent to the mine and found a great mass of it. Workmen who had once handled alum in Asiatic Turkey were brought from Genoa and when they had thoroughly examined the nature of the place, they declared it was like the Asiatic mountains where alum was found and, weeping for joy, they worshipped God on their knees three or four times and blessed His goodness Who had bestowed such a gift on our age. They smelted the rock and produced much finer and better alum that the Asiatic product.

It was sent to Venice and Florence. Experiments were made and the result surpassed their expectations. First the Genoese contracted for 20,000 ducats worth. Then Cosimo dei Medici invested 75,000 ducats, and the first year brought in so much more than anyone expected that Pius thought Giovanni deserving of extraordinary honors and of having his statue erected in his native city with the inscription: "To Giovanni da Castro, discoverer of alum." Nor was he allowed to go without a share of the profit. The brothers who were lords of Tolfa on whose land the mine had been found were granted immunities and given a percentage of the profits.

This revenue came to the Church of Rome by the grace of God during the pontificate of Pius. If, as is just, it escapes the hands of tyrants and is shrewdly administered, it will increase from day to day and be of no small aid to the Roman pontiffs in bearing the burdens of the Christian religion.

There was no lack of poets to celebrate this event in verses, among which the following epigram of Campano is conspicuous:

He who says that only the heavens are thine mistakes and is grievously deceived as to Pius's empire. The earth too has brought to thee what she has and gives thee herself, prodigal of her very vitals. From one place she has struck out crude bronze, from another alum, and a third vein in another place produces silver. They lay hidden in the bosom of the earth so many years and today are revealed only to their master. Now, O richest Earth, that thou mayst not be charged with theft, render likewise to Pius the gold that remains.

After the cardinals had been created as described, the Cardinal of Arras, now that he knew his ship was in harbor and he need have no more worry about the dignity he had too much coveted, began to write what he had heretofore kept silent, about Louis's attitude toward Sicilian affairs, namely that the King's little daughter had been betrothed to the son of Jean of Anjou, grandson of King René, who was nearly of the same age. Louis wanted a kingdom for his son-in-law and would make every effort to drive Ferrante from his throne; it would not be for the Pope's advantage to oppose the royal line of France; the help he had sent Ferrante must be recalled; in this way he would appease the King and make absolutely certain that the Pragmatic Sanction would be abrogated.

Louis soon sent to the Pope as ambassadors Richard, Cardinal of Coutances, and Jean, Cardinal of Arras, who were followed by the Bishops of Angers and Saintes and a number of abbots and most exalted nobles headed by Pierre, Count of Chaumont, whose character and years gave him authority. There were also among the envoys certain doctors and secretaries of the King. It was a brilliant embassy befitting a sovereign, with a great number of horsemen and a long line of attendants.

After many days on the journey they at last entered Rome on the thirteenth of March and were met by all the college of cardinals except those who were themselves in the King's embassy. A public consistory was held in the Apostolic palace to which the envoys were escorted in solemn procession. The Pope was seated in majesty on his high throne, the cardinals on their usual benches. Bishops and notaries sat as usual at the Pope's footstool. The rest of the assembly, which was very numerous, either stood or sat on the floor, occupying the space between the cardinals and the Pope's tribunal. The King's ambassadors, after kissing the Pope's feet and presenting the royal letter, were allotted a place behind the cardinals opposite the Pope and were bidden to stand there and explain what they wanted.

The Bishop of Arras delivered a long speech about the nobility of the French, the glory and extent of their kingdom, the valor of the Gallic people, the peerless virtues of Louis, the Pragmatic Sanction, the way it had entered the kingdom, and how Louis had abrogated it. He then produced public documents to prove that King Louis had banished the Pragmatic Sanction from all his kingdom and dominion, had destroyed it root and branch, had completely annihilated it; that he had renewed his true and entire obedience to the Holy See of Rome and to Pope Pius as the Vicar of Jesus Christ and was now again renewing it, since it was his purpose to act as the son of the Pope and never to disregard his slightest wish. He mentioned also the Turks, whose sword was hanging over the necks of Christians to the great danger of the Catholic Faith. Louis was reflecting on the way to safeguard religion. If the kingdom of Sicily should be open to the house of Anjou and

Genoa came under the French yoke, as was just, he would send to
Greece against the Turks 40,000 cavalry and 30,000 archers, a force
which could easily drive Mahomet from Europe and recover a second
time Syria and the most holy sepulcher of Christ. He spoke on these
matters at length with *more* magnificence *and ostentation than truth,*
interspersing bombastic words and *barefacedly* alleging *Gallic fictions
and* patent falsehoods as facts.

The Pope, when the Bishop of Arras had reached his long expected
and desired end, praised at length the King's embassy and his pious
purpose. *He touched as briefly as possible on the chimerical and fanciful
and meaningless offer of 70,000 fighting men, so as not to seem to be
taking nonsense seriously. All listened to him with profound attention
appearing to refresh themselves from the boredom they had suffered
in listening to Arras. Men are reluctant to hear braggarts and cannot
suffer calmly open lies and empty grandiloquence. The truth appropriately expressed finds friendly listeners. Thus Arras's speech seemed
endless, the Pope's very short.*

When Pius had finished he bade the Bishop of Arras approach and
in the same consistory placed upon his head the red hat and directed
him to take his seat among the cardinals. He also proclaimed a three
days' holiday with thanksgiving in all the churches and processions
carrying sacred relics through the city.

When the consistory was dismissed, the entire Curia and the populace
burst into exultation. At nightfall fires blazed, all the trumpets and bells
blared and rang; the young cavorted, adults danced and sang, and old
men congratulated one another that they had lived to see the Pragmatic
Sanction abrogated. They praised the Pope during whose pontificate
this boon had been granted; they extolled the King whose heart had
been filled with such piety. The event seemed so much the more right
and marvelous as it had been unexpected. For there was no one who
had had any faith that the disease of the Pragmatic Sanction, which had
been deep-rooted for twenty-four years, could be cured under Pope Pius.

About this time Pius called together six of the cardinals whom he
thought most loyal and wise and said to them, "My brethren, perhaps
you, like almost everyone else, think that we are neglecting the common
weal because since our return from Mantua we have neither done nor
said anything toward repulsing the Turks and protecting religion, and
that too though the enemy has pressed us harder every day. We have
been silent; we do not deny it. We have done nothing against the enemies of the Cross; that is evident. But the reason for our silence was

not indifference but a kind of despair. Power, not will, has been lacking. Over and over again we have pondered as to whether we could muster the strength of Christians against the Turks in one way or another and take measures to prevent the Christian peoples finally falling a prey to them. We have spent many sleepless nights in meditation, tossing from side to side and deploring the unhappy calamities of our time. Our heart swelled and our old blood boiled *with rage.* We longed to declare war against the Turks and to put forth every effort in defense of religion, but when we measure our strength against that of the enemy, it is clear that the Church of Rome cannot defeat the Turks with its own resources. No man of sense provokes a stronger foe to fight. The challenger must be superior or at least equal to the challenged. We are far inferior to the Turks unless Christian kings should unite their forces.

We are seeking to effect this; we are searching out ways; none practicable presents itself. If we think of convening a council, Mantua teaches us that the idea is vain. If we send envoys to ask aid of sovereigns, they are laughed at. If we impose tithes on the clergy, they appeal to a future council. If we issue indulgences and encourage the contribution of money by spiritual gifts, we are accused of avarice. People think our sole object is to amass gold. No one believes what we say. Like insolvent tradesmen, we are without credit. Everything we do is interpreted in the worst way *and since all princes are very avaricious and all prelates of the Church are slaves to money,* they measure our disposition by their own. Nothing is harder than to wring gold *from a miser.* We turn the eye of the mind in all directions. We find nothing certain, nothing solid, nothing that is not utterly unsubstantial.

"What are we to do in such difficulties? Shall we rush into certain danger and have ourselves to thank for surrendering to the enemy? Or shall we embark on an undertaking that will make us ridiculous? To labor in vain and for our pains get infamy would be the extreme of folly. Our mind has long been perplexed and sorely anxious and our soul could not be comforted, since we saw everything growing worse and no slightest hope of success. But while, during our silent days and nights, we have been coming more and more to this decision, that we must seek out some plan for the common salvation, one remedy has at last occurred to us. In our opinion it is most effective and perhaps there is no other. Listen and we will expound it briefly. Then you shall judge of our plan.

"In the year when Constantinople was lost Philip, Duke of Burgundy, publicly made a vow that he would go against the Turks and wage war with them and challenge Mahomet to single combat, if the Emperor Frederick or Charles of France or Ladislas of Hungary or any other great prince whom it would not be beneath him to follow would set out for the same war. Thus far no one has been found among those named who has girded himself for so great a contest. Philip believes himself excused, since the terms of his vow have not been met. He is excused but not absolved. His obligation still stands. His vow speaks and his oath is not silent. The condition may still be fulfilled. Some great prince may still gird himself for this crusade and summon Philip to follow him. If he does not obey, he will be guilty of breaking his oath and his vow, which we are certain he could not endure.

"We are resolved, old and ill as we are, to undertake war against the Turks in defense of the Catholic Faith. We will set out on the crusade. We will summon Burgundy to follow us who are both king and pontiff and we will claim the fulfillment of his vow and oath. No excuse will be open to him. A greater than king or emperor, the Vicar of Christ, will declare war. It will not beseem a duke bound by a vow to stay at home. If Philip accedes to our desires, he will not come without a great and mighty army. Many will follow so noble a prince. The King of France, who has publicly promised 70,000 men, will be ashamed to send fewer than 10,000. From Germany, England, Spain, many will enlist voluntarily. The Hungarians, whose own cause is at stake, cannot fail us. Nor will the Venetians, when they see such great preparations, refuse a fleet. Who does not know that the Pope of Rome with the Venetians and Hungarians followed by the Duke of Burgundy and aided by the King of France can wipe out the Turkish race?

"But first of all we must be certain of the Venetians and we must get their advice, since they are acquainted with the habits and the power of the Turks and know what strength and what strategy it will take to conquer them. It would be useless to persuade the Burgundians and the French to this expedition without the assistance of the Venetians, to whom the seas are open. They must first of all be told our purpose. If they do not approve, all our planning has been in vain. If they applaud it, we will send an embassy to exhort France and Burgundy not to fail the Christian religion. We will call on France for troops. Burgundy we will hold to his vow. When they agree, as they must, we will proclaim our purpose and our crusade.

"We will command a five-year truce between all Christians now at variance. On those who obey we will bestow Heaven's blessing; those who rebel we will smite with anathema. We will bid the bishops, abbots, and men of every ecclesiastical rank to aid this task with all means at their command. The disobedient we will excommunicate and consign to the devil as slaves of everlasting fire. The others, who are faithful to Christ, we will induce to aid us to the extent of their powers by indulgences and spiritual graces, and who will there be who will not move when he hears the Pope has moved? Unless we are mistaken, this is the one way we can rouse the sleeping Christians and stir the hearts of kings and peoples. When this resolve is spread abroad it will shatter sleep as with a thunderclap and rouse the hearts of the faithful to protect religion. Not arms or horses or men or ships will be lacking. On land and sea we shall easily equip the war when it once becomes known that the Pope of Rome with the holy senate is marching straight on to win salvation for all and desires no man's silver since he is resolved to risk not only his own gold but his own person for Christ's sake.

"This is what has come to us; whether of our own wit or God's inspiration it is for you to judge."

The cardinals listened to the Pope with wonder and stupefaction. They did not doubt that words which pleaded God's cause were of God, but in a situation so critical and strange and unheard-of they begged time for consideration. This was granted and after conferring together for a number of days they returned to the Pope and said that his purpose was worthy of the Vicar of Jesus Christ, who like a shepherd did not hesitate to lay down his life for his sheep. Nothing could be said against so praiseworthy and noble a plan, though there seemed to be some difficulties in the way. When however they specified what these were, the Pope, who had thought out everything, easily answered them.

They decided to write to the Venetians, urging them to keep the matter secret and communicate it to no one except those without whom a matter of such importance could not legally be decided. They were to be assured that this was necessary. The letter was written by the Pope's own hand and may be found in the volume of his letters.

The Venetians convened the necessary number of their senate, who adjudged the Pope's plan to be divinely inspired. They replied that their state would do all the Pope desired to defend the Faith.

Then the Pope, at the instance of the same cardinals, sent Lorenzo, Bishop of Ferrara, who was pre-eminent for integrity and learning and knew French ways, to France to persuade the King and the Duke to come to the defense of the Faith at the Pope's desire. Lorenzo set out shortly after the French embassy (except the cardinals, who remained in the Curia) had been dismissed.

It was now the Holy Week during which Pope Pius decided to transfer to Rome the sacred head of St. Andrew which had long been kept in the citadel of Narni. Since this ceremony was carried out with remarkable devotion and special pomp, we will describe it from beginning to end *and go into some points in greater detail.*

BOOK VIII

ANDREW, Apostle of Jesus Christ, brother of St. Peter, after the passion of our Lord, at which he was present, and His resurrection and ascension into heaven, of which he was witness, having received together with the other disciples the Holy Ghost, crossed from Asia into Greece and betook himself to Achaia (now called Morea), a province of the Peloponnese, where it had fallen to his lot to preach. And whereas, when he left his ship and abandoned his nets for the Lord, he had received the promise that he should be a fisher of men, he was not disappointed, for he became a great preacher and teacher of the truth and with the hook of his eloquence caught countless men whom he won for Christ. Furthermore the province under his teaching accepted the holy tenets of our religion: it recognized Christ, the Son of God, together with the Father and the Holy Ghost to be one God; it worshipped the Holy Trinity. The holy Apostle himself, when already worn out with age, was crucified under the proconsul Egeus in Patras and received the same crown of martyrdom as his brother Peter and his master, Jesus Christ. Therefore, when he stood by the Cross and had greeted it most lovingly, he said, "Receive the disciple of Jesus Christ who hung on thee."

Andrew was illustrious both during his life and after his death, for many miracles, which are related in his biography. His body was embalmed with spices and buried by a pious woman named Maximilla, but long afterward it was removed to Italy and buried in the city of Amalfi, which was made a metropolitan out of reverence for him. His tomb is famed for the magnificence of its workmanship and the throngs that visit it. His head however remained at Patras, where it was closely guarded with the utmost veneration till 1460, when it was transferred in the following manner.

When the Turks invaded the Peloponnese, two tyrants were ruling there. They were Thomas and Demetrius, brothers of the Greek Emperor Constantine, who had been killed shortly before in the fall of

Constantinople. Demetrius, the elder, when he found he could get no adequate help from Christians, went over to the Turks and received possessions elsewhere which would afford him the means of livelihood. But Thomas, the younger, *who was regarded as the heir to the throne,* could not be induced to submit to those who had murdered his brother, robbed the Greeks of their empire, and defiled Christian altars. Since he realized that he was no match for the might of the Turks and saw no hope of assistance, he decided to leave the Peloponnese, a large part of which had been surrendered by Demetrius and was in the hands of the Turks. But before he left he went to Patras, which was still his, and from the sanctuary, of which he himself was the keeper, he took the most precious head of St. Andrew, the Apostle. Then with his wife and children and many Greek nobles he took refuge with the despot of Arta on the island of Santa Maura off the coast of Epirus, for he thought so precious a treasure ought not to be abandoned to the enemy (though indeed they would have trampled it like rubbish). He saw to it that God's saint should not be thrown to the dogs and he thought too that his own journey would be more prosperous if the Apostle went with him. Thus he came safely to his royal kinsman, with whom he stayed for some time, guarding the sacred head as closely as he did his wife and children.

Meantime many Christian princes, both in Italy and beyond the Alps, hearing that the Apostle's head had been taken out of Greece, sent ambassadors to Thomas to offer large sums for the holy relic. When Pope Pius heard of it he was indeed distressed to think that so sacred a head should be an exile, but now that it had actually been driven from its abode and could not easily be restored, he thought there was no more fitting asylum for it than beside the bones of its brother, St. Peter, Prince of the Apostles, and in the Apostolic See, the citadel of the Faith, the safe refuge for all who are driven from their own churches. Therefore he too sent envoys to Thomas to say that he had acted piously in removing the most precious head of the Apostle from a city that was on the point of falling into the hands of an infidel foe and thus saving it from destruction. He would however be acting impiously and cruelly if he surrendered it to any but the Pope, whose prerogative it was to decide on the honors paid the saints, and if he desired it to rest elsewhere than with the bones of its brother at Rome. He must bring it to Rome himself. Someday, God willing, it would come about that with the help of its brother it would be restored to its own throne. Thomas must not trust so sacred an object to anyone without the Pope's orders, unless he wished to incur the anger of the Apostles. He need not plead poverty as an excuse, for if he would come to live at Rome, he should be maintained in the style befitting a prince.

The despot was persuaded by the Pope's words and promised to set sail for Ancona with the sacred pledge. He kept his word and in 1461 he landed at Ancona, having escaped unhurt (with the Apostle's help, we may well believe) from the violent and terrific gales which that year more than usual lashed the Adriatic and sank innumerable ships.

Pius when he heard of Thomas's arrival, sent Alessandro, Cardinal presbyter of Santa Susanna, a man celebrated for his holiness and learning, as his legatus de latere. If he recognized the relic of the holy Apostle, he was to take it from the hands of the despot and with the ceremony and reverence due to so sacred an object carry it to Narni and deposit it in the citadel, where it was to be guarded by the commandant till it could be brought to Rome with fitting rites and honors. (This was impossible at that time because of the fierce war which the tyrants about Rome had declared on the Pope.)

Alessandro went to Ancona and after carefully examining the head and recognizing its distinguishing marks, pronounced it to be the genuine head of the Apostle and did it reverence. He then received it from the despot and after giving Thomas sufficient funds for his journey to the Curia, he carried it with a splendid escort in solemn procession with many tapers to the citadel of Narni, where he entrusted it under seal to the commandant. Here it was kept for some time in due honor with lamps always burning before it.

Several months later, when the Pope's campaign had succeeded, when peace was restored in the territory of Rome and the people round about were enjoying security and rest, when the clash of arms was no longer heard, the Pope decided to send for the sacred head. Since the more people were present the more magnificent would be its welcome, he promised plenary remission of sins to those who came to Rome for its entrance or took part in its reception. A proclamation to this effect was sent to the chief cities of Italy naming the day when the head would come. When this was at hand he chose three cardinals: Bessarion, Bishop of Tusculum, a Greek at home in both languages and a man of high repute; Alessandro, mentioned above; Francesco, administrator of the church of Siena, *the son of his sister Laodamia and his nephew after the flesh*. These he directed to go to Narni and bring away the sacred pledge deposited there.

Meantime at Rome all the preparations were made that were thought fitting for the solemn and magnificent reception of the holy Apostle. The Pope was afraid of seeming niggardly in the honors paid to so great an Apostle and thought nothing good enough. He intended to carry out to meet him the glorious heads of the Apostles Peter and Paul, which are buried in the Church of St. John in the Lateran, and with them to greet the sacred head of Andrew outside the city. This however proved to be impossible because of the mass of silver in which the heads are imbedded. It is said to weigh more than 4,000 pounds and there is besides a great quantity of iron, which could neither be broken away without great inconvenience nor carried with them. The idea of carrying out the heads was therefore abandoned and orders were given that on the afternoons of the days when the head of St. Andrew was carried through the city in the morning the heads of the Apostles should be exhibited publicly in the Lateran, a ceremony which each time was attended by large crowds.

When the cardinals sent to Narni arrived there, after having recognized the distinguishing marks, they did reverence to the sacred bones and taking them up with emotion and profoundest veneration, carried them as far as the Ponte Molle on Palm Sunday, April 12, 1462. All along the way they were greeted by countless throngs praising God and commending themselves to the Apostle Andrew. Two miles from Rome they deposited the venerable relic in the tower on the bridge for safekeeping during the night. Two archbishops, Perotti of Manfredonia and Alexis of Benevento, were left on guard.

On the same day the Pope, after celebrating according to ancient custom the feast of Palms at St. Peter's in the Apostolic palace, decided to go in the afternoon with the holy senate of cardinals and all the clergy to the church of Santa Maria del Popolo, where he planned to pass the night, that he might start out the next morning to meet the sacred head; for the church is close to the Porta Flaminia on the road that leads to the Ponte Molle across the Tiber. He was however disturbed by fear of rain, which seemed imminent. Clouds had obscured the sky, lightning flashed all around, claps of thunder were heard from every direction, and there seemed no prospect of clearing. For many days before this the weather had been wet and cloudy, but now it looked more threatening than ever and a terrible storm seemed to be brewing. Winds from all directions were driving clouds toward Rome and no one thought he could make the trip without being caught in drenching rain. But (marvelous to relate!) great Andrew kept his own fair weather and did not suffer rain to interfere with the clergy's coming to do him honor. Though it had poured for whole days and nights that month, yet during the time that the sacred head was on the way and the Pope was going to meet it not a drop of water fell on the ground where they had to pass and all that flood of gathering rain that had seemed likely to prevent the Pope's progress held off till evening, so that he walked dryshod. A rainy night however made them despair of carrying out the ceremonies planned for the next day and it was thought they would have to be postponed. But at dawn the rain ceased and the sun shining brightly on the earth seemed to invite them to proceed. At once the three cardinals, who had left the sacred head at the Ponte Molle, went back to get it and escorted it in procession to the city.

Near the Ponte Molle on the left as you approach Rome are broad meadows, which were then covered with grass and flowers and so gay that they seemed to be laughing. In the middle of them the Pope had ordered a wooden tribune to be constructed large and strong enough to hold all the clergy present and high enough for all in the meadows to see clearly what took place upon it. In the center was set up a high altar.

Soon after the three cardinals had been sent ahead (as has been mentioned above) the Pope himself with the rest of the senate, all the clergy, the ambassadors of princes, the nobles of the city, and a great throng of the populace passed through the Porta Flaminia carrying a palm branch, as did the cardinals likewise. The other prelates carried the palms given them the day before by the Pope himself in memory of the Savior. The whole road was thronged with people; the fields and vineyards could not be seen because of the crowds that swarmed everywhere. As soon as they reached the meadows mentioned above the Pope ordered the cardinals and prelates to dismount and after putting on their sacred robes and priestly ornaments to walk the distance of a bowshot and ascend the platform with him. The robes of all the priests were white, as were their miters and all their vestments, and in the green meadow they seemed to gleam even whiter. All were spellbound by the marvelous dignity and solemnity of the procession of so many priests carrying palms in their hands and offering prayers to God as they advanced through the meadows two by two with slow steps and grave faces, the Pope in their midst and the populace standing about.

The platform was approached by two flights of easy stairs, one opposite the Ponte Molle, the other toward the city. While the Pope followed by the sacred college and all the clergy ascended the latter with tears of joy and adoration, Bessarion with two other cardinals mounted the former. He carried a reliquary containing the sacred head, which he deposited on the center of the altar while a chorus intoned hymns. Then amid profound silence the keys were brought and when the seals had been recognized, the casket was opened. Bessarion in tears, taking the sacred head of the Apostle, offered it to the weeping Pope. But the Pope himself, before touching the holy bones, knelt at the altar and with pale and downcast face and streaming eyes said in a tremulous voice:

"Thou hast come at last, most sacred and adored head of the holy Apostle (Fig. 19). The fury of the Turks has expelled thee from thine own abode. In exile thou hast come for asylum to thy brother, Prince of the Apostles. Thy brother will not fail thee. God willing, thou shalt be restored to thy throne with glory. Some day thou shalt say, 'O happy exile where such aid was found!' Meanwhile thou shalt tarry a space with thy brother and shalt enjoy like honor with him. This city thou seest close at hand is mother Rome, hallowed by thy brother's precious blood. To this people standing here thy most loving brother, St. Peter the Apostle, and with him the chosen vessel, St. Paul, gave a new birth in Christ the Lord. The Romans are thy nephews through thy brother. They all revere, honor, and worship thee as their uncle and their father and they doubt not that they enjoy thy advocacy in the sight of Almighty God.

"O most blessed St. Andrew, preacher of the truth, great champion of the Trinity, with what joy thou dost fill us today, while we behold thy sacred and venerable head, the head of thee who was found worthy that the Holy Ghost in the guise of fire should alight upon thee on the day of Pentecost! O ye who journey to Jerusalem out of reverence for the Savior, to see the places His feet have trod, behold the abode of the Holy Ghost, the throne of divinity! Here, here the Spirit of God alighted, here the Third Person of the Trinity was made visible, here were the eyes that often beheld God in the flesh. This mouth often spoke to Christ, these cheeks surely Jesus often kissed. Behold a mighty shrine! Behold love and piety and sweetness of soul and consolation of the spirit! Who is there who is not stirred to the depth of his being, whose inmost heart is not on fire? Who does not weep for joy at the sight of these *venerable and* precious relics of the Apostle *of Christ?* We rejoice, we exult, we shout in jubilation at thy coming, most divine Apostle Andrew. For we cannot doubt that thou art with thy *carnal* head and with it dost enter the city. It is true that we hate the Turks as the foes of Christianity, but in this we do not hate them, that they have been the cause of thy coming. For what blessing more to be desired could befall us than to behold thy most venerated head, to inhale its supreme fragrance? Our one grief is that we do not pay thee at thy coming the honors thou dost merit and cannot receive thee as becomes thy matchless sanctity.

"But do thou accept our intention: *measure the will not the deed*. Graciously suffer us to touch thy bones with our polluted hands and, sinners though we are, to accompany thee within the walls. Enter the holy city and be propitious to the Roman people. May thy coming bring safety to all Christians, thy entrance bring peace. May thy stay among us be happy and auspicious. Be thou our advocate in Heaven and together with the blessed Apostles Peter and Paul preserve this city. Take loving thought for all Christendom, that by thy intercession the mercy of God may be upon us and that, if He is angry with us for our sins, which are many, His anger may be transferred to the impious Turks and the barbarian nations who dishonor Christ the Lord. *Amen.*"

The Pope's prayer drew tears from all eyes. There was no one on the platform, clergy or laity, who did not weep and beat his breast imploring the protection of the blessed Apostle. There were some on whom the Pope's words made so profound an impression that on reaching home they wrote them down verbatim and gave them to him. Among these was Theodore, Bishop of Feltre, a man distinguished alike for his learning and character. When the Pope had read his copy, he marveled at the man's memory and praised his ability.

While the Pope was speaking there was profound silence except for the sobs of those who beat their breasts and could not control their tears. Torches were burning all around and the throngs in the fields waited in silence for him to finish. When he ended, he kissed the sacred head and all on the platform weeping did likewise. The Pope then prayed again:

"Omnipotent and everlasting God, Who dost rule Heaven and earth, Who hast today deigned to solace us with the coming of the precious head of St. Andrew, Thy Apostle, grant, we pray, that through his merits and intercession the insolence of the faithless Turk may be crushed, all infidels may cease from troubling us, and Christians serve Thee in freedom and safety. And this we ask in the name of Christ our Lord."

When all had answered "Amen," he took the venerable relic of the Apostle in his hands and elevating it made the circuit of the tribune showing to the people the gift so much desired. There was no one who did not have a chance to see it and presently voices from the multitude were heard crying aloud and imploring God's mercy, so that all the valleys echoed the sound. After this the canticle beginning, "Te deum laudamus," which is said to have been written by the celebrated Fathers of the Church Ambrose and Augustine, was loudly intoned and after it the choir sang the following hymn in Sapphics:

"He was first to follow Jesus's call; he first like Him endured the Cross, martyr revered forever on the shores of Greece. But when the Turks were conquering the Greeks, that he might not fall a prey to ravening hounds, Pius II carried him away and received the exile into the holy city. The Pope himself came to meet him with the holy senate, while Rome was fragrant with festal flowers and priests sang songs of praise. The priest in shining robes carries the sacred relic in his hand; the people in bright array raise the chant, 'Be thou, we pray, the prop, the father of our fostering city. O thou great champion of the holy Faith, first to hear the Lord's summons, first to triumph by a death like His, protect Rome. O gracious God, bless this day to us. Sharpen Thy three-forked bolt against the Turks.'

"Andrew gives ear to the people's prayer and answers with his own: 'I pray Thee, Creator of heaven and earth, put an end to bloodshed and punishments and at last in pity for Thy people crush the Turks!'

"This is the prayer of the great and good shepherd Pius as he kneels before Thee: 'Pity the wearied; stretch out Thine arm to a world on the brink of ruin, omnipotent King of kings.' This is the suppliant prayer of the princes of our city, Paul and Peter, and Rome, leaning upon them as upon two columns, humbly offers the same petition. Grant Pius life, we all implore Thee. He alone with unfailing courage dared to cross the Alps and raise the call to arms against the Turk. He gladly offers his own life that the world may worship the name of Christ and the faithless foe be brought to see the way of our salvation. Amen."

This hymn was written at Pius's orders by Agapetus, Bishop of Ancona, a Roman citizen of whom it would be hard to say whether he was more illustrious as jurist, orator, or poet.

The Pope now descended from the tribune surrounded by lighted tapers and carrying the sacred head in his hands. He proceeded to carry it to the city, accompanied by the cardinals, bishops, and other prelates in the order of their rank bearing palms. On the road many persons were trampled in the crowd of men and horses and it was almost impossible to make a way through such a throng. At the city gate they found some of the clergy who had come out to meet the Apostle with sacred relics. After doing him reverence they returned with him into the city. The Pope, entering the church of Santa Maria, laid the head of the Apostle on the altar before the image of the glorious Virgin, mother of our Lord, which they say was painted by St. Luke the Evangelist. Then he blessed the people and appointed from the Referendarii certain bishops to keep watch during the night. He too spent the night in the church in a chamber prepared for him.

The sun had not yet set when of a sudden the wind changed and rain drove in from the south, continuing all night till dawn. The storm was so violent that there was no hope of carrying the head through the city to the basilica of St. Peter the next day as had been intended. There was universal grief that the solemn rite that had been planned should be prevented and such eager expectation on the part of the populace disappointed. Countless strangers had flocked to Rome from Germany, France, Hungary, and other Transalpine countries, not to speak of innumerable commoners of Italy and many nobles, who were eager to see the sacred head, so that not even at the jubilee celebrated under Pope Nicholas V, which is agreed to have been the greatest ever held, was a larger throng seen on a single day. All were dejected, especially those who had not been in the meadow: for many had not arrived in time.

Pope Pius too was equally distressed and apprehensive for the populace, whose dearest wish he saw was being disappointed, and he sympathized alike with citizens and strangers, who were equally heartbroken. But now the whole city began to implore God to vouchsafe clear weather on the morrow and the Divine Mercy was not deaf to their prayers. Indeed it is probable that St. Andrew was listened to as befitted his dignity and obtained calm weather for his head. For suddenly a little before sunrise Aquilo or Boreas or some other wind scattered the clouds, leaving the sky bright and clear, and the sun himself appeared in the east extraordinarily dazzling and radiant, so that many, especially the Pope himself, recalled the couplet:

It rained all night; the shows are resumed in the morning. Caesar divides his empire with Jove.

But Pius altered the verses and said to those about him,

"It rained all night; now our weather has returned. The past night was the enemy's; the day will be God's."

And he added,

"The wet weather is past; the dry has returned. The hostile night has gone; the friendly day has shone."

The Pope gave orders that the cardinals should be summoned *at once* and the necessary preparations for the processions be made. He himself celebrated mass in his chamber and read the Passion of our Lord according to St. Luke. When the mass was over and the full senate and all the clergy were assembled, he called the cardinals and asked what they had better do; for though it had been decided to carry the Apostle's head in procession, whether on foot or on horseback was still unsettled. Although the people on the preceding day had cleaned all the route to be traversed, the rainy night had overlaid it thick with mud and it looked as if the slippery ground would be very difficult for the priests carrying the sacred relics and clad in their ceremonial robes. Furthermore the route seemed too long for the older men, for it was about two miles through the heart of the city from Santa Maria del Popolo to the basilica of St. Peter. Therefore many thought that cardinals, bishops, and abbots should have the privilege of riding while the rest walked.

This however did not please the Pope, who did not wish to have the procession divided nor to have it look as if the priests failed in devotion or paid less reverence to the divine Apostle. He therefore ordered that all should go on foot and do honor to the sacred head by their own exertions and earn the indulgences. However if any were too old or ill to be equal to such an effort, they might go on horseback by another route to St. Peter's and there on the steps before the doors await the arrival of the procession. Those who could not walk all the way but could manage a part of it were to walk as far as they thought they could, choosing the place from which they estimated that their feet would carry them to St. Peter's.

It was a fine and impressive sight to see those aged men walking through the slippery mud with palms in their hands and miters on their white hair, robed in priestly vestments, never lifting their eyes from the ground but praying and invoking the Divine Mercy upon the people. Some who had been reared in luxury and had scarcely been able to go a hundred feet except on horseback, on that day, weighed down as they were with their sacred robes, easily accomplished two miles through mud and water.

Guillaume, Bishop of Ostia, a noble of royal blood, had hard work to support the burden of his flesh, for he was fat and old. Alain, Cardinal of Santa Prassede, *a tall man with a huge paunch,* also had difficulty in propelling his great bulk. Both however cheerfully finished the course. But Juan, Bishop of Porto, a Spaniard learned in civil law, who had shortly before returned from an embassy to Hungary, excited particular admiration, for though he was old and ill, nevertheless he covered the whole distance with good courage and a joyous countenance, praying as he walked. Love carried the burden and nothing was difficult for the lover. No small difficulty was experienced on the road by Alessandro, Cardinal of Santa Susanna, and Jacopo of Sant' Anastasia, one weighed down by ill health and the other by his sixty-six years. Their devotion however conquered and they did not drop out of the procession anywhere. Latino Orsini, who was frail and usually unable to endure any exertion, on that day got new strength and seemed to have no difficulty at all in walking. All the rest were young and vigorous, as for instance Pietro of San Marco, nephew of Eugenius IV; Lodovico of Santi Quattro Coronati, nephew of Calixtus III; Richard of Coutances, who had been counsellor to King Charles of France; Niccolò of Teano, who had once commanded the armies of the Church and subdued the Narsi; Jean of Arras, who had but just returned from France after the abrogation of the Pragmatic Sanction; Jacopo of Pavia, a great classical scholar; Rodrigo, the Vice-Chancellor, nephew of Calixtus and an extraordinarily able man; [1] Francesco of Siena, mentioned above; Francesco of Mantua, related to the noblest families of Italy and Germany. The faces of all expressed solemnity, reverence, and devotion. There was not a single unseemly gesture and the procession of cardinals passed with such dignity that the watching crowds along the way were stirred to worship. A like impression was produced by the bishops and other prelates and all the clergy manifested a remarkable spirit of humility.

There were present the priests of all the churches of Rome carrying sacred relics; Roman citizens splendidly dressed; the conservators of the camera; the chiefs of the sections and other magistrates. There were also ambassadors of kings and princes and the nobles of the city carrying lighted tapers and marshaled according to their rank. Some of the ambassadors and nobles were stationed about the Pope, holding over the head of the Apostle a golden canopy (baldacchino we call it nowadays) like an umbrella to keep off the sun's rays. The rest of the clergy brought up the rear. Some say that on that day in the procession of the clergy and laity 30,000 lighted candles could be counted as they crossed Hadrian's bridge two by two, and there were so many priests carrying sacred relics that the head of the procession reached St. Peter's before the Pope started, though the marchers left no space between them and trod close on one another's heels.

[1] Borgia, future Alexander VI.

When everything was ready and the procession was well started, the Pope came down *from his chamber* carried on men's shoulders in his golden chair, as had come to be his custom, since gout had long since deprived him of the use of his feet. He dispatched the Bishop of Ostia with two cardinals to bring him the Apostle's head from the church of Santa Maria, since he could not himself get through because of the great crowds. They received the famous relic at the altar and put it into the Pope's hands while all the people looked on and invoked God's mercy. The Pope kissed it and then carrying it before him and blessing the crowds who surged about him he began his progress.

It was already the thirteenth hour and such throngs had blocked the streets that the soldiers massed around the Pope could scarcely open a way with their cudgels, though for some distance the route led outside the buildings of the city where the streets are broader: for the Pope turned to the right toward the Tiber and proceeded along the bank of the river leaving on his left the tomb of Augustus. In this district, though at other times there are plenty of wide spaces, that day there was not a foot of empty room and the crowds were so closely packed that if you had thrown a grain of wheat it would hardly have fallen on the ground. All the way to St. Peter's they found the streets just as crowded and it was not the same crowd leaving one place and filling up another but everywhere new faces were seen.

The route followed the Tiber till they reached the closely built districts on the right. Then the procession turned left and through narrow streets between high buildings came to the Pantheon, which the heathen consecrated to all the gods, that is demons, and our ancestors to the glorious Virgin, Mother of our Lord, and to all the saints. There after crossing the great square before the church it turned to the right till it passed the chapel of San Eustachio, where it turned left again till it reached the house of Berardo Cardinal of Santa Sabina, a most virtuous man and an authority on law. Here, bearing a third time to the right, it followed the street called the Pope's to the newly erected church of Maximo, where it again turned left to the Campo dei Fiori. Crossing this on the right it reached the square of San Lorenzo in Damaso, where it took a street to the left which brought it to the Tiber bank, and finally a road to the right which brought it to Hadrian's tomb. Here it crossed the bridge and proceeded to St. Peter's by the Via Sacra, which was everywhere strewn with flowers and fragrant herbs.

In all the city wherever private houses were built close together the street was covered with canopies and branches of trees to keep off the sun and all the houses were decked with hangings and tapestries which completely hid the walls. The Romans displayed extraordinary joy and reverence and members of the Curia and strangers alike vied with one another in honoring the Apostle. All the decorations the houses possessed were lavished to adorn the streets for the sacred head. There was no precious robe that was not displayed that day. In the floors and windows matrons and maids with lighted tapers, dressed as befitted the occasion, watched the procession, praying and adoring the sacred head. At the crossroads and in all the streets altars sent clouds of smoke. Everywhere incense and branches of fragrant shrubs were burning. Whoever had in his house paintings or fine and lifelike statues displayed them outside in the portico before his door. In many places there were actors in costume; children represented angels, some singing sweetly, others playing musical instruments. There was no instrument that might not be heard and praises of the Apostle filled the air. Besides fountains of wine and divers wonders hanging everywhere caught the attention of the marchers.

The efforts of all his inferiors and equals were surpassed by Melchior, Procurator of the Knights of Rhodes, an excellent and learned man. He had erected in front of his house an altar smoking with clouds of incense and had added various embellishments. Singers, flute players, *and trumpeters* honored the relic of the Apostle as it passed with varied and delightful harmony. All the cardinals who lived along the route had decorated their houses magnificently. (*There was one exception whom I forbear to mention out of respect, for fear he might be thought irreligious.*) The Cardinal of Spoleto, though not present himself (for he had gone to his own church to minister to his people and his sheep during Holy Week), had left stewards at his house who had covered the adjacent square with carpets and decorated the house walls most beautifully. He was outdone however by Alain, Cardinal of Santa Prassede, generally called Cardinal of Avignon. He lived in the Campo dei Fiori where they say the Genius of Pompey the Great once stood on the site of the present palace of the Orsini, which was erected at great expense in a strange land by Pope Eugenius's nephew, the Cardinal of Porto. Alain had built in the square an altar covered with a canopy of cloth of gold with many perfumes burning on it; the lofty walls of the palace he adorned with precious tapestries which he had brought to Italy from the French city of Arras.

But all were far outstripped in expense and effort and ingenuity by Rodrigo, the Vice-Chancellor. His huge towering house which he had built on the site of the ancient mint was covered with rich and wonderful tapestries, and besides this he had raised a lofty canopy from which were suspended many and various marvels. He had decorated not only his own house but those nearby, so that the square all about them seemed a kind of park full of sweet songs and sounds, or a great palace gleaming with gold such as they say Nero's palace was. Furthermore on the walls were hung many poems recently composed by great geniuses which set forth in large letters praises of the divine Apostle and eulogies of Pope Pius.

Nor did the Tuscan merchants and bankers who lived near Hadrian's bridge leave their houses without ornament, but they tried to outdo one another in lavishness and effort and originality. There was no square or street where there were dwellings that did not display something worthy of admiration.

Thus the Pope was carried through so many wonders, himself carrying the sacred head, and came finally to the great broad square before the basilica of the Prince of the Apostles, which was already filled with a crowd of strangers; for the Romans, except those in the procession, remained in their own districts, especially the women. Here arose a great noise of voices like the murmur of many waters, since at the sight of the Apostle's head all fell to beating their breasts and with groans and wailings commended themselves to it. The Pope mounted the many steps of the marble staircase before the great doors which he himself had recently built at great expense (Fig. 18), for the old one built by Constantine had given out. On the top stair he turned to the crowd and blessed them, exhibiting to them the sacred head.

On entering the atrium the Pope turned his eyes toward the statue of St. Peter which sits before the vestibule and, fancying that the statue wept with joy at the coming of his brother, he himself burst into tears as he reflected on the meeting and embrace between two brothers who had been so long separated. Then he entered the church, which seemed one blaze of lights, for it too was full of men and women and there were very few who did not hold lighted candles or tapers in their hands. Furthermore there was the glow of innumerable lamps and candelabra and all this was made still more marvelous by the music of the organ and the singing of the clergy. They passed to the high altar with considerable difficulty through densely packed crowds who would hardly give way before swords. Under the altar lie the bodies of the two Apostles, Peter and Paul, which are objects of worship the world over.

Here the precious head of St. Andrew was deposited and all the prelates and distinguished persons present kissed it.

The preceding year Isidore, Bishop of Santa Sabina, cardinal of the Holy Roman Church, a Greek from Peloponnese who had once been assigned to the Roxani who live in the far north, had had a stroke of apoplexy which had deprived him of speech but not of intelligence. He had remained at home ill, but when he beheld the sacred head passing his house, he could not be restrained from following the holy relic. He came therefore on foot to the basilica of St. Peter and entering the iron grill that encircles the Holy of Holies and guards the high altar, he approached the Pope and indicated by signs and gestures that he desired to kiss the divine head of the Apostle. On receiving permission he knelt and with sobs and tears and profound reverence satisfied his yearning and gave vent to his exultation as if he had received an answer to prayer. Then he returned home rejoicing, for he was delighted in that he had beheld the founder of his country, and the venerable old man appeared much happier when he left than when he came.

Then Cardinal Bessarion (Fig. 19), holding the right horn *of the altar,* with the Apostle's head on one side and the Pope on the other, spoke as follows:

"O most blessed Peter, Prince of the Apostles, and thou, chosen vessel and teacher of the Gentiles, who, though called last to apostleship, dost share equally with St. Peter the primacy, behold your brother! Behold, I say! your Andrew, who, first to be called, showed the rest the way to the Savior. Lo! your Andrew is here, that he who is united with you in heaven and sits beside the Creator and Savior of all the human race and enjoys the sight of His glory may now be united with you in his body on earth and dwell with you after so long a time, he who has been severed from you more than 1428 years since the Ascension of our Lord. For, as you know, Achaia, which he once dedicated to God with his own blood, kept him and guarded him most faithfully far from you and from the city of Rome which had obtained you, the founders and teachers of the Faith, its holy and true shepherds.

"The reason for this his coming is assuredly not unknown to you who behold not only all things past but much that is to come. But that this fact may come to the knowledge, not of you, but of any Christians who may be ignorant of it, he says, 'Brother Peter, behold your Andrew! After I was sent first by the Savior and then by your orders to preach the Gospel, after traveling through many and diverse nations whom I dedicated to the true Faith and the name of Christ, I came at last to

Achaia, a province of Peloponnese filled full of men not only noble but
learned; there I sowed the truth of the Gospel so widely that I converted the entire province from the worship of idols to the religion of
the true God. Wherefore at the hands of the proconsul Egeus, whose
wife I had rescued from him by the sword and fire of the spirit and
offered to Christ, I too met death on the most holy Cross, as did you
and our Lord and Master Jesus Christ. I was buried by Maximilla, the
proconsul's wife, and until now have rested there, honored by the worshippers of Christ and extolled by their fervent praise.

"But when the Mohammedans (ah, piteous and tragic tale!) following the son of Satan, the antichrist Mahomet, after seizing the rest of
Greece and the Orient, finally in these latter days most impiously subjugated Achaia too and perverted it with infamous worship, then by
God's aid I fled thence from the clutches of the heathen and I have come
to thee, *most holy brother, to thee, teacher and master, to thee* appointed
by God the universal shepherd of Christ's flock, as to the safest haven,
that, as thy Paul (or rather ours) let down from the walls in a basket
by the brethren, escaped the most cruel hands of the governor of Da-
mascus, that he might finish his course and complete his ministry of
the Gospel, so I too taking refuge with thee, may by thy power and help
restore to their former liberty the sons whom I had begotten to myself,
or rather to thee, nay to Christ our Lord, who are now subject to an
impious and most savage enemy and not only deprived of physical
freedom but in danger of losing the integrity of their faith; and that I
may bring them back to the worship of the true God and present them
safe and cleansed of all heathen vileness before Christ our Lord, a
purpose assuredly welcome and most acceptable to thee.

"What wilt thou do now? Wilt thou be inert or slow against the
impious Turks, the bitterest enemies of the most holy Cross of our salvation, through which He Who redeemed us by it gathers to Himself
both thee and me against barbarians who are savagely rending asunder
Christ's limbs and continually assailing Christ Himself with blasphemy
and insult? Wilt thou endure such deeds? Thou hast today a successor
who besides his other virtues cherishes in his heart this supreme purpose, this yearning to avenge by righteous punishment the innocent
blood of Christians that has been most cruelly shed. Now plowshares
must be beaten into swords, now the tunic must be sold and the sword
bought, now must thy zeal blaze forth, now must thy Paul's blade be
whetted, that by thy power and aid, working through the mightiest
princes of the west, the faith which thou didst preach and approve, by

which thou didst become the father of all, *may be defended and* the Church founded on the rock that is Christ may prevail against the gates of hell through the authority and testimony of our Lord, Jesus Christ Who is very truth.

"Enough then for thee. Now I call upon thy most worthy successor and the true vicar of Christ, the Pope, who has received me with the highest honors, who welcomed me yesterday with such faith and devotion, who addressed to me such words that he himself wept and moved almost all his hearers to tears—and indeed he would easily have drawn tears from hearts of stone. Thee, Pope Pius, I beg, implore, beseech that what I have asked of my brother thou who deservedly sittest in his seat, who art his most worthy successor in the pontificate, wilt pursue and consummate. Strengthen daily the purpose thou hast thus far cherished, to avenge the blood of Christians. Cease not to exhort Christian princes and despair not because they have so often been approached by thee. One day they will come to reverence Christ, one day they will reverence Peter, and calling upon thee and me, they will put on the spirit of Christians and kings. They will at last act as becomes them and by assaulting the most cruel foe will win everlasting fame to the great glory of thy name and to the salvation of Christendom. For this may God preserve thee safe and fortunate for long time to come, to steer the course of Peter's See with all temperance and seemliness and may He in His mercy grant thee grace, that thou who hast received me this day in this city with great glory may one day restore me to my country with even greater honor, as thou didst voluntarily promise yesterday with deep emotion."

Bessarion was heard with attention and favor, though the Fathers wearied with the march, desired rest and it was already the sixteenth hour. Nevertheless when he ended they did not find it burdensome to listen to the Pope's reply, which was as follows:

"If the most holy bodies of the blessed Apostles which lie beneath the altar could speak, they would assuredly rejoice exceedingly at the coming of thy most reverend head, divine Andrew, and would express their joy in noble words and voluntarily promise the aid thou hast asked. But they lie voiceless till the day of Resurrection. Nevertheless they experience today, we think, a wondrous sweetness and an inner gladness at the presence of a head so beloved and so closely akin; and especially is this true of the bones of thy brother Peter, whose joy is enhanced by fraternal affection. But their souls are in heaven *in God's kingdom,* in Christ's kingdom, nor can we doubt that they are thinking of thee and invoke the divine aid to restore this head of thine to its own throne.

"As far as concerns us (since mention has been made of us too), the unworthy holder of thy brother's place, we will be brief. To thee Andrew, most worthy Apostle of Christ, whom from our youth to this day we have venerated with especial devotion and have chosen with many others among those who dwell in heaven to be our advocate and protector, we promise willingly and eagerly all the aid in our power to recover thy sheep and thy home here on earth. For nothing is closer to our heart than the defense of the Christian religion and the orthodox faith, which thine enemies and ours, the Turks, are striving to trample underfoot. But if Christian princes *and people* will hear our voice and follow their shepherd, all the Church will see and be glad that we have not neglected the duties of our office and that thou hast not in vain come hither to obtain thy brother's aid."

After these words and the singing of the collect, he rose and laid the famous relic on the altar, that it might be exhibited that day for all to see, and the auditors of the holy palace were set to guard it. Then while the cardinals and bishops sang praises to God with a loud voice, he went to a place where he could be seen by all and blessed the multitude, and the Cardinal of Siena, his nephew after the flesh, announced plenary indulgence. They then returned to the palace. On the following days of Holy Week the divine services assigned to each by long usage were observed and the Passion of our Lord was celebrated with profound devotion on the part of the populace.

On Saturday, April 17, after high mass, when the Pope blessed the people, he promised that the next day, in reverence for the Resurrection, he would himself celebrate mass in the church of the Prince of the Apostles and would bring thither the sacred head of Andrew so that it might be repeatedly seen. (It had been removed from the altar of St. Peter and locked up in the palace.) This was a strange and unexpected event, for because of the illnesses and absences of the Pope it was four years since the Romans had seen their pontiff elevating the divine Host; and because Pius could not stand on his feet they contrived a way for him to celebrate practically seated.

From the time when the sacred head was brought from Narni until that Saturday it rained every day and night except while it was on the road. The pious took this for an omen, thinking that God granted that fair weather to his Apostle when he went abroad, and the superstition was increased on Easter day: *for although it had rained all night, with morning it was clear again and as long as the ceremony and the sacred procession lasted the sun shone, so that the Pope said a second time, "It rained all night, but in the morning fair weather returned. Lo! the night was Satan's; the light will be God's."*

So the Pope came down into the apostolic church carrying before him the sacred head. He celebrated mass, offering to God the most acceptable of all offerings, His own Son, and he administered the most holy Body of Christ with his own hand to great numbers of the clergy and the laity. At the close of the mass the Pope took the venerable head and walked in procession with the cardinals and clergy to the part of the church where holy Veronica is kept (this is what they call the miraculous likeness of Jesus Christ imprinted on the towel which the celebrated woman Veronica *is said to have* offered him). Then standing at a little distance he ordered the towel to be displayed. Pietro, Cardinal of San Marco, a noble Venetian, Eugenius's nephew, and archpresbyter of that church, ascended the steps and exhibited the venerable and holy face of our Lord while the people, as is the custom, thrice implored mercy. It was a marvelous and awesome thing to behold on one hand the holy face of the Savior and on the other the precious relic of His apostle and furthermore to see the Pope with the cardinals and all the clergy praying bareheaded on their knees.

After this they proceeded to the place of benediction where there was as great a throng as there had been recently at the earlier procession. Even those who had come last saw the famous head of the Apostle and those who had prepared themselves through confession and contrition received the Pope's blessing and plenary remission of their sins. The Pope then withdrew to the palace carrying with him the sacred relic of the Apostle, which he deposited in the castle of Sant'Angelo to be kept till a proper receptacle could be prepared for it.

At this time Pius brought up in the senate the question of raising his native place to the rank of a city-state. This was unanimously voted and the name of the place was changed from Corsignano to Pienza.

A few days later he left Rome to go to the baths at Viterbo. The first night he spent in a Campanian villa, the second in Città Castellana in the palace of his friend the bishop; the third day he had lunch prepared in a quiet grove not far from the town of Fabricia. On the way he passed through Faleri. This is a very ancient monastery situated in a level plain, but there are no monks or other inhabitants. It has very high walls constructed of square stones without mortar and the great rocks are so cunningly fitted together that the joints can hardly be detected.

The area surrounded by the wall is extensive enough for a large town but there are no buildings inside—only the church in the middle still intact, though the monks' cells and the offices are mostly in ruins *and the church itself was for short time used to stable horses—such is our age's reverence for religion!*

From Fabricia the Pope went to Soriano along roads which at that season were most delightful. Masses of flowering broom gave much of the country a golden hue and some of it was covered with other shrubs or various plants that presented purple or white or a thousand other colors to the eye. The world was green in that month of May and not only the meadows but the woods were smiling and birds were singing sweetly. The town of Soriano lies on a high hill toward the eastern slope of Monte Cimino looking toward the Tiber. On the very summit is the citadel, an ancient structure fortified on all sides by rocks and steep cliffs and so high that it could hardly be reached by stones shot from engines. The place was made famous by the Bretons who were brought in by a French pope and down to the time of Martin held the citadel and the town and harassed all the patrimony of St. Peter in Tuscany. Pope Calixtus had put in command a Catalan whom Pius with difficulty got rid of by loading him with promises. In his place he put Lorenzo, his niece Montanina's husband.

Pius spent a whole day and two nights in Soriano since his sister Laodomia and his niece Montanina were there. He could not refuse them an audience and they urged at length their own causes and those of their friends. Seven cardinals accompanied him on this journey: two Frenchmen, Rouen and Arras; one Spaniard, the Vice-Chancellor; four Italians, Teano, Pavia, Siena, and Mantua; and with these he proceeded to Viterbo. Two others, Bologna and Spoleto, met him on the way near Viterbo. He looked at them grimly and did not think they deserved to be spoken to since they were so uncouth and ignorant of etiquette that they did not dismount as soon as they saw the Pope as was the custom. Later they apologized for their ignorance and begged his pardon.

Pius was received with the highest honors by the people of Viterbo, who were delighted beyond measure. Soon afterward he was followed by almost all the cardinals who had remained at Rome when the plague began to ravage the city and in a short time the Curia at Viterbo was enlarged and not uncomfortably lodged. All were pleased with the country, the kindness of the people, and the pleasantness of the city, in which there is hardly a house without its spring of unfailing water and a garden. Furthermore there was an abundance of dainties, wines of various kinds not inferior to those of Florence or Siena, white bread with a delicious taste, and flesh of cattle pastured on thyme and other fragrant herbs. Fish were supplied in plenty by the Tuscan Sea on one side and the nearby lake of Bolsena on the other. There was plenty of fodder for the horses too. As to prices, the members of the Curia might set their own.

The Pope lodged in the citadel and had hot water brought to him there to be used according to his doctor's orders. Almost every day at dawn he would go out into the country to enjoy the sweet air before it grew hot and to gaze on the green crops and the blossoming flax, then most lovely to see with its sky-blue color. Nowhere are there more or larger fields of flax than around Viterbo, either because of the character of the soil or because the best water for steeping it is found here. From this industry they derive their chief income. The Pope inspected all the meadows and crops riding on different roads every day, but he did not neglect the consistories or the Signatura. As he rode he heard suppliants and envoys and when he returned he either held a consistory with the cardinals before lunch or a Signatura with the referendarii. The latter he often held in the convent of the Minorites, who are called Observant-ists, in a peaceful spot outside the city called Paradise.

While the Pope was thus enjoying himself, numerous letters were sent from the Roman Curia to King Louis of France asserting that Pope Pius was his enemy and was prosecuting the war for the Kingdom of Sicily more ardently ever. *They said that* when Pius had received the letter telling of the abrogating of the Pragmatic Sanction *he had exult-antly cried out, "War! war!" because now that the Pragmatic Sanction was abolished France was going to contribute money that would amply finance the war. Some asserted that the Pope had contemptuously thrown the King's letter on the ground and trampled on it.*

When the credulous king heard this he was furiously angry and with-out considering whether what was written him was probable or not he at once dictated a letter to the Pope as follows:

"Louis, King of France, to Pope Pius greeting. Your Holiness, I thought to win your affection by benefits. I abrogated the Pragmatic Sanction. I freely tendered you obedience. I offered aid against the Turks. To those who demanded a council and rebellion against the Apostolic See I returned harsh answers. It has never been possible to persuade me to anything incompatible with your dignity. Who would not think that by these services I ought to have softened the harshness *which you seem to have conceived against the French nation?* I was convinced that you were becoming, if not gentler, at least not more severe. The opposite is the case. You are taking this opportunity to eject from the Kingdom the Duke of Anjou, my kinsman. *My daughter, whom I offered to marry to your nephew, you actually scorned, and preferred a connection with Ferrante. When you heard that the Pragmatic Sanction had been abolished at my command, you cried out twice, 'War! war!' and some say you publicly trampled on the letter I sent you on the subject.* What am I to do if I cannot appease your fierce spirit by good offices? Shall I try the opposite way? No! I cannot bring myself to persecute Christ's Vicar. I shall pursue the road I have started on, though all my counselors advise against it. Perhaps you will one day regret having cherished hatred *against the French* and will become a friend to our nation and will at last be won over by my persistent devotion. Farewell."

This letter was endurable and easy for the Pope to answer. More harsh was the message brought by the King's envoy, the Marshal of Toulouse, a man noble in his own country, though uneducated and ignorant of Italian. He spoke through an interpreter to the following effect:

"Louis, King of France, requested you to withdraw the aid that you sent into the Kingdom to Ferrante and finally to cease persecuting his kinsman. That you might be more willing to do so, he abolished the Pragmatic Sanction in the Gauls and became once more completely obedient to you. You have returned evil for good. You have sent fresh forces into the Kingdom and you are pressing the Duke of Anjou even harder. The King again begs you to desist and consent to regard the kingdom of France as a friend. If you persist in supporting Ferrante's cause, all the French, even the cardinals, must leave the Curia. I am charged to give them this message. They will obey (have no doubt of that) rather than be deprived of their worldly goods."

The Pope answered: "Although Louis's kindnesses to us are numerous and great, they have given him no right to make unjust demands nor does it become us to depart from the path of honor for his sake. In accordance with our compact we sent aid to Ferrante and we have warded off violence so that the holder of a throne might not be deposed without a trial. Let Louis withdraw his support from the Angevins and refer the quarrel about the Kingdom to law. Ferrante will do the same or he will find me his enemy. More I cannot offer. The Frenchmen shall be free to leave the Curia when they will. The gates will be closed against no one. *We have no doubt that, as you say, the bishops and cardinals will obey the King's commands. For what Frenchman would not obey his king rather than his God? Undoubtedly they will prefer to Christ's Vicar him whom they prefer to Christ Himself.* As for us, we will await calmly the lot God sends."

When Arras heard this he said he must defer his answer and wait for new orders from the King before communicating his message to the curials. For Louis, although he had publicly given the Marshal instructions in regard to recalling the members of the Curia, had secretly directed him by no means to carry them out. He had meant to strike terror by words but not by deeds. Arras was aware of this and therefore he temporized to see if the Pope might not perhaps be frightened into recalling his troops.

By now the whole Curia was buzzing with the rumor that the King of France was angry at the Pope and making grave threats and that there was no doubt that all the French would leave unless Ferrante's cause were abandoned. Cardinals and many others came humbly to beg the Pope to consider the good of himself and of the Church. They repeated what they had heard about the King's anger and declared that the Curia would be deserted if the French left it; they were the strongest part and must not be allowed to withdraw. The Pope said to them: "This is all empty talk. They will not carry out their threats. The French will stay, though they pretend they are going.

"But let them go if they will. What of it? Will the Curia therefore be destroyed? On the contrary it will be remade. Avarice and simony and luxury and ambition will go with them and all evil practices will leave when the French leave. For what disgrace in the Curia was not brought in by the French? Happy the pope who never saw a Frenchman in the Curia! And what has the obedience of the French in abrogating the Pragmatic Sanction brought us? Only danger to our conscience? Every day we are forced to fight with the French who make outrageous and improper requests. Our soul is at stake. They bring gain to our coffers and ruin to our conscience. It were better that they should depart and stay away. Only thus shall we be able to live in peace and virtue."

When the Marshal had waited some days in vain for the Pope to change his mind, he said he must carry out the King's orders and begged the Pope not to take offense. Pius answered, "On the contrary, you have put it off too long already. Go and obey the King as soon as possible." Nevertheless the Marshal did not dare do as he threatened, but for a long time after that remained at the Curia.

Meanwhile since the time was at hand for the feast of the Most Holy Body and Blood of Christ[2] which is celebrated yearly in the Christian world with the greatest devotion and profound worship by all nations, the Pope decided to observe it with all possible reverence and particular honors. With this in view he gave orders first of all that the street leading from the citadel through the city to the cathedral, which was cluttered with balconies and galleries and disfigured with wooden porticoes, should be cleared and restored to its original splendor. Everything that jutted out and obstructed the view of the next house was removed and everywhere the proper width of the street was restored. Whatever was removed was paid for from the public funds. No wall was allowed to project further than another and no roof to overtop another.

Next the cardinals were directed to choose each a portion of the street to cover and adorn with tapestries. The rest was divided among the bishops and other curials. Some of the cardinals undertook also to decorate walls and houses. In the cemetery of San Francesco which was opposite the great entrance to the church, the Pope constructed a wonderful tabernacle of many colored stuffs hung from hastily erected beams and pulled taut by many ropes. In it he erected an altar with rich hangings on either side and placed on it many marvelous objects to attract the attention of the spectators. There was a vestibule decorated with silk and cloth of gold and a chamber next it with a purple-covered couch, tapestries with ancient tales woven in silk, wool, and gold, portraits of illustrious men, and representations of various beasts.

Countless arches of flowering broom and myrtle and laurel constructed with admirable skill lined both sides of the road from the citadel to the fountain at the foot of the hill. The way was strewn with flowers; in the middle near the tabernacle was erected a triumphal arch. The house walls were concealed by representations of the cardinal virtues and the fluttering banners not only of the Pope but of kings and cardinals or by embroidered hangings or flowers.

The Pope, attended by the cardinals and all the clergy, before a great throng of the populace, began the celebration with vespers in the tabernacle he had erected. The sun was still high and its rays, penetrating the woolen walls which imitated the varied colors of the rainbow, gave the tabernacle the appearance of a celestial hall and the dwelling of the King of Kings. It seemed indeed like a kind of paradise since choristers like angels were singing sweet hymns and lights, disposed with marvelous art, imitated the stars of heaven, and now human voices

[2] The Feast of Corpus Christi at Viterbo, June 17, 1462.

were heard raised in sweet strains and now the melodious harmony of musical instruments.

The next day at dawn the Pope came down again from the citadel in solemn procession with the cardinals, bishops, and all the order of curials and taking the most sacred Host from the altar began the journey to the cathedral. There were crowds of people who had swarmed from the neighboring towns for the sake of the indulgences (for the Pope had promised to all present plenary remission of their sins) or to see the show. Every square was full and every street packed with men, women, and children so that it was difficult for the Pope and the procession to pass. Nevertheless they finally made their way through the crowded populace though not without much pushing and effort. Where the Pope's decorations ended Rouen's began. Then came those of the cardinals of Coutances and Lebret, who, after the custom of their country, had covered the walls with tapestries (which they call arras) and constructed altars rich with gold and silver and heaped with incense. After them came the houses decorated by the Referendarii. Under an altar raised aloft they had put a youth impersonating the Savior, who sweated blood and filled a cup from the healing stream from a wound in his side. And they had added boys winged like angels who sang epic verses or elegiacs by learned scholars. Next came the Cardinal of San Sisto, who, as befitted his ecclesiastical dignity, had a representation of the Last Supper with Christ and the disciples and the institution of the sacrament in memory of the Passion and of the everlasting protection of mankind against the wiles of the devils to the end of time. And he had represented St. Thomas Aquinas administering that holy and solemn sacrament.

After him the Cardinal of Mantua covered a long expanse of road and adorned it with very famous stories which clever weavers had wrought in rich tapestries. Next came the Cardinal of Porto, in whose exhibit a huge dragon and the shapes of many malignant spirits seemed to be making some horrible threat. But as the Pope passed, an armed soldier, playing the part of St. Michael, cut off the dragon's head and all the demons fell headlong baying like hounds. The sky was covered as with a cloud by a reddish canopy and the walls with leather embossed with golden flowers in the Spanish style. Next the Cardinal of Nicaea had erected an altar and had boys singing like angels. Everywhere numberless altars smoked with incense, priests in many places were celebrating divine service, and all the sacred vessels and holy relics in the city might be seen exposed on the altars covered with gold and silver.

Nicaea was followed by Spoleto, whose display was enclosed between two arches cunningly contrived of flowers and green foliage. There was a shrine and an altar in the middle and clouds of fragrant smoke and a chorus of singing boys. The sky was hidden by a canopy of varied colors called a saium. Next came the display of the Vice-Chancellor occupying seventy-four feet. A rich purple curtain enclosed statues and representations of stories and a richly decorated chamber and a splendid bed and a fountain which poured out through many pipes *various kinds of* the finest wines as well as water. As the Pope approached, he was met by two boys singing as sweetly as angels, and after genuflecting before the Host and saluting the Pope, they went back behind the curtain and chanted in sweet high voices, "Lift up your gates, O princes, and King Pius, lord of the world, will come in." Inside five kings in magnificent attire with an armed escort pretended to prevent his entrance, but when they heard the angels, they replied, "Who is this King Pius?" and the angels, because of the sacrament which Pius was carrying in the procession, said, "The lord of the world." At these words the curtain was drawn to reveal the entrance and at the same time trumpets and organs and countless other musical instruments sounded and the kings, doing reverence to the Pope, recited alternately in sweet and ringing voices heroic verses in his praise. As he passed along he was met by a forester leading a captive lion with which he often wrestled. A canopy of tapestry made a rich roof over all the square around the fountain and banners hung there on which were the arms of Pope Calixtus and of Borgia, once prefect of the city. Draperies no less rich in material than in workmanship and art hung down on the sides attracting the attention and charming the minds not only of the ignorant mob but even of learned men. At the exit a triumphal arch built like a citadel was held by armed soldiers who imitated thunder with bronze engines and struck terror into the passers-by.

The Cardinal of Santa Susanna had followed nature in the part of the road next the Vice-Chancellor which had fallen to him, covering it with tapestry the color of the sky spangled with gold stars. He had made a fountain of white wine decorated with flowers and a perfumed altar and statues which seemed to laugh and sing and there was a chorus which delighted the crowd with their clear voices and musical instruments. Niccolò, Cardinal of Teano, to please the Pope who liked distinction in everything, had brought from his native Pistoia actors and boys who sang sweetly.

Next Pius came to the square around which the magistrates of the

city live. This was covered with blue and white canopies. It was decorated on all sides with tapestries and there were many arches covered
with green ivy and many kinds of flowers and every column had a boy
representing an angel sitting on it. There were eighteen boys like angels
in face, voice, and dress, and they sweetly sang responsive verses. In
the middle of the square he had built a model of the tomb of our Lord,
where our Life for our sake fell asleep in God. About it armed soldiers
lay buried in slumber as if dead and angels stood on guard to prevent
the chamber of the Heavenly Bridegroom from being violated. When
the Pope came to this place, lo! of a sudden there was let down along a
rope as if flying from heaven a beautiful boy with wings like an angel,
the face of a seraph, and a heavenly voice, who made a gesture of salutation to the Pope and sang a hymn announcing the immediate Resurrection of the Savior. There was sudden silence; no one spoke; all listened
with delight as if an actual event were taking place and it were a real
messenger from heaven. *When he had finished,* fire was applied to
powders which had been mixed in a bronze urn and the flash of the
explosion waked the sleeping soldiers and dazed them with terror.
Thereupon the actor who represented the Savior was suddenly revealed
to the sight of all, a sandy-haired man of the stature and age of Jesus
holding the banner of the Cross and wearing a diadem. He pointed to
the conspicuous scars of his wounds and proclaimed in Italian verses
that salvation was won for Christendom.

Next to Teano the Cardinal of Avignon had built an altar which was
far from insignificant and had lavished the wealth of France to make
splendid the part of the road assigned to him. Then came Pavia who
had shut out the sky with awnings of four colors and covered the walls
with tapestries from Arras. He had built flowery arches and on either
side had stationed a crowd of boys representing angels who held lighted
tapers in honor of the divine Sacrament.

After this came less elaborate decorations. Instead of canopies there
were flowers and leaves and green branches that indicated poor owners,
though altars and priests and vestments and singing and clouds of incense were nowhere lacking. Ambrogio of Siena, an official of the papal
court, again adorned the road in front of his house more handsomely
and by shutting out the sun and covering the walls did his best to equal
the great men with his display.

Next the Cardinal of Arras canopied the road from the stone bridge
that connects the two parts of the city as far as the cathedral square with
stuff that he had recently had sent from Florence *to make new dresses*

for his household. It was of English wool of a color between red and russet. The sides of the street he had reinforced at the expense of his city. Because the surrounding houses seemed to him too humble he had erected at intervals high posts connected with ropes from which he had hung tapestries. *The night before the feast there had been a great gale which beat and buffeted the ropes back and forth and tore a good part of the fabric, thus depriving his servants of some of their expected dresses.*

The great square before the cathedral the Cardinal of Santi Quattro Coronati had canopied all over by erecting great posts connected with ropes and he had decorated it lavishly with wonders. He had erected an altar in a suitable place on the right of which was set the papal throne and benches for the cardinals, on the left seats for the bishops, protonotaries, and abbots. It was a chapel like that in the apostolic palace. In the higher part of the square was built the tomb of the glorious Virgin Mary and above the roofs of the houses the palace of the King of Heaven with God Himself seated in majesty and companies of holy angels and burning stars and the joys of supreme glory expressed in marvelous ways. Divine service was held here with profound reverence on the part of the people. The Cardinal of San Marco celebrated mass; the Pope blessed the people. Then a boy representing an angel proclaimed in sweetest song the assumption of the Virgin, whereupon the tomb opened and a most lovely girl came forth upborne on the hands of angels. *When she had risen a little in the air* she dropped her girdle *into the outstretched hands of an apostle.* Rapt with joy and singing sweetly she was carried up to Heaven where her Son, who is likewise Father and Lord, met her and kissing His mother on the forehead, presented her to the everlasting Father and set her at His right hand. Then all the ranks of heavenly spirits burst into song and played on their instruments. They rejoiced and made merry and all Heaven laughed.

This brought to an end a celebration in which the greatest marvel was that arranged by the Pope's officials: Christ was represented by a man naked except for a loincloth with a crown of thorns on his head, painted so that he seemed to be exuding blood, carrying the cross on which he seemed to have hung. He was borne in a chariot from the church of San Francesco to the cathedral and while mass was being celebrated and the assumption of the Mother of God represented, he stood motionless as a statue. Since the square would not hold all the people, the Pope gave orders that they should go down into the fields behind the papal palace, and there from a window he again blessed the multitude and gave them plenary indulgence for their sins. Such was the honor paid by Pius to the most divine Sacrament of the Body and Blood of our Lord Jesus Christ.

After the ceremonies the Pope lunched with the Cardinal of Santi Quattro Coronati who was then living in the papal palace, a large ancient structure adjoining the cathedral. It had been built in earlier days by the Popes of Rome because they often stayed at Viterbo. It has dining rooms and chambers fit for a prince, and the Cardinal had decorated it throughout magnificently. The great vaulted hall was flooded with light and commanded a charming view; in the middle was a marble fountain which sent out clear jets of abundant water through numerous pipes. This was draped with gold and silver cloth; on the walls precious tapestries depicted famous tales and showed forth the noblest genius on the part of the artist. The Cardinal had planned a banquet such as kings have served and he kept many of the cardinals to lunch. There were dishes of heavy gold and silver *and most delicious and elegant food*. There were lyre-players and singers. Nothing you could possibly desire was missing. Pleasant conversation and wit seasoned with wisdom made the hours seem short.

After lunch, when he had rested a little as was his custom, the Pope with the College returned at evening to the citadel by the way he had come. All who entered Viterbo that day and beheld so many marvels and such an array and succession of sights as they walked through the city thought they had assuredly entered the dwelling of gods, not a habitation of men, and said that while living in the flesh they had beheld Heaven.

But what joys of mortals are lasting? All that pleases is too brief. Grief succeeds happiness. Lamentation follows hard on laughter. While the Curia was exulting over such a state of affairs and the city was elated with excessive joy, they were stricken by a sudden plague. A wasting poison and fatal pestilence carried off many, both citizens and curials, so that the terrified cardinals urged that the Curia be moved. The Pope kept a few with him and allowed the rest to go where they pleased to escape the fatal sickness. He himself wished before he left to visit the convent of St. Martin on Monte Cimino, which he had entrusted to his nephew. It is three miles from Viterbo but not actually on the summit of the mountain. It has a lofty vaulted church of hewn stone, a noble work made splendid by many columns, in which, as we have said, the body of Cardinal Egidius is said to have been buried.

Once many monks sang praises here to God, but now crows and doves nest in it and sometimes the screech owl utters her ill-boding cry. The splendid refectory still stood but all the rest had fallen in ruins or seemed likely to fall soon. The Pope's nephew assumed the responsibility of restoring it. The site is most delightful with an abundance of clear bubbling springs. It is surrounded by chestnut forests and there are meadows and vineyards close by. The view toward Siena extends as far as Amiata. To the west it commands Mt. Argentario and is bounded by the sea. Its climate makes it a pleasant place to stay in summer.

When the Pope had returned from here and was going home through the city in the dusk, men, women, boys, girls and aged persons from the whole city carrying lighted tapers met him with wondrous plaudits, shouting, "Long life and prosperity to Pius!" No other cry was heard. All marveled at him and hailed him as if he were God descended from heaven. There was no toddler who did not lisp "Pope Pius" with his baby lips though too young to say the words plainly. All this affected Pius and moved him to tears when he reflected on the calamities to come and he said to himself, "Behold the hard lot of mortals! Alas for the mind that cannot know the future! Men and matrons joyfully applaud us; maids and brides exult; the most lovely young people of both sexes are given over to happiness and express their gladness; the streets are gay with throngs of little children. But how many will escape the fatal summer? The plague will devastate the city; it will carry off children and youths; it will spare no age. If it is granted us to return one day, we shall find but few of those who today honor us so highly. O flesh! O life of men! how fragile and how fleeting ye are!" and without saying more he returned to the citadel.

The next day since almost all the Curia had gone, he thought he too ought to retreat before the fury of the plague and he went to the estate of the noble Farnese family. This is a castle called Capodimonte situated in a most delightful spot on the lake of Bolsena. Three sides are washed by the lake, the fourth is protected by a strongly fortified citadel. A rocky mound almost a stade high in the middle and difficult of approach rises from the water. On the top is a plateau surrounded by a wall, where are the houses of the rustics and the stables and barns of the nobles. Between the walls and the cliff they have laid out a vineyard six or eight feet wide which bounds three sides of the town. It is level and easy to walk on and in summer affords pleasant shade. It is never entirely exposed to the sun. The west is shady in the morning, the east at evening. There are vines which in their season give pleasure with the shade of their leaves. The cliff, where there is no flint rock, is planted with vines and fruit trees. There is a path almost like steps down to the lake and here among rugged stones and jagged boulders grow many evergreen ilex trees which make a grove beloved of thrushes. Between this and the vineyard they have hewn out a path wide enough for two persons, where they often set snares for birds.

Here the Pope stopped and was lodged with a few companions in the citadel. The referendarii were accommodated in neighboring towns and came to him by boat on stated days. *The Pope held the signatura on the road which we have said encircles the town.* When he had leisure he rode out into the nearby groves to breathe the mild breezes. He explored the immediate neighborhood and made excursions by water and land. The cardinals of Spoleto and Teano were close by (eight stades distant) in a town called Marta from the name of a river formed by the lake which has its emissary at this point. Here there is good fishing for eels which are considered particularly large and fine. When the south wind ruffles the clear water they retreat to the end of the lake and following the course of the river fall into a trap. For where the river drops, the inhabitants have built a tower with a wooden receptacle at its foot which lets out the water through many small holes in the floor but keeps the eels in. Since they cannot climb up again against the force of the river flowing down from above, they are left high and dry and are caught. The tower is kept under guard and returns a very considerable revenue. When the water rises too high it is possible to turn its course away from the tower. The Pope visited this place too, that he might see with his own eyes what he had heard of.

In the lake are two islands worth mentioning on which there were once numerous buildings. Traces of ancient ruins may still be seen. It is generally known that the princes used the islands as prisons, for we read that the maid Christina was banished here and also Amalasunta, most noble queen of the Goths, who was impiously and treacherously murdered by her own people. The larger island is today called Bisentina from the town of Bisentinum whose ruins are to be seen on a mountain nearby. Here live Minorites who are thought to observe special rules and are therefore called Observantists. They are indeed exemplary men whose riches are poverty and abstinence, *unless they deceive themselves more than they do others.* Ranuzzo Farnese built them a chapel and a monastery and gave them the fields of the island, where they have *planted vines and trees delightful for fruit or shade. Part of the island is* a carefully cultivated garden with broad level paths in which they

grow cabbages and legumes. There are meadows too and some parts
are left to rabbits, many of which make their holes among the brambles
and are hunted by the monks to supply their table. They have dug out
a path among the thorns and brambles where they stretch nets a cubit
high. Then they beat the thickets with clubs and stones and drive out
the beasts, which fall into the nets and are easily caught. A third of the
island is high rough cliffs, though that part too is planted with olives
and almonds. There are vines too and on the summit ilex trees grow.
There are many oratories there, which are reached by steps cut out of
the rock. Pius had a new shrine built at the very top and endowed it
with spiritual graces.

On the other and smaller island live the Augustinian friars called
Eremites. Part of this too is level and made into a garden; part is rough
and rises to a high rock difficult of access. There are two ancient and
venerable churches, the larger on the plain surrounded by the monks'
quarters and recent plantings of trees and vines, the other on the summit, in which are the bones of St. Mary Magdalene who washed the
holy feet of the Lord with her tears and wiped them with her hair. These
are said to have been discovered recently by a miracle and attract crowds
of worshippers. The story of the finding is supported by ancient tradition and the fame of the relics, and the fact that the island has long been
called by the name of that glorious and holy woman. When the Pope
visited the island, he sailed around it, attended mass in the upper church,
and examined the sacred bones, which he kissed and revered. At that
time the quarters of the monks were just being built with the aid of the
Bishop of Corneto, by whose zeal the brethren were first brought there,
and the island, which had been deserted, was inhabited again. The Pope
and two cardinals lunched with the bishop.

The lake between the two islands is said to be unfathomable. Sailors
have often tried to touch the bottom with rocks tied to ropes but have
never succeeded. Here is a safe refuge for the fish which can only be
caught near shore.

The Pope, having decided to celebrate the birth of St. John,[3] the
precursor of our Lord, in the chapel of the Minorites on the island of
Bisentina, ordered plenary indulgence to be proclaimed for all who
should be present. Gabriele Farnese, lord of the place, to make the feast
more numerously attended, offered prizes for any who would come and
engage in boat races.

The Pope sailed at dawn from Capodimonte to the island and with

3 June 24.

him the Cardinals of Spoleto and Teano. Rouen, who was not far away, joined them. There were present too the referendarii and the Bishops of Corneto and Foligno. The populace of the neighboring towns came in throngs. Mass was celebrated at the appropriate time with reverent devotion. Rudolf, Dean of Worms, officiated at the altar and offered the Host beloved of God. He was a learned man and had been a friend of the Pope from their youth.

After this they lunched in the meadows in the poplar shade. The lunch had been begged by the monks many days before from the surrounding towns, that they might receive the Pope with all possible honor and they besought Pius not to despise their food nor disdain the preparations they had made. Nor did he. He ate the courses offered him and drank the wine they had begged, that he might not seem to scorn the poor table. He breakfasted one day with the brethren, but he fed them many days.

After lunch the captains of the boats which were to race presented themselves and also lusty young men who were the rowers. Out of a great number of boats five were chosen. The first had been equipped by the Bolsinians, who were as boastful and confident as if there were no doubt that they would carry off the prize. The second belonged to the Clarentani, the third to the Cornetani, the fourth to those who live in Crypte San Lorenzo, the fifth to the Martani. All were extraordinarily confident and even more boastful. Everyone despised everyone else and exalted himself, and the more they had to drink the more they lauded their own exploits. They had been winners in the past and beaten their rivals by a long distance and won the prize; there was no doubt that now too they would win. Arguments also arose about the size of the boats, the number of oarsmen, the length of the oars. Gabriele Farnese, Alessandro the papal major-domo, and Pagalia his bodyguard were chosen as judges to decide all disputes.

First the course was laid out at Capodimonte. The goal was set up in the harbor of the island and prizes for the victors deposited there: pieces of cloth of the best Florentine purple eight ells long for the winners and other gifts for those who came in next. The boats, which were not larger than skiffs, were to have each four rowers and a coxswain. When they reached the shore at Capodimonte, they drew lots for positions from which they were to shoot off as from barriers. The coxswains sitting at the tillers wreathed their heads with white linen and poplar leaves and so did the rowers, who were naked except for loincloths and glistening with oil. On their benches, with arms extended toward the oars, they awaited the signal. Their hearts beat fast with excitement and they were carried away with a mighty longing for glory. When the trumpet gave the signal, at once all darted from their places. Hoarse shouts rent the sky, the water foamed under their strokes. They cleave the furrows side by side and the lake yawns to its very depths under the oars and beaks. They were followed closely by a fleet of smaller boats filled with spectators shouting and applauding one crew or another and making the air ring with their cries. The woods and the neighboring mountain took up the sound, the shores sent back the voices, and the hills re-echoed. The first to get away in all the excitement and confusion was the Bolsinian boat, a whole length ahead of the rest. Next came Cornetani and Martani together, with the rest slightly behind them.

Although the Pope was in a quiet spot some distance from the harbor discussing political matters with the cardinals, still he beheld the boat race with pleasure and amusement. The referendarii, other prelates, and many nobles stood on the shore near the harbor and the prizes. *Among them was a certain Guicciardo related to the Pope on his mother's side and on that account made prefect of Bolsena. When he had heard that his clients were ahead (unsupported rumor had brought the news) he cried, "Did I not tell you so? and you would not believe me. I knew the strength of the Bolsinians. Nowhere will you find stronger arms. Our men are made lusty by exercise and by drinking unadulterated wine. It is useless for the Martani to contend. I have no fear of the Clarentani or the Criptenses, I snap my fingers at the Cornetani. Soon our boat will come in victor. Award the prize now and declare for us, judges, The palm is ours. We have won. The prize cannot slip through our hands."*

Gabriele answered him, "If the palm belongs to heavy drinkers I do not deny that your clients are famous for that. But it is not so easy to pull an oar as to drain a goblet. This contest was first instituted by the Bishop of Corneto. For many years now boats have contested and it has never been heard that the Bolsinians won. The Martani have often carried off the prize. They will do so this year, I hope—unless you have seen to it that your clients can get a drink every time they smite the water with their oars."

It was not yet possible to recognize the boats and tell which was ahead, since they were more than a mile from harbor and the whole course was about two miles. Meantime the coxswain of the Martani's boat cried out, "What are we about, boys? We are already left in third place, we who are not used to being anything but first. For shame!

Where is the strength of our arms? We are contending today with those whom we have often beaten. What has made them better or us worse? Can we who have never been conquered before endure the disgrace of being conquered today *before the eyes of the Pope?* Death would be better. Up, boys! Renew your strength! Bend with more vigor to your oars! Save our nation from such an outrage!"

The spirited youths heeded his words. Putting forth all their strength, with mighty strokes they smote the flood and stole the ground from under their quivering boat. They passed the Clarentani and came up with the Bolsinians. For a time they were neck and neck but from then on the victorious Martani were ahead of the rest. The Clarentani passed the Bolsinians as did also the Cornetani for by now the dry lips of the drinkers were panting and the men were streaming with sweat that there was no wine to recompense. *When Guicciardo saw that, he left the crowd heartbroken.*

The Martani came in far ahead of the others and carried off the prize of victory. The second prize went to the Clarentani. The Bolsinians, left among the last and dreading the reproaches and abuse of Guicciardo, did not come into harbor at all. The Cryptenses shared their disgrace. The Cornetani were midway between glory and ignominy. After the race all went off, though a strong wind had risen which was making the lake rough and was the precursor of a storm. Rouen did not reach his house without some danger of drowning, as the Clarentani, in whose boat he was, were so drunk that they could not steer straight nor bend well to their oars. *As all were withdrawing the referendarii, who had equipped two ships, gave a realistic imitation of a naval battle after the manner of the Ethiopians, fighting now with pikes and now with bows. The battle was interrupted by the gale from which at last they barely escaped after being submerged many times shaking with cold.*

The Pope returned to his lodging where he remained a few days. Then when the plague had left the neighborhood, he crossed the lake, blessed the people who had gathered in great numbers on the other side, and through green fields and a lovely valley watered by clear streams went to the town of Crypte. It is a rocky mound two stades high, pregnable by one approach, which is however fortified by a moat and a high wall. Everywhere else it is steep and protected by very deep valleys. The townspeople have dug out caves in which most of them live. There are also houses of hewn stone. The tufa hardens in the sun and can be used like rock.

The joy of the people, who had never seen a vicar of Christ, was incredible. All brought out their treasures to adorn the streets as the Pope passed. He went to the house of the parish priest, who was an old friend of his, an excellent man, wiser than he was handsome, to partake of the elaborate lunch which the townspeople had prepared for the occasion. While he was at table with the cardinals, such a drenching rain fell that it seemed as if it would flood the neighboring valleys and submerge the town itself, high as it was. But the rain ended with the meal and the Pope proceeded the same day to Acquapendente where he spent the night. Then [4] he proceeded through Piano to Abbadia which he had selected as a suitable refuge from the July heat.

[4] After giving up plans to visit his native Siena because of hostile demonstrations there. The Sienese had feared he would make it the occasion for a restoration of the nobles to power. Despite Pius's patronage of Siena, his efforts to restore the nobles remained unsuccessful.

BOOK IX

MOUNT AMIATA is in Sienese territory. It is as high as the
Apennines and in all Italy only the Pistoian Alps *and two other
mountains* are said to be higher. It is clothed to the very summit with
forests. The upper part, which is often cloud-capped, is covered with
beeches; below are chestnuts and below them oaks and cork trees. The
lowest slopes are covered with vines and cultivated trees, tilled fields
and meadows. In a secluded fold of the mountain there grow also lofty
firs, which furnish splendid timber for the buildings of Rome as well
as of Siena. Here Pius bought the beams for his palace at Pienza. The
only bare strip on the mountain is between the firs and chestnuts, but
even this is grassy and good for grazing.

On the west the mountain slopes toward the Sienese coast. To the
south it overlooks Santa Fiora, of which we shall speak a little later. To
the north it has a view of Pienza, many strongholds of the Sienese,
Siena itself, and the River Orcia. On the east it looks to the citadel of
Radicofani and the River Paglia, which unites with the Chiana and
empties into the Tiber. On it are many populous towns. The one called
Abbadia is unsurpassed in natural beauty. It lies on the east side about
equally distant from the summit and the Paglia. In the center of this
region there was a natural plain about eight stades long covered all over
with chestnuts and ending in rough cliffs. There the ancients built a
town protected on one side by precipitous crags and on the other by a
wall and a moat kept full by running streams. In it they constructed
very comfortable houses of squared stone with roofs of material that
would resist the snow. In front of the town the woods were cut away
for about a stade to make room for gardens and a little pasture land.
There is an ancient monastery here dedicated to the Savior with an
extremely well built church and monks' quarters. It is said to have been
founded and endowed with great possessions by Rotharis, King of the
Lombards. The abbot had absolute and comprehensive authority over
many castles and this town was called Abbadia because it was com-

pletely under the abbot's jurisdiction. It owned precious sacred vessels
and a splendid library, of which only a few volumes remain. Among
them is a large and admirable copy of the Old and New Testaments in
majuscules, which Pius beheld with envy. Today (seeing that nothing
on earth is not subject to change) the monastery is poor. Tyrants have
plundered it of everything. Nor have the townspeople remained loyal,
for they spurned the yoke of the monks and went over to the Sienese
whose power they thought would give them greater protection against
hostile attacks.

In July the cherries there were not yet ripe. Nearby an abundant
spring gushes from the rock and after he had lunched beside it, Pius
heard embassies and petitions there. Many, after leaving the Pope,
climbed to the top of the mountain by a steep and precipitous path
which no one would dare to attempt except that numerous beech trees
screen the danger and promise to intercept a fall. On the top they found
an open space and in the center a great rock with another just as large
upon it. They climbed both and reported that they could see the mountains of Sicily and Corsica.

The chestnuts which follow the beeches are very tall towering into
the sky. You would find many trunks which four men could scarcely
get their arms around. Some of the hollow ones provide stabling for
twenty-five sheep. Grassy fields spread out beneath the chestnuts and
are always shady except that after the autumn frosts when the leaves
have fallen the sun's rays penetrate the branches. Surely here, if anywhere in the world, sweet shade and silvery springs and green grass and
smiling meadows allure poets. Here they will spend the summer and
for our part we think the slopes of Cirrha and Nysa, though they are
often mentioned in literature, cannot compare with these; nor should
we prefer Peneian Tempe. There are no snakes or dangerous wild
beasts; no annoying swarms of flies; no gnats or gadflies sting your
face; no bugs scent your bed with their vile odor; no mosquitoes buzz
in your ears. A tranquil peace pervades the grove and no brambles or
briers prick your feet. The trees are so spaced that they shade all the
ground between with their lofty branches and their leaves. The ground
is covered with grass and wild strawberries through which clear streams
glide and chatter ceaselessly.

The Pope had noted this place the preceding year when he was
passing that way and had chosen it as the most congenial refuge from
the summer heat, since he was a lover of woods and liked a change of
surroundings. The learned poet Campano, whom Pius made a bishop,

when he observed Pius's successful wars and his frequent withdrawals into the forests, composed the following verses:

Marvel not that you see Pius victorious in so many battles and the arms of his enemies grown weak. Victoria was the mother who bore him. Thus from his mother's breast he learned to conquer. As to his loving forests and traveling over the great world, his father Silvius begot him to this lot. With good right then he roves afar and conquers all. Travel is his heritage from his father, conquest from his mother.

The Pope lodged in the monastery. Six cardinals and many of the curials stayed in the town. The referendarii found accommodations two miles off in a place called Piano, which is not without charm of its own nor inferior to Abbadia. On fixed days they came to the signatura, which Pius held in the woods under one tree or another by the sweet murmur of the stream. Every day he changed the place, finding new springs in the valleys and new patches of shade among which it was hard to choose. Once when the Pope was affixing his seal, it happened that hounds came on a huge stag which was lying nearby, but it flung them off with its horns and hoofs and darted away to the mountains. Sometimes too Pius held a consistory with the cardinals under the chestnuts and heard embassies in the meadow. He rode daily through the woods accompanied by the curials and dispatched private and public business on the way. When evening came on he would go a little beyond the monastery to a place where the Paglia could be seen and would sit conversing delightfully with the brethren. It was wonderfully pleasant. In the valley below the sun had parched everything and every tree was dry in the thirsty fields. The earth seemed to have undergone Phaethon's fires and to have been burned to ashes. Around the monastery and the higher places everything was green; no heat was felt and a sweet breeze stirred. You would have said that here was the abode of the blest; in the valley the punishments of the damned. The curials sometimes went down to the lower ground to hunt and on returning they would say they had found the heat intolerable. On the other hand those who had been ranging the mountains and the loftier haunts of wild beasts would declare that they had been stiff with cold.

When July was almost over, the Pope had a desire to see the source of the famous river called Vivo. It was about forty stades away in a lonely spot on the north slope of the mountain. The ascent of some three miles among meadows and chestnut trees was not very difficult; the descent through oaks was only two thirds as long but steep and rough. On the brow of the hill there were treeless meadows where there grew an herb called Carolina, because it had once been divinely revealed to Charlemagne as a cure for the plague. The story is that on his way to Rome he came to this spot with his army already plague-stricken. When he lay down to sleep, worried on this account, he saw an angel who said to him, "Rise and when you have climbed the mountain, throw a javelin and pick the plant whose root you wound with its tip. Parch it in a fierce fire, crush it to a powder, and give it to the sick in wine to drink. It will drive out all the poison and save your army for you." The danger made him believe the dream. It is a plant with thorny leaves which grow close to the ground and are set around a flower like that of the thistle but of a different color. It has a sweet root as large as chicory which by divine dispensation always displays the scar of the wound, so that the miracle may be remembered forever. This is the story the natives tell. Pius thought it a mere tale made up by Charlemagne's admirers, who did not hesitate to ascribe to him not only his own marvelous exploits but those of Alexander of Macedon who subdued the East.

The Pope set out along the path and a little before noon arrived at a spring which burst cool and abundant from a grotto. Nearby a shrine of squared stone still stands, although the roof threatens to fall and the dwellings which once surrounded it are in ruins. Chestnuts and beeches form a thick grove. Lunch was prepared in the shade by the spring. The cardinals and referendarii had arrived and the Pope decided to hold the Signatura before eating. It was a clear day and the sun was almost overhead, yet its heat had not tempered the extreme cold. They had to set the table and sign the petitions in full sunlight. Thus the Pope, who had found more coolness than he had wanted, lunched in warmth and comfort.

After lunch they descended sixteen stades along the stream which rises from the spring and flows with a great noise and rush over precipitous rocks and through rugged valleys. At the bottom of the valley is a little plain and a field which once felt the plow and produced bearing apple trees. That there was formerly a fine convent here is proved by the ruins. Camaldolese monks used to live in it; now it is the home of screech owls. The not inconsiderable church is still standing. Nearby runs a stream called Vivaremo because it flows from the upper to the lower hermitage and its waters never fail but replenish the Orcia, which shrinks and sometimes dries up altogether. It turns mills, which during the summer months, when all others stop, furnish flour to Pienza and the neighboring towns.

In the lower monastery lived the abbot and the brotherhood of monks who liked regular and communal living. In the upper hermitage dwelt the brethren of a rougher mode of life who liked solitude and fasting. Now both places are deserted.

The Pope crossed the river and returned to Abbadia by another road which led through lofty forests of tall oaks as perfectly straight as firs. He carefully observed the configuration of the ground to see whether, as he had hoped, he could divert the river's course, turn it into the Orcia above Bagni di Vignoni, and there by damming the stream, a project he had often planned, make a lake which should cover the more level regions and supply the province with fish as well as protect it from a hostile invasion. It would be an expensive operation and need a pope with plenty of leisure.

Pius went also to Santa Fiora at the invitation of the tyrant of the place who has the title of Count. The town lies on a high rock with rough and jagged cliffs falling steeply to very deep valleys all about; except that at one point close to the mountain side there is a level approach cut across by a deep moat. Here they have built a citadel and while that is safe they have nothing to fear. Many crystal springs bubble up all around. On the west a great volume of water gushes out and after it has filled a broad pond it is drawn off through pipes and falls with a roar into the valley below. In this pond trout a cubit long are preserved as in a vivarium. While the Pope was there they caught a great many. Pius also went down to the lower stream, which provides the most flavorsome trout in all Italy. The inhabitants fished while he was there and took a large catch.

As the Pope was returning through the cattle grazing in the meadows, the cowherd, who had never seen the Pope, in his wonder at the cardinal's robes and the ornaments of the courtiers hesitated a little as to which he should venerate as the supreme pontiff, but finally, on seeing the golden chair carried on men's shoulders between horsemen, he decided that he who sat in it was the one to be adored. He then milked the nearest heifer and joyously offered the Pope milk in the bowl from which he himself was accustomed to eat and drink; for he thought the heat must have made him thirsty. The Pope, remembering the man who offered water in his two hands to Artaxerxes as he passed by, smiled and did not disdain to touch the black and greasy bowl with his lips, pretending to drink, nor to hand it to the cardinals to taste; for he would not appear to scorn the attention and reverence of a poor peasant who had offered him his most precious possessions; and he pondered on a heart which was generous with what it had and would surely have offered richer gifts if it had possessed them.

The Pope fell ill at Abbadia and had been in bed twenty-four hours with the gout when the terrified cardinals suddenly brought the news that the plague had broken out in the town and that some of their acquaintances had succumbed to it. They urged Pius to flee from the foul infection. The Pope lost no time in ordering a litter and by sunset, though he was faint and in great pain, he set out with all his household followed by all the cardinals. This was the end of the pleasures of Abbadia. Joy is always followed by grief.

It was very late when Pius reached Pienza and he could not go to see his buildings at once as he desired. He was confined to his bed for some days but when he was better he carefully inspected all the details and did not regret what he had spent, though he had laid out more than 50,000 ducats on the work. The beauty and dignity of the buildings made him forget his annoyance at the cost.

The palace (Fig. 20) was square, built of hewn stone smoothed from bottom to top by the workmen's tools. The blocks were cut back round the edge a finger's breadth and the joinings made at the cuttings, so that the surfaces of the blocks stood out like tiles. On the roof a cistern of larger blocks set five feet back from the wall received the rain water that collected in gutters and distributed it to a distance through iron pipes. The wall was nowhere less than four to six feet thick. Three of the palace walls were constructed in this fashion. The northern wall was 126 feet long; the eastern and western 18 feet longer on account of the porticoes which projected to the south from the main square of the palace. The entire building was 540 feet in circumference.

There were two rows of windows remarkable for size and design, twenty-three windows in each row equidistant from one another. Three men could look out of each window which was divided in thirds by slender columns. Under each row of windows were two ornamental bands commonly called cornices, made of stone like the Tiburtine, splendidly wrought and encircling the palace like two garlands. The architect had set square pilasters reaching from the ground to the compluvium with appropriate bases and capitals. At the corners of the building and in many places between the windows he had hung stone shields on which by the art of the sculptor and the painter the arms of the Piccolomini shone in gold and silver and other colors. There were

also many iron rings and here and there devices to hold torches by
night and banners by day. There were also smaller square windows to
light the lower apartments. These had metal gratings. Seats two and
sometimes three steps high of the same stone as the cornices ran around
the building.

The magnificent great main door was on the north side. In the east
side, where an entrance could not be made in the middle there were two
smaller doors symmetrically placed, one of which was walled so as to
appear closed and other left open for everyday use. The west side was
treated in the same way. On the fourth side (Fig. 21), which has a
most delightful view of Mt. Amiata to the south, were three porticoes
raised above one another on stone columns. The first with its high and
splendid vaulting provided a most delightful promenade near the garden: the second, which had an elaborately painted wooden ceiling, made
a very pleasant place to sit in the winter. It had a balustrade which with
its cornice was as high as a man's waist. The third was similar to the
second but less elaborate in its coffering. So much for the exterior of
the palace.

The reservoir on the roof carried off some of the rain outside, as we
have said, and carried some down into the court, so that, after being
filtered through gravel, it might fill the cisterns, of which there were
three: two in the palace and a third very large one in the garden, which
was ample to provide for a numerous household. On the very top of the
roof, where the smoke from the chimneys emerged, were built twenty-
three towerlike structures ornamented with pinnacles and buttresses
and various paintings, which could be seen from a distance and added
much to the splendor and charm of the building.

As you enter the palace by the main door you face a large and lofty
peristyle carried round the square court on monoliths sixteen feet high
and proportionately thick with bases and capitals skillfully set. There
are dining rooms for winter and summer and the seasons between,
chambers fit for kings, and storerooms for various things both over and
under the cellar vaulting. For when they excavated for the foundations
of the palace they quarried out the very hard rock to a depth of about
sixteen feet and constructed vaulted cellars for wine and oil and other
provisions. Certainly a noble larder and one it would be hard to fill.

From the main door to the peristyle there extends a gleaming arched
portico as long as the width of the dining rooms on each side. After
passing through this and entering the peristyle, if you turn to the right
you will find a staircase leading to the rooms on the second floor by

some forty easy steps a foot high, two feet deep, and nine wide, each made of a single great stone. Twenty of the steps turn right and twenty left and there is a window at the turn to light both flights. At the top is a gallery which on three sides looks down into the court through square windows divided by a stone cross. Its ceiling is skillfully constructed and decorated in various colors. As you follow it to the right you come to a square hall out of which open two splendid chambers, one of which gets the western sun and the other the north light as well, and this also has a strong room where valuables can be kept. At the end of the gallery is a hall seventy-two feet wide and a third again as long with six doors. Two look into the gallery, two give access to the middle portico that looks toward Mt. Amiata, and the others to two large and elaborate chambers, one of which receives the light of the rising, the other that of the setting sun. The hall itself is lighted not only by the doors but by large windows toward the court and smaller ones toward the portico. It has a fireplace cunningly wrought of white marble and the coffered ceiling is remark- able for the precision of the woodwork and the variety of the paintings. There is never a time when the place is not comfortable since it does not feel the extremes of heat or cold.

If you turn left in the gallery you will come on another staircase exactly like the first leading to the third floor. Passing by this you come to a door which divides the gallery into two parts. If you choose to turn right you enter the hall which we have said adjoins the second portico, but if you go left you will find yourself in a summer dining room or hall larger than any of the others with four windows on the north giving on the street and two on the east giving on the square. From this hall you pass into an oratory and the eastern apartments, that is three chambers, the last of which is connected, as we have said, with the hall of six doors and the adjoining portico. In this room the Pope lodged and he had given orders that it should be paneled in fir so that the dampness of the new walls should not trouble him. Every chamber had its fireplace and everything else that was necessary. Everywhere were paneling and fir beams worth one's notice and suitable in size and beauty to the building itself. The beams and timbers contributed magnificence not only of themselves but by the painting and gold leaf upon them. The floors were of polished brick and without any unevenness whatever—every- where the same level surface; in going from room to room and place to place you never had to step up or down.

The plan of the third floor is like or very nearly like the second. The ceilings are a little lower; they have no painting or color and are conspicuous only for the dignity of the beams. If, as some think, the first charm of a house is light, surely no house could be preferred to this one, which is open to all four points of the compass and lets in abundant light not only through outside windows but through inside ones looking on the inner court and distributes it even down to the storerooms and the cellar. The view from the upper floor extends to the west beyond Montalcino and Siena to the Pistoian Alps. As you look to the north diverse hills and the lovely green of forests are spread before you for a distance of five miles. If you strain your eyes you can see as far as the Apennines and make out the town of Cortona on a high hill not far from Lake Trasimeno, but the valley of the Chiana, which lies between, cannot be seen because of its great depth. The view to the east is less extended reaching only as far as Poliziano, *a continual source of apprehension to the Sienese,* and the mountains which separate the valley of the Chiana from that of the Orcia. The view from the three porticoes to the south is bounded, as we have said, by towering and wooded Mt. Amiata. You look down on the valley of the Orcia (Fig. 22) and green meadows and hills covered with grass in season and fruited fields and vineyards, towns and citadels and precipitous cliffs and Bagni di Vignoni and Montepescali, which is higher than Radicofani, and is the portal of the winter sun.

The palace had no kitchen. A square building as high as the palace itself was built near the cistern in a corner of the garden toward the winter sunset and in it were three kitchens with their various offices built one above the other and connected with the palace by porticoes, thus making it possible to serve the three floors with the greatest convenience. They were not troubled by smoke or wind and drew water with a rope from the nearby cistern. Beyond the porticoes and kitchens, extending up to the town walls, was a space as large as that occupied by the palace itself. Here Pius had intended to plant a garden, but the ground was uneven and sloped sharply. Very thick walls were built on a stone base and between columns of brick or stone it had arched openings which could provide stabling for a hundred horses and workshops for blacksmiths. Above them was left some twelve feet of solid wall and above that was a second row of arches. On these was heaped earth deep enough to make a hanging garden with vines and trees, care being taken that the rain should not penetrate to the vaults below or wet the stables.

Around the garden were stone seats and a balustrade breast-high ornamented with painted pinnacles, which from a distance presented a very gay appearance. If you entered the palace by the great north door you could see straight through the peristyle and court, then through a back door to the lower portico and as far as the very end of the garden and could walk the whole length smoothly without stepping up anywhere.

Such was the palace and next it stood the church (Fig. 23) built in honor of the Blessed Mary Ever a Virgin. Because of the unevenness of the ground it was really two churches, an upper and a lower. When they started to dig for a foundation, they went down fully a hundred and eight feet before they found any and even then it was none too good, since, when they cracked the crumbling stones in their effort to strike a solid base, they kept coming on fissures and sulphurous exhalations. While they were trying to shut out the fumes, the sides of the pit, which were not sufficiently protected, gave way and some of the workmen were killed. Therefore they constructed very broad arches from rock to rock and laid the wall on them without having sufficiently investigated the solidity of the rocks. Though they were very large it was uncertain how firmly they were set in the earth and a crack in the building running from bottom to top gave rise to a suspicion as to the security of the foundation. The architect thought the crack was caused by the settling of the mortar while it was hardening and that they need not fear for the safety of the structure. Time will tell. The walls are very thick and adequate to carry their own weight and that of the two rows of arches above them.

The lower church was reached by a door and thirty-six broad steps. Two columns in the middle supported the entire structure. Three large windows let in ample light for the whole church and the four altars and the beautiful white marble font in one of the chapels. The very aspect of the church rouses emotion and a devout reverence in all who enter. The upper church is 140 feet long, 60 high, and as many wide, not counting the space taken by the chapels which add to both the length and the width. Of necessity its greatest length, contrary to custom, is from north to south.

The square before the palace was paved with bricks laid on their sides in mortar. Three steps of hard stone ran the width of the church façade. By these you ascended to the church which was entered through an open space fifteen feet wide instead of a vestibule. The façade itself is 72 feet high, made of stone resembling the Tiburtine, white and shining as marble. It was modeled on those of ancient temples and richly decorated with columns and arches and semicircular niches designed to hold statues. It had three beautifully proportioned doors, the center one larger than the others, and a great eye like that of the Cyclops. It displayed the arms of the Piccolomini, above them the papal fillet wreathed about the triple crown, and the keys of the Church between. The façade is of the same breadth all the way from the foundation to the roof. From there to its top it has the form of a pyramid decorated with charming cornices. The other walls are of less precious material but the stones are squared and well polished with projections like ribs interspersed at regular intervals to strengthen the fabric.

As you enter the middle door the entire church with its chapels and altars is visible and is remarkable for the clarity of the light and the brilliance of the whole edifice. There are three naves, as they are called. The middle one is wider. All are the same height. This was according to the directions of Pius, who had seen the plan among the Germans in Austria. It makes the church more graceful and lighter. Eight columns, all of the same height and thickness, support the entire weight of the vaulting. After the bases were in place and the columns with four semicircular faces had been set upon them and crowned with capitals, the architect saw that they were not going to be high enough. He therefore placed above the capitals square columns seven feet high with a second set of capitals to support the arches of the vaulting. It was a happy mistake which added charm by its novelty. The side naves are of the same width as far as the third column; there they begin to narrow and the entire church ends in a semicircular apse. The further part, like a crowned head, is divided into five small chapels which project from the rest of the structure; it has the same number of arches, as high as the naves, in which are fastened gold stars and they are painted the color of the sky to imitate the heavens. The vaulting in the naves was painted in various colors and the columns, which we have said were added together with their capitals to correct an error, contributed the colors of porphyry and other precious marbles. The lower columns were left in the natural white stone. The walls of the church and all the rest of the building gleam with a wondrous white luster.

In the central chapel were the episcopal throne and the canons' seats, made of precious wood decorated with sculpture and designs in the work called intarsia. In the other four chapels were altars adorned with paintings by illustrious Sienese artists. In the second to the left of the throne was the repository for the Host, of finely carved white marble. Every chapel has a high and broad window cunningly wrought with

little columns and stone flowers and filled with the glass called crystal.
At the ends of the naves were four similar windows which, when the
sun shines admit so much light that worshippers in the church think
they are not in a house of stone but of glass. On the two columns nearest
the door are two fonts, the work of no mean genius, from which those
who enter sprinkle themselves with holy water. The high altar stands
between the last two columns and is ascended by four steps. The priest
and his attendants when celebrating mass, have the people behind them
and the choir in front next to the pontifical chair. In the body of the
church are two other altars to serve the congregation.

To the right of the main church is a sacristy, to the left a bell tower
which was to be 160 feet high. A third of this was still unfinished. From
the lower church on the right and left 132 spiral stairs cut in the thickness of the walls led to the upper church and the roof.

In the square before the palace was a deep well of living water, the
mouth of which was decorated with very beautiful marble columns
supporting an entablature artistically sculptured. There were also chains
and buckets for drawing water. All these buildings except the bell tower
which was still unfinished were completed from foundation to roof in
three years.[1]

The Pope had received many insinuations against the architect[2]:
that he had cheated; that he had blundered in the construction; that he
had spent more than 50,000 ducats when his estimate had been 18,000.
The law of the Ephesians, according to Vitruvius, would have obliged
him to make up the difference. He was a Florentine named Bernardo,
hateful to the Sienese from his mere nationality. In his absence everyone
abused him. Pius, when he had inspected the work and examined everything, sent for the man. When he arrived after a few days in some apprehension, since he knew that many charges had been brought against
him, Pius said, "You did well, Bernardo, in lying to us about the expense involved in the work. If you had told the truth, you could never
have induced us to spend so much money and neither this splendid
palace nor this church, the finest in all Italy, would now be standing.
Your deceit has built these glorious structures which are praised by all
except the few who are consumed with envy. We thank you and think
you deserve especial honor among all the architects of our time"—and
he ordered full pay to be given him and in addition a present of 100
ducats and a scarlet robe. He bestowed on his son the grace he asked

[1] Between 1459 and 1462.
[2] Bernardo Rossellino.

and charged him with new commissions. Bernardo, when he heard the Pope's words, burst into tears of joy.

In order to preserve the dignity and brilliance of the church Pius issued the following bull:

Pius, Bishop, Servant of the servants of God, for the record of the future. In this church which we have erected and dedicated to the Blessed Virgin Mary, Mother of our Lord and God, no one shall bury a dead body except in the tombs assigned to priests and bishops. No one shall deface the whiteness of the walls and columns. No one shall draw pictures. No one shall hang up tablets. No one shall erect more chapels and altars than there are at present. No one shall change the shape of the church either the upper or the lower. If anyone disobeys he shall be accursed and unless in articulo mortis may be absolved only by the authority of the Pope. Given at Pienza September 16, in the year of the Incarnation of our Lord 1462 and the fifth year of our pontificate.

The Pope also built a house adjoining the church on the left where the bishop and the canons might be comfortably lodged, from which they could without interference pass to their duties by night or day through a little door let into the side of the church for their convenience. Across the square from the palace was an old house where the prior and other magistrates of the town were accustomed to live. This Pius bought and handed over to the Vice-Chancellor on condition that he should build on the site an episcopal palace and present it to the Blessed Virgin Mary. He bought also other houses of the citizens on the side of the square opposite the church and gave orders that they should be razed and a third palace erected with a portico, a great hall, chambers, storerooms, a tower with bells and a clock, and a prison. He intended this to be the residence of the magistrates of the city and a meeting place for councils of the citizens. He himself hired the workmen and contributed a large part of the expense, wishing the square to be surrounded by four noble buildings.

Other magnificent houses were built in the city. The Cardinal of Arras erected a large and lofty palace behind the Vice-Chancellor's. Next to him the Treasurer and after him Gregorio Lolli laid their foundations. First of all the Cardinal of Pavia built a most convenient and beautiful square house, covering an entire block. The Cardinal of Mantua bought a lot with a view to building as did also Tommaso, a papal official, and many of the townspeople tore down old houses and built new ones, so that nowhere did the aspect of the town remain unchanged.

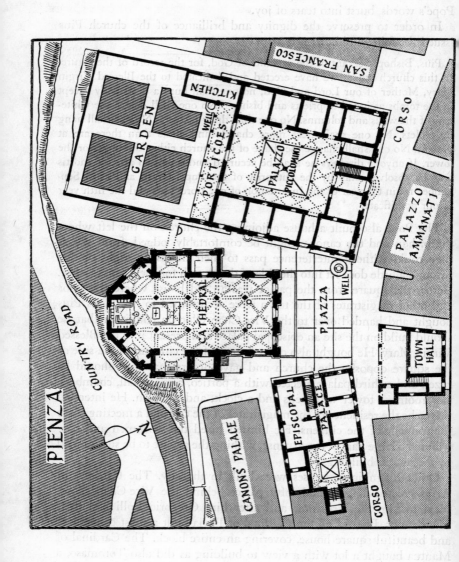

On the Feast of the Beheading of St. John the Baptist the Pope dedicated the church and the altars, the Cardinal of Ostia officiating. He himself anointed the front of the high altar and when the relics of the saint had been deposited in it he affixed the seal.

The townspeople worship devoutly St. Matthew the Apostle and on his feast, which they were used to celebrate in September, they have a crowded market and give prizes for races. Pius, in order that the festival might be celebrated while he was there, presented all the consular citizens with new robes and gave money for the necessary expenses. They offered prizes for races as follows: for horses *eight ells of scarlet cloth;* for asses *four ells of another color;* for men *the same;* for boys *geese.*

When the appointed day dawned mass was celebrated very early in the church in the presence of the Pope with profound reverence of all the people. Then the crowd thronged outside the town to the tents where cooks had roasted thirty great oxen taken from the plow and many smaller animals, all of which they consumed at one meal. The time from then till evening was devoted to buying and selling.

After this positions at the barrier were assigned the horses and the signal was given for the races to begin. The sight was less impressive than it might have been because their speed was unevenly matched and the victory undisputed. Alessandro's horse left his competitors far behind and came in with no close second. Among the asses there was a sharp contest and now one and now another goaded by frequent lashings took the lead. Finally Sacchino's ass, which had often before been a winner, after throwing its rider reached the goal first. The man who came in next still seated on his mount claimed that the prize belonged to him rather than to Sacchino who had been thrown. The judges refused his plea on the ground that the prizes were offered for asses not men.

Many lusty, active youths who had often run in the stadium competed in the foot race. There had been a light rain and the track was slippery. They ran naked and now one, now another was ahead and often one or another could be seen to slip and fall and roll on the ground and mud and those who had been last were now ahead. In this way they ran four stades as far as the gate with very little space between the victor and the vanquished and they were so befouled with mud as to be unrecognizable. *Then a cook from the Pope's kitchen named Trippes, throwing off his boots and clothes except only his cloak, dashed out from a corner and unrecognized started to run through the town as if he were one of*

the contestants. Being fresh he quickly passed the two foremost runners
and triumphantly seized the prize, to the great chagrin of the next
runner who thought himself beaten when already victor and resented
having the victory snatched from his grasp. But he realized at once that
this victor was not muddy enough and that he was wearing a cloak in
which he could not possibly have finished so long a course. The judges
shaking with laughter rejected the cook and gave the prize to the youth
from Sarteano who came in first.

The boys' race was the best of all. There were many young lads who
leapt forward naked at the signal, each trying to outstrip the others and
competing with extraordinary keenness. They could not shake their
feet clear of the sticky clay and now they would lose their breath and
fall, now get it back and rise again. Their parents and brothers cheered
them on with repeated shouts of encouragement. The course was about
a stade to the town gate and victory wavered among many. *Then a*
house slave of Alessandro's who was very small and being beardless had
been taken for a lad and allowed to enter the race, darted to first place
and running swiftly through the town touched the goal and claimed the
prize as victor. He was followed closely by a boy of Pienza with fair
hair and beautiful body, though disfigured with mud, who realizing
that he had been beaten by only three or four feet, burst into tears and
was furious at himself for not running faster. His mother, a very pretty
woman, was present and comforted her son with sweet words and
wiped off his sweat with a towel. The judges were just on the point of
giving the goose to the first runner, but when Alessandro realized this,
he cried out. "What are you doing? My slave is eighteen years old and
got himself enrolled among the boys by a trick. Do not let him profit
by his fraud." When the judges understood the situation they preferred
the Pienza lad, who was carried home on his proud father's shoulders
followed by a great crowd and greeted with joy by the entire neighborhood.

The Pope watched these contests *from a very high window with a*
good deal of pleasure though while they were going on he was consulting with the cardinals on public business.

BOOK X

BOOK X

NOT long after this [1] the Pope, having as we have said sent the Legate against Sigismondo, went from Pienza to take the baths at Petriolo. His way led past the monastery of Sant'Anna. This is situated on a rocky and barren mountain, but nevertheless the monks who live there have by their industry made some of it bear fruit, planting almonds and setting out other trees from which they get part of their livelihood while they pay pious service to God. Their order is called the Order of Monte Oliveto and their chief convent and the head of the whole Order is six miles distant. Thither the Pope went over roads passable only in summer when the sun dries up all the moisture. In the rainy season you would say the place was inaccessible for the clay is so deep that no paving stones can be laid. The earth gives under the horses' hoofs and will not let them go unless the horse makes the most violent efforts. Besides, the rains have made ditches on each side of the read leaving narrow paths which can be followed only with the greatest difficulty. If you make the slightest misstep you will fall headlong.

Thus they came to the monastery of Monte Oliveto, which is not far from the village of Chiusure, where the Tuscans think the cheese is among the best in the world. The monastery is situated as follows. There is a high hill of tufa and clay about a stade in length and much narrower looking to the west. If you ask its shape, it is like a chestnut leaf. Around it on all sides cliffs drop sheer to a very deep ravine which one shudders to look into. Where the hill joins the surrounding country by a gentle ridge a brick tower has been built, which bars any hostile approach, and a ditch has been dug which discharges water into both chasms. It is crossed by a bridge and when this is raised no approach to the monastery is possible. The hill is steep and halfway up is the celebrated church and the usual refectories, ambulatories, and porticoes for the monks besides the various service quarters which they think necessary. There is nothing that is not of the best, nothing that is not elegant and

[1] Late summer or autumn of 1462.

that you would not behold with envy. *The monks of that place regard the Piccolomini as their founders as much as the Tolommei, though no one doubts that the original founder was a Tolommeo.* The rule of the Order is almost the same as that of the Benedictine Observantists. In their dress you would observe a difference. The dress of the Benedictines is black, that of these monks is an immaculate white. The eating of flesh is forbidden to both alike *unless illness requires it.* In their ritual you would find a number of differences, but they have substantially the same rule of life and up to now these monks have lived blameless.

The mountain itself is planted with native trees, among them a great many olives, whence the name Oliveto. There are figs and almonds and many varieties of pears and apples. There are also groves of cypress trees where in summer one may find pleasant shade. Vineyards too and leafy vines and vegetable gardens and swimming pools and an unfailing spring and cisterns and wells, and on the cliffs themselves oak forests and juniper. Many paths wide enough for two men wind round the hill and cut it in two. They are planted on both sides with vines and rose beds or rosemary, delightful refreshment for the monks and even more delightful for those who are at liberty to depart after seeing them.

The monks received Pius on his arrival with the greatest joy and showed him every possible honor. There was a market at Chiusure and therefore a great crowd came to meet the Pope and descend to the tower, which we have said marks the foot of Monte Oliveto, to obtain his blessing. It was a Thursday when he arrived. The cardinals and all the papal household were expecting to have meat for dinner but the Pope ordered all to abstain from meat in that place since he had seen that this would please the monks. He thus set an example for ecclesiastical dignitaries who might thereafter stop there not to ask for meat knowing the Pope had abstained out of reverence for the place.

Pius spent the following day also here and dined with the monks in the common refectory. He introduced musicians who sang to them, while they ate, a new song about St. Catherine of Siena so sweetly that they brought tears of joy to the eyes of all the monks. He also granted generous indulgences to the place and wide privileges to the Order.

In this monastery Matteo of Sicily, called Runta, was passing his old age. He wrote verse with such facility that Ovid's words might properly be applied to him: "Whatever I tried to say turned out verse"; though his poetry was meter without elegance. He translated Dante's poem from the vulgar tongue into Latin and put it into hexameters, though they lacked polish. *In his old age he became foolish, and tempted by his craving for meat, would often leave the monastery and in secret with his friends ravenously devour squabs. Otherwise he led a blameless life.*

When Pius left here he descended along the Ombrone River which he crossed to Buonconvento, but he did not enter the town as the plague was raging there. He spent the night beyond Arbia with his nephew, the Cardinal of Siena, on an estate belonging to the Church called Sant'Innocenzia. The next day he reached Petriolo, the site of which we have described earlier. Here he took the baths in accordance with the advice of his physicians and when he had leisure often went out into the country and sat sometimes under the trees, sometimes on the bank of the Farma or the Mersa talking with the cardinals about state affairs or hearing embassies. The Cardinal of Santa Susanna, who had chosen himself an estate three miles from Petriolo, came from there to the Pope on the days when there was a consistory and took part in public business. The Pope desired to see his house, which he had heard highly praised, and went there on an appointed day. It lies in a wooded valley protected from the north winds and open to the south and west. The view of the sea is blocked by Monte Amiata. The woods are full of cork trees and chestnuts, oaks and ilex from which in season acorns fall and furnish food for droves of wild boars, which make their lairs in the depths of the valley. The ancients, having found a perennial spring in the middle of this vale, cut down the surrounding forest and built a chapel of hewn stone to Sant'Antonio, which is reverenced for its antiquity. Near it they built dwellings for the monks, planted vines, cultivated gardens, and grafted fruit trees. Brethren of the Eremites live here but never more than four to six at a time, since they have to go a long way to beg alms. Only exemplary men are sent here and those who love solitude. They get wine from the vineyard and vegetables from the garden and gather chestnuts in the woods. Sometimes too they get meat by hunting. Everything else the begging brother provides. They rarely see a human guest. Wolves and bears often appear and it is hard to protect the vineyard from them nor is it safe to walk alone in the forest. Except for that, the spreading shade of the evergreens is delightful. The Pope was here toward the end of autumn but before the vintage had stripped the vines of the abundant grapes which hung in great clusters from their stems and presented a most delightful sight. After the Pope had lunched he rode for some time with the greatest pleasure through the shrubbery where there were many laurels and after inspecting everything he returned at evening to Petriolo.

While the Pope was at Petriolo the Sienese often sent him gifts of food and drink and also envoys to beg him to visit his own dear city. Pius gave as an excuse the unhealthful climate (for some had died of the plague at Siena) and said he was sorry that he could not grant the prayers of his very dear sons as he would like to do. When he had finished the baths, he returned to Pienza where he was kept one day by illness. Then by way of Montisculo and the high wooded ridges adjoining Montepesio he went to Sarteano, whence he at once crossed the Chiana near Chiusi and descended into the Perusine country, passing the night in the town of Panicale in the mountains above Lake Trasimeno. After crossing these he entered a pleasant valley thickly dotted with castles from which Perugia can be seen. He then crossed still other mountains and came into the broad valley of the Tiber and after spending a night at Marsciano he succeeded the next day in finding a good ford where he crossed the Tiber. He then went on to Todi to rest until he should hear that the climate at Rome was again healthful. He had been preceded by embassies of kings and states and by a good many cardinals who all came out to meet him on his arrival. The papal state, which had not seen its lord for many years, welcomed him with unspeakable joy and the highest honors in its power to bestow.

Todi (or, as the ancients called it, Tuder) is a not inconsiderable city and the most important one of Umbria. It lies on a hill some twenty stades from the Tiber. Wherever you go in the town you always have to climb.

Pius chose to stay in the episcopal palace though the citizens had prepared for him the town hall and a splendid house in the piazza. The palace seemed to be a more healthful place to lodge, less exposed to the winds which continually sweep over Todi so that you would call it a second house of Aeolus. Wherever you turn a most delightful prospect meets the eye. You can see Perugia and all the valley between with its numerous castles, its spreading and fertile fields, and the noble river Tiber which winds about like a snake dividing Tuscany from Umbria, then entering the many mountains below the city itself, through which it descends to lower ground with loud murmurs as if resenting its enforced confinement. The hills below the city planted with vines and olives are a delightful sight and no less charming are the more distant slopes clothed with forests or good for pasturage.

At this time the Pope's sister Catherine came from the city of Spoleto to see him, accompanied by his niece Antonia and her bright beautiful baby whom Pius had directed should be named Silvio after his own father. He was not yet twenty months old but already mimicked everything he saw and gave many signs of future intelligence which amused the Pope immensely.

There arrived also envoys from Rome, important men, one of whom was the jurisconsult Pietro Mellino, a member of the conservatori of the camera of the city. The embassy was accompanied by sons of nobles with horses and attendants splendidly accoutered. They reported that the plague in Rome was ended, the air of all the surrounding districts had been purged, and everything was perfectly safe. They implored the Pope repeatedly and earnestly to make haste to return to his own Rome and restore his presence to his sons who yearned for him unutterably. The Pope consented and though winter was still at its fiercest and the ground frozen stiff, he left Todi on December 13 before daylight and traveled through country by no means without charm to the town of Acquasparta where he was met by great throngs carrying olive branches. Among them was a woman beating her breast and tearing her cheeks, lamenting loudly her brother's death and imploring vengeance for the crime. Pius, when he had heard the case, turned the matter over to the Priors of Todi, who soon afterward settled it, though families of some importance were involved in the feud.

Then over rough mountains already white with snow Pius came to the town of San Gemini situated on a high hill, where he passed the night. The ruins show that the place was once populous. It has fine vineyards and olive groves and commands the valley watered by the Nera, being equally distant from Narni and Terni. After leaving here the Pope was received by the people of Terni with enthusiasm and all the splendor the city could afford. He dined there and then departed by way of Collescipoli to Stroncone. The road lies over cultivated and most delightful slopes where Bacchus seems to vie with Ceres and Pallas. The fertile land between olive groves and vineyards produces abundance of wheat. There are also figs, nuts, and other fruit trees of all sorts. The people of Collescipoli had set tables before the gates of the town and regaled the throng of pedestrians with food and drink. The citizens of Stroncone, where Pius passed the night in the Minorite convent just outside the walls, entertained all the Curia. Both these towns are independent, subject only to the Pope whose service is freedom.

Stroncone is four miles from Terni in a straight line. It is set on a rocky hill accessible to an enemy on only one side and that strongly fortified. Some include it in the Sabine district, as they do also Collescipoli, on the ground that the Sabine territory extends as far north as the river Nera. That the west boundary is the Tiber no one doubts and from this the Sabine territory extends eastward to Lake Velino, the city of Riete, the Marsians, and the mountains of the Equicoli today called the Tagliacozzi. From the point at which Lake Velino plunges down over the rocks a high mountain ridge runs through the Sabine country to the Aniene and overhangs Tivoli. The ancients called it Severo; today part of it is called Monte San Giovanni and part Montenero. In our times the Sabines are placed between this mountain and the Tiber and are thought to extend no farther east.

When Pope Pius left Stroncone he crossed a number of hills difficult because of the rough cliffs and descended into the valley enclosed on the left by Monte Severo and on the right by Monte Luna, which extends as far as Narni, is as high as Severo, and has numerous towns on its slopes. Through the valley flows a never-failing stream which empties into the Nera not far from Narni. Following this upstream the Pope reached the watershed where Monte Luna and Monte Severo join. *It is a little lower than they are and was then covered with snow*. Thence the waters fall in two directions, some to the north swelling the river which we have said flows into the Nera, others to the south by a long descent.

Pius after passing over this ridge descended into a pleasant valley overlooked by a number of towns, among which Asola may be seen perched on a high mountain.

Next he proceeded along the river till it turned sharply south. Then as it ran to the right among boulders and rough cliffs, he left it and proceeded up the hill, coming down again at a town of the Orsini called Turres. This is exposed to attack only on one side where it is overlooked by a higher elevation, though separated from it by a deep moat. The other sides are protected by very deep valleys. The town does not occupy the entire hill but on the west is a large empty space where there is an ancient ivy-covered temple. If this part were taken, engines could easily shell the town from it, but the ascent is steep and difficult. It is generally believed that the whole hill was once inhabited but when the populace was reduced they reduced the circuit of the walls also.

Pius after spending the night here descended into a very deep valley and crossed the river which flows from the mountains where there is the considerable town of Aspra belonging to Savello (the only one left him except Palombara), which is protected by the rough ground from which it takes its name. Guides from Cures led the Pope through out-of-the-way paths from which he did not emerge without difficulty and danger since the cliffs were precipitous and difficult. It was then that Pius first realized their perfidy and sent them away with sharp rebukes.

He next came to Cantalupo, where he found the town still in ruins and the fields waste. The townspeople poured out to meet the Pope commending themselves to him with earnest prayers. They said they had resisted the Church of Rome against their will but nevertheless they begged for forgiveness. The Pope not only pardoned them but granted them certain privileges and favors. Then he descended to still another valley and after crossing a little stream and climbing a neighboring hill came to the town of Poggio Mirteto. This is on the lofty hill of the monastery of Farfa under the precipitous Monte Severo which it adjoins on the east. On that side only it is exposed to attack but it is defended by a very strongly fortified citadel. All the other sides are protected by unscalable cliffs and rough precipices. In the citadel is a very large and almost royal dwelling, and an abundant and limpid spring of sweet water, always very cold even in summer, falls from the mountain. The Abbot of Farfa, a member of the Orsini family, who was also Archbishop of Trani, lodged the Pope in the citadel and loaded him with most distinguished honors.

After leaving Mirteto Pius came to the Farfa River which is thickly shaded on both sides and descends to the plains through the monastery to which it gives its name. Everywhere it is clear and full of trout. It empties into the Tiber. After crossing this river by a bridge and climbing a lofty hill nearby Pius came to the marshes crossed by a little stream which some say is the Curesium which gave its name to Podio Cures. The Pope passed the night at Monterotondo with nobles of the Orsini family. Monterotondo is a considerable town producing abundance of corn and wine and well adapted to raising sheep. It is situated twelve miles from Rome. The Pope observed everything along the way with no little pleasure and refreshment.

BOOK XI

(Sept.-Dec. 1462)

PIUS returned to Rome on December 18,[1] crossing the Aniene by the Ponte Nomentano, a famous work of Narses, where the Roman populace was awaiting him with the greatest enthusiasm. The state, which had been plunged in grief on account of his absence and the terrible plague which had raged there, regained its old merriment at the return of its lord, put off its mourning, and made holiday.

Meantime Adolf,[2] Archbishop of Mainz, though it was icy winter weather, collected some eight hundred soldiers and attacked Mainz in the dead of night. Bold fighters scaled the wall at the point where it encloses vineyards and orchards. The city was thrown into confusion when the army entered; there was a general rush to arms and the most stubborn fighting among the crowded buildings with Diether's garrison on one side and Adolf's soldiers on the other fiercely pressing forward. The loyalties of the citizens were divided, but Adolf was finally victorious and, after killing or routing Diether's men, took possession of the city. All were amazed that he had succeeded in taking with so small a force so large a city which was defended both by its own citizens and by outside aid. The thing had been done by favor of the night and terror caused the enemy's forces to be thought larger than was actually the case. The citizens of the opposite faction went into voluntary exile. This was the war's compensation to Adolf for the princes captured by Palatine—so shifting is Fortune which exalts now one party, now the other.[3]

[1] 1462.

[2] Adolf of Nassau.

[3] The attack occurred late in October of 1462. The sack of Mainz begins a new chapter in the history of printing. The rival archbishops had enlisted the printers of Mainz—Gutenberg among them—in the war of words which accompanied the dispute, thereby calling into being the broadside or partisan newssheet. After the successful attack upon the city here referred to, some of the printers fled to nearby cities like Cologne and Strassburg, carrying the new invention with them. Thus the spread of printing in Germany from its original center in Mainz is usually associated with the capture of Mainz by the armies of Adolf of Nassau. Gutenberg accepted an appointment under Adolf of Nassau in 1465.

About the same time, when the Venetians were pressing hard for the pardon of Domenico Malatesta and were offering themselves through an envoy as mediators, the Pope consented and announced terms of peace as follows: If Domenico asks forgiveness for his sins, if he restores to the churches of Ravenna and Sarsita the property he robbed them of, if he gives back to the power of the Church the towns which deserted to him after they had been captured by the Church, if he pays the tribute due the Apostolic Camera, if he takes measures to insure that, in the event of his dying without legitimate issue, Cesena, Bertinoro, Meldola, and the other towns he now holds shall return to the sovereignty of the Church, if he promises to be henceforth a loyal vassal, he may have peace. He need not hope to regain what has been taken from him by arms with the exception of a single castle which Pope Pius in his generosity intends to bestow on him.

These terms were satisfactory but some difficulty arose as to what measures could be taken to prevent Domenico's states from falling into the hands of others than the Church after his death. The condition itself was thought just and the only difference of opinion concerned the manner of enforcing it. To attain this end the Pope commanded the citizens to bind themselves by oath that if Domenico died childless they would submit to the rule of no one except the Pope. The Venetian envoys declared that this was an unprecedented demand and could not be met without insult to Domenico.

While this discussion was going on the Venetians *with the good faith characteristic of barbarians or after the manner of traders whose nature it is to weigh everything by utility paying no attention to honor,* bought Cervia from Domenico, agreeing to pay 4,000 ducats yearly to him for his lifetime and on his death to those he might designate, and in addition two hundred bags of salt. There are salt mines at Cervia where the very best salt is found. It is taken to the cities of Romagnola and brings in a very large profit to the Malatestas. Since the Venetians supply the Ferrarese with salt (though much against the latter's will), fearing that it might be secretly furnished them from Cervia, they resolved to lay hold upon the place in any way they could, right or wrong. It was a fief of the Church of Rome and bound to return to it if the male line of the Malatestas should fail; and the Malatestas might not in any circumstances transfer it to any other family or gens; nor had the Venetians the right to buy it without the consent of the Church.

But what do fish care about law? As among brute beasts aquatic creatures have the least intelligence, so among human beings the Venetians are the least just and the least capable of humanity and naturally, for they live on the sea and pass their lives in the water; they use ships instead of horses; they are not so much companions of men as of fish and comrades of marine monsters. They please only themselves and while they talk they listen to and admire themselves. When they speak they think themselves Sirens. Furthermore when they are in Egypt or Africa or Asia they adopt barbarian ways and hate the practice of our religion, although they make a certain show of Christian piety. They are hypocrites. They wish to appear Christians before the world but in reality they never think of God and, except for the state, which they regard as a deity, they hold nothing sacred, nothing holy. To a Venetian, that is just which is for the good of the state; that is pious which increases the empire. The Venetian is bent on founding a new monarchy; he is already convinced that the destiny of Rome is his; the descendants of Aeneas, who of old set out from Troy and became the masters of the world, were succeeded by the Antenoridae whose sons the Venetians are. They are allowed to do anything that will bring them to supreme power. All law and right may be violated for the sake of power. What wonder that they bought Cervia from one who did not own it, when a little earlier they seized Ravenna which belonged to the Church? *and wrested Aquileia and all Forlì from the patriarchate and drove the Carraras from Padua and the Scaligers from Verona and Vicenza and won over Brescia and Bergamo and many other towns from the Lombards.* Cervia also contributed to increase their empire because her salt was very useful to Romagnola. Now salt must be got from the Venetians unless imported from a distance, which would be a very expensive business.

All Italy condemned the action of the Venetians in buying Cervia, which was a state of the Church, from a man who had not the right to sell it. *It was thought a base and detestable thing, but it was condemned, not punished. Everyone pitied the innocent sufferers, but no one helped them. What harm does the talk of the populace do a robber? or a usurer? While he is amassing wealth gradually he appears mean and wicked and not fit for human society, but when he has become rich and powerful, who does not call him fortunate? Who does not seek his friendship? His house is filled with clients. When he walks in the city all rise and bend their necks. It is a mark of success to touch his hand. So with the Venetians. Now that by many crimes they have extended their empire, though men hate them in their hearts and curse them behind their backs, there is no one who does not praise them to their faces. This is the way of the world but before Almighty God no crimes go unpunished. Verily, verily the Venetians too will have their day. The calm of the sea will change. The sons will bear the transgressions of the fathers.*

When Pius learned the facts about Cervia, he sent for the Venetian envoy and asked the reason for this and what excuse he had to give. He admitted what had been done *with embarrassment and shame* like a man who knew *a base act* could not be defended, but he put forward motives of expediency seeing that the Venetians' income from salt (which is very large in the territory of Ferrara and neighboring districts) was being seriously reduced by the secret importation of salt from Cervia. The state had been unwilling to stand the deprivation and had therefore bought the place as a means of recouping its losses.

The Pope replied: "At the intercession of the Venetian Senate we promised peace to Domenico. We recognized you as mediator in the Senate's place. Among the terms of peace the chief was that if Domenico died without male issue the states which he had received from the Church whether in fief or as vicariate should revert to the Church. You approved this condition. It was approved also by Domenico's agents though there was some disagreement about the method of enforcing it. Meantime the Senate buys Cervia from a man who cannot sell it. One obstacle is the nature of a fief, another is its confiscation on account of rebellion, another is the controversy now pending, another the apostolic letter of investiture which forbids any alienation, another is honor itself. We are discussing in regard to Cervia and others of Malatesta's states how they shall return to the Church after his death. We are discussing this with the Venetians and while we are consulting together the Venetians seize Cervia. *Truly a noble act! Behold the integrity of the Senate! Behold the glory of the Venetian republic!*

"*Is this the way you keep faith? Is this your regard for honor? The republic is a sluggish thing. It does not know the meaning of shame. It does not blush or grow pale or feel embarrassment. It presents always the same countenance and that insolent and shameless. They measure honor by the decree of the Senate, not by right reasoning. What the Senate approves is holy even though it is opposed to the Gospel. Divine law is abrogated by the decrees of the Senate.*

"'*Cervia furnished salt secretly to the Ferrarese. That reduced our income from taxes. We considered how to secure our indemnity. Therefore we shall not be defrauded if Cervia is bought!' Fine reasoning indeed! You seek your own gain at another's loss. Your cause is one with that of thieves and robbers and rests on expediency. On that basis anything that men do may be approved. What man in his senses does not defend his acts by some sort of expediency? The slavedealer and the harlot are in pursuit of gain.* You have been considering how much your state would gain, not how much loss you would inflict on the Church of Rome.

"*There is no limit to your avarice or your ambition. It does not matter whether you amass wealth justly or unjustly provided you amass it and neither right nor wrong stands in the way of your extending the boundaries of your empire. Honor follows in the train of power. God in Heaven you despise. The state is your god. You worship this and abandon the Creator of the universe. This god of yours will perish, I say will perish! Do not think it is immortal. The Athenians were greater than you; so were the Spartans, so were the Carthaginians, yet they perished utterly because they were unjust. No power was ever greater than the Roman Empire and yet God overthrew it because it was impious and He put in its place the priesthood because it respected divine law.* Rome became a sacerdotal city and the greater part of Italy became the patrimony of St. Peter, who keeps the keys of eternal life, and of his successors.

"All kings and emperors bow before the Pope of Rome as the Vicar of Jesus Christ and kiss his feet *and you Venetians spurn the Church of Rome and encroach upon its rights and possessions. You defy its mandates and censures and you think your republic will last forever. It will not last forever nor for long. Your populace so wickedly gathered together will soon be scattered abroad. The offscourings of fishermen will be exterminated. A mad state cannot long stand. Your power is wasting away. A state attacked in its youth by most foul and incurable diseases will not live to be old. Within the memory of our fathers Venetian justice was rated very high. The state was held to be virtuous and temperate and devoted to religion. In our age all piety, all temperance, all regard for justice, has disappeared. In their place have come avarice, greed, ambition, envy, cruelty, lust, and all wickedness. With such a character you cannot stand. An empire built on evil foundations must crash. You will pay the penalty for your crimes and your mockery of the Church of Rome will not go unpunished.*"

When the Venetian envoy heard this *he shook with terror and for a long time stood dumb but at last,* having no further defense for his city's cause, *he said he hoped that the Venetian Senate would in the future*

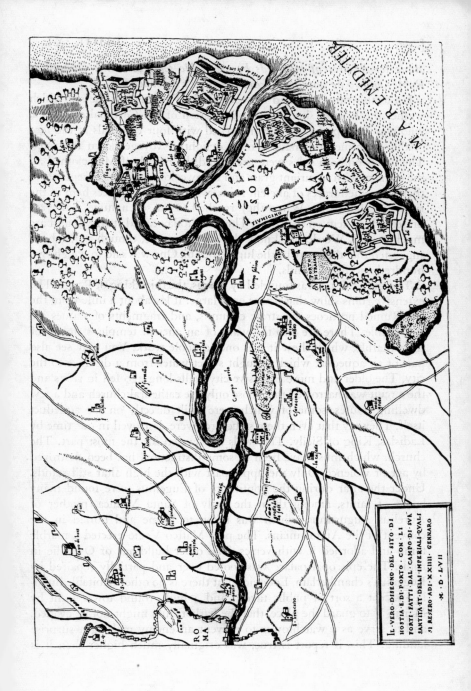

IL · VERO · DISEGNO · DEL · SITO · DI
HOSTIA · E · DI · PORTO · CON · LI
FORTI · FATTI · DAL · CAMPO · DI · SVA
SANTITA ET DELLI IMPERIALI QVALI
SI RESERO · ADI · X XIIII · GENNARO
M · D · L · VII

atone for its present misdeeds by profitable services to the Church of
Rome; and so he withdrew from the Pope's presence.

Up to this time Pius had not seen Ostia Tiberina nor the sea which washes the Roman shore. At the invitation of the Cardinal of Rouen, who was Bishop of Ostia, he embarked with four cardinals at the foot of the Aventine and made a most delightful voyage down the river. The banks on both sides were green and the month of May clothed all the country with luxuriant grass and many-colored flowers except where there remained traces of ancient ruins, which in many places hem in the river bed like walls. When they reached Ostia seven huge fish were presented to them on the shore. These are today called sturgeon and are much prized. We do not know the ancient name, though it has been suggested that they may be the lupi Tiberini. One was said to weigh two hundred and fifty pounds.

The city of Ostia was founded by Ancus, the third king of Rome. The extensive ruins show that it was once large. It lay about a mile from the sea. Ruined porticoes, prostrate columns, and fragments of statues are still visible. There are also the walls of an ancient temple, stripped of their marble, which show it was once a noble work. You may see also part of an aqueduct which brought sweet water from a distance to the city. The older and more extensive city walls long ago fell in ruins and the circuit was narrowed to enclose only the cathedral church and a few dwelling houses, some of which were built directly on the aqueduct itself. They say that even these structures were destroyed in our time by Ladislas, King of Sicily. The walls are leveled for the most part. The church, which must have been of some distinction, has been destroyed by age or violence. Only the upper part with the high altar still stands. Under the altar during the pontificate of Eugenius were found many bones of saints, among them the body of Santa Monica, mother of Aurelius Augustinus, which was taken to Rome and buried in the convent of the Augustinians. The poet Maffeo Vegio erected a marble tomb and adorned it with verses. The other buildings of Ostia lie in ruins. The episcopal palace was roofed over and partially repaired by Eugenius's chamberlain, Lodovico, but there is no other habitable building except a sort of public tavern and a high, round tower built by Martin V to guard the place, that the harbor dues might not be evaded, and to serve as a watchtower to prevent an enemy making a surprise landing. This, if report is true, was originally much higher than it is now. They say it has settled under the shock of earthquakes and is underground more than a man's height.

Such today is Ostia whose fame was great in antiquity. Only a few fishermen from Dalmatia and the guards of the tower live there. It lies on a triangular tract cut off along two miles by the sea and encircled by the Tiber for an equal distance. The rest is bounded by a lagoon where there are saltworks. An aqueduct built in antiquity through this lagoon serves today as a bridge and over this a footpath leads straight from Ostia to Rome. Swans lay eggs and rear their young on the bank and in the marsh grass and it is delightful to see and hear the flocks. The lagoon is hardly fifty feet from the Tiber so that it would be easy to turn the peninsula into a real island. At its widest point the lagoon is a stade across and it is no deeper than a man's height. It narrows toward the sea and is like a canal hedged on the sides with trees in which birds sing sweetly. It is not connected with the sea except when the ocean swells and then the sandy shore between the lagoon and the sea is covered with water and the lagoon thus enlarged becomes one with the sea. The whole peninsula is covered with grass and is suitable for cattle although in many places and especially near the sea it is very sandy.

The actual mouth of the Tiber is larger and admits galleys and moderate-sized freighters, though not without some danger as there are said to be only three cubits of water above the sand and the sand itself is continually shifting. On this account they have to have a steersman who knows the nature of the place (he is called a pilot) and they have to hire him. If anyone omits to do this, his stinginess is punished with shipwreck. They say that Carthage was directly opposite this mouth not more than five hundred miles away and that fresh figs were brought from there to Rome. It was on this account that Cato argued that an enemy of the Roman people so powerful and so near ought to be utterly destroyed.

Juan, Cardinal and Bishop of Porto,[5] when he heard that Pius had gone to Ostia, sailed over to ask him to visit his church too and the Pope accepted. With the cardinals he went on board and was towed upstream. *They had scarcely gone two stades when a heated dispute arose as to whether a certain palace was in Ostia or on the island opposite. The Pope said it was in Ostia and so did Gregorio Lolli; the rest held the other view. The sailors and Romans supposed to be familiar with the region were questioned and they said it was on the island. Gregorio and the Vice-Chancellor, who were on opposite sides, agreed that the loser*

[5] Carvajal.

should pay a forfeit of the largest sturgeon. The subject was continued
till their return with various arguments and no results. Their perplexity
and uncertainty was caused by the fact that the river was very winding
and the ground, which was practically a continuous meadow between
the island and the palace, was so low that from a distance no water
could be seen. The question was so difficult to settle that men who rode
across the island toward Ostia to within about three stades of the palace
still thought it was connected with the island until runners sent to reach
the palace found their way blocked by the river and reported Lolli the
victor. Afterward all were able to see the topography for themselves.

Two hundred miles above Ostia the Tiber branches; the larger part,
which is much the wider, runs to the left toward Ostia, the smaller
bends to the right and flows toward the west, whether because such is
its natural course or because man has so diverted it.[6] These two arms of
the Tiber encircle a good-sized island with abundant pasturage which
is excellent for cattle. On it is the church of Porto.[7] It is unroofed and
only the walls and the fine bell tower without its bells are standing.
There is no other building on the island, but wherever you dig you find
pieces of marble, statues, and huge columns. They say the marbles were
brought here from the Ligurian mountains and other regions by traders
and offered for sale to the Romans. Scattered about are many rough
and unpolished fragments *marked on two sides with numerals which,*
according to Pliny,[8] indicate the weight of the stones, but according to
others the order of the pieces sent by the merchants, but almost everything has been covered by the rising soil. The island is level and grassy,
about ten miles in circumference. In time of peace it is full of herds.

At the point in Tuscany where the smaller branch of the Tiber
enters the Tuscan sea the Emperor Claudius built a harbor protected
right and left by the jetty, with a mole at the entrance where the sea
is deep. To facilitate the building of this mole he first sank the ship
in which the great obelisk had been brought from Egypt and built on
it a lofty tower supported on piles after the manner of the Pharos of
Alexandria, that ships might steer by its light at night. There are still
traces of this tower which can be seen from far out at sea. Everything
else has perished utterly.

The neighboring city of Porto gets its name from the harbor. Whether

[6] Although Pius is traveling upstream, "left" and "right" branches are here in *down-*
stream terms.
[7] Cathedral of Santa Rufina.
[8] We have not found this reference to Pliny. Had Pius some other author in mind?

it was built by Claudius or by Trajan, only the ruins are now to be seen. There is the city gate stripped of its marbles and part of the ruined walls. Traces too can be seen of the pagan temples and the corpses of Christian churches. In the center was a dock said to be the work of Trajan and vulgarly called Trojan instead of Trajan's. It was capable of accommodating many galleys but now it is choked with mud and looks like a lagoon. Once a canal two miles long brought ships from the sea and the harbor and mingled the salt and sweet waters. Of the rows of columns around the lagoon, to which ships used to be moored, some are still standing. Nearby are arches very convenient for storing merchandise and larger workshops suitable for building or repairing ships. A Roman named Pamachius built an inn here, which St. Jerome commends, but no traces of it are to be seen. The city was once destroyed and then reduced to a mere fortress. This also is now uninhabited.

The Cardinal of Porto spread canopies over the ruins of the destroyed city and erected arbors of branches where he received Pope Pius with smiles and flattering words. He talked a great deal about Trajan, saying that he was succeeding him as one Spaniard another.

When Pius returned to Ostia he found that fishermen had caught an enormous dolphin which the servants of the French Cardinal of Rouen had cooked in many different ways and devoured greedily, *as they prize very highly this sea fish and consider it one of the sovereign's perquisites. The Italians were disgusted either because of the foul odor or because they had gorged themselves stupid on sturgeon.* The catching of a dolphin is said to be the sign of a coming storm. The next night, May 15, the sea, which during the last few days had been continuously disturbed and rough, became much wilder than usual. A violent tempest arose, a south wind churned the waters to their very depths, huge waves lashed the shore, and you could have heard the ocean groaning and shrieking. The force of the winds was such that it seemed nothing could withstand it. They fought savagely together and seemed now to rout, now to flee from one another. They tore down forests and everything in their path. The sky flashed with repeated fires, the heavens thundered, and terrible bolts shot from the clouds. One of them struck the tower bringing down a buttress and a bell which came near crushing a monk who was lying there buried in *wine and* sleep. Herds of cattle were stabled nearby and heifers that had just calved bellowed horribly in their anxiety for their young, either because they were terrified at the thunder or because they were afraid that wolves might attack them in the dark. The utter blackness of the night (though there were frequent flashes of lightning) doubled the terror, and such sheets of water fell that you would have said it was not rain but a deluge, as if the Creator had resolved once more to drown the human race.

Since there were not accommodations in the episcopal palace or the tower for all the attendants of the Pope and the cardinals, many lay under tents and some had gone to bed in the ships. Among the latter were Roman citizens, some of the Pope's household, and Rouen's steward. When with the rising storm winds buffeted the ship and rain filled the hull, in their fear and dismay they did not know what to do. The steward to escape from water plunged into water and nearly drowned. Being by good luck near the bank he seized hold of a rope and when he shouted for help was finally rescued. He emerged from the river dripping and half dead. One of the Pope's household took the only light in the ship and leapt with it to land. Then the Romans, left in darkness, embraced one another and prayed that they might not be abandoned. They cried that theirs was a most miserable fate if they must die in the dark; they bitterly bewailed their lot and never doubting that their last day had come, entwined in each other's arms and soaked to the skin, they awaited the outcome.

The wind had torn down all the tents. Outside the wall were two tents where the household of the Vice-Chancellor [9] were lodged. These were caught up in a violent whirlwind which snapped the ropes, splintered the poles, and slit the canvas to ribbons. One of the poles fell on the leg of a man lying close by and came near breaking it. Everyone fled from the ruined tents but in the dark they could not see the way. The violence of the storm drove them naked as they were among the thistles with which the place was overgrown and they were wounded by the sharp prickles. Finally a pitiful sight, covered with blood, stiff with cold, and almost dazed, they reached the Vice-Chancellor who was lying in the palace terrified at the fury of the dreadful storm. When he saw his men had left the tents and come there naked, he did not ask whether they were all safe but where they had left the plate (*gold is so much more regarded than a man*) and he refused to be comforted till he learned that it was safe. Everyone in the palace was in a panic. There was no one who did not fear for his life except those who had drunk more than usual at dinner or had been lodged in the lowest rooms. These were sunk in deep sleep and heard nothing.

Pius in his room had begun, as was his custom, to dictate to Agostino

[9] Rodrigo Borgia.

Patrizzi [10] and for almost an hour thought little of the storm and felt
no alarm. But when the fury of the rain increased and the wind buffeted
the walls and made them quake and the whole house shook and the roof
tiles were torn off and sent flying hither and yon, he began to fear there
was danger, and when he looked at the walls and ceiling and saw they
were all very old, fearing that they might be rotten and collapse, he bade
Agostino get up and call the servants. When they came he said, "Bring
me my clothes so that I may go outside." They said that would be un-
wise because it was not safe to stay outside in the furious rain and in
the palace there was no safer place than his room. But the Pope answered, "You don't know what you are talking about! The wind is
easier to bear than a falling house. Dress me at once. I shall have better
protection under the sky. The walls are cracking and do you put confidence in a room?" The servants obeyed but when Pius was half
dressed the storm suddenly abated and all the winds subsided as if they
had been afraid to cause the Pope inconvenience.

The Cardinal of Porto, who had remained in his own city, passed a
similar night. When his tent collapsed and was torn to pieces, finding
himself out in the open air he covered himself up with his clothing and
so got through the storm and that dangerous night. At Rome too there
were thunderstorms as severe as those at Ostia.

The next day the Pope returned home to the delight of the expectant
people *who supposed the pontiff had gone to Tivoli for the summer.*

At this time the people of Aquila were pressing the matter of driving
back to the mountains the flocks of sheep which had been wintering in
the pastures of the Church and the coast regions. The Pope answered
that the Aquilani had violated the terms of the treaty in furnishing provisions to Piccinino when he was besieging Sulmona, admitting the
enemy's forces to their towns, buying up booty taken in the lands of the
Church, and committing numerous other acts contrary to the terms of
the treaty and their pledged word. On this account they had often
incurred a fine of 50,000 ducats and their sheep were to be held as
security. The Aquilani on the other hand said the sheep were free and
could not be held because of a violation of the truce or any other offense,
even if it involved charges of treason; an agreement to this effect had
been made with the Church's tax collectors when the sheep were sent.
The fiscal procurator asserted that the tax collectors had no authority
to make such an agreement. When the matter came to be disputed, the
Pope summoned the Auditors of the sacred palace as if for another

[10] Friend of Pius's student days, now reader and secretary.

purpose and bound them by oath to investigate the truth quietly and report to him whether in their judgment, notwithstanding the agreement with the tax collectors, the flocks of the Aquilani could be held on account of their violation of the treaty.

They asked for time to consider and after discussing the point at issue for a week they told the Pope that they had come to a decision in regard to the law and the matter in hand. Pius summoned the cardinals and called a public consistory at which he ordered the ambassadors of the Aquilani to be present, and addressed them as follows: "Although when there are two claimants for the throne of Sicily it is the duty of the Aquilani to acknowledge and revere as king him to whom the Holy Apostolic See allots the throne, nevertheless forgetting honor and justice Aquila, as if the Church of Rome had no authority of its own, after Ferrante was declared king by us, set itself in opposition and obeyed René and his son; attacked our generals who were fighting for Ferrante; furnished infantry to Piccinino when he was ravaging the Church's lands; and did not fear to show hostility in every way to their rightful lord, the Pope of Rome. Though our forces were superior in war and the land of the rebellious Aquilani was being plundered, we were asked to end the war and embrace a truce.

"In pity for our sons we consented to lay down arms and grant the Aquilani a truce on these conditions: that they should not furnish supplies to the enemy or admit Piccinino's army within their boundaries or buy the booty taken from our fields. If they violated these conditions they were to be fined 50,000 ducats for every time they offended. When these terms had been agreed upon between us, they sent their flocks to our coast district (because there was no other place where they could be kept safe for the winter), taking the word of the tax collectors that they could not for any reason be withheld. After this they violated the terms of the truce two or three times and on this account we have asserted that they have lost their sheep. You, their envoys, though you admit guilt and the violation of the compact, nevertheless claim that there is no ground for our holding the sheep since it is contrary to their agreement with the tax collectors. We have referred the whole matter to the Auditors of our palace who constitute the Rota and judge the world. You shall hear from them whether your cattle are lost to you. Auditors, declare what is the law in the question at issue."

Then the Dean of the Rota, an aged Spaniard who for many years had devoted his services to administering justice in the apostolic palace, said: "Most Holy Father, we are present here as your chaplains and

Auditors of the Rota. We have carried out your instructions. We have examined carefully the question laid before us and with the same diligence have made ourselves acquainted with the facts of the case. We have seen the regulations of the Camera and the agreement between the Aquilani and the tax collectors in regard to their sending the sheep. We have seen the terms of the truce. We have considered the notorious rebellion of the Aquilani, the crime of lèse majesté committed against you and the clear violation of the truce. We have found that your tax collectors had no authority to promise what they did and that you are not bound by their compacts which are forbidden by the rules of the Camera. For these reasons we say that it is clearly the law that the sheep of the Aquilani may be kept by you without any blame attaching to you."

Then the Pope said: "Is this the opinion of all of you or did some dissent?" Among those present was Sanchez, one of the Auditors, himself a Spaniard and the last but one in seniority. He now rose and kneeling said, "All the rest, as our Dean says, are of the opinion that has been given. I alone dissent and I told my colleagues the reason." The others said that it was true that Sanchez had dissented but that he had given no reason of any weight. The Pope then said: "Envoys of the Aquilani, you have heard the opinion of the Auditors of the sacred palace. Your sheep are lost to you and have become ours. We may lawfully keep them and if we do, your punishment will be lighter than your fault. No man of intelligence could call an act unjust which the first tribunal of the world had declared to be just. We have the power to exact punishment from rebellious and ungrateful sons. We shall not do it. Our clemency shall be greater than your perfidy. Go and drive home the beasts that you have legally lost. We make a present of them to your state, though it ill deserves it. Learn how great is the difference between ecclesiastical and secular rule. No one who had offended any king on earth as you have offended the Church would have received from him the grace that you today receive from us. Unless you are utterly ungrateful you will refrain in the future from injuring the Church of Rome."

The envoys of Aquila, who as if stunned had been anxiously awaiting the Pope's decision, on hearing this breathed again. Having got a far better result than they expected they confessed the error of their state and thanked the Pope. All marveled at the Pope's generosity for on that day he presented to the Aquilani more than 100,000 sheep.

Some days earlier the Pope had sent the Protonotary of Bologna to

the Aquilani with the decree of the Rota, that he might make clear in
their senate that the sheep had been lost and then restored to their
former owners by the generosity of the Pope. This he did to prevent the
envoys from attributing to their own efforts what was really due to the
Pope's graciousness. It did not however lessen at all the perfidy of the
Aquilani. They took the sheep but were not a whit reformed. *It is not
the nature of mountaineers to be won over by kindnesses. Like asses and
mules mountain men are moved by the lash.*

While this was happening Everso, Count of Anguillara, who never
for a moment forgot to be false, contrived many schemes against the
Pope to see if he might in any way destroy him by the sword or poison.
His chief adviser in this was Piccinino's chancellor, Broccardo. Letters
between them were found which made it clear that they had tried many
plans to murder the Pope and had some still in reserve. There was also
found a letter to Everso from the Florentine Piero Pazzi, who on being
sounded by Everso about the murder of the Pope, had answered that he
was a friend of the French; in their cause he had heretofore spared
neither his fortune nor his person; he was prepared to do likewise in the
future; but he desired to save his soul for God and to plot against the
life of the Pope was not right for any man nor could it be done without
harm to one's soul; Everso was not to ask such a thing of him again.
Broccardo said he had discovered a poison such that if a very little were
rubbed on the Pope's chair it would kill him when he sat down. They
must bribe one of Pazaglia's followers who regularly carried the chair.
When the Pope was dead Ferrante would be utterly undone and the
Kingdom would be in the hands of the Angevins from whom Piccinino
and Everso would get all they wanted.

On the discovery of these letters the Pope took what extra precautions
he could but trusted more to the protection of God than of man.

Meantime Everso had certain of his household arrested on the charge
of plotting with Gregorio Lolli for his death. It was said he had imprisoned a father and two sons in a dry well at Vetralla to die of hunger,
blocking the mouth of the well so that their cries could not be heard;
that he had murdered others in various ways; that some who confessed
their treachery he had spared with a pretense of clemency; that he had
sent letters throughout Italy saying that the Pope was plotting against
his life. He did not realize that the character of a man who says he is
betrayed when he has vainly tried to betray others is known to everyone.

Meantime Pius after celebrating in St. Peter's the feast of the Ascension of Our Lord, was invited by the chamberlain of the Cardinal of

Aquileia [11] to visit the monastery of St. Paul in Albano that he might make himself acquainted with those ancient sites. He accepted readily and went thither accompanied by three cardinals and his household. Going out by the Porta Appia on the road toward Naples, he viewed on the way many ruins, chief among them the hippodrome near St. Sebastian's, a huge shattered obelisk which once served as a goal post for two- and four-horse chariot races, and the noble tomb of Caecilia Metella now called "bull's head." He came on many ruined villas and an aqueduct borne on lofty arches but broken in many places. In the groves near Albano they found the Appian Way paved with very hard black stone and on either side the huge bulk of towerlike tombs stripped of their marbles.

The Chamberlain, Lodovico, had acquired the ruined monastery of St. Paul in Albano, founded by Pope Honorius III, and had restored it. The church, which was roofless, he repaired. He erected splendid houses and where once he hunted wolves and foxes he planted gardens and made the place delightful. There is a never-failing spring there but nevertheless he built cisterns from which better water could be obtained. The climate is not unhealthful though the place is exposed to the sea winds which blow from Africa. Lodovico kept animals of various kinds here, among them peacocks and pheasants and goats from Syria with very long ears hanging down and covering their cheeks. The whole aspect of the place was changed under him and the monastery repaired.

Quite different was the care given to his church by the Cardinal de Foix. *He is the Bishop of Albano, of noble birth, rich and powerful, who when he was legate in Avignon amassed so much money that he literally drained the citizens dry. His church in Albano lies without roof or altar or doors. Only the ivy-covered walls are standing and even they will soon collapse. Meantime they serve as stables for goats and cattle. These are the canons appointed by the Cardinal of Albano to perform divine service day and night in his church!*

I am inclined to believe that Albano was once the little city sixteen miles from Rome where Ascanius, Aeneas's son, ruled, which got its name from the sow with the white piglets. It was destroyed by Tullus Hostilius, who moved the inhabitants to Rome and settled them on the Caelian Hill. It was afterward rebuilt and enlarged, as is shown by the ruins of ancient walls which enclose an area as large as Bologna, for it extended in length from the edge of the Alban lake to the fortress now called Albano and was as wide across. There remain traces of public

[11] Scarampo whose lavish expenditures won him the nickname of "Cardinal Lucullus."

and private buildings built of unusually large squared stones. You may still see the theatre, of which the central part, which is quarried into the stone of the mountain itself, still retains its old seats and has kept its outline intact though overgrown with brambles. An addition was built of baked brick supported on numerous arches which still exist. The town has many large reservoirs. The Florentine Battista Alberti, a scholar and a very clever archaeologist, said that more than thirty were to be found hidden among briers and brambles. Pius saw four very large ones still standing.

Henry III, Emperor of Germany, was the last to destroy the larger Alba. On the ruins the Savelli built a small fortress which in our day the Patriarch of Alexandria demolished because it was hostile to the Church of Rome. This is now restored and can be defended. In it they say Ascanius's palace still exists, but that is a mistake. There were once baths here, a great and splendid work of the empire. Lofty arcades are still standing and show traces of the channels for warm water. The baths were as large as all Albano is today and her walls are strengthened by their ruins. In the part looking toward Ariccia is to be seen a square pile despoiled of its outer wall, on the summit of which rise five lofty pyramids. Three are stripped of the hewn stone with which they were once faced while two still retain their ornament. Time, the foe of all things, has so shaken some of the stones that they threaten to fall and in many places it has allowed that foe of walls, the wild fig tree, to wedge itself in. This is popularly called the tomb of the Curiatii, who fought with the three Roman Horatii in defense of their liberty and fell in the battle. They say that two pyramids were added for the two Horatii who fell at the same time. This seems to me improbable, for the three champions fell fighting between Rome and Albano and one lived to win the victory for his country. I should suppose that the ancients set up inscriptions where the event occurred and that the tombs were erected where the bodies were found or at least not far off. As you go from Rome toward Albano they point out three piles gnawed by time which are thought to have been dedicated to the Curiatii, for they are in Alban territory.

Behind Albano on the north hidden in a deep valley is the Alban lake today called Castello from the Sabine Castel Gandolfo which overlooks it. The castle was once destroyed by the Patriarch but is now in process of restoration. Pius went there to see whether there might be any ancient remains. The lake is remarkably lovely, surrounded by lofty cliffs of which the lowest toward Rome has a drop of a stade. The others are higher and inaccessible. All are covered with forests in which are many evergreen ilex trees. The lake is shaped like an egg, a little longer than it is wide, with a circumference of five miles. It is a very suitable place for a naval battle with room for innumerable spectators. The water is clear and furnishes excellent fish, especially huge eels. It is said that the depth is unfathomable; all agree that it is very great. There is a tradition that during the Veientine war a seer said that if the water were let out of the Alban lake the Romans would take Veii. An outlet was made with great labor and the Alban Mount itself tunneled for a distance of fully two miles. This proved to be of the greatest practical use. Mills were built which are always operating; the industry of catching eels was started; the thirsty fields were irrigated; and the lake prevented from spreading. Pius inspected the opening made for the water to drain off and the place where it enters and found both worthy of admiration. He saw too the cave hollowed in the rock and enlarged with ancient walls to give it the appearance of a temple, and the places where idols evidently were set up. This is on the west side near the lake. You would say it was a grotto where the dryads lived. Between the lake and the grotto are wide fields. Whether it was used as a place for a market or sacrifice or games nothing was lacking to make it pleasant.

From here the Pope returned to Albano and the next day went to see Lake Nemi which he had heard much admired. He went by the Appian Way, the pavement of which is still visible. The road was in many places more beautiful than at the height of the Roman Empire since it was shaded on the sides and overhead by leafy filbert trees which were at their greenest and most flourishing in that month of May. Nature who is superior to any art has made the road most delightful. There are ancient ruins on the mountains to the left at the foot of which are the remains of old buildings called Bovillae. It is said to be the spot where Milo killed Clodius. Fresh springs bubble up here and the land is fertile. About a mile to the right is a pond called the Ariccian Lake. From there you may ascend the mountain on which is the Castello di Cynthia belonging to the Colonnas and named after Cynthia whom the pagans also called Diana.

At its foot lies Lake Nemi which the ancients called Diana's mirror, and not without reason for it is shaped like a round mirror and the clear water reflects those who look into it. It lies in a deep valley reached by a steep descent of not less than two stades wooded from summit to base. The lake is two miles in circumference or a little more. All around it runs a path on which you may stroll and a strip of level ground of varying widths, the narrowest part ten feet wide, the broadest two hundred or more. Then come cliffs and a steep ascent into the mountains. The entire plain and the cliffs as far as the brow of the mountain are covered with fruit trees, here splendid chestnuts, here taller walnuts set out in ranks, here filberts. There are also tall apple trees of various kinds and beneath them grow low medlars and young pear trees and quinces and plums. Under them there is pleasant shade and green meadows inaccessible to the sun and obstructed by no brambles. In a good year enough fruit is carried into Rome from here to supply the whole population. In summer you could find nothing more delightful than this shade. It is a most congenial place for poets to stroll. If the genius of a bard is listless here it will not be roused anywhere. You would call it the abode of the Muses, the dwelling of the Nymphs and, if there is any truth in legends, the retreat of Diana.

Under the castle called Nemi, which is in the direction of the Castello di Cynthia on the other side of the lake, a spring of cold and very clear water bursts forth and runs down into the lake, so full and strong that it turns the wheels of numerous flour mills in its course. This lake too had no outlet. The Romans constructed an emissarium by digging through the mountains with great difficulty for a long way and through this a stream of water of such size as a man could embrace with his arms flows into the Ariccian lake. Some think this is the source of the river Numicus where Trojan Aeneas disappeared. We cannot believe it, for the Numicus swallowed up Aeneas before the outlet was made. Still this water may have flowed into the Numicus, the marshes of which are to be seen today near the sea not far from Ardea. Julius Caesar built a villa near the west shore of the lake but he had it destroyed because it did not come up to his expectations. The ruins are still there.

That this place was a special favorite with the Romans is indicated by many things but especially by the ship which in our day has been found in the lake under nearly twelve ells of water. Cardinal Prospero Colonna sent to Genoa for sailors who could easily remain under water and attempted to raise it. He got out some fragments which showed the shape and the construction. The hull was of larch wood three fingers thick. The outer surface was smeared with pitch. This was covered with silk stuff of a saffron or red color which in turn was overlaid with lead plates fastened with bronze nails, their gilded heads set so close together that no water could get in. To prevent its catching fire the inner surface had besides the pitch an incrustation made by mixing iron and clay (a process our experts do not understand). This was as thick as the material it enclosed so that the ship was clearly fireproof. The separate parts of the keel and hull appear to have been put together to form a ship not less than twenty cubits long and of proportionate width. They say that on this ship was erected a palace such as that of Borso of Ferrara on the Po or Lodovico of Mantua's on the Mincio or those of the Prince Electors on the Rhine. The divers who went to the bottom of the lake say that in the hold they saw a chest of iron or copper fastened by four hoops and a clay water jar with a cover of gilded bronze. The ship is thought to be a work of Tiberius Caesar because in the lake were found numerous lead pipes inscribed in capital letters TIBERIUS CAESAR. Pope Pius saw on the shore beams taken from the ship made of larch wood which is very like fir.

After inspecting these with a good deal of pleasure he ascended to Nemi but did not enter the fortress, though he passed close under the gates. The populace swarmed out to meet him and received the blessing they begged. You might have seen aged men weeping for joy, embracing each other and saying, "And who would have thought that before we died we should see a Roman pope here? God has vouchsafed us this grace."

When the Pope was returning by the Appian Way he found that by the efforts of the Romans a place that had been difficult to climb had been made easy, the mountain cut away on one side and on the other a retaining wall of huge squared stones constructed. Here a man was digging out the pavement and destroying the road, breaking up the great rocks into small pieces to build a house near Nemi. The Pope sharply rebuked him and instructed Prince Colonna, the owner of Nemi, not to allow the public road, which was the Pope's responsibility, to be touched thereafter.

The next day after returning to Albano he went down to the groves which are worth seeing below the castle called Savelli, from which the Savelli family takes its name. Here he visited the Lake of Juturna [12] into which Turnus's sister is said to have flung herself on hearing of her brother's death. This pool (or lake if you will) has no outlet either. It is shallow and small but has a great many fish.

After this Adoardo, Duke of Marsia, of the Colonna family begged the Pope to be so gracious as to visit the citadel called Rocca di Papa and if he found the place pleasant, to spend the summer there. The Pope consented because he wished to make it understood by everyone that the

[12] Laghetto di Turno.

Colonnas were not less dear to him now that Cardinal Colonna was dead. On the way he visited the monastery of Santa Maria Palazzuola and attended masses there.

This is an ancient church, not very large, with one archway and a vestibule supported on marble columns. There are dwellings for the monks and service quarters convenient enough but not very attractive and fallen into disrepair with age. The place overhangs the Alban Lake. The rock has been cut away far enough to give room for the monastery and garden. Grottoes too have been quarried out where abundance of water bubbles up and the clear springs fill the fishponds. It is delightful in summer to see the cold sparkling water thrown high into the air through pipes and it is available for all the needs of the monks. *In a corner* beyond the beautifully terraced garden is a *large natural* cave always shady till noon, which is like a hall where a number of tables can be set out. There too an abundant spring of clear and never-failing water gushes forth and fills a fishpond nearby. Isidore, Cardinal of Ruthen, when he took refuge there from the summer heat, usually had lunch in that grotto. The Carthusians used to live here to escape the summer climate of Rome; now it is the dwelling place of the monks of St. Francis who are called Observantists from their rule of observance. The very narrow approach to the monastery can easily be guarded by a few men. To the right very high precipices fall to the lake, to the left is a towering cliff in which the ancients hewed out a path with iron tools. At the left before you enter the monastery there is a high wall-like rock on which according to ancient custom were sculptured the fasces of a Roman consul and twelve axes. Six were covered with ivy, six were still visible. Pius ordered the ivy to be cleared away to encourage the memory of antiquity.

From here the Pope went to Rocca di Papa which is on a lofty mountain strongly fortified by the nature of the place and the work of man. Prospero Colonna strengthened it greatly and it is impregnable except where a road leads toward the highest mountains, though here too nature has set a rock on which a tower with very massive walls has been built. The other sides which overhang the town—itself set on a beetling crag— an enemy would attack in vain.

The Pope was received at Rocca di Papa graciously and hospitably by the commandant and after lunching there he went out into the broad meadows that are spread before the citadel. At that season everything was bright with grass and flowers. Then he entered the pleasant shade of a forest of filberts and beyond them many chestnuts and other trees of various kinds. Above the meadows and Rocca di Papa a hill towers some thousand feet and dominates all the surrounding heights. The Pope climbed this hill and on the summit found a plateau a stade or a little more in circumference. The foundations of the ancient walls are preserved for their entire circuit and there are great stones smoothed by the axe and a ruined shrine in the center on the remains of which some Dalmatian constructed for himself a hermitage of stones piled together without mortar. That a castle or the country house of some rich Roman once stood here is proved by the road up the mountain paved with Appian flint which is still perfectly preserved to the very top. Some conjecture it to be the citadel of Gabii because the mountain is commonly called Monte Cavo, which might be a corruption of Gabii. Its height may be realized from the fact that from it you can see Monte Amiata, though Monte Cimino is between.

The Pope sat there with the cardinals for some time gazing at the seashore and surveying all the coast belonging to the Church from Terracina to Monte Argentario. They beheld the mountains of Civita-vecchia, which enrich our times with the newly found alum, and the thickly settled Tuscan shores as far as the port of Rome. Then came Ostia in Latium and the Tiber like a snake twisting its many coils through the plain. He saw too Ardea, Turnus's city, ringed round with forests, and toward the sea the pools of the Numicus from which alone it was lawful to draw water for Vesta, and the ruins of Ariccia, where they say Augustus's mother was born, and the hill town of Lavinium named for Latinus's daughter Lavinia who married Aeneas. He saw too on the coast Nettuno, built on the ruins of Antium, where the people live by fishing, hunting, and fowling. In spring they attract the quails coming back from Africa by playing on pipes and catch them in nets. The sport lasts thirty days and one day's catch is often 100,000 birds. They take also a great quantity of pigeons when they are preparing to leave Italy and cross the sea.

The Pope also turned his eyes toward Monte Circeo and its fabled heights and the island of Ponza famous for King Alfonso's imprisonment there, and finally to Terracina itself, which the Volscians called in their tongue Anxur. The lakes of Nemi and Ariccia and the one named for Juturna and the Alban Lake could be seen from the mountain as clearly as if it were on their very brink. You could form a true idea of their size and shape and of the intervening space, which being at that season covered with leafy forests and green grass presented a variety of gay colors. Most charming of all was the broom which covered a great part of the fields with its flowers.

After this all Rome presented itself to view and Soracte and the Sabine country and the range of the Apennines glistening with snow, and Palombara and Tivoli and Palestrina and many places in the district we now call Campania. He could also see Lake Regillus, which is today called Pantano Secco. The ruins of Tusculum too were visible. The Romans destroyed that city after their defeat by Frederick I, which is said to have been disastrous. Strabo says there was a magnificent palace there and the foundations are still to be seen supported on numerous arches. Below them are the ruins of Molara. Visible also is Rocca Priora which belongs to the Sabines and Lucullanum, once L. Lucullus's villa, today called Frascati, and Marianum now called Marino, a town sixteen stades from Rocca di Papa belonging to the Colonnas.

The Pope after seeing the view from the mountain returned to Rocca di Papa where he passed the night. The next day at dawn he proceeded to Grottaferrata. This is an ancient monastery in the Tusculan territory between Marino and Lucullanum. It is thought that Cicero's villa where he wrote the Tusculan Disputations was there. The monks of the monastery wear beards after the Greek fashion and chant praises to God and the offices in Greek. The ancient and noble church has a most beautiful image of the glorious Virgin, Queen of Heaven, to whom it is dedicated. It is reported to be a work by the Evangelist Luke and every year in September crowds flock to see it at the time of the fair, *which seldom passes without bloodshed among the drunken populace.* At the Feast of Pentecost the monks purify the water after the Greek custom and keep it all the year in a marble urn in the vestibule of the church to give as remedy to those suffering from fever. At a little distance are fine lodgings for the monks and the abbot and beautiful vegetable gardens and, best of all, a cold and very abundant spring, which bubbles up in front of the entrance of the church and is piped to all the service quarters as well as filling a large pond. The monastery was presided over by a Calabrian abbot. He was given to litigation but his lawsuits had recovered a great deal of lost property. The Romans disliked him *and often tried to murder him* because he disturbed the holdings they had had for a long time and persisted in stirring up old quarrels that had long slumbered. Pius transferred him to Sicily and made him Archimandrite there. Grottaferrata he gave to Bessarion, Cardinal of Nicaea, who proceeded to restore the monastery itself with new and very handsome buildings.

The Pope lunched here and then, as it unexpectedly became very hot, he returned to Rome by the Via Latina through the ruins of many ancient buildings. He stopped at the Lateran and after he had prayed a few minutes at the high altar and inspected the roof of the church of which he had restored a great part and given orders for the restoration of the rest, he went on through residential streets to the Trastevere quarter and from there to his palace by St. Peter's. Next day[13] he celebrated the Pentecostal mass with solemn pomp in the church of St. Peter and blessed the people.

On June 6 of this year there died Flavio Biondo of Forlì, a distinguished historian who had long been Apostolic Secretary and in high favor with Pope Eugenius IV. He wrote a universal history from the time of the Emperors Honorius and Arcadius, with whom the decline of the Roman Empire is said to have begun, to his own day, a work which is certainly painstaking and useful and deserves to be revised and emended. Biondo was very far from possessing the eloquence of the ancients, did not examine carefully enough what he wrote, and was less concerned with the truth than with the quantity of his writings.[14] If someday a scholar and accomplished writer sets himself to emend and embellish his works he will be doing posterity no small service and will make himself famous by bringing to light the history of many ages which is now almost buried. Some one may perhaps say the same of us and rightly, for though what we write is true, yet *we set down the important or unimportant alike,* we are without eloquence, and have woven together a rude and unorganized narrative. Perhaps someday another will shed light on what Biondo and we have put together and will reap the fruit of others' toil.

There are extant other works of Biondo which are of considerable value though they should be read with caution, that you may not take the false for the true, since in many points he has been found in error. He wrote Italia Illustrata, Roma Instaurata, and Roma Triumphans, the last finished just before his death. He died at Rome, poor as became a philosopher, leaving a family of both sexes well educated. His slender means he divided among the girls as their dowry. To the boys he bequeathed nothing except learning and good character. He died contented that his sons were of an age to look after themselves.

Here I shall insert a very trifling matter but one not wholly without

[13] May 29, 1463.
[14] Biondo none the less served as one of Pius's main sources, enjoyed his favor and dedicated his "Roma triumphans" to him.

*its use, since though referring to small things it may serve to furnish
counsel for great ones. Pius had a little bitch not yet eleven months old
named Musetta. It was not extraordinarily handsome but pretty and
charming and it knew how to win its way and make itself liked. While
the Pope was sitting in the garden hearing embassies the dog, who was
sniffing about hunting for something to eat, jumped up on the edge of
a cistern and fell into the water. No one saw it fall and when it was
tired out with swimming it was on the point of drowning. It barked
for help but no one came; they thought it was just barking as usual.
The Pope hearing the dog's repeated cries and thinking something had
happened to it told his servants to hurry and see what it was. The dog
was found at its last gasp no longer able to keep itself up and was
rescued and taken to the Pope to whom it continued to whimper for a
long time as if it wanted to tell about its danger and stir the Pope's pity.*

*The next day when the Pope was dining in the same garden a large
monkey that had happened to get loose set upon the dog and bit it. The
servants who were standing by with difficulty rescued it from the beast's
jaws. Almost dead with fright the dog again seemed to be lamenting
and moaning to the Pope. The Pope thought these were signs that the
dog could not survive, since within a few days it had twice narrowly
escaped death. And he was right. A fortnight passed. The dog, as it
often did, climbed up on the sill of a very high window overlooking
the vineyard. Suddenly there arose a violent and terrifying whirlwind
which seized the dog, hurled it outside and dashed it dead on the rocks.
When the Pontiff heard this he said, "It was decreed that the puppy
should die a violent death. This was predicted by its two escapes from
danger: it could not escape a third. We find in animals examples from
which men may learn. If anyone escapes two dangers let him beware
of a third. After two warnings he should know that the third is per-
emptory. Let him correct his way of life before he is summoned by a
third. A dog who has no conscience to reproach it awaits death
unafraid."*

BOOK XII

WHILE this was happening Napoleone[1] the captain of the
Church's army, collected twelve troops of horse and some thousand infantry and marched into the territory of Sora belonging to the
proud and insolent Duke Pietro Cantelmo, who had long been hostile
to Pope Pius, to punish his *mad* presumption. In his first raid he attacked and took by storm the fortress of Casale, handed it over to his
soldiers to plunder, and devastated the country far and wide, ruining
the ripening grain everywhere. The people of Isola after suffering the
destruction of their fields were the first to surrender. They were foolish
not to have done so sooner. Isola is a town adjoining the lands of the
Church completely surrounded by running water with high banks. The
river which encircles the island is called Viridis. It either is the Liris or
flows into it. It abounds in trout. There is no point on the island where
it can be forded. Such is said to be the situation of the town. The river
gliding calmly and quietly from its upper regions comes up against a
broad, high rock on which it splits into two parts and rushes headlong
on either side into the abyss below. Then after flowing with complaining murmurs around a considerable tract it again unites in a single
stream. On the rock that divides the river is a citadel fortified by
nature and art. The rest of the island is occupied by a town lying lower
than the citadel and between them is a moat which can be flooded to
keep the townsmen from the citadel.

After the town was surrendered there still remained the citadel,
which was hard to storm because of the river and its height. They
decided however to attempt even this difficult feat and fortune favored
their bold undertaking. Bombards were placed across the river to batter
the citadel at the point where we have said the rock on which the river
divides rises. The citadel was assaulted for several days without any
prospect of victory until the larger tower, shattered by incessant stones
from the bombards, collapsed and by its fall opened a path by which,

[1] Napoleone Orsini. The campaign took place in 1463.

steep though it was, the fortress could be scaled. Then an Ethiopian soldier who had been for some years in Napoleone's service and had finally entered the army said, "Comrades, I see a way open into the citadel; we can climb up on the ruined tower. Believe me, the citadel is as good as taken. Follow me. I will go on ahead and clear a path. Be as bold as I am and do not let me go alone."

With these words he hurled his lance across the water at the ruined tower and throwing off his clothes leapt naked into the river and swam swiftly to the other side. Then recovering his lance he strove to climb the heap of ruins, a black and revolting figure. Every bold man in the camp followed his example. The river was full of swimmers. Two were sucked down in the rapids, swept away by the current, and dashed upon the jagged rocks far below. One of these is said to have escaped. The rest caught up with the Ethiopian unharmed and clambering together over the ruins, marvelous to tell, naked and armed with spears as they were, by hurling rocks and weapons they dislodged the armed defenders of the citadel who were stationed before the walls, entered the citadel and completely destroyed it. A bold and incredible feat, but one actually performed in our time. An Ethiopian's courage stormed what was believed to be impregnable. Posterity will think it mythical; for how will a future age believe on hearsay a thing which our own age has actually seen and yet regards as a dream? Those who were captured in the citadel, when they saw themselves the prey of naked men, were plunged in unspeakable gloom because they thought that from that day they would be a byword and laughingstock to the populace.

The army next proceeded to Arpino, once a famous Roman provincial town, the birthplace of C. Marius and M. Cicero, one of whom conferred luster on the town in arms, the other in letters. The Arpinates at once surrendered to the Church and the two citadels in the town which the Duke of Sora had fortified were taken by storm. It is said that almost all Arpinates today are named either Tullius or Marius because they think that thus the memory of their most illustrious citizens is perpetuated.

When the Sorani learned that the citadel of Isola had been stormed and that Arpino had surrendered, they sent envoys to the Bishop of Ferrara, who was the Pope's Legate in camp, and offered to obey his orders on condition that they should have no other lord than the Pope; they were weary of tyranny; the rule of the Church of Rome was that of a father and they would gladly obey it. The Bishop agreed to their conditions and received the submission of Sora in the name of the Church of Rome. The bishop of the place was chiefly responsible for this event.

The Duke of Sora, as a result of these blows, asked for peace or at least a truce during which he might obtain peace from the Pope. A truce of a few days was granted him and three strongly fortified towns were taken from him on condition that if he could not obtain his request from the Pope, he should understand that he had lost them permanently.

The Duke's ambassadors arrived at Rome and peace was agreed upon on the following terms: The Duke of Sora was ordered to restore at once to the monastery of Cassino, to the Marchioness of Pescara, to his brother the Count of Popolo, and various others all that he had taken from them; Sora, Arpino, Isola, and many other places remained in the possession of the Church; only a very few unimportant places were to be restored to the Duke. Thus chastised and constrained, the Duke of Sora abandoned the French and returned to his allegiance to Ferrante, assured by the Pope's decree that he would not have to suffer any indignity from the King.

Before the capture of the King of Bosnia [2] the Venetians, learning that there was no Turkish army in the Peloponnese (for almost all the troops had followed the Sultan to Bosnia), thought the time had come when they could subjugate the largest and most famous peninsula of Greece. They therefore equipped a great fleet and put in command Aloisio Loredano who was esteemed a man of high spirit. Under pretense of defending Euboea they ordered him to sail to the east and empowered him to make war on the Turks, if he thought it for the interest of the state, and to wrest the Peloponnese from them and its other masters by any possible means. They had the support of the Albanians who of themselves were calling upon the power of Venice. .The Albanians live in great numbers in the mountains of Arcadia and of other parts of the peninsula and are hostile to the Greeks. Numerous cavalry and infantry forces were transported from Italy and they sent to Crete for 3,000 archers. Various kinds of aid had arrived from the various islands and there was no doubt that when the Albanians joined the Venetian camp the army could go into battle with more than 30,000 fighting men. The alleged object of the war was to avert aggression and defend the Christian religion. They accused the Turks of taking Argos and sacking Lepanto in violation of the treaty.

None of these considerations impelled the Venetians to arm so strong a fleet and incur such heavy expense. Traders care nothing for religion nor will a miserly people spend money to avenge it. The populace sees

2 The capture and beheading of Stephen Thomasevich occurred in 1463.

no harm in dishonor if their money is safe. It was lust for power and insatiable greed of gain that persuaded the Venetians to equip such forces and undergo such expense. They were well aware of the profits to be derived from the Peloponnese which brought in 300,000 gold ducats yearly in taxes. They were not ignorant that this region, once called the citadel of Greece, lay in the middle of the sea which washes Asia, Syria, Egypt, Libya, Spain, France, Italy, Illyria, Macedonia, Epirus, Boeotia, Attica, Thessaly, and all Thrace and connects with the Euxine sea; that it is a region most convenient for the whole world's commerce, a veritable abode of merchants, abounding in wine, wheat, and everything requisite for human existence. *They were possessed with the desire of conquering a very rich province. They spent money to get more money. They followed their natural instincts. They were out for trade and barter. This course was urged upon them by an overcrowded city which could no longer endure itself. Those they call nobles, who have control of the government, had increased to a remarkable degree, though all are slaves to the sordid occupations of trade. They thought they ought to send out a colony and that there was no better place to found one than the Peloponnese. These were their real reasons for equipping a fleet; all others were pretended. He is a fool who thinks a people can be persuaded to noble deeds unless it is to their material advantage.*

The Venetians reckoned that the Peloponnese was all but theirs when it was reported that the King of Bosnia had been captured by the Turks and it was evident that all Illyria was in the greatest danger. They reported what they had heard to the Pope, they summoned all Christians to their aid by a letter, and they who so recently were threatening others were now in deadly fear for themselves. Those who had begun to terrorize others abroad now did not feel secure at home.

The Ragusans too and Georg of Albania and the Despot of Arta and numerous others sent to Rome to ask advice and help. The Pope took thought for all so far as he could. He dispatched Bessarion, Cardinal of Nicaea, to Venice as Legate of the Apostolic See to bring the Senate hope of aid and relieve them of fear of the enemy; to assure them that the Pope would summon Christian princes to arms and that it would not be long (God willing!) before a great host under the banner of the Cross would be led against the Turks. Infantry forces and a large supply of grain were voted to aid the Ragusans.

After these measures had been decided on the Pope, fearing the heat of the city, withdrew to Tivoli the day after celebrating the feast of St.

Peter Martyr in his church.[3] On the way he had the pleasure of visiting the spring of Salone. There are two bubbling springs near the Aniene ten miles from Rome so abundant that each alone could easily turn a mill with only a slight fall of water. The water is crystal clear and very cold, a circumstance which in summer causes the death of many rash persons. Nine cardinals accompanied the Pope and lunched with him under shelters which their attendants constructed of branches near one of the springs and the stream which flows from it. The lunch as befitted a pope was elegant rather than sumptuous *and elaborate*. A great deal was left over though more than six hundred men had eaten all they could. While the heat was still intense the Pope and cardinals engaged there in pleasant conversation; then when a breeze came up inspiring false hopes of coolness they continued the journey and came to Tivoli just before sunset.

That year Ferrante, because of the carelessness or the treachery of his captains or because his treasury was empty and he could not pay his soldiers, took the field much later than had been agreed upon nor did he bring with him the Sforzeschi in the companies specified. Only twenty-six troops of horse and two thousand infantry joined the expedition. Advancing with these into the territory of Teano and the adjoining districts subject to the Duke of Sessa, he ruined everywhere the crops standing ripe and ready for the sickle. The enemy were unable to prevent the devastation of the fields though they had sixteen troops of light-armed horse under arms. The soldiers, greedy for plunder, treated other men's harvest as if it were their own. The infantry wielded sickles, carried the sheaves of grain to the threshing floors, and after carefully separating the wheat from the chaff are said to have sold the Capuans more than 200,000 pecks of corn and barley stolen from the enemy. What could not be carried off was trampled and burned and all the peasants' hopes of a harvest were swept away. There remained the territory of Sessa which contains a great many of the buildings they call casalia. It is very rich in wine and grain and abounds in everything pleasing to mankind. You would call it blessed both for mildness of climate and fertility of soil. It is sheltered from the east and north winds by lofty mountains, bounded on the south by the Tyrrhenian Sea and on the west by the Liris which is too deep to ford and broad enough for galleys. An ancient tower fortified like a citadel guards the point where vessels cross. There is but one approach over level ground, a very narrow one on the coast between the mountains and the sea, but this

---

[3] Thus the Pope left for Tivoli on June 30.

too had been rendered impassable by a moat and rampart. Furthermore a citadel at the foot of the mountain strongly fortified by nature and art prevents the approach of an enemy.

Within this territory all was security, peace and quiet. The lord of Sessa had put everything else in the hands of Fortune. The plain of Sessa he believed to be quite outside the range of the war and he had no apprehension that the enemy would enter or that they would even make the attempt. His subjects had brought all their most valuable possessions from the neighboring districts to this place as to the safest of strongholds. Ferrante ordered Roberto San Severino and Antonio Piccolomini with infantry and some of the cavalry at the fourth watch of the night to occupy the lofty and almost inaccessible mountain commanding the citadel which we have said guarded the approach. He himself with the rest of his forces moved just as dawn was whitening. Arriving about the third hour at the entrance called the Torre de' Bagni he ordered the army to wait a little till the fleet, which was proceeding under full sail in command of Admiral Villamarina, should put in to land; for he had decided to attack both by land and by sea.

Meantime he ventured on a skirmish and when that succeeded the soldiers crossed the moat at the first onset and climbed the rampart. They were at first thrust back but when rank after rank had climbed after them with increasing fury and the infantry who had occupied the mountain attacked from above, the King's army was in possession of the rampart before the fleet put in. The rampart was quickly demolished and then two companies of horse were sent in who met the enemy's cavalry beyond the rampart and routed them. By the time the lord of Sessa came up with the rest of his forces the rampart had already been surrendered to the King. The routed enemy renewed the battle but when the King's troops launched a more vigorous charge they were not strong enough to withstand it and fled in their turn. The royal troops pressed them hard and after pursuing the fugitives a long distance took many prisoners. The pursuit did not end till they were driven as far as the church of San Francesco which lies under the very walls of Sessa. Some fifty helmeted knights were captured. A large number of common soldiers were also taken. The tyrant of Sessa himself, throwing away his arms and decorations and ripping off his horse's trappings, saved himself by flight though his horse was almost exhausted. Almost all the numerous villages in the territory of Sessa were sacked and many of the inhabitants taken prisoner. Finally late in the day the army returned to camp loaded with plunder. The plan of the King and the captains was to pitch camp close by the church of San Francesco but since, owing to the utter weariness of the soldiers, they had not been able to destroy the defenses of the rampart or fill the twelve-foot ditch and had no way of getting their baggage across, and since moreover it was already evening they decided to encamp for that night on the edge of the moat and then after this was leveled up and the fortifications razed, to assault Sessa with the entire army.

The next day the whole territory of Sessa was overrun and so many cattle driven off that cows were sold for a gold piece and pigs for a silver one. Traders sailing up from Gaeta bought up the booty. The Sessans rushed upon the royal troops while they were scattered and captured a number of the infantry, but when the cavalry dashed up they were repulsed with some loss. Camp was pitched two miles from Sessa and plundering expeditions were carried up to the very gates.

Napoleone, who was now called on by the King to bring up the Church's forces, with the Pope's permission obeyed the summons and on his march took many towns east of the Liris belonging to the tyrant of Sessa which fell to the share of the Count of Fondi. René's son Jean had set out with two troops of horse and two hundred infantry to aid the lord of Sessa but he did not inspire sufficient hope in the besieged to prevent their negotiating for peace. Ambassadors were sent to the King to ask a few days' truce till they could agree on terms of peace. The King did not reject peace negotiations but refused the truce and meantime sent men to besiege the tower which, as has been said, commanded the crossing of the river. After a few volleys from the bombards it fell, killing some of the garrison; the rest were panic-stricken and surrendered. There was a second tower at the mouth of the same river but though it was much more strongly fortified the commandant did not dare to await the bombards but surrendered at once after stipulating for safe-conduct. The citadel commanding the rampart, which had been demolished by the charge of the King's forces, and the tower called de' Bagni were taken on the very day the troops entered and were later burned and demolished.

Meantime the peace negotiations were proceeding. The Duke's ambassador, Antonio da Trezzo, was summoned by Sessa and after a long conference he thought he had persuaded the tyrant to accept terms of peace. He was so certain of it that he returned to the King carrying an olive branch and assured him of an agreement. He said that the next day Sessa's envoys would come to the camp and bring with them the signed pact. Antonio had believed a liar and had committed the grave error of trusting the oath of a perjurer. The envoys did not come as had been arranged and the excuse given was that Antonio had not been invested by Francesco, Duke of Milan, with the authority to bind that prince; he had merely presented general instructions which Sessa did not trust sufficiently. He was nevertheless eager for an agreement and he begged that his friend Colantonio might be sent; he would trust him.

Colantonio was sent; terms of an agreement were stated and accepted; everything was satisfactory. "Go," said Sessa, "inform the King that day after tomorrow I will send proctors who shall publicly accept in my name the terms of the agreement and swear allegiance to Ferrante." Colantonio replied, "You made the same promise to Antonio da Trezzo and did not keep your word. See that you do not trick me. If you have no intention of doing what you promise, rather say so now and do not mock me with empty hopes." Sessa answered, "Go. My promises are sure. I shall not change," and pointing to his young son who was present he said, "If I prove false to you may I be forced by hunger to eat him!" He lied to Colantonio also; his promises were empty words; he said he could not trust those intermediaries either; he must have more important men. The Bishop of Ferrara invested with apostolic authority was proposed. His powers too were asserted to be inadequate. Then his brother the Cardinal of Ravenna, Legatus of the Apostolic See, was summoned from Benevento. Again and again peace terms were discussed; it was all mere words and nothing definite was accomplished. The more assiduously an agreement was sought, the more reasons for delay were invented by Sessa, the greater difficulties he piled up.

Meantime the King pitched camp near the town of Mondragone and moved up the bombards, which however were useless either because of the carelessness of the server or because the situation of the place was such that it could not be injured by bombards. The stones discharged passed beyond the town without doing any damage. Then they had hopes of forcing the townspeople to surrender from thirst, since their access to the spring where they were accustomed to get water was cut off and the summer heat had dried up all the cisterns. There was a mountain ridge over which the Sessans had a path to bring help to the besieged. Here Ferrante built a fort of timber and posted guards to prevent the Sessans from crossing. Their commander was the distinguished Sienese soldier Possa. Antonio Piccolomini was stationed a little lower down to guard the bombards. The King's camp was at the foot of the mountain five hundred feet away. Marco of Cremona, who had recently deserted from the enemy, was ordered to watch the spring that the townspeople might not get water at night.

When these arrangements had been made, Sessa chose a thousand or more lusty young foot soldiers and ordered them to go in the dead of night by paths unknown to the enemy. They were to capture or drive away Antonio and seize the bombards. They succeeded in getting by the royal pickets and were upon the wooden fort before the guards heard the approach of an enemy. The fort was attacked in the dark and defended with the greatest vigor. The commandant Possa showed himself a hero and his comrades also did every man his utmost to repulse the enemy, but their garrison was small and the great numbers of their adversaries enabled them to demolish the inadequate defenses of the fort. Their archers let fly fifty arrows at one volley. Possa was wounded many times and all his men were wounded and captured. Then there was a rush to the mound where Antonio and Giovanni Conto Romano were. As soon as the enemy reached the tents the alarm was given, but Giovanni and Antonio had barely time to arm and in the dark danger is greater in proportion as it is unseen. The Sessans rushed down from the mountain and attacked Antonio. When he had seized his arms and found Giovanni at his side, he said, "Look, Count! We promised to guard this position. We must either rout the enemy or die here. While I live Sessa shall never carry off the engines entrusted to my loyalty."

Giovanni applauded Antonio's resolution and both hurled themselves against the enemy. They were followed by only four, some say six, servants. The Sessans who had first broken in were repulsed. Meantime Antonio's comrades had armed and joined him. Giovanni's strength too was augmented, but the enemy's still more, since a great horde of Sessans rushed down from the mountain and by this time it was very difficult to defend the mound. The enemy ran to the bombards and seized the smaller ones. The townsmen came out to do battle and the situation was critical. Marco of Cremona, hearing the tumult and realizing its meaning, dashed up with a troop of his men and plunged into the battle unrecognized by either side and suspected by both. When he saw that the enemy were frightened he shouted to identify himself and charged upon them, followed impetuously by Giovanni and Antonio. The enemy turned and fled into the mountain abandoning the bombards and all their booty and leaving behind a considerable number of dead. The townsmen withdrew in panic into the fortifications just as dawn was glimmering. Thus the dangers of that night were escaped. Sessa, who the day before had broken off all negotiations for an agreement, when he saw that trickery had been useless and that the night battle had failed, as usual offered false excuses and again asked for peace. Through the mediation of the Cardinal the question was discussed for many days. When all details were arranged and nothing remained except to sign the actual document and seal the compact, Sessa raised a new difficulty. He said he had so deeply offended the King that he could not hope for pardon unless the King's daughter married his son. His request was granted. The marriage was promised, the dowry specified, an agreement next day was regarded as a certainty.

Meantime the south winds or others had gathered clouds and caused violent rains so that the cisterns of the besieged were filled and the besiegers deprived of their one hope of taking the town by thirst. There came also a letter from the Prince of Taranto to Sessa urging him not to make terms with the King and promising aid. This revived the faithless man's courage and from day to day he invented new reasons for delaying the agreement and wanted new terms. The Cardinal, realizing that he was being kept there by mere words, finally left the camp in indignation and returned to Benevento. The King raised the siege of Mondragone with great discredit to himself since he had encamped against it contrary to the judgment of many and without having sufficiently thought out his plan of action. When a man's attempt does not succeed, the populace always thinks it was stupidly planned.

In the King's camp was a Roman named Gentile Molara, whom the Duke of Milan had often sent to Sessa in regard to peace. Shortly before returning to Milan he went to Sessa and in an interview with the tyrant asked him why he rejected peace and why he had lied so often. The tyrant replied, "I have lied to no one except my friend and that boldly. It is the custom of our country to keep no promises between friends. He will turn the tables when he wishes and balance lie with lie. The reason that I do not embrace the peace which is necessary to myself and my subjects is distrust. I have tried to kill the King by trickery; I cannot hope for pardon. Who can doubt that if I fall into the King's hands he will some day exact punishment for so heinous a crime? I cannot be easy unless I have exalted vouchers."

To this Gentile answered, "But Antonio da Trezzo offered you the Duke of Milan as guarantor; the Cardinal offered you the Pope. Why have you not trusted such great names?" Then the tyrant said, "Do you bid me have confidence in the miserable chancellor? Antonio's eminence is not such that I could safely trust myself to him. As to the Cardinal, what shall I say? I have never liked any priest. *I should be*

happy if I could see every priest in the world hanged. They are a faith-
less and base set of men and not fit for princes to listen to. It would be
well for the human race if this scourge of mankind did not exist."
Gentile replied, "You are angry and speak wildly. He who hates priests
hates also God, whose servants they are. Farewell. If you have any
message for my master, I will gladly deliver it." Then Sessa said, "Commend me to the Duke and tell him to send me someone from his court
with authority I can trust. I will do everything he bids me"; and Gentile
answered, "I will do so though I know that these words of yours have
no more weight than the earlier ones." Then he departed and went and
repeated all these conversations to the Pope at Tivoli. The King proposed to attack Sessa in another way.

Federigo of Urbino and the Cardinal of Teano had meantime raised
a force and had intended to besiege Rimini. They changed their plans
however because they thought their strength was not adequate to take
a large and strongly fortified city and they marched against Fano. They
pitched camp an arrow's flight away and invested the city with fourteen
troops of horse and a few infantry. They brought up three large bombards and proceeded to batter the ramparts and dig subterranean passages which would give them direct access to the walls. To prevent the
bringing in of supplies or any other kind of aid by the sea on which the
city is situated they brought from Ancona and Pesaro a transport of
seven hundred amphorae (so they say) and triremes and smaller craft,
which they armed, and thus closely guarded the coast of Fano. The
army of the Church was increased by ten troops of cavalry from Forlì
and Faenza.

The besieged were now suffering from hunger and they went to Sigismondo's son [4] Roberto threatening to surrender the city unless corn were
brought to them. They declared that soldiers could fight, go without
sleep, suffer hardships, and endure anything except hunger. Roberto
bade the soldiers and townsmen be of good hope and he presented to
them as the Doge's envoy a Venetian merchant, *a natural liar,* who
happened to be present, saying that the Venetians would soon send sure
and certain aid. Meantime he wrote to his father urging him to come
with all speed to the help of the besieged; if he did not make haste, he
himself would have to lose the city. Sigismondo loaded some ships with
grain, armed a very large vessel and some smaller ones called fustae,
and ordered the fully equipped fleet to sail straight to Fano. When
Federigo learned of this through his scouts, because he had very little

[4] I.e., Malatesta.

confidence in a mob of sailors, he at once put on board the fleet at Ancona picked and daring soldiers from his camp, bidding them show themselves heroes and attack the enemy's fleet whether it approached by night or day.

Every word had its effect. The fleet of Rimini with all sails set reached the coast off Fano after midnight. The Church's fleet met them and a fierce struggle followed. A ship of Rimini taller than any of the others injured a galley of Ancona and some smaller craft with showers of missiles. The Church's fleet replied with small bombards, javelins, and every kind of engine. There happened to be present a spirited priest fitter for armed than for sacred warfare, who suddenly hurled a brand which set the sails of the larger ship on fire. The crew rushed to put out the flames but meantime the Church's men had boarded the ship on ladders and won a speedy victory. All the ships were captured, transports as well as battleships, and just as day was dawning they were brought gloriously into Ancona, all but the largest, which could not be towed, as it had no sails and was shattered in many places. Soldiers were put on board to guard it.

During this time the Venetians had summoned four galleys from Dalmatia and ordered them to sail to Rimini on the pretext of preventing piracy, but in reality to aid Sigismondo's cause by their presence. Two had already arrived and when they learned that Sigismondo's fleet had been captured and saw the abandoned ship, they at once attacked it and defeated the guards in a brief contest. Then they fitted it out with new sails and took it to Rimini. The Cardinal of Teano sent to ask the captains of the galleys why they had attacked a ship which was his prize of war when there was peace between Venice and the Pope. They said they had not taken the ship; *and after the way of traders took refuge in deceit and lies;* they said that the sailors who had been shut in the hold had tricked the soldiers set to guard them; they had invited them to a conference and coaxed them down to the lower part of the ship while they themselves got out one by one and made themselves masters of the upper part. Then they had imprisoned their jailers in their own prison and become victors instead of vanquished; the Venetians had supplied them with the necessary sails since they were now free men; *and other fairy tales.*

This greatly increased the courage of the people of Fano to withstand the siege, for they were convinced that the Venetians favored Sigismondo and would shortly send aid to overrun the camp of the Church. But the Venetians had other plans, for they did not want Sigismondo either to conquer or to be conquered. Their object was to prolong the war and wear out both sides with the expense of it, for they thought that this would result in Sigismondo's being abandoned by everyone and selling to them for money Rimini and any other places he held. *Such is the trickery and deceitful nature of an envious people. By such wiles they tried to subjugate the Duke of Milan when they withheld corn from a people besieged and perishing of hunger, with whom they were allied.*

Meanwhile Alessandro Sforza had with great difficulty crossed the mountains which divided Apulia from Calabria and with eighteen troops of picked cavalry had come down into the lands of the Caldori not far from the town of Castello d'Arce. There he was met by Matteo of Capua, Roberto Orsini, Alonso the Spaniard, and Jacopo Piccinino called Cavallo, masters of horse who had been all winter defending the King's cause in the Abruzzi. Jacopo Piccinino when he learned of Alessandro's approach tried to intercept him. When he failed he withdrew to Castello d'Arce and pitched camp before the town with an army of ten troops of horse, counting those of Caldora, and a force of infantry neither small nor inexperienced. Alessandro after consulting his colleagues and finding them all agreed decided to provoke Piccinino by repeated attacks in the hope of inducing him to give battle.

There was a field a stone's throw from the enemy where they decided to pitch camp and harry them. A picked cavalry force was sent ahead to occupy the field and Piccinino led his own men to keep off the Sforzeschi. You would call their operations preliminaries to battle rather than actual battles. The Bracciani charged and after breaking a lance with their adversaries at once retreated without venturing to dash headlong into a battle. A large body of Sforzeschi hurried to the aid of their comrades, drove the Bracciani from the field and forced them back to the fortifications of their camp. They then proceeded to taunt them with all sorts of insults and when no one came out to fight again Alessandro set up his camp in the spot he had selected, under the very eyes of Piccinino. Piccinino in the silence of night moved his camp and fearing to have the enemy too near, marched up the mountain and put the town between himself and them. The next day he sent to Alessandro to ask for a parley. The matter was discussed in a conference of the generals and it was decided to hear this famous captain to see if he would make any proposal favorable to King Ferrante.

Piccinino came down into the camp accompanied by the brothers Caldora and valiant officers. They were conducted to Alessandro's quarters where all the masters of horse and prefects of infantry were assembled. It was a great gathering of famous men. They stood looking at one another reflecting on the exploits of each individual and weighing the superiority of each. Then Piccinino spoke. "Gentlemen," he said, "you have all united against me. You who are many seek to destroy me who am one. I admit I am no match for your strength nor can I with this weak body of troops engage with you in a pitched battle. On the other hand you cannot force me to fight against my will. I am protected by the nature of the ground and the loyalty of my soldiers. When winter comes you will have to raise the siege. Meanwhile you will be wasting your time. A new year will bring new plans of campaign.

"But suppose it were possible to defeat Piccinino and imprison him. I ask you, generals, whom will you defeat? *I ask you, comrades, whom will you imprison?* Is it not I who support you? It is I who bestow on you wealth, luxury, and power. While I am a captain in arms and disturbing the peace of the Kingdom you are called out to war when otherwise you would be sitting idle. It is I who have got for you the gold with which you glitter, your arms, horses, dress; and you who were but now nameless I have made illustrious. Do you then persecute me who am the source of your safety? Suppose I am taken or fall in battle. What profit would be left for you? Will you take thought for yourselves or for others? Will Italy be at peace when I am dead? Who finds peace advantageous except merchants and priests? You will fatten the priests if they are not already fat enough. You will enrich the merchants if they are not yet sufficiently wealthy. Let me go. I am your fowler. It is for you I hunt. Your safety depends on mine. What is richer than the Roman Curia? What more opulent than the Venetians and Florentines? Everything desirable in the world is conferred on them by peace in Italy.

"But unless Italy is ablaze with war we can scrape together nothing from her. In peace we are looked down upon and forced to the plow. In war we are famous. Our trade is to bear arms. Do not let them rust in idleness. Consult for the common good. Vote for war and arms. *Why should priests have such wealth and power? Who can endure that the pride of the Venetians should lord it over land and sea? What more shameful than that the Florentines should rule Tuscany?* It is fair that those who wield arms should be the ones to rule kingdoms. I applaud the power of Francesco Sforza which was won by military prowess. It is base and disgraceful that loafers should be kings. Let merchants sweat at buying and selling wares. Let priests administer the sacraments. Lord-

ship belongs to us. If you will believe me we shall easily draw to ourselves the wealth of the Pope of Rome, the Cardinals and all merchants.
Do you ask how? The means is at hand. Do not desire to conquer. Our
best strategy is to prolong the war, for when it ends a soldier's profit
ends too. No man in his senses is in a hurry to terminate a thing the
end of which means the end of his own advantages."

Piccinino's words were received with great enthusiasm. Only a few
did not believe he spoke the truth. Officers and common soldiers alike
declared it was outrageous to press a brilliant general so hard that he
could not retreat. If Piccinino were taken, there would be an end to the
quarrel for the Kingdom. "Where shall we go then?" they said. "All
Italy is at peace. We shall have to return to the hoe. Peace is death to us.
War is our life. Let the man live who provides us with the means of life.
Let us shut our eyes and give Piccinino a chance to escape. Let us be
satisfied with having had the upper hand. Let there always be some
remnants of war left. Only thus shall we be safe."

There were present veteran soldiers who said that the same thing had
been done repeatedly in earlier wars. One said he had once had the
opportunity of capturing Niccolò Piccinino when he was careless; another that Francesco Sforza had deliberately refrained from putting an
end to war; and others cited other instances.

Then Alessandro said, "Have no fear, comrades. Italy will never be
without war unless it is governed by one lord—and you see for yourselves how easy that is to bring about! Many sovereign powers cannot
fail to have war so long as one threatens another and desires to rule
alone. Unless Venice can snatch the lordship of Italy I do not see who
else can possibly bridle this indomitable province. It is she you must
fear, she you must resist, and if you ever fight in her service take care
that victory does not bring you defeat.

"Now there is another way to look at war. When this war is over we
are summoned to greater ones. And you, Piccinino, do not take to yourself the glory of being the only one who supports fighting men in Italy.
The French would have conquered Ferrante; they would now be in
possession of a peaceful kingdom and would have ceased long ago to
pay you wages if the Pope and the Duke of Milan had not sent help to
Ferrante and fed this four years' war which has fed you. But you say the
French would have yielded long ago if you had not been their captain.
I do not deny it, but it was not without dishonor to yourself that you
consented to lead the French. You wear the insignia of Aragon and you
have attacked Ferrante of Aragon. You were born under the Church

and you have served against the Church. You are the son-in-law of my brother, the Duke of Milan, and you have not hesitated to harry your father-in-law. Is this your loyalty? Is this your regard for honor? Do you call yourself responsible for our safety? Before ever you wore arms many of our comrades here saw me a general. Our lives do not depend on you; rather do you depend on us. We can save or ruin you though you seem to have put your hope in the mountains. These soldiers will storm Heaven itself, not to mention mountain ranges. Why not rather yield to fate and come over to our side? If you consent, I will reconcile you to the Pope, the King, and the Duke. Thus you will save both your army and yourself. All the rest of what you say is nonsense. We at any rate are completely loyal to the masters we fight for."

Piccinino replied, "I was compelled to serve the French because no one else wanted me. I was unwilling to be abandoned by the army, bred as I have been in arms. I would rather have declared war on my own father than have seen my soldiers leave me. I took the pay of the French; I had to serve the master who paid me. Now I am free. I will go wherever I am called, provided I can find terms worthy of me."

After this the two generals withdrew to a private room and discussed at length an agreement. At last they came to the following terms: Piccinino shall be commander in chief of the royal troops so long as he remains in the King's service. His pay shall be 90,000 ducats a year; he shall retain the states and towns in the Abruzzi which he now holds; he is free to invade and take the possessions of the Count of Campobasso. Whenever occasion requires he shall put into the field 3,000 horse and 500 infantry and shall wage war anywhere in all Italy at the King's pleasure; he shall harry the French forces; half his pay he shall get from the taxes due the King in the Abruzzi, the rest shall be paid in equal parts by the Pope, Ferrante, and the Duke of Milan. Count Broccardo shall be chancellor of the realm and have the city of Vieste in Apulia. Piccinino shall swear allegiance to the King and raise his standard as soon as he has received a fourth of his pay; he shall serve a year and, if the King pleases, another year on the same terms provided that he declares his purpose before the end of the first year; on the termination of his engagement he shall be free to serve whom he will, so long as he does not bear arms against the King.

Some time before this the Pope had sent a certain Dalmatian named Luca into the Gauls to see whether what Gerard had written was true. Gerard was a Frenchman who had kept a brothel in Bologna and had got together a little money by that most dishonest traffic. Then after the fall of Constantinople, when he heard that preachers in their sermons in churches were publicly declaring that those who took arms against the Turks earned Heaven, he was carried away by zeal for the Faith and religious fervor and when under Calixtus III a crusade against the enemies of the Faith was proclaimed, he wound up his affairs, converted all his substance into cash, and came to Rome at the head of three hundred infantry with the intention of going to Greece if he could be assisted by pay. When he got nothing he went off in dejection and abandoning all his enthusiasm moved to Savoy.

When however Pius was on his way to Mantua, Gerard went to him and said he had many comrades who were eager to fight against the Turks if they might only be allowed to form a society under the name of Jesus, enrollment in which should ensure plenary remission of sins. Bessarion, Cardinal of Nicaea, supported him, vouched for his reliability and thought everything he asked should be granted. He said he could easily muster 10,000 men, which would be a great help to their cause; Peter the Hermit, a mean and lowly man, had repeatedly done the same thing when Godfrey had crossed with an army into Asia. Why should our time not be able to produce what earlier times had produced? Why shall that not happen again which has happened once? The Pope consented on condition that no one should be admitted to the society who could not serve against the Turks for a year at his own expense.

The man went off with the letter he wanted and proceeded to canvass the Gauls,[5] but it was not till after four years had passed and he was completely forgotten that he sent one of his comrades to the Cardinal of Nicaea, when the Pope was at Pienza, with the message that up to that date 4,000 soldiers had been enrolled in the society and in a short time more than 10,000 might be expected to assemble. He needed a standard and somewhat larger funds and 200 ducats to free his son from the clutches of his creditors. Nicaea on hearing this went joyfully to the Pope. He took the messenger with him and showed the letter Gerard had sent him. He begged that such an opportunity of advancing their prospects should not be let slip. The Pope said the story was like a dream and was a scheme contrived to make money. The standard asked for could not be lightly entrusted except to a man known and proved. The funds requested amounted to no inconsiderable sum and could not be granted to anyone who asked. It was to be feared that they were to be used for some new trickery and were designed for personal

[5] The French.

gain. It was not much for the Pope of Rome to lose 200 ducats but to lose his honor was too much. He would send a trusty man to Gaul with the money to inquire into the truth of the matter and if he found the situation satisfactory he should deliver the money to Gerard. The other things could be dispatched the moment it was clear there was no trickery involved. The Cardinal of Nicaea approved the Pope's plan. Luca was sent to have an interview with Gerard and see whether what he had written was true. He was also directed to go to the Duke of Burgundy and remind him of what the Bishop of Ferrara had said to him the preceding year and of the answer he had made; to ask why he had not kept his promise and to urge him to fulfill his vow.

When Luca arrived in Savoy and had found Gerard, he inquired as to the Society of Jesus and learned that a number of noble and excellent men were enrolled in it and that the Duke's son Philip would join if the Pope would appoint him General of the Society. This encouraged Luca somewhat but when he reached Burgundy, where it was said 4,000 members had registered and many arms had been collected, after a careful and thorough scrutiny he found nothing at all. He accused Gerard of lying. Gerard protested that he had told the truth but by Burgundy he had meant Brabant and Flanders, since Burgundy was lord there too. Luca must go there and he would find many thousand recruits. Luca therefore went on to Brussels, encountering many traps on the way. He escaped them all but was left in no doubt that Gerard was a rascal. The Bishops who had been adduced as witnesses to the facts were now questioned. No one of them admitted knowing Gerard nor could anyone be found who had heard anything about the Society of Jesus, but some of the Duke's council told the following tale. Gerard had been at the French court before King Charles's death and had asked permission to form a society. He said he would lead a large army of French as if intending to march against the Turks and to cross the sea at Ancona, but in reality he would go to Piceno, cross from there to the Abruzzi, expel Ferrante's party and assure the Kingdom to René. The King had spurned the scheme of this scoundrel who proposed to make a mock of religion.

This is what was learned about Gerard. Evidently his conversion had no roots. The parable in the Scriptures about the sown seed is true. The word of God found no good soil in Gerard. His pious resolutions lost their strength because they were not seasoned with salt. His confidence exceeded his powers. When he found his mistake he became a crooked bow. On learning that Luca had arrived safely in Brussels, knowing that his deception would be discovered he took care to disappear completely.

Luca had an audience with the Duke of Burgundy and delivered the Pope's message. Burgundy blamed the English for his slowness; he had been unable to arrange a truce; it had not been safe for him to make a long journey while his own domains were unsettled; negotiations for peace had been in process down to that very day; on the birthday of St. John Baptist French and English ambassadors were to meet at St. Audemar and at his instance would agree to a a ten-years peace; he was now on the point of being able to fulfill his promise to the Bishop of Ferrara; he remembered that promise and had no intention of breaking. it.

Luca was pleased with his answer but when he asked that it should be confirmed by a letter he was sent to one person after another and wasted many days, for Burgundy, who though an old man was given to a life of pleasure, forgot all about religion while he amused himself with dancing and wrestling and elaborate banquets that lasted till midnight. Furthermore his courtiers thought a crusade against the Turks would be ruinous; it was a mad idea for a prince weighed down with years to leave home and make war on unknown provinces; war in Greece was too far off for Burgundians; he would never return if he went. Everyone measured his own dangers. Some feared the toil, some the expense; some reflected on a possible change of sovereign when, in place of an excessively mild father, a son would reign whose character they did not thoroughly know.[6] They were afraid that a most kindly master might be succeeded by a cruel one. At any rate it was unavoidable that a new lord would be followed by new ministers. They would have to leave the court whether they went to war or stayed at home. All loathed the Prince's project and, though they dared not oppose their lord openly, they secretly devised reasons for delay and no one applied a spur to the Duke's natural sluggishness.

He seemed to be undergoing a change of heart and nothing more was said about the Turks when suddenly one night after the third watch Burgundy fell ill and so completely lost all his senses that for a time he was thought dead. His physicians hastened to his bedside and administered all sorts of remedies. Some held out very little hope of life,

---

[6] Philip's son and successor, Charles the Bold, was indeed at odds with the Duke at this time and gave promise of a very different kind of regime. Philip, grown old and worn out by his excesses, relinquished his power to Charles some two years before his death in 1467.

others utterly despaired of it. The next day, whether because of a strong constitution or by God's miracle, Burgundy came to himself and being seen restored to his former vigor called a counsel of his nobles and said to them, "My lords, that I am alive and you see me preserved is due to God's grace. I deserved to die for not having fulfilled my vow. You know what I vowed and what I promised Pope Pius. Though I always meant to keep my promises, yet I delayed overmuch, beguiled by pleasures at home. Meantime the power of the Turks has increased to the great injury of Christianity. Justly has an indignant God scourged me with sickness, but in His mercy though He chastened me, He did not give me over to death. Contrary to your expectations and my own I have quickly recovered my former health. This has been a warning. God has called me. There is no reason for me to delay longer. Go, all of you who are my friends and who made the vow with me. Gird yourselves for the march so that when Pope Pius commands you may be ready."

All said they must obey God and delay no longer. Every man offered his life and his person. The Prince summoned Luca also and said, "Return with all speed to Rome and tell Pope Pius that my envoys will be with him on the feast of the Assumption of the Blessed Virgin Mary and I will do his behests. The envoys will explain how we may best go against the Turks. Let the Pope see to it that on the appointed day he have present embassies from all Italy with whom the actual business may be transacted."

Luca asked for a letter in witness of this and having obtained it returned to Rome the day before the Pope left for Tivoli. When Pius had heard him he was overjoyed and wrote to all the potentates of Italy of Burgundy's purpose, bidding them send envoys to Rome about the middle of August.

While this was happening King Louis of France, who had been heartily devoted to the Pope, seemed to have slipped a little in his allegiance, either because he was too elated with prosperity or because he resented that Ferrante had the upper hand in Sicily by the Pope's favor. He wrote a letter to Pius and also to the cardinals which was unworthy of his dignity, and as if he were the Pope's superior condemned his acts and laid down rules as to his conduct. He accused the Pope of harrying the Kingdom of Sicily with war, of being a foe to his own kinsmen, of desiring neither peace nor a truce, of subjecting the church of Mainz to dire calamities, of persecuting the Count Palatine of the Rhine and Sigismund, Duke of Austria, with too severe edicts; of calling the King of Bohemia a heretic, of leaving no one undisturbed; and he said he would do better to foster peace among Christians and turn his schemes against the Turks. He asked the cardinals to send him an answer regarding the Pope's intentions as soon as possible.

This letter was read in a secret consistory. The Pope vindicated his own innocence. The cardinals, amazed at the King's letter, said that either he was sadly astray or the letter was not as he had dictated it.

This however was not the King's only mistake; others soon followed. He issued three edicts. In the first he declared that he and no other was the competent judge of all lawsuits which might arise concerning regaliae. (Regaliae is the term applied by the French to the right claimed by the French kings, when cathedral churches fall vacant, of appropriating their revenues and conferring benefices till a new bishop is invested.) In the second edict he confirmed the presidents of the parlement and all his ministers, even in cases involving benefices, in those privileges which the Apostolic See is said to have conferred on the University of Paris. In the third he laid down the principle that the decision as to the possession of any ecclesiastical benefice belonged to him and that no one else in his kingdom might presume to exercise it. Punishment was fixed for anyone who should transgress these edicts. His devotion in having abolished the Pragmatic Sanction appeared less than his sacrilege in issuing such decrees.

Pius thought no answer should be sent to the angry King's letter, which, once read, had nothing further to say and could not answer if questioned. Two envoys were dispatched, one from himself and one from the college. They were both eminent men long distinguished in the college, Teodoro, Bishop of Feltre, and Lodovico, Archdeacon of Bologna and notary to the Apostolic See. One would be at a loss which to admire more, their learning or their eloquence. They were instructed how to clear the Pope of the accusations made against him and appease the King. This was to be the main object of their efforts. They were also to bring up the subject of making war on the Turks and to do their best to persuade His Majesty to that undertaking, offering him the opportunity of a five- or at least a three-year truce if he would take arms against the Turks.

About this same time envoys of the Burgundians waited on the Pope at Tivoli. They were Guillaume, Bishop of Tournai, who had long been known to the Pope and had been transferred by him from Toul to Tournai, and with him three influential nobles of the Duke's court. When they were given private audience they said that their prince,

Philip, had decided to do all that the Bishop of Ferrara had asked of
him in defense of the Faith. The delay had been due to the English
who had seemed to be planning to declare war on France and prevent
the Duke's marching. Now there was a sure prospect of a ten-year
truce and the Duke was free to go where he would. They would deliver
the rest of their message at Rome, where they had heard the Pope was
soon to go. Pius applauded Philip's holy purpose and said he was a
prince deserving of the highest honors from the Apostolic See.

During these same days the allegiance of Louis of France (Fig. 27)
was shown to be of quite a different character. Imbued with a spirit
of rebellion he was so rash as to dare to seize the Apostolic Legate,
Giovanni Cesarini, auditor of the sacred palace, as he was leaving for
Brittany and to take from him all the documents he carried. Not content with this he deprived Alain, Cardinal of Avignon, who had been
the cause of the Legate's being sent, of the revenues of all his benefices
(or, as it is called, temporalities) and appropriated them himself. He
inflicted the same punishment on two of his nephews who were bishops,
though they were completely innocent. He also made many threats
against the Cardinal of Rouen on the grounds that he too had conspired
with Avignon. He held the embassy of Cesarini to be a crime because
he was going to Brittany to judge concerning the feud between the
Bishop of Nantes and the Duke of Brittany. The King said they were
his subjects and that the right to decide the feud was his, not the Pope's.
This was truly a tyrannical and false utterance. Neither Duke nor
Bishop acknowledged himself subject to the King of France, though
both revered the power of the great king. As Louis declares himself
emperor in his own kingdom, so the Duke of Brittany asserts himself
king in his own principate and the Bishop of Nantes holds that his
church was founded and had temporal dominion and so-called regalia
iura before the constitution of the kingdom of France where Louis rules.

It was proper therefore that the Pope should be the judge in a quarrel
between the Duke and the Bishop. But who can persuade a king of
such facts when avarice is his law and he listens only to teachers with
itching ears? *There is nothing in the world more dangerous than a
sovereign who has no wisdom in himself and will not be guided by
another's. In France madness has long been king. There it is proverbial
to say when making excuses for madmen, "It's no wonder. They're of
royal blood."*

At Tivoli audience was given to the ambassador of Georg, called
Skanderbeg, Lord of Albania, who spoke to this effect: Mahomet had

come to Scopia with a huge army with the intention of taking Georg off his guard. Georg had had no time to fortify the province. His one way of salvation had been to sue the enemy for peace. This he had done in order to save the province but he would go to war again whenever the Pope wished. He now begged that if he should be driven from his kingdom by the Turks he might find asylum in the lands of the Church. The Pope did not blame this forced peace if, as Georg said, the power of the Apostolic See was unharmed. He assured him that in case of defeat he should not fail to find a refuge in the Church's lands if he should be driven out by the enemy of the Faith while fighting in the cause of religion.

Since the Italian embassies which had been summoned to discuss the affairs of the Faith were now on the way to Rome, the Pope decided to leave Tivoli and hasten to receive them. First however he went to Frascati, which was once the villa of Lucullus and is now a little hamlet. Its ancient ruins attest its early splendor. He also climbed the mountain of Tusculum, once a city strongly fortified by nature and almost impregnable, which the Romans destroyed three hundred years ago. The foundations of the splendid palace, which we have said Strabo mentions, are extant as well as lofty arches facing west and south. This must have been a magnificent structure, whether a palace or a senate house. Everything else is razed to the ground. After seeing these things the Pope again visited Grottaferrata where he saw a very high waterfall and gave orders that mass should be celebrated according to the Greek ritual. It was not till September 9 [7] that he returned to Rome, where he was met outside the walls by the cardinals, all the clergy and populace, and the ambassadors of princes.

After some days he summoned the Burgundian envoys to a public consistory and bade them state their wishes. Guillaume, Bishop of Tournai, a professed monk and head of the mission, delivered a long speech packed with learning in which he discoursed at length of the Turks, their insolence and foul practices. He described their deeds and told what great injuries they had inflicted on the Christian religion. He dwelt still more on the nobility, antiquity, and learning of the Greeks, lamented their ruin, pointed out the dangers threatening Christians if they did not speedily arm in their own defense. He urged the Pope, the cardinals, and all the embassies present not to delay longer in such a crisis but to take thought for Christendom and go to meet the enemy. He said that Philip, Duke of Burgundy (Fig. 24), who had sent him,

[7] Actually September 19.

had determined to lead a fleet against the Turks the next spring and
prosecute the war with all his might in defense of holy religion. Though
an old man he would not spare his own person; he would march with
the army and perform the duties not only of a captain but of a soldier
unless he were prevented by illness; in that event he would send a
substitute.

The Pope on hearing this spoke as follows: "Reverend brethren and
most beloved sons, having heard the Burgundian envoys I suppose you
are awaiting with eagerness our answer in which we shall praise as he
deserves our most loving son, Philip, Duke of Burgundy, and speak of
his exalted merits. Your desire is more just than attainable. We have
not the eloquence to satisfy your expectations. Many fine things ought
to be said about Philip which could not be adequately set forth except
by the most eloquent of orators. Mention should be made of the exalted
rank of his family which traces its origin back to Ilium, of his physical
and mental endowments, his justice, courage, temperance, humanity,
and all the other virtues which are always found in the noblest degree
in the noblest man. Mention should be made too of his glorious exploits
alike in time of peace and war. His victories have been as many as his
battles, yet he has fought with his country's foe more often than any
other man of our day has quarreled with his private enemy. All France
is filled with trophies erected by him and he has set up monuments of
victory even across the Rhine among the Germans. Such things as these
our discourse could not touch upon, much less fully set forth. They call
for subtle genius and noble rhetoric. Our old man's dry style is not
equal to so great a task. Nor does Philip wish this. His true virtue is
content with itself and desires no flattering words. His great and noble
deeds have been done not from desire for praise but to please God. He
looks for his reward from Him, not from man, who can bestow nothing
that is not mortal.

"But granted that we cannot praise Philip as he deserves and that he
does not want such praise, shall we therefore ignore this most august
embassy and show it no honor? Never in the world! Some answer must
be made to the proposal laid before us and so distinguished an embassy
must not be cheated of the praise due it. What has Philip's embassy for
us? What are its instructions? What does it offer? It says that the
Turkish arms are threatening our lives. It calls attention to the disasters
which the Christian religion has suffered and seems destined to suffer.
It urges us to go to meet the enemy before they grow stronger. It says
that if war is declared on the Turks, if a sufficient army is raised, Philip

will take part in this crusade and will not spare his person in order to consult for the safety of holy religion.

"What do you think of all this, brethren? Who would not say that these are great and splendid words? Who could adequately extol this prince? No Christian has less reason to fear the Turks than Philip, yet he is the first to promise to march against them and wage war for the Holy Gospel. O purpose worthy of a prince! O peerless spirit! O most noble blood! A long, long journey is before him; the frozen Alps must be traversed from the west to the east. He has the courage to surmount all difficulties. He thinks no toil is to be refused in God's cause, no danger avoided. This has long been Philip's purpose. On the day that the Turks stormed Constantinople he made this vow and he has never departed from it. For almost ten years he has persisted in this aim. Now perhaps God will have pity on us and at long last will grant that a strong army under fair auspices shall be marshaled against the Turks, since the flourishing republic of Venice too has equipped a very powerful fleet and sent it against the enemy. And Matthias, King of Hungary, now that he has attained the crown and peace in his kingdom, will be able to arm such forces as he desires, and this exalted prince promises that he will come to the war with a picked company. The other potentates of Italy will, we hope, join us, and the western sovereigns will not refuse aid. Holy Jesus will show that the vileness of Mahomet is hateful to Him and fighting on our side will crush the enemy before our eyes.

"But, to address our words at last to you, most distinguished ambassadors, you have brought us comfort today by your speech and Philip's magnificent promise, which is indeed worthy of his blood and his name. When you urge us to put forth every effort in the defense of the Holy Faith you are spurring a running steed. Nothing is so dear to us as the defense of holy religion. At the Congress of Mantua all the Church heard our plans and our yearnings. We were unheeded. We toiled in vain. Nevertheless we were not therefore discouraged. We are resolved not to desist from our purpose till we rouse Christian princes and peoples to defend the most Holy Gospel and the divine law. On this account during these last days we have summoned to our presence the princes of Italy. You see their embassies here that we may consult with them and with you in regard to protecting religion. And if the aid of the faithful and especially of the Italians does not fail us, not Rome only but all Italy and all Christendom itself shall soon know that we have not been lacking in solicitude and courage to take thought for the Christian state. May the Grace of Almighty God and of our Lord Jesus

Christ be with us and may He weigh His mercy rather than our iniquities."

With these words he dismissed the audience while all praised to the skies Philip's name and spirit.

The following day the Pope summoned the Italian embassies and asked what they would finally offer in defense of the Catholic Faith now that they heard Philip's promise and were aware of the necessity for war. When they answered that all were waiting to learn what burden the Pope would impose on them and that no one would fail in so holy a work to do all in his power, the Pope said, "Why need we waste time with many words? We have the decree of Mantua. We will keep to that if you so please. In it burdens are apportioned according to strength: one tenth of their income for three years is imposed on the clergy, one thirtieth on the laity, one twentieth of all their property on the Jews. This was approved by all peoples, though afterward its execution was delayed because Italy was in confusion with new internal wars. Now peace is almost restored. Now it will be possible to wage war with the Turks. The necessary money can be collected according to the decree. We can think of no easier method or fairer distribution."

The envoys answered that as private individuals they approved the Pope's words but as envoys they were not empowered to answer them. They requested permission to inform their masters and ask their consent. Only the Venetian said, "My prince is far from needing this urging. He is already at war. He has sent a large and strong fleet against the enemies of the Faith and has already wrested part of Peloponnese from the Turks. He has accepted the tax of tenth, twentieth, and thirtieth and on his own initiative, with the consent of the Senate, has imposed further burdens on his subjects. Everything is being done which is thought necessary for victory. Our republic will not fail you in any respect."

The Pope, after praising the Venetians for having undertaken the war in so courageous and noble a spirit, turned to the other ambassadors and said, "Go and tell your masters what we have said and add one thing more: that we do not ourselves want their money nor wish so much as to touch it. Let them themselves require of their subjects funds for soldiers and ships for us to use in war. Let them choose their own captains and raise their own standards on the ships. We should rather receive from them such aids to war than money." His words were received with approval and nothing further was done that day.

The Florentine ambassador had heard none of all this with satisfac-

tion, for he suspected everything that seemed to increase the prestige of
the Venetians. He went to the Pope in private audience and said,
"Your Holiness, what are you thinking of? Are you going to wage war
on the Turks that you may force Italy to be subject to the Venetians?
All that is won in Greece by driving out the Turks will become the
property of the Venetians who, after Greece is subdued, will lay hands
on the rest of Italy. You know that people's *pride and* insatiable greed
for power. It is their continual boast that they are the successors of the
Romans and that the sovereignty of the world belongs to them. *They
say that the successors of Trojan Aeneas ruled in their time but that
now the sovereignty belongs to the descendants of Antenor and they
claim it for themselves.* You are helping them in this by aligning your
arms with theirs *against the Turks* and you do not see into what an
abyss you are hurling Italy. *You are weaving a net of perpetual slavery
for your country.* To say nothing of the losses to Italy, what will become of the Church of Rome? Do you think it will maintain its
dignity? *Will it not rather be the handmaid of the Venetians? The
Venetians are not men to prefer divine to human things. They value
worldly above ecclesiastical power. They hold the authority of the Pope
less than that of the Doge. And do not think that the office of Vicar of
Jesus Christ will help you. 'This is our will,' they will say. 'Thus the
Senate has decreed.' It will be useless to bring forward the sacred
canons. Either the apostolic eminence will be destroyed entirely or the
Venetians will arrogate it to themselves and unite it with the dogate,
whether they choose to call it empire or kingdom.*

"These are the dangers your wisdom must meet, *not those lesser ones
which we fear from the Turks.* The Venetians are at war. They have
dealt the Turks a heavy blow and have almost succeeded in taking from
them the Peloponnese. There is no chance that the Turks and the Venetians can ever be reconciled. Undying hatred has been born between
them. This in my opinion was what was most to be desired by us. Let
them fight it out between them. Their strength is well matched. Turk
will not utterly conquer Venetian nor Venetian Turk. The war will
last a long time and *at last the Scripture will be fulfilled, 'When the
strong meets the strong both shall fall.' And what result could be more
desirable for us than that the strength of both the Turks and the Venetians should be so exhausted that* at last they will let us have peace.
Your purpose, as I understand it, is to free Italy and all Europe from
fear of the Turk and to that end you are making a military alliance
with Venice. I propose a more advantageous plan when I tell you that

not only the Turks who are threatening the lives of Christians but the Venetians too must be thrown back and without expense or toil or danger and in perfect peace. You are wise enough, I think, not to despise or belittle the advice of the Florentines. This proposal I have brought you from the midst of the school of our wise men. We beg you to embrace a course which will be for the good of all Christendom."

The Pope was astounded when he heard this and finally replied as follows: "If we were in your position and neither in holy orders nor honored with the vicariate of Jesus Christ we should perhaps feel as you do and should succumb to your specious reasoning. But the mind of a prince is not that of a private individual nor the spirit of ecclesiastics that of the laity. Many things are tolerated in the people which no one would listen to in the clergy. Sins venial in the populace are held to be mortal in a priest. The princes of this world and governors of cities care not by whatsoever means they protect their power so long as they do protect it, and therefore they often violate the law of nations and act contrary to honorable practices. The people praise the victors and do not count it base to have conquered through trickery and fraud provided that he who has laid low the enemy is of the laity; but if a priest has destroyed a foe by guile, nay, if he has slain one who was manifestly plotting against him, he is held to be in the wrong. The people expect the clergy to be so much more righteous than the laity! Do not be surprised then, my very dear Otto, if in regard to the matters now in hand our opinion differs from yours and that of the Florentines. If their own state is safe they will let the Christian state go to ruin. If they neglect religion and the Faith, *although they are guilty of a heinous crime before God* yet they keep their place among men. But if we are the least remiss in anything concerning the Faith we are at once torn to pieces by the cries of all Christendom. 'See,' they say, 'is it becoming that Christ's Vicar should thus postpone the defense of the Faith? We must have a council to punish his negligence and elect a better man.' In a pope no fault is so small that the nations do not think it enormous. They expect him to be an angel not a man.

"Listen then to our words, Otto, words though not of an angel at least of a cleric and one raised above the common lot of mankind. We admit that the Venetians, as is the way of men, covet more than they have; that they aim at the dominion of Italy *and all but dare to aspire to the mastery of the world. But if the Florentines should become the equals of the Venetians in power, they would also have an equal ambition for empire.* It is a common fault that no one is satisfied with his lot.

No state's lands are broad enough. If the Venetians conquer the Turks and become masters of Illyria and Greece, they will perhaps try to subdue Italy (*we do not deny it*), provided only they are free from fear of barbarians and are not distracted by foreign wars.

Suppose they do subdue Italy, *which would be very difficult to do;* what then? Would you rather obey Venice or the Turks? *No Christian who deserves the name would prefer the rule of the Turks under which the sacraments of the Church must finally be doomed and the gate to the other life be closed to those who desert the Gospel. You will admit that the worst thing of all would be to become slaves of the Turks and the best to serve neither Turks nor Venetians. You desire the latter and you think it will come to pass if we do not aid the Venetians now that they are involved in war with the Turks. Your plan is neither expedient nor honorable.*

"We went to Mantua. We exhorted all Christendom to arm against the Turks and not allow the enemies of the Faith to advance further against Christians. The Venetians spurned our exhortations. Almost everyone else also spurned them—to the great detriment of the Christian religion. Now the Venetians have changed their minds. They have listened to our Legate and declared open war on the Turks. They have equipped a great fleet and put fear into the enemy. They ask help from us, having no doubt that they are not a match for their foe. We urged the Venetians to wage war in defense of religion. They have obeyed. Now when they ask aid shall we refuse? Who that hears of this will approve it? God may put it into the hearts of the enemies of the life-giving Cross to abandon their partners in time of war. We may not for any reason withhold aid from those who are fighting for the Holy Gospel.

"You will say that the Venetians have been brought into this war not by any desire to defend the Faith but by greed for power; that they were seeking the Peloponnese *not Jesus.* So be it. It is enough for us that if Venice conquers, Christ will conquer. The victory of the Turks means the overthrow of the Gospel, which we are bound to try with all our might to prevent. You have asserted that if the Turks and Venetians fight each other, both will collapse, assuming that the resources of the Turks are no greater than those of the Venetians. You are mistaken. Venice is far inferior to the Turks, though her fleet is judged to be superior. It can harass the islands and coast towns. It can do very little in the Mediterranean. But if the Turkish captains should lead land armies against the shores of Dalmatia, as they seem to have planned, they could finally make it impossible for the Venetians to man their fleet, since they get their rowers and naval allies from Dalmatia. It is not so easy to get control of the land as of the sea.

"We must not then think that the Turkish empire, which is far-flung in Europe and in Asia, can be wiped out by the Venetians even though they range the seas at will; since if they must fight on land they cannot match armies with armies, being as they are so inferior in numbers and strength of cavalry and infantry. If they are not aided by us and other loyal Christians they will soon break down—to the disgrace and ruin of our religion. It costs a great deal to maintain a large fleet in the east and it cannot be done for long. But if the fleet is withdrawn, everything that has been won there must at once go over to the enemy whose army will be on hand, unless indeed the Turks are compelled to move out of Europe. There is very little in Greece that the Venetians can take or keep. Your plan therefore is not advantageous, since it neither saves the Venetians nor destroys the Turks. But if the Venetians are destroyed it will be vain to think of saving Italy. They have engaged in a great and perilous war in which their defeat would mean the destruction of the Christian religion. They must receive aid in their difficulties. They must have added strength and reinforcements of troops and we must make every effort that they may not be forced to yield to the enemy. The war is our common war. We must put forth all our energy to win it. We for our part together with Philip, Duke of Burgundy, shall not fail the Venetians. We will join fleet to fleet and make all the coast cities hostile to the Turks. In the other direction Matthias, King of Hungary, will harry Upper Moesia, Macedonia, and the neighboring districts with a land army. It will be hard for Mahomet, who has powerful enemies in Asia too, to resist on all fronts at once. He will, in our opinion, be conquered and utterly driven out of Europe unless a just and merciful God, offended by our iniquities, judges otherwise—which may Heaven forbid!—concerning His people.

"Nor do we think that on this account the Venetians are going to put a yoke on Italy when they have triumphed over the Turks. Not all the Turkish possessions in Europe will be theirs. Peloponnese will fall to them and perhaps Boeotia and Attica and numerous maritime districts of Acarnania and Epirus. In Macedonia Georg Skanderbeg will claim the chief role. In other parts of Greece there will be no lack of Greek nobles to seize the power when the Turks are expelled, and they will have to be allowed their independence. The other regions bordering on the Danube (namely Bulgaria and Rascia and Servia and Bosnia; and beyond the Danube Wallachia in Sarmatian or as some say Scythian, territory, called Dacia by the ancients, right up to the Euxine) will all come into the hands of the Hungarians to whom they once belonged. No one will profit more by the defeat and expulsion of the Turks than the Hungarians, who will be far more powerful than the Venetians. *With added wealth and power they will demand Dalmatia of the Venetians. It will be refused. War will then break out between them which will free Italy after a long time from the tyranny of the Venetians. Meantime one hope after another will spring up.* Now the Hungarians and the Venetians are allies against a common foe whom they fear more, and nothing is said about the Dalmatian quarrel *which will be stirred up again the minute the fear of the Turks is dispelled.* There is no occasion for our being so frightened about Italy and we need not fear the precedent set by the Romans. The Venetian character is very different from the Roman. We shall see many snows before the Venetians bridle Italy. But unless we put up strong resistance to the Turks it will not be long before both the Hungarians and the Venetians give way and then our liberty too is doomed. We must meet the immediate danger that threatens us from the Turks. About the Venetians we will plan at the proper time if necessary and we shall not fail to find potent remedies.

"Your state will act more wisely if it equips the best fleet it can, joins us and goes after a share of the plunder of the East. In this way it will have regard to both honor and expediency. But if the Florentines stay idly at home while the Pope goes to war and all the rest of Italy rushes to arms, the city's name will be dishonored. God Himself will be angry with it and no one will blame the Venetians when they march against you or will come to your aid. You will experience God's righteous judgment and you who have abandoned Christians in their peril in war against the Turks will yourselves in your hour of need be deserted by all."

When Otto heard this he said he thought what the Pope said was true and that he was not likely to change his mind; he had himself been convinced by almost adamantine arguments; he would write to the Florentine senate everything he had heard and did not doubt that finally all would be arranged as the Pope wished, though not without some trouble and delay; they would have to deal with a people who hate nothing more than risking their money. Then he departed without further words.

The next day [8] the Pope called a secret consistory and addressed the cardinals as follows:

" 'What is the purpose,' you ask, 'of this long story?' Why, that you may understand the blessings of Almighty God which He has heaped upon the Church of Rome and you and us; that you may plan with us to repay and to be grateful to the Giver. We are now free to turn our arms against the Turks. We cannot delay longer nor do we wish to. Now we may fulfill our dearest desires. You have often begged us to do this thing. Now we will beg you. Take care that what you have blamed in us we cannot blame in you. We will set you an example, that as we shall do you may do also. We shall imitate our Lord and Master Jesus Christ, the holy and pure Shepherd who hesitated not to lay down His life for His sheep. We too will lay down our life for our flock since in no other way we can save the Christian religion from being trampled by the forces of the Turk. We will equip a fleet as large as the resources of the Church will permit. We will embark, old as we are [9] and racked with sickness (Fig. 26). We will set our sails and voyage to Greece and Asia.

"But someone will say, 'And what will you do in war? You are an old man, a priest weighed down with a thousand ills and will you go into battle? What will an army clad in togas avail in a fight? What good will the whole order of cardinals do in a camp? They will hardly endure drums and trumpets, not to speak of the bombards of the enemy. They have spent their youth in luxury and will you torture their old age with arms? You are ill-advised. Better stay at home wtih the cardinals and all the Curia and send against the enemy a fleet supplied with funds and manned by brave soldiers used to hardships, or furnish money to the Hungarians that they may lead as strong a force as possible against the Turks.'

"Well said and wisely! if we had the money. But where are we to scrape it together? Our treasury is exhausted by a long war and the revenues of the Church are not sufficient for such an undertaking, though by God's grace a vein of alum has been discovered which continually puts us in greater debt to the Divine Mercy and encourages us to protect religion. The entire sum which can come to our Camera yearly does not reach 300,000 ducats. Half of it is spent on guards for citadels, prefects of provinces, military captains, our court; and the

---

[8] September 23, 1463. A very long address follows in which Pius reviews the whole story of his efforts for a crusade, his disappointments, etc. The review is omitted here.
[9] Pius was nearly fifty-nine years old.

Apostolic See cannot do without these expenses. Who would say the remainder was enough to finance a decisive war against the Turks? You are wise enough to understand that we need a far larger sum. A million a year would hardly suffice for a Turkish war which the experts at Mantua estimated would last three years—probably more.

"We hear you whispering. You say, 'If you believe the war to be so difficult, how can you go on without securing adequate strength?' We are coming to that point. An unavoidable war with the Turks threatens us. Unless we take arms and go to meet the enemy we think all is over with religion. We shall be among the Turks in the position in which we see the despised race of Jews among Christians. It is either war or infamy for us. 'But,' you say, 'war cannot be waged without money.' It occurs to us at this point to ask where we are to look for money. You will answer, 'From loyal Christians.' We press you further, 'How? By what means?' All ways have been tried. No one has answered our prayers. We called a congress at Mantua. What good came of it? We sent envoys to the provinces. They were scorned and derided. We imposed tithes on the clergy. They set the pernicious precedent of appealing to a future council. We ordered indulgences to be proclaimed. They said this was a trap to extort money and a scheme of the greedy Curia. On every single thing we do the people put the worst interpretation. We are in the position of insolvent bankers. We have no credit. The priesthood is an object of scorn. *People say that we live in luxury, amass wealth, are slaves to ambition, ride on the fattest mules and the most spirited horses, wear trailing fringes on our robes and walk the streets with puffed-out cheeks under red hats and full hoods, breed hunting dogs, lavish much on actors and parasites and nothing on the defense of the Faith. And they are not entirely wrong. There are many among the cardinals and the other members of the Curia who do these things* and, if we are willing to tell the truth, the luxury and pride of our Curia is excessive. This makes us so hateful to the people that we are not listened to even when we speak the truth.

"What do you think we ought to do in such circumstances? Must we not seek out a way to recover our lost credit? Naturally you will say, 'And what path will lead us thither?' Certainly none trodden in our time. We must change to paths long disused. We must ask by what means our elders won for us this far-flung rule of the Church and employ those. For a principate is easily kept by the same means that won it in the beginning. Abstinence, purity, innocence, zeal for the Faith, religious fervor, scorn of death, eagerness for martyrdom, have

set the Church of Rome over the whole world. Peter and Paul were the
first to dedicate it by the glory of martyrdom. Then there followed one
after another a long series of popes who were dragged off to heathen
tribunals and while they accused false gods and openly confessed Christ
as the true and supreme God met death by the most agonizing tortures.
Thus they took thought for a new planting. Disciples believed that
teachers who by their teachings were steeled to face death and could not
be forced to give them up by any torments had spoken the truth. They
were indeed true and approved shepherds who laid down their lives for
their sheep in imitation of their Lord and Master, Jesus, the eternal and
supreme Shepherd who was slain for His sheep on the altar of the Cross
and reconciled the human race to the Heavenly Father.

"Then when the Romans turned to Christ and churches were opened
and the Gospel spread everywhere, martyrdom ceased and there came
the holy confessors, who by the light of doctrine and the brightness of a
pure life served Christian peoples no less than the martyrs had done,
for they put a bridle on the vices of men which in peace are most likely
to run riot. By martyrs and confessors alike our Church was made great.
It cannot be preserved unless we imitate our predecessors who founded
the Church's kingdom and it is not enough to be confessors and preach
to the peoples, to thunder against vices and extol virtues to heaven. We
must draw near to those earlier saints who gave their bodies as witnesses
of their Lord.

"If this method does not rouse Christians to war, we know no other.
This path we are resolved to tread. We know that it will be a crushing
burden for our old age and that we shall in a sense be going to certain
death. We do not refuse. We trust all to God. His will be done. We
must die sometime and it matters not where so long as we die nobly.
Blessed are they who die in obedience to the Lord. A noble death re-
deems an evil life. We shall think we have fared well if it pleases God
that we end our days in His service. What we are doing is of necessity.
We promised Philip, Duke of Burgundy, that we would go. He had
vowed to march against the Turks if the Emperor or the King of France
should propose to do the same. We realized how important it was that
Philip, who is followed by a large part of the western world, should go.
We were eager that he should start and, as the saying is, be first to break
the ice, never doubting that a mighty host of chieftains and nobles
would follow him. But neither the Emperor nor the King of France
nor any other prince superior to the Duke brought himself to bear arms

against the Turks and Philip was beginning to think himself freed from his vow since its terms had not been met.

"Then it occurred to us to snatch the excuse from him. Some two years ago we summoned six cardinals whose loyalty and discretion we had proved and revealed our plan to them. At our first words they were thunderstruck. They could not approve a thing so momentous and never heard of before. But after repeated consultations, when the dangers to the Faith and the loss to the Church of Rome were fairly weighed, all came over to our opinion. Accordingly we wrote to the Venetian Senate of our proposal, enjoining secrecy and calling on their princes for advice and aid. The Venetians approved our plans. They promised aid and kept the secret with the utmost loyalty. Then we sent the Bishop of Ferrara to King Louis of France who scorned all our words as being but dreams, thinking we had devised such schemes to divert his attention from Italian affairs, though indeed he was indulging in much loftier dreams when he boasted that in one year he would conquer England and settle the disputes in Spain; then after subduing the Genoese and reducing the King of Sicily he would easily cross through Italy into Greece and make himself master of all the barbarian nations.

"The Bishop of Ferrara scorned the *braggart* king and went straight to Philip, as he had been directed. He found the Duke ill in bed. When he had told him among other things that he must arm against the Turks and fulfill his vow, for we ourselves who were both king and priest purposed to set out on the crusade, he said, 'You come at an opportune time, your Eminence, for in this message you bring me health. I will do as the Pope bids. I will follow where he goes and will soon send him envoys to arrange the whole matter.' See, here are the envoys and you have heard their demands. They urge us to the defense of the Faith and war against the Turks. They claim the promises made by the Bishop of Ferrara. They say their prince will come if we go first. If not he will remain at home.

"What are we to say? We cannot refuse to set out, as we promised the Duke and the Venetians, without dishonor and the blackest disgrace. There is no longer room for choice. We must go. The road on which we are setting out is full of peril—at least for us who are old and frail. It is not the same for the others and high hopes of victory are before them. For we do not go alone against the enemy. The strong fleet of the Venetians which commands the sea will accompany us.

There will also be other Italian potentates and the Duke of Burgundy will bring with him the west. On the north the Hungarians and Sarmatians will press on; Christians throughout Greece will revolt and flock to our camp; the Albanians, Servians, Epirotes will rejoice that the day of liberty is at hand and will aid our cause. In Asia too there will be risings of the Karamanians, the Iansae, and others who hate the Ottomans. If only God's favor is with us everything else speeds us on to victory.

"We do not go to fight in person since we are physically weak and a priest whom it does not befit to wield the sword. We shall imitate the holy Patriarch Moses, who when Israel was warring against the Amalekites, stood praying on the mountain. We shall stand on a high stern or on some mountain brow and holding before our eyes the Holy Eucharist, that is, our Lord Jesus Christ, we shall pray Heaven for the safety and victory of our fighting soldiers. A broken and a contrite heart the Lord will not despise. You too will be with us, all except the aged whom we shall permit to stay behind, and you likewise will pray and by your good works will win God's grace for Christian peoples.

"While we are speaking you are wondering how the Church of Rome will be governed in the meantime. You are thinking, 'The Transalpine nations will not follow you across the sea and in your absence the patrimony of the Church will not be safe.' We are coming to that directly. Everything has been provided for. Listen. We shall leave in Rome the Roman Curia and all its offices and also two Legates of your rank, one to preside over spiritual, the other over temporal matters. All will find what they seek if their requests are just. Only the more important and the very difficult and unusual cases will be referred to us. Our vicar will administer justice and confer benefices. He will provide for churches which may become vacant and succor the needy; he will grant dispensations; he will confer favors according to the dignity and deserts of the persons concerned. Our second representative will administer justice to the subjects of the Church and repulse its enemies with the support of an army to be commanded by our nephew Antonio. We shall leave him a force of 3,000 horse and 2,000 infantry, part of which will remain in the Picenum. Thus so far as human reason can foresee we shall leave everything safe. But there is nothing in which we place greater hope than in the aid of the Most High. For unless God guards the State any other guard watches in vain. For our God we leave our own See and the Church of Rome and commend to His protection this white head and this frail body. He will not forget us. If He does not grant that we return He will grant us entrance into Heaven and will keep the Holy See and His bride unharmed.

"You have heard the outline of our plans. It is now your turn to express your opinions."

The Pope had often shed tears as he spoke nor could the *more right-minded* of the cardinals keep from weeping. The first member of the college to answer was the Cardinal of Ostia, Bishop of Rouen, a Frenchman and long averse to the project, *a devotee of luxury and ease who* when he was bidden to express his opinion did not dare oppose the plan. The man's nature was conquered by the nobility of the subject. "Your Holiness," he said, "for my part I approve your plan and admire your courage and I will follow you wherever you bid me—though nothing is harder for me than sailing. Whatever burden you impose on me I will bear."

The Cardinal of Porto, a Spaniard and very old, who was weeping bitterly and could not master his sobs, said, "Heretofore, Your Holiness, I have thought you a man. Now I deem you an angel. You have surpassed my expectations. May God bless your undertaking! I will always be at your side, whether we must go by land or sea. Even if you go through fire I will not desert you, since you are going straight to Heaven."

Those who came after said substantially the same things till it came to the Bishop of Spoleto. He was one of the cardinals with whom we have said the matter had been discussed from the beginning. He had heard the arguments on both sides and had known that the objections put in the way had been confuted. Nevertheless that he might seem to know somewhat more than the rest, he said he was not sure whether the Pope's plan, though noble and praiseworthy, could be carried out and he brought up difficulties that had already been answered a thousand times, as if that day were the first time he had so much as heard the expedition mentioned. But he did not speak with impunity. The Pope easily confuted again one whom he had so often confuted before.

Spoleto was followed by the Cardinal of Arras whose opinion was as follows: "As I see it, this is not an open question. You have promised to set out and you must go. Many will praise this act but just as many will blame it. They will say that you have devised this scheme to block the French designs on the Kingdom. As to your saying that the cardinals are bound to follow you, I do not agree. To go to martyrdom is a matter for counsel not command." He had long before this begun to oppose the Pope and as if out of his senses had burst into actual insanity.

He could not even speak peaceably to the Pope. The reason for this change in him we shall tell later. The Pope disregarded the madman's words and when he asked the others their opinions he found no one who did not heartily approve and urge his going nor anyone who did not offer his property and his person. The Pope was happy at the approval of the Curia but imposed silence till an appointed day.

Meantime the Cardinal of Teano and Federigo of Urbino after a long siege of Fano, in which they had suffered unspeakable hardships, being not only terribly harried by the missiles and engines of the enemy but tormented by the inclemency of the weather and the rains which flooded the camp till it was like ponds and great lakes, at last decided to attack the defenses of the city by constructing right up to the walls mines and open ditches through which the soldiers might advance with their flanks safe from attack. Sigismondo came from Rimini to Fano to see whether the town could be saved, and had brought by ships such provisions as he had been able under the circumstances to get together. When he had surveyed the city and considered the strength of the enemy and their siege works, he summoned his son Roberto, whom he had put in command of the place, and said, "I must return to Rimini. Do you go on as you have begun, defending the city stoutly. But if the enemy's strength proves superior or if the citizens themselves attempt to surrender, do not allow the city to fall intact into the hands of the Church. Either set fire to the buildings or let the enemy plunder it." With these words he departed.

Antonio and the Cardinal, having learned what was going on in the city, attacked the walls with the engines they had ready. A fierce battle took place. Weapons and stones flew in all directions. The soldiers of the Church scaled the walls which by this time had been mostly ruined by the bombards. The citizens had built up a second line of ramparts of timber and earth farther in and while they struggled to defend this and the Church's forces to demolish it many were killed and many on both sides left the field wounded. Without doubt the rampart would have been taken and the city given over to plunder if the Church's missiles had not given out. When Federigo heard this he sounded the retreat. The people of Fano, realizing their danger and not daring to await a second battle, then sent envoys in the dead of night to the Cardinal and after coming to terms with him surrendered on September 25. Roberto had no chance to carry out his father's orders. He soon surrendered the citadel and fearing his father's fury passed by Rimini and went to Ravenna.

During the siege of Fano there was in the town a certain monk, an unworthy member of the Franciscan order, such as are often found in convents, who desire nothing so little as virtue though they are usually well versed in theology. So long as he could he urged the people of Fano not to open the gates to the Church and he did not fear to fight before the walls and to drive back the enemy with arrows. But when the Church's army entered he would not endure the Church's yoke and fled to Sigismondo, who, because he spoke his mind too freely, flung him from a high tower into the sea. Some say that Sigismondo stabbed him with his dagger—fitting wages for a soldier.

Pius happened to be at table when the Cardinal's messenger brought the news that Fano had fallen into his hands intact. He at once raised his hands to Heaven and gave thanks to Almighty God Who had heaped such blessings on him; and he said to himself, "Now there is nothing to keep me at home. God calls me to His war and opens the way. There is no cause for further delay."

Meantime the Italian embassies, having received their masters' replies, waited on the Pope and said that the decree of Mantua as to the tenths, twentieths, and thirtieths had been accepted. Let collectors be sent and there would be no delay in fulfilling the Pope's wishes. This was the answer of Ferrante, King of Sicily, Francesco, Duke of Milan, Borso of Modena, Lodovico, Marquis of Mantua, the Bolognese and Lucchese. The Genoese, though invited, sent no representative to the Congress, nor did the Duke of Savoy though he owned a wide territory in Italy, nor the Marquis of Monteferrato. The Florentines sent an embassy but offered nothing but words. They said that some of their foremost citizens were in business in Constantinople and they were afraid that if they involved themselves in war against the Turks their citizens would be made to suffer. Their magistrates had decided to send three of their large vessels called galleys to Constantinople under pretense of trading, to bring home their citizens and all their possessions. They thought this would be accomplished before Christmas; then the state could easily be persuaded to make war or contribute money for it. Till then it was no use to approach the people, who are harder to induce to give money than anything else. The Sienese, after long consultation and fruitless wearing out of the senate benches, at last promised to contribute 3,300 ducats to the expedition. So much they promised their Lord Jesus Christ! So much they gave to please the Pope of Rome, their own citizen, who since his elevation had bestowed on the city of Siena more than 50,000 ducats!

The Pope despised his ungrateful countrymen. He had passed the same judgment on the Florentines *as traders and a sordid populace who can be persuaded to nothing noble.* The Sienese however corrected themselves some days later and wrote that they would contribute 8,000 instead of 3,000 ducats. Though this was far from satisfying the Pope it was accepted with an appearance of gratitude, since Pius was influenced by love for his native city and thought he ought to agree with it even when it was mistaken.

The Venetians, as we have said, had declared open war on the Turks. Meantime Lemnos and many other islands in the Aegean called Cyclades threw off the Turkish yoke and deserted to the Venetians. When the Pope heard that, he decided that a bull in regard to his departure must be circulated.

In order to do this many questions had to be discussed with the cardinals, among whom the Cardinal of Arras, seeing that he had long been hostile to the Pope, always showed himself opposed, and actually rebellious. *The man was blinded by ambition and avarice and had an ingrained hatred of the Italian race. Furthermore he was shameless and had sunk to every vice. For Arras before he became cardinal made every effort to conceal his wicked nature and since he was regarded as learned because of the fluency of his discourse, he wished to seem good also with assumed virtue. But after he attained the red hat he could control himself no longer. He dashed at full speed into every crime. Lies and perjury were so familiar to him that he often deceived himself and told the truth when he thought he was lying. When he read to the Pope the letters of the King of France he often perverted the meaning and asserted that the King desired this or that which had never entered his head. Pius had noticed this and when he had caught a manifest error (for Arras read far more than the page could contain), he said, "Give me the letter so that I may see whether you are reporting the truth." The man blushed but, quick as a woman to deceive, he said, "There are some private matters of the King's that I do not wish you to see." At this the Pope exclaimed, "Well done! You are acting like an honorable cardinal indeed! You do not blush to lie to your master nor to deceive the Vicar of Jesus Christ. Your villainy has led you astray. Two cardinals have read the letter and bear public witness that none of the things you read were in it and no secrets of the King. The Bishop of Mirepoix was commended in it. Depart from our sight and do not return till you have cleansed yourself of a sacrilege." The cardinals understood this open rebuke and Arras went away in confusion.*

Some months before this two important churches in France had fallen vacant, one the metropolitan of Besançon in Burgundy, the other the cathedral of Alby in Auvergne, both of them very rich *and bringing in to the incumbent over 7,000 ducats yearly.* (*The church of Besançon is believed to be the more distinguished, that of Alby the richer.*) Arras applied for both and going to the Pope said *with shameless face and bold speech,* "You cannot refuse me the church of Besançon where I was born. *Thus you will provide for my brother and my nephews.* The King of France asks you to give me Alby. You promised him this long ago."

The Pope answered, "You know our custom. We do not give two pontifical churches to anyone unless one of them is a titular church. Choose one of these. Do not expect to have two." Arras was very angry and as if he had been insulted began to abuse the Pope for refusing him the rewards due his labors. He said he had hastened the abrogation of the Pragmatic Sanction and the friendship of the King of France which had been obtained by his efforts. The Pope remained firm. *Then Arras had recourse to Gallic wiles. He promised the Pope 12,000 ducats if he got what he wanted. The Pope burst out furiously, "Go to the devil, you and your threats! and your money go to hell with you!"* From that time Arras was never friendly to the Pope *though he sometimes concealed his feelings. He wrote the King of France many things about the Pope which were not true, saying that the Pope hated his nation and would not keep his word to him. All the decrees of the Curia, although secrecy was imposed on pain of anathema, he reported to the enemy and a letter in his handwriting was found in which he revealed to Jean of Anjou the Pope's secrets and said that he himself was hated by the Pope because he was most devoted to the Angevins.*

The infamy of these acts was increased by the man's hypocrisy and fits of passion. He wished to seem devout and would perform mass now in the Basilica of St. Peter, now elsewhere; by expression and gesture he would appear actually rapt, would heave sighs from the bottom of his heart; would weep and pretend to talk with God; but before he had taken off his vestments and left the altar he struck with his fist one or the other of the attendants who had made some slight mistake in his office, and the Pope was told that one of the attendants at the altar had his ears boxed so hard by him that he fell down and, as the saying has it, he boxed one ear and the ground the other. When he was dining he would be angered at the least offense and throw silver dishes and bread at the servants and sometimes, even though distinguished guests were

*present, in his rage he would hurl to the ground the table itself with all
the dishes. For he was a glutton and an immoderate drinker and when
heated with wine had no control of himself. Therefore his servants
could seldom stay with him more than a month.*

*Only one saw through the man's character and knew how to take
advantage. He used often to drink at the inns in the Campo dei Fiori
and then, flushed with wine, he would return home when he thought
the Cardinal was at table. When the Cardinal asked him where he had
been and he said, "In the Campo dei Fiori," he would ask him what
news he had heard there. He would say, "The very best, for all the
members of the Curia, many of whom were wont to stroll in the piazza,
were praising Arras alone among the cardinals as excelling the rest in
wisdom and learning; no one doubted that when Pius died the papacy
would be offered to him. For whom could the cardinals choose who
would be better qualified or more acceptable to kings?" When Arras
heard such things he could not restrain his tears for joy. He would rise
from the table as soon as possible and go to his room. There he would
summon the rogue and talk at length about the papacy, for he said the
King of France too had prophesied that he would be Christ's Vicar.
How blind is the cupidity of men! It is easily caught by flattery and
cannot rightly measure its own vices.*

*Arras, abandoned to drunkenness and dissipation, did not fail in the
third vice, lust. He was fond of women and often passed days and
nights among courtesans. When the Roman matrons saw him go by—
tall, broad-chested, with ruddy face and hairy limbs—they called him
Venus's Achilles. A courtesan of Tivoli who had slept with him said
she had lain with a wineskin. A Florentine woman who had been his
mistress, the daughter of a countryman, angry with him for some unknown reasons, waited for the time when the Cardinal on his way from
the Curia should pass her house and then, as he was going by, she spit
out on his hat saliva that she had held a long time in her mouth and
mixed with phlegm, marking him as an adulterer by that vilest of
brands. The Cardinal of Avignon, who was present, sympathized with
his colleague whom the woman had dared to insult publicly. All the
rest who saw it burst out laughing. Arras himself kept on quietly as if
he had noticed nothing.*

*What shall we say of the fickleness and inconstancy of the man? He
could never hold long to the same purpose. What pleased him in the
morning displeased him in the evening. He made the dignity of cardinal
so cheap that he was not ashamed to go to meet kings' couriers outside*

*the gates. What he said now he denied soon after. He could not be
bound by promises or oaths. He often quoted that line of Euripides,*[10]
*"I swore with my tongue. My mind did not swear." He committed to
memory a great deal of literature both sacred and profane. He had run
through all Latin letters and had stocked the larder of his mind with
selected sayings of philosophers and poets. On any subject that came up
in conversation he was prepared to say something and he would quote
the words of ancient scholars. But he lacked wit and judgment. He
mixed up together all sorts of incongruous things. He pursued what
agreed with his whim not with justice. The saying is true: Folly without letters is less dangerous. Learning makes a wicked character even
worse and as steel is sharpened by the whetstone so by learning a good
character is whetted for piety, a bad one for wickedness. It is wisdom
which perfects a man and wisdom cannot live in a wicked heart.*

*The Cardinal of Arras was made mad by much learning and he had
such confidence in it that he thought there was no argument he could
not win in debate nor did he fear the stigma of inconstancy. For what
he defended yesterday he dared attack today. The war which Pius
waged against René he said was most righteous while King Charles of
France lived. When Louis came to the throne and began to favor Jean
of Anjou, he changed his mind as if a new king had brought down
from heaven new justice. And when, as we have said, Giovanni Cesarini
who had been sent to Brittany was detained in France at the King's
orders and stripped of all his decorations and Pius had condemned this,
he put out a little pamphlet in which he tried to defend his change of
heart about the Kingdom and the King's seizure of the Apostolic messenger. He prattled foolishly and at length also about the authority
which the French boldly presume to exercise in ecclesiastical matters,
and since the Cardinals of Avignon, Rouen, and Coutances had been
deprived of the temporality of their churches by royal edict and everyone was saying that it was a bad precedent, he tried to defend this too,
subordinating the authority of the Pope to that of the King.*

*When the Pope heard of such things he often summoned Arras to
him privately, rebuked him and warned him with a father's affection to
change his way of life. The man would weep when he was admonished
and promise to obey, but as soon as he was out of the Pope's sight he
would return to his true character and behave worse than ever. Three
friends were brought as witnesses, according to evangelical law. They
were of no use. He was rebuked in a consistory before the brethren.*

10 Hippol. 612.

Every effort came to nothing. The rush of the river could not be stemmed.

When the Pope realized it was hopeless to try to save the man, he listened to him no longer. He refused his requests for an audience, rejected his demands, ignored his words. He spoke more graciously to the cardinals to whom Arras was unfriendly and listened to their suits. When Arras learned this and was at last an object of scorn to everyone, having finally obtained an audience with the Pope, he said that he could no longer remain in a Curia whose head he saw was his enemy and he wished to go to France to a king who was his friend. He begged that he might be permitted to withdraw. The Pope said he must consult with the brethren about his departure. He must on no account go before that. The Cardinal resented this as though he were being held against his will and wrote to the King that plots had been laid against him; he was afraid of being thrown into prison.

And indeed his suspicions were not unfounded. The Pope did not think it safe that a seditious man should go to France to stir up rebellion nor on the other hand did he want to keep in the Curia a man who would report the Curia's secrets to the enemy and make the barons of the city friendly to Anjou. He thought it better that he should be arrested and punished for his sins. He had the votes of the cardinals for this, the greater number of whom voted that the insolence of Arras deserved severe punishment. One thing saved him. When the Pope considered what the populace would say about the arrest of the Cardinal it became perfectly clear that the more powerful side would be criticized, for the crowd always favors unhappy defendants and calls just punishment violence. Fearing this the Pope gave the Cardinal permission to go to France when he wished; there he would finally pay the penalty for his crimes. After the decree against the Turks was issued, he departed dejectedly to France.

In these circumstances the Pope, meditating on the magnitude and the dangers of the war he had decided to undertake against the Turks and the advantage its conduct would derive from the prestige of Francesco, Duke of Milan, if he joined it, sent the Duke a long letter which has been published with others of his. In it he tried to persuade Francesco to accompany him on the crusade in the capacity of commander in chief of the whole apostolic army with the certainty of winning undying fame and the salvation of his soul, and the assurance that he would be acting for the best interests of his descendants in the principate of Milan. But his efforts were in vain. A mind enslaved by the pleasures of this world scorned those to come and he made farfetched excuses.

Pius with unshaken confidence in the aid of the Most High on October 22 in the sixth year of his pontificate called a public consistory, which was largely attended, for the ostensible purpose of answering the Burgundian envoys. He directed Gregorio Lolli to read the decree which had been issued with the advice and consent of all the cardinals, in which he dwelt on the necessity of making war against the Turks and of his going himself, the grounds for hoping for victory, the prizes for those who fought, and the punishments of obstructionists. The decree [11] was listened to with profound attention though its reading could barely be finished in two hours. The charm of the style, the novelty of the subject, the readiness of the Pope to offer his life for his sheep, drew tears from many of those present. The Burgundians thanked the Pope warmly for enabling them to take back to their master so welcome and so splendid an answer.

But the Romans when they learned the Pope's resolve were reduced almost to despair as if they were certainly going to lose forever the Roman Church and the emoluments from it. When the Pope realized this he said, "Be of good courage, my Roman sons whom we love as our own life. When we go against the Turks we shall leave here the Apostolic Camera and the Rota and the Chancery and the Penitentiary and the other offices of the Roman Curia and two Legates, one to preside over temporal matters, the other to administer spiritual affairs and to take our place in aiding those who throng to the city. There will remain also the aged cardinals who are prevented by illness from going on the crusade. We too (God willing!) shall soon return bringing victory. Be of good heart! The God of consolation and peace will not refuse His protection to this city hallowed by the martyrdom of the holy Apostles."

With these words the assembly was dismissed amid the greatest enthusiasm on the part of all. The Pope, who was suffering from very sharp pains in his feet and had for a long time had difficulty in concealing his distress, hastily withdrew to his chamber.

Sigismondo Malatesta, who was shut up in Rimini with only a few fortresses in his possession, sent ambassadors to the Pope and said, "I am beaten and sue for peace. I am ready to submit to any terms you set. The glory of the victor is to spare the vanquished. I admit I have sinned grievously against you but neither has the punishment I have suffered been light. If I am spared I will henceforth refrain from harming the Church." The Pope gave orders that his terms should be drawn up. After the lawyers had approved them he granted peace to Sigismondo

---

[11] The Bull *Ezechielis prophetae.*

on the following conditions: In the Basilica of St. Peter on a feast day during mass Sigismondo's representatives should testify that he had confessed and acknowledged the errors savoring of manifest heresy of which he had been accused and should recant and abjure them in his name, especially those which denied the resurrection of the dead and the immortality of the human soul. Sigismondo himself should do the same at Rimini. For the crimes of treason and heresy he should understand himself to be deprived of all his power and other gifts of Fortune. By the Pope's grace he should receive Rimini under the new title of vicariate and pay a yearly tribute of 1,000 ducats. He should at once withdraw from his other towns, citadels, and fortresses wherever situated. The Church he had injured should be indemnified in full for its losses. Federigo of Urbino should recover what had been his. When these terms were complied with peace should be declared.

Sigismondo's agents, who had been sorely afraid of losing Rimini, accepted the terms and the next Sunday at mass at the altar of Holy Mary in the Basilica of the Apostles, before a large congregation in the presence of many bishops, in a loud and distinct voice they publicly confessed Sigismondo's heresy and in accordance with the powers delegated to them abjured it. On the appointed day Sigismondo, as commanded, handed over to the Count of Teano the possession of his various towns and citadels.

After this the Bishop of Sessa, in obedience to the Cardinal's orders, went to Rimini to raise the excommunication. All the populace went out to meet him and Sigismondo too craving pardon for his errors. The Bishop proceeded to the Cathedral where he showed clearly how greatly the tyrant and the people had erred in defying the mandates of the Church. He ordered that divine services should be discontinued for three days and that the people should fast in order to be prepared for absolution. After three days the people gathered in the Cathedral and Sigismondo kneeling before the Bishop at the high altar confessed his errors, implored pardon and vowed allegiance to Pius. The people did likewise promising thenceforth to observe forever the mandates and censures of the Church. After this the Bishop absolved the penitents and blessed the state. The priests who had profaned the divine office during the interdict were suspended according to the nature of their offenses. Thus at last the war in the Picenum came to an end and with it Malatesta's rebellion and insolence, an end too severe considering the clemency of the Apostolic See, too mild considering the enormity of the crimes.

These things resulted fortunately for Pius as did also the action taken at the same time in regard to the affairs of the church of Mainz.

Pius, as we have said before, had sent the Bishop of Tricarico to Germany to settle the affairs of that church. Meantime Diether, whether broken in spirit by the long-continued reverses in war or recalled by the Divine Will from his unjust purpose,[12] began to take pity on the Church whose son he was, which he had too long afflicted, well knowing that the Count Palatine had no other object in waging war than to crush all the sinews of the See of Mainz and utterly extinguish a dignity which seemed to cloud his own brightness. Therefore without the Count's knowledge Diether requested an interview with Adolf, since he had resolved to grant him peace. They met, each accompanied by friends and their military allies (except Palatine) at Frankfurt, a city on the Main, famous for its frequent fairs and as the place where the emperor is elected. For when the German throne becomes vacant the electors convene here and, shut in in the pretorium, choose the Emperor, though he is not called Emperor till he is crowned at Rome. After he is crowned at Aix he is called King of the Romans; before that Electus.

In Frankfurt there are most magnificent churches dedicated to the Deity and splendid private houses though most of them are of wood. They are all roofed with small pieces of a thin lead-colored stone which we call abacus, so fitted together that they look like fish scales and when the sun shines they sparkle marvelously. The Main River rising in the neighboring mountains of Bohemia flows west through Würzburg and many other cities of Franconia. At Frankfurt it is spanned by a stone bridge with fourteen arches, one of which has been left open for fear of the town on the opposite bank, and in time of peace the two sides are connected by wooden beams. The river abounds in fish, especially eels. It flows into the Rhine near Mainz. Every day without fail a ship capable of carrying three hundred persons, towed by horses, crosses from Mainz to Frankfurt and another from Frankfurt to Mainz—such is the demand for ferrying merchandise.

Here Adolf and Diether met and having called in Pietro Ferrici, the Apostolic Nuncio, by whose authority the matter was to be conducted, discussed terms of peace. They finally agreed that Diether should definitely resign the rights to the church of Mainz, which he had declared

---

[12] Diether was tricked into submission by being shown a letter supposedly written by the Count Palatine offering to recognize Adolf of Nassau in return for certain concessions. This perfidy on the part of his ally led Diether to offer submission at once in the hope of better terms. The letter is thought to have been forged by Palatine's brother, newly elected Archbishop of Cologne.

belonged to him, and revere Adolf as his lord and archbishop appointed
by the Pope. Then before the gathering of illustrious men he at once
laid down his sword, the badge of princes, which Electors are used to
have carried before them and, humbly kneeling and asking forgiveness,
was absolved by the Apostolic Nuncio. He left the pretorium deprived
of his office and soon restored to Adolf Aschaffenburg and other towns
and strongly fortified citadels which he held; retaining some for his
lifetime according to the agreement, that he might not be reduced to
want, seeing that he had dissipated his patrimony by long wars. His lot
and that of Sigismondo were almost alike. Both had resisted the Apostolic See and were excommunicated. Both came to know how greatly
Pius was favored by the Divine Mercy though they experienced his compassion rather than his severity.

The Germans regard the Archbishop of Mainz as a second God and
do not think the authority of the Pope extends to him. Therefore when
Pius had removed Diether they derided him as if he had attempted a
thing that could not be. Even in the college of cardinals there were some
who felt the same and secretly blamed the Pope for excessive boldness.
Firmness conquered vain opinions and it became evident that those
who thought the Pope mad were mad themselves. *Among these cardinals was the Cardinal of St. Peter in Chains,*[13] *a German too devoted to
his nation*. Adolf was the second of the house of Nassau who had
deposed an archbishop of Mainz at the Pope's bidding and being
elevated to his place occupied the chair with dignity. Pius won great
fame for this and was enabled to conduct operations against the Turks
with a freer mind.

There remained in the Kingdom of Sicily the Prince of Taranto who
seemed likely to interfere with the Pope's expedition against the Turks
and to stir up a new conflagration against Ferrante. Though he had
been reconciled to him after the victory at Troia the preceding year, still
remembering his own perfidy he thought war more healthy for him
than peace. He therefore pretended good will to Ferrante and openly
displayed it but secretly he promised aid to Jean of Anjou and urged
him not to leave the Kingdom; if he had no other safe place to stay he
offered him his own fortresses; he bade the people of San Severo be of
good courage and not surrender to Ferrante; he promised help, furnished money for mercenaries, and was already leading twenty-two
troops of light-armed horse into Apulia to stir up rebellion. Two letters

[13] Nicholas of Cusa whose outburst against the papal policy and the entire Curia is
recorded in Book VII.

of his written on the same day were found. One sent to Ferrante professed a very special affection for him, the other directed to Jean urged him not to lose heart and voluntarily offered him aid.

When this became known Ferrante thought he must hasten into Apulia, and already Lucera of the Saracens had ejected the French garrison and come over to him. Choosing therefore from his whole army twenty-four troops of horse he hastily crossed into Apulia, but did not dare attack San Severo which was strongly defended. He made for Manfredonia which was soon surrendered to him by the citizens though it did not escape plundering. The commandant of the citadel, seeing a French galley sailing toward him and deceived by hopes of fresh aid, ventured to make a sally and while Ferrante's troops were resisting him and the soldiers in excitement and confusion rushed in from the camp the looting of the city could not be prevented. The commandant was repulsed and retreated into the citadel with some loss. The French galley was intercepted and the defenders on land taken prisoner. The captured ship was manned with fresh soldiers and being commanded to sail as if toward another not far off, it captured that also before the trick was discovered.

When this news was brought to the Prince of Taranto he was plunged into sudden despair and attacked by pains in the stomach. He was the victim of intense terror, for he was a weakling, haughty and swelling with pride in prosperity, frightened and broken in adversity. His sickness increased daily and his physician held out no hope of recovery. Therefore after he had wrestled with the disease more than twelve days he decided to return to his own dominions. He was carried in a closed litter to the town of Altamura and when they came to set him down there on November 15 they found him dead. He had made no will nor had he been reconciled to God by confession nor fortified by the sacraments of the Church like a Christian.

His end was like his life. He lived without religion and without religion he died. The townspeople heard nothing with more pleasure than his death. It was a strange situation. No state mourned his demise. Everywhere there was public rejoicing, public dinners and revels, general joy, as is usual at the death of a rich miser who is popularly said to do nothing rightly except die. For Giovanni Antonio had been the worst of misers and so bent on gain that he kept the trade of his principality for himself alone. He bought from his subjects at his own price everything that was for sale and sold it to foreign merchants. He rarely paid his creditors. He kept in his dominions great numbers of Jews

whom he could most easily plunder. He had commercial dealings with
the Turks. He wished his household to be content with a meager living.
He used no lights except tallow candles and those very sparingly. Thus
his death was, as it were, his subjects' life and resurrection.

Ferrante when he learned of the Prince's death left a few men at
Manfredonia to storm the citadel and with all his cavalry hastened to
Altamura where he was received by all with the utmost joy. A great
change in conditions took place. Within some eight days ambassadors
of all the more than three hundred states and towns that had been under
the power of the Prince enthusiastically surrendered to the King. The
Prince's widow too and her son-in-law Giulio and the captains of the
army at once submitted to the King's commands and swore allegiance
to him. Enormous treasure was found and nothing escaped the King.
Wealth that had been kept for many years and treasures too closely
guarded suddenly came to light. It was reported that the value of everything belonging to the Prince in treasuries, warehouses and flocks
amounted to a million ducats and all this came intact into the King's
hands.

After this stroke of good luck the citadel of Manfredonia and the city
of Vieste were taken. The people of San Severo opened negotiations
with the Apostolic Legate concerning a reconciliation, since they
realized their situation was utterly hopeless. Lucrezia, who had once
been Alfonso's mistress, fearing to meet his son Ferrante, fled into
Dalmatia with the son of Giovanni Cossa and is said to be still living
there with her lover. In the Kingdom everything is subject to Ferrante
except San Severo (unless that has by now surrendered), the citadel
of Lucera, a few fortresses of the Counts of Bari in Apulia, Ortona in
the Abruzzi, Mantea in Calabria, the island of Ischia in the Tyrrhenian
Sea where Jean of Anjou is hiding, and the so-called Castel dell' Ovo
near Naples which has been almost destroyed by bombards. Everything
else does his bidding and there no longer seems any doubt that the
Kingdom enjoys peace.

There is henceforth nothing to prevent Pope Pius from going on the
crusade against the Turks and many advantages may result. Confident
in this hope he is girding himself for this enterprise and preparing for
the greatest of all wars (Figs. 28, 29). We pray that the Divine Favor
may attend his undertakings.

This is what we had to write about his history up to a point in the
sixth year of his pontificate, in twelve books, the last of which was
finished December 31 in the year of the Incarnation of the Word, 1463.

BOOK XIII

WITH the completion of twelve books of the Commentaries of Pius II we thought to have finished our work, since after the expulsion of the Angevin party from the Kingdom of Sicily and the subjugation of Sigismondo Malatesta not only the Church of Rome but almost all Italy was enjoying the sweetness of peace. We had decided to share ourselves in the general tranquillity or at least to exchange the toil of writing for the delight of reading, but, since Pius, weighed down by age and illness, did not discontinue any activity but rather planned greater and heavier ones every day by declaring war on the Turks, our mind recoiled from rest and purposed to write the history of the Turkish war if life should last. We did not refuse. We will begin and so long as Heaven permits we will continue.

In this task we have not the same privilege that all other writers have, namely to begin with the magnitude or length of the war, the changes of fortune or the barbarity of the combatants or other matters that challenge wonder, a procedure by which the good will of readers and hearers is generally secured. That is done by those who record wars long past and write the history of antiquity. All the material is before their eyes. They understand what was praiseworthy, what was to be blamed. They see the magnitude of their subject and can divide their work and decide on the number of books and make definite promises to their readers. We however must approach an event hardly begun and certainly far from ended. The foundations of a very great war have been laid. We shall begin with those and set down whatever worth recording may take place from day to day. We shall imitate the architect who, having begun a great building, goes on with it according as his patron supplies the funds. If he furnishes what he needs in abundance he promises him a splendid house. If he withholds what is needed he either discontinues his work or produces something inappropriate or ridiculous. We shall be dependent on the outcome. The nature of our history will be shown by the result of events—if we live so long. In this

work we shall pursue the same practice which we were careful to observe in the earlier one. We shall include not only what concerns the
war with the Turks but contemporary acts of Pius and other sovereigns
and peoples worth transmitting to posterity. You who are to read,
though you will not be reading history (since we are setting down
recent events), must yet understand that we have kept the law of history, not to depart from the truth.[1]

---

[1] Book XIII remained a fragment. Like the crusade, it was cut short by the Pope's death
at Ancona (Fig. 30). On that final journey neither Duke Philip of Burgundy nor Pius's
old ally Sforza accompanied him.

INDEX

CAPRICORN TITLES

201. *Hauser,* DIET DOES IT. $1.55.
202. *Moscati,* ANCIENT SEMITIC CIVILIZATIONS. $1.85.
203. CHIN P'ING MEI. $3.45.
204. *Brockelman,* HISTORY OF ISLAMIC PEOPLES. $2.65.
205. *Salter,* CONDITIONED REFLEX THERAPY. $1.95.
206. *Lissner,* LIVING PAST. $2.75.
207. *Davis,* CORPORATIONS. $2.45.
208. *Rodman,* CONVERSATIONS WITH ARTISTS. $1.65.
209. *Falls,* GREAT WAR. $2.15.
210. MEMOIRS OF A RENAISSANCE POPE. $1.95.
212. *Viereck,* UNADJUSTED MAN. $1.85.
213. *Cournos,* TREASURY OF CLASSIC RUSSIAN LITERATURE. $2.45.
215. *Guerdan,* BYZANTIUM. $1.65.
216. *Mandeville,* FABLE OF THE BEES. $1.65.
217. *Bradford,* OF PLYMOUTH PLANTATION. $1.85.
218. *Taylor,* COURSE OF GERMAN HISTORY. $1.65.
220. *Shelby Little,* GEORGE WASHINGTON. $1.95.
221. *Peterson,* ANCIENT MEXICO. $1.95.
223. *Isaacs,* IMAGES OF ASIA. $1.85.
224. *Krafft-Ebing,* ABERRATIONS OF SEXUAL LIFE. $1.95.
226. *Grekov,* SOVIET CHESS. $1.65.
227. *Ernst-Loth,* REPORT ON THE AMERICAN COMMUNIST. $1.45.
228. *Adler,* THE PROBLEM CHILD. $1.85.
233. *Barraclough,* ORIGINS OF MODERN GERMANY. $2.45.
235. *Skeat,* ETYMOLOGICAL DICTIONARY. $2.95.
236. *Hauser,* GAYLORD HAUSER COOK BOOK. $1.65.
237. *Fulop Miller,* THE JESUITS. $2.45.
238. *Shenton,* RECONSTRUCTION. $1.75.
239. *Blitzer,* COMMONWEALTH OF ENGLAND. $1.65.
240. *Wright,* GREAT AMERICAN GENTLEMAN. $1.65.
241. *Braeman,* ROAD TO INDEPENDENCE. $1.65.
242. *Bridenbaugh,* CITIES IN THE WILDERNESS. $2.95.
243. *Bridenbaugh,* CITIES IN REVOLT. $2.65.
244. *de Riencourt,* COMING CAESARS. $1.95.
246. *Weinberg,* THE MUCKRAKERS. $2.45.
247. *Hays,* FROM APE TO ANGEL. $2.65.
248. *James,* ANCIENT GODS. $2.25.
249. *Green,* LUTHER AND THE REFORMATION. $1.65.
250. *Filler,* THE ANXIOUS YEARS. $1.95.
251. *Ehrlich,* EHRLICH'S BLACKSTONE: RIGHTS OF PERSONS, RIGHTS OF THINGS. $2.95.
252. *Ehrlich,* EHRLICH'S BLACKSTONE: PRIVATE WRONGS, PUBLIC WRONGS. $2.95.
253. *Lissner,* THE CAESARS. $1.95.
254. *Collis,* QUEST FOR SITA. $1.45.
255. *Nabokov,* INVITATION TO A BEHEADING. $1.65.
256. *Wedeck,* PUTNAM'S DARK & MIDDLE AGES READER. $1.95.